THE DINNER PARTY, BY SARGENT

MUSICAL INTERLUDES IN BOSTON

1795-1830

By

H. EARLE JOHNSON

1943

COLUMBIA UNIVERSITY PRESS

NEW YORK

THE SONNECK MEMORIAL FUND IN THE LIBRARY
OF CONGRESS, THROUGH AN AWARD IN 1942, AND
THE AMERICAN COUNCIL OF LEARNED SOCIETIES
HAVE GENEROUSLY CONTRIBUTED FUNDS TO
ASSIST IN THE PUBLICATION OF THIS VOLUME.

To

L M H

who would have been pleased

COLUMBIA UNIVERSITY STUDIES
IN MUSICOLOGY

BOARD OF EDITORS

OTTO KINKELDEY, Professor of Musicology and Librarian, Cornell University, Honorary Chairman

PAUL H. LÁNG, Associate Professor of Musicology, Columbia University, Executive Chairman

ARCHIBALD T. DAVISON, Professor of Choral Music, Harvard University

GEORGE S. DICKINSON, Professor of Music and Music Librarian, Vassar College

CARL ENGEL, Honorary Consultant in Musicology of the Library of Congress, Editor of *The Musical Quarterly*

ERNEST HUTCHESON, President of the Juilliard School of Music

CARLETON SPRAGUE SMITH, Chief of the Music Division, New York Public Library

FOREWORD

Books about music in America are becoming more numerous. This is as it should be; for we still have much to learn about the musical doings of those who dwelt in these United States during the formative period. The knowledge can be brought to us in detail only in such special studies as Mr. Johnson offers us in this picture of musical life in Boston in the early part of the nineteenth century. We need similar pictures of New York, Philadelphia, Baltimore, and Charleston,—monographs on local musical history which will continue the minute and thorough eighteenth-century studies with which Oscar G. Sonneck set the standard and the model for American musical historians.

The period surveyed by Mr. Johnson is approximately contemporary with the period that saw the beginning and the whole course of Ludwig van Beethoven's activity in Vienna. In fact, one of the figures that flash across our vision in Boston, James Hewitt, theater musician, composer and publisher, a somewhat stormy petrel of New York and Boston, was an exact contemporary of Beethoven (1770–1827).

We can well afford to ignore the lifted eyebrows of censorious or captious readers who will point out that the musical life of Vienna and the musical life of Boston in these years were not the same. It is perfectly true—Billings was no Bach, Hewitt was no Haydn, and Graupner was not even a Gelinek. But they were all we had. And according to their lights and their gifts they worked as honestly, as sincerely, and as effectively in the American musical vineyard as the great European masters did in the state of life to which it pleased God to call them. For this we honor our musical forebears. They really did pave the way for the Boston Symphony Orchestra and the Metropolitan Opera.

Occasionally the upheaval of world events shook both hemispheres alike. The wars that on several occasions thrust themselves into

Beethoven's life or work, had their reverberations on this side of the ocean. At least one English-born Boston musician, the ponderous but active and able George K. Jackson, was sent into exile for the duration of the war into the far-off town of Northampton, because he had neglected to register as an enemy alien when the young republic a second time took up arms against the mother country.

Although many of the musicians who lead the way in Boston came to us from the European continent, most of the visiting artists were English, particularly those connected with the theater and the vocal art. Practically all our music came to us by way of England. Handel and Haydn, Pleyel and Mozart, were known here because they were known in England. We were not ready for Beethoven at this time. In spite of the pioneer efforts of the London Philharmonic Society (founded 1813) in behalf of Beethoven, the Boston awakening to Beethoven did not come until after the period covered in Mr. Johnson's study. Among the English singers was one who gave to America a more precious gift than the pleasure experienced by those who listened to her tuneful voice. For several years, just before the birth of her gifted son, the mother of Edgar Allan Poe appeared on the Boston stage and sang in concerts. The poet was born in Boston on the 19th of January, 1809. We do not know much about the quality of Mrs. Poe's performances, but at any rate she did not merit, or she escaped, the caustic criticism which Joseph T. Buckingham, a few years later, aimed at Mrs. Mills, "whose voice is not unpleasant if she would contrive to get it in unison with Mr. Hewitt's violin, instead of running parallel to it at a distance of a semitone above."

To his lively picture of the actual Boston scene Mr. Johnson adds several lists, bibliographical and historical. Even these have their charm for one who cares to read life into them. The long register of the publications of Gottlieb Graupner conceals the names of Boston composers who remained inglorious if not entirely mute Beethovens. Who was R. W. Wyatt, who composed "Five Waltzes" in 1820? And there was Joseph Wilson, organist of the Rev. Dr. Porter's church in Roxbury, who wrote a "Welcome Lafayette" for the great Frenchman's visit to America in 1824, and the modest violet, Miss Caroline Clark, who composed "Lafayette's March" for the same occasion. Marches were in the air, and Massachusetts governors must have been regarded as especially susceptible to their charm, for we have "Governor Jones' March," and "Governor Knight's March" both by Oliver Shaw, while "Governor Strong's March" bears no composer's name. Perhaps governors' marches were a specialty with Oliver Shaw, and he should be credited with the anonymous composition. Or again, we may be sure that the sinister meaning of the word in our own troubled days did not attach to the term in Graupner's time, but we are a little curious as to what is behind Thomas Hamley Butler's composition, "The Tank, a favorite air with variations," which Graupner evidently republished in America, for Butler (1762–1823) was a London pianist and theater musician who seems never to have come to America.

Even the list of Massachusetts musical copyrights provided by Mr. Johnson yields items of interest. Patriotic battle music for the piano was not restricted to Prague and Marengo. Francesco Masi, in 1815, upheld the honor of America with the "Ballad of Lake Champlain and Plattsburg, a grand sonata for the pianoforte." And we may confess to an honest shudder, when we run upon "The Murderous Bride" by P. D. (!) Moran, who is, of course, P. K. Moran, Boston musician and sometime organist of St. John's Church in New York. A strange subject for a church musician, although not unknown in the realm of folk song.

No, Boston may not have seen the birth of Eroicas, Fidelios, or Creations; but something was going on there in those days. The Muses were not wholly unknown in the new world. The Handel and Haydn Society could not have come into being in 1815 on a wholly infertile ground. The cultivators of this ground are pictured in these pages.

OTTO KINKELDEY

March 1, 1943
Cornell University

PREFACE

I N HIS CONCLUSION to "Concert Life in America," Oscar Sonneck defers expressing an opinion on the lessening of musical activity until another historian "attempts to span the bridge between the eighteenth and nineteenth centuries." For the most part, historians, having covered the formation of a new government and envisioned the Jeffersonian reforms, leave the political and social welfare of the young nation to struggle on as best it can until the more exciting reign of Andrew Jackson. Or, on the other hand, historians fall into "the sink of antiquarianism" against which Henry Adams warns. This volume is an attempt to span that part of the bridge between the centuries which rests in New England.

A large part of the pleasure gained from compiling these notes has been owing to the courtesies extended by individuals and institutions. Above all to Dr. Otto Kinkeldey, to whose hospitable door all musical scholars, lay or professional, gladly come, more gratitude is due than can be easily expressed. His kindness and encouragement have been constant and inspiring. Dr. Archibald T. Davison early showed his interest, and Mr. Harold Bauer has been most cordial. The Harvard University Library, the Music Room of the Boston Public Library, and the American Antiquarian Society permitted wide use of their treasures; research in the British Museum was finished two days before war was declared. Miss Osborn and Miss Tapley of the Essex Institute gave cordial assistance, the John Carter Brown Library and the Massachusetts Historical Society showed Von Hagen and Graupner imprints, and the Trustees of the Handel and Haydn Society permitted examination of early records. The collection of newspaper findings compiled by Mr. Donald Tilton, under the auspices of the Elizabeth Sprague Coolidge Foundation in the Library of Congress, was of inestimable value by reason of its accuracy and scope. Without them, this study would have been burdensome.

Miss Emma Forbes Waite of the American Antiquarian Society spent many hours discovering wanted items of sheet music from the carefully organized collection housed there; Mr. J. Francis Driscoll of Brookline generously gave information from his unexcelled stock of Graupner imprints, and Dr. Carleton Sprague Smith carefully read the manuscript and saved the author from many embarrassing errors of statement. Mr. Henry Mason was alert to any possible relationship between Gottlieb Graupner and Lowell Mason. Professor Andrew Hoover of Oberlin College offered good counsel in organizing the opening chapters, and Dr. Harold Spivacke combined sound advice with kind deeds. Miss Elizabeth Sherwood, in carefully editing the manuscript, has made suggestions and corrections of the most valued sort. The Boston Museum of Fine Arts is to be thanked for courtesies in connection with the illustrations, and Mr. Stephen Alvord Buckingham for consenting to the use of the Trumbull miniature.

For permission to quote from their publications, acknowledgment is made to the following publishers: Dodd, Mead & Company, for quotation from Schouler's *History of the United States of America;* Harvard University Press, for quotation from Foote's *Three Centuries of American Hymnody;* the Beacon Press, for quotation from the *Life of William Ellery Channing;* and G. Schirmer, for quotation from the *Musical Quarterly.*

There are many others to be reckoned in any complete acknowledgment of favors generously bestowed, or courage inspired by friendly interest. Particular gratitude is extended to the American Council of Learned Societies and to the Sonneck Fund in the Library of Congress for grants which make the publication of this book possible.

The author is aware that the music of this period is not discussed at length. This can be explained, if not excused, on the grounds of limited space, and by the conviction that the publications of the period, the developing standards of taste, and the local compositions are subjects for more than a regional survey. Another volume of equal size will be required when the time for such a study has come. An explanation is due also for the omission of a formal bibliography. The chief source of all research has been the newspapers, scanned page by page. Their factual commentary on the immediate present is far more reliable than the faulty memoirs of contemporaries whose recollections were often written years after the events they discussed. Mr. Sonneck's scholarly works remain unchallenged, but many other histories, recollections, or compilations are in such varying measure untrustworthy that it has seemed wiser to record the source materials as they occur by copious footnotes rather than to perpetuate a bibliography of doubtful value.

H. E. J.

Boston, Massachusetts
January 10, 1943

CONTENTS

ILLUSTRATIONS

Part I

BACKGROUND

I. THE SCENE

*I am a great friend of public amusements for they
keep people from vice.*—BOSWELL

THE BOSTONIAN of 1800 looked at the world and found it good.
It was good because he had helped make it so, and by the turn
of a bright new century firm conviction as to its merits had developed from two hundred years of toil in an undeviating line of
progress. An important part in the founding of a nation had given
the Bostonian courage to face the world and eternity with frankness,
boldness, and a naïve curiosity. So it was with all New England,
which aligned itself, with minor shades of difference, in thought and
custom to the key settlement at the head of Massachusetts Bay.

There was time now to look about, take pleasure in the good already
accomplished, and enjoy some of those arts and graces which make
society not only estimable but pleasant. Philadelphia had already
done so with no loss whatever to her prestige or her prosperity, and
New York was developing along the same line. The South had taken
that point of view from the beginning. Boston's own experience with
the theater had proved very tempting, indeed, and rather more exciting than the endless and literal challenge of hell-fire and brimstone
enjoined by the tiresome proponents of theological disputation, whose
popularity either as rational entertainment or as moral influence was
perceptibly on the decline.

Boston was not a metropolis at the turn of the century; it was more
the village, with twenty-five thousand persons inhabiting a township
laid out in precarious and winding streets and alleys whose names
often suggested either the charming byways of the English countryside or the forthright designation of common trade. Salutation Alley,
White Bread Alley, Frog Lane, Distil-House Square, or Oliver's Dock

were sufficient guides to unnumbered houses and unpaved roads, conditions no worse in Boston than in Vienna but so recognizably inconvenient that special notice in the press assured concert-goers that planks would be strewn on the way for shipwrecked mariners to make the distance from carriage to hall.

The citizen at home was frugal and contented, kept alert by a constant inflow of new ideas but cautious about accepting them; some good things got away during this exercise of extreme wariness, but the net gains were acquisitions of permanent value for the most part, and Boston continued to grow rapidly. Predominantly Federalist, she relaxed not one jot or tittle until well after 1812, while the vast majority of her citizens cast their lot with the American nobility of the time, the moneyed classes, and the English trade relations. Yet a few influential New Englanders—among them John Quincy Adams, son of "old John"—had joined the Republican Party, a defection which was neither here nor there, culturally speaking. Federalism controlled the state legislature and selected the executive from the first and most cultivated families long after Jefferson came to power in that distant "other government" at Washington. Following Adams's retirement the fury of a jealous press belabored Jefferson with singular aversion to the type of breeding which he embodied, and the clergy joined the fray with glee, not hesitating to mention Jefferson and the Devil in one and the same breath. The New England clergy, likening his regime to all the worst excesses of the French revolution, dubbed him a Paine; so excited did they become in their fury that they thundered from their pulpits the warning that his election would result in the burning of Bibles and breaking down of sacred altars. As a specimen of continental degeneracy Jefferson was condemned because he kept a French cook and liked French dishes—"abjuring his native victuals" quoth Patrick Henry.

New England's cultural interests were consistent with her business connections even to the extent of defying the policies of the Federal government. The leading citizens of Boston openly admitted that they considered the best interests of the United States to be inalienably connected with those of Great Britain and that their safety depended on hers. Moreover, a handful of New England's daring and independent legislators envisioned complete secession from the Union in these years, as their sentiments were expressed by President Dwight of Yale in his sermon on the text "Wherefore, come out from among them, and be ye separate, saith the Lord." All these signs of earnest conviction arising from minds independent and free spoke well for the progress of the arts once the serious interest of a cultivated public was gained. The undercurrent rebellion of New England political leaders formed subject matter for discussion on the cracker barrels of country stores and pointed to a thorough and conscientious survey of all intellectual and social movements washed up on the shores of New England's stern and rock-bound coast.

Part of this independence of thought and action may be attributable to the fact that New England's front door was the sea, and that all things, either from distant lands or from other parts of her own Union, came under sail. These days of her maritime glory were possible because overland transportation was difficult and costly. Not until the quarter of a century had passed did land and sea transportation assume a comparable footing.

At the turn of the century New England's cultural experience was confined to forms sanctioned by the ecclesiastical eye, admitting literature, music, and painting strictly on the basis of their moral standards and probable influence on the community. Regularity of conduct in artists—a variable factor, indeed, when tied to the ridgepole of strict theology—was scanned even more rigorously than the work of art itself, for the narrowest ecclesiastics still had imagination enough to envision evil where it was not apparent on the surface. But the broadening of the cultural horizon came, as it needs must come, with a broadening of outlook and a relaxing of proscribed standards of conduct. Enforced concentration on the establishment of a new nation with a consequent turning away from entire reliance on northern Europe was succeeded by a vigorous interchange of ideas and merchandise with the Orient and way stations, a sudden world of empires in which Americans were free to move. The changes were apparent all along the line in Salem and Boston, and they spread with greatest rapidity to the veriest outpost of New England, every community a little Boston with its own wits, literary hacks, and powerful clergymen who tended the souls of their flocks like shepherds, giving due care to the ninety and nine but saving plentiful energy for pursuit of the lost hundredth. The Unitarian and Universalist movements were soon to widen the scope of religious thought to include foreign cultures, to see good (or perhaps good entertainment) in the theater, to recognize fresh and Christian exaltation in the new hymnody, and merits, other than completely papist ones, in the painting and sculpture of Italy. Boston was very late in coming to this pass, but the turn of the century was made at an accelerating speed, and the development of the arts was accomplished with that painstaking thoroughness comparable to building a bridge or laying out a curriculum.

There were tempests in New England teapots to stir up mighty controversies. Utter lack of any recognition of Christmas with all its attendant preparation strikes the student as more heathen than Christian, yet the day remained unmarked by observance in Boston, except for an occasional church service, until 1818. In fact, the strict Baptist clergy proposed a severe penalty for any one apprehended making special observance of the 25th of December! Yet Philadelphia and New York had celebrated Christmas for many years. Once the right to worship according to conviction was reaffirmed on this point, the same intense feeling was displayed with regard to claims of the secular realm in so far as their public practice was concerned. However, throughout all these struggles one must bear in mind that there were liberalizing influences no less powerful toward the establishment of New England as a completely civilized community. The New England gentry enjoyed pleasures and comforts comparable to the best anywhere. Providence had its "Nob" Hill, and Salem its Chestnut Street in process of building; Newburyport, Portland, Portsmouth, and a host of lesser towns now dimmed by decline held high the torch of a new world refinement, in its way quite as culturally enlightened as the more luxurious hospitality of the South.

One observing visitor remarked:

Better tables are nowhere spread than in Boston; and nowhere does a guest find himself more at ease, more secure from solicitations, or entertained with more graceful or cordial hospitality. The best bred women here are charming examples of grace and amenity.

The people of Boston are characteristically distinguished by a lively imagination, an ardor easily kindled, a sensibility soon felt and strongly expressed, a character more resembling that of the Greeks than that of the Romans.[1]

[1] "Boston at the Beginning of the 19th Century," from *Travels in New England* by Timothy Dwight (Old South Leaflets, No. 136).

In such a home might be found an imported pianoforte by Clementi of London or an American instrument made by Osborn or Crehore, and a wide array of fashionable songs, marches, duets, or polite dances. Music was a ladies' pastime in so far as the keyboard instrument was concerned, but gentlemen played the flute or the clarionet —though rarely the violin—and all sang the affecting ballads "What Is the Bosom's Commotion," "Let Me Borrow for a While," or "Eveleen's Bower." There were new books and recent London magazines in these homes, looked down upon by the grim visages of ancestors as painted by Copley, Sargent, or Dunlap. There was silver from Paul Revere's seemingly inexhaustible supply and furniture which we seek out today as finest embodiment of the American tradition.

Boston was a town of small homes, for the most part, all snugly placed together, with precise, formal frontages. In summer the tightness and strictness of the pattern was softened by the gracefulness of the landscape and by white fences marking green lawns overarched with stately elms; the broad doorways wearing shining brass knockers on their bosoms were often framed in lavender fanlights. This mannered, dignified, arrangement was also a practical measure for protection against the winter's cold and an economical means of assuring warmth and comfort when the forbidding snow piled the ground; the stillness of the deep, white blanket gave a sense of patient waiting until another season should allow for frugal expansiveness into the polite New England air. The everyday life of the family was best observed from the rear, for the houses extended by a variable series of attached "ells," leading, even in the central parts of the town to a woodshed, stable, or kitchen garden; well-trod paths to the several buildings and to the neighboring lanes afforded exodus and return for the small boys at play and for the cows at pasture on the already historic common. The Charles River and the marshes of its winding course with their charm of pastoral scene resembled the countryside immemorialized by Constable and Bonington, but to the philosophical Yankee beauty was more often a thing forever in the abstract and not consciously applicable to Pond Street or Frog Lane. To him the insatiable curiosity for distant vistas, rendered into moral and improving influences on character, were more worthy of attention than the prodigal commonplaces of nature. Not in this generation was the beauty of the landscape a compelling factor in literature or art; rather the grim problems of the soul's redemption and the stern visages of those concerned in the process were subjects for the artist's earnest endeavors.

But a change was at hand. These peaceful days bore within them the seeds of dissatisfaction, of longings for the conquering of other and metaphysical worlds, worlds that were not far distant in point of time, as indeed they were revealed to be not unobtainable in point of space. When the earnest New England boy read: "I will lift up mine eyes unto the hills, from whence cometh my help" his thought may have turned to the Berkshires, or to the White Mountains, with entire conviction that they were explicitly intended and that those noble ranges were under no particular obligation to the psalmist for mentioning them. Such a longing for new vistas of the mind was present in Concord and Salem, in Cambridge, and in Roxbury, where the minds of the new day were stirred by the still small voice suggesting that great ideas often come from humble beginnings and that they were chosen to mark the age of maturity in thought for this heaven-sent land. They glimpsed the simple truth that the making of pencils, the surveying of an acre or marking of a sparrow which God had made, that in the lonely, silent room where they were confined through youth, or between the disciplines of becoming self-educated in the classics preparatory to accepting the universe, and the seemingly unrelated teaching of small children, between the gay and sophisticated wanderjahr and the forsaking of the clergy—that in all these there was intimate relation to the Infinite. They were the elect who divined these things.

Education came through the colleges, but not revelation. That came in the silence of the night, in the intervals of pause during a day of toil; it came like a star shining in sparse heavens and its promise was compelling. One reached out his hands and made ready his mind and the revelation came. It came through books and sermons, by listening in the synagogue and watching in the field. To men standing on the shore or before the mast the winds brought the spirit of the Greek argosies, laden with new understanding and spoken with new tongues. On dark winter nights in the town young men gathered in the Palaestra to hear wisdom taught, and at bright noon walked on the shore of Galilee to hear strange new meanings given old familiar doctrines worn thin by the black-robed theologians. All this went side by side with the increase in material prosperity and wealth through-

out the first quarter of the century and brought forth a new and
eager society. There appeared furtive "signs of luxury . . . in an
increasing taste for comfort and the fine arts . . . for now the colonial times and colonial distinctions were fast vanishing . . . and a
sort of upstart vulgarity, which offended the old school of American
social leaders, whose influence was sensibly declining," [2] was current.
The parallel development of the commercial and the intellectual could
have heralded a mighty struggle, but first things came first in the
majority of instances, and New England cultivated the things of the
spirit and adhered to the dictates of the mind with gratifying constancy.

The educational system within the town of Boston and throughout
New England was a matter of pride and a fruitful basis for her
dominant part in the intellectual life of the young nation. The public
schools freely offered the elements of sound learning, possibly with
more literal exactitude than imagination in method, and progressive
steps for the brighter young men to the very doors of Harvard, Dartmouth, or the new colleges at Brunswick or Williamstown.[3] The

[2] Schouler, *History of the United States of America,* II, 248, 253.
[3] President Dwight reported that Boston was the only town to his knowledge
which had formed schools into a system. There were 8 public primary schools,
including one school at the Alms House, providing the elements of education for
2,400 pupils, while 162 private schools had more than 4,000 pupils attending. Children from 4 to 7 years were accomodated with alphabet, spelling, and reading, and
from those subjects they advanced to grammar schools until the age of 14. If sufficient progress warranted they entered Latin School at the age of 9 and English
High at 12, fitting for college which might be entered at 15. In these upper schools
the curriculum was somewhat expanded to include the classics, language and literature, and—for girls, who were in the majority—the refinements of sewing and
music. For an intimate description of the young ladies' seminary, readers are referred to Mrs. Rowson's moral tale, *Charlotte Temple.* A typical curriculum of a
private school in 1815 is appended: plain and ornamental needlework; rug work;
tambour; embroidery; geometry and drawing; painting; reading and writing;
arithmetic; English grammar; geography, including manners and customs; use
of maps and chronology; history, ancient and modern; composition; French and
Latin languages. Mr. Graupner heads the music department.
    It will be recalled that, according to the Mock Turtle, superior schools had
"extras."
    "Yes," said Alice, "we learned French and music."
    "And washing?" said the Mock Turtle.
    "Certainly not!" said Alice indignantly.
    "Ah! Then yours wasn't a really good school," said the Mock Turtle in a tone
of great relief. "Now, at ours, they had, at the end of the bill, 'French, music, *and*
washing—extra.' "
    The budget for primary schools in Boston was $5,000 in 1818 but rose threefold
in a decade, owing in part to the decline in the number of private schools and to a
higher standard of instruction and maintenance.

majority of the sixty young men entering Harvard each year were dedicated to the ministry, but many of those poured in at the opening came out in strange shapes, while some of those who tried the ministry and suffered ordination gave it up after a few years, as did Emerson and Dwight two decades later, the one in Boston retiring to the metaphysical air of Concord, and the other in Northampton finding a career in the practical Christianity of Brook Farm and eventually as musical missionary to the nation. The strength of the clergy, undisputed during two centuries, was clearly broken, but a new life of influence opened to them with the age of speculative philosophy guided by the German and French metaphysicians.

America's growth in the realm of the mind came not so much from any remarkable augmenting of population or immigration as from a new and inspiring contact with the culture of Europe and the Far East. Books and magazines were becoming common property of the citizen whose middle name was self-improvement and whose constant diet was sound moral instruction. The college libraries were growing apace, with Dartmouth owning 12,000 volumes, a collection surpassed in size only by that in Cambridge which, as everyone knew, had been in existence for nearly two centuries and comprised a very learned pile indeed.

A few well-to-do citizens and a number of clergymen had private libraries, and the general public was rapidly acquiring the habit of purchasing books as American publishers bought up plates from English booksellers and issued reprints. But the circulating library was an active institution, although the nature of the contents would hardly meet with the enthusiastic approval of the eager seeker for "light reading" today. One library had 7,000 volumes,[4] bound and unbound, while another leading bookseller advertised a stock of 18,000; of these latter the larger part was comprised of theology, including pamphlets, sermons, and moral miscellany. Books too numerous to mention were advertised in the press, and the following are selected from a library whose other parts included law, medicine, anatomy, and midwifery:

Robertson's Scotland, Moore's Journal, Scott's works, Pope's do. Bolling-broke's do, Don Quixote, Robertson's America, critical and monthly reviews, monthly magazines, Bible, 2 vol. with plates, Paley's Philosophy,

[4] *Columbian Centinel,* Oct. 17, 1819; Parker's Circulating Library, 12 Cornhill.

Winchester's Lectures, Haller's Physiology, Marshall's Life of Washington, Smalley's, Logan's, Porter's, Taylor's and Dana's Sermons, Wright's Book of Martyrs, Jefferson's Notes, Darwin's Zoonomia, Ferguson's Astronomy, Newton and the Prophecies, Smith's Wealth of Nations, Hume's England, Goldsmith's Animated Nature, Dodridges Expositions, Ainsworth's Dictionary, Stewart's Philosophy, Simpson's Algebra, Life of Sir William Jones, Washington's Letters on Agriculture, Locke's Essays, Bacon's do. Newton's works, Romance of the Forest, Blair's Rhetoric, Bellisarius, Boyle's Voyages, Sheridan's Lectures, Plutarch's Lives, Bonaparte, Thompson's Seasons, Gay's Fables, Watts' Psalms and Hymns, American Preceptor, Hubbard's American Reader, do. Geography, &c. &c. &c.[5]

Verily, Sydney Smith's scornful remark in the *Edinburgh Review:* "Who reads an American book? Who looks at an American picture?" had few instances to justify a resounding negative in 1810 or in 1820.

So overwhelming did the book trade become in these years of awakening that another merchant advertised in 1823 a lot of 20,000 volumes of elegant publications from London, Paris, and Leipzig, an advertisement smacking of some exaggeration of numbers. These worthy items were included: Quentin Durward; Scott's Poems; Gibbon's Rome; Smart's Horace; Bradford's Massachusetts; Morse's Geography and Atlas; Scott's Novels; O'Meara's Napoleon; Byron's Works; Cowper's Poems; Thompson's Seasons; Mather's Magnalia; Plutarch; Robertson's Works; Lives of the Poets; Gregory's Dictionary of Arts and Sciences; Village Sermons; Law's Call; Whitfield's Life and Sermons; Orlando Furioso; Scot's Bible; Tacitus, etc.[6] This array of foreign books shows the course of popular interest and offers an interesting commentary on the materials for a thorough education obtained by such zealous souls as Margaret Fuller, then a little girl of nine.

The "Great Unknown," author of the Waverly novels, was the most popular writer after 1815 as every work from his pen became a momentous release for the readers of polite fiction. *Guy Mannering* followed *Waverly* in that year and was immediately performed as a play.[7]

5 *Ibid.,* Jan. 31, 1810. 6 *Columbian Centinel,* Aug. 9, 1823.
7 "One is used to hearing Harriet Beecher Stowe blamed for helping foment the Civil War with Uncle Tom's Cabin, but the same charge has been brought against Scott, and by no other than Mark Twain: 'Sir Walter Scott had so large a hand in making Southern character as it existed before the war, that he is in great measure responsible for the war.'" David A. Randall, "Waverly in America," *Colophon* (New Series), Vol. I, No. 1.

The humble mechanic—term for the working man—was not neglected, for the Mechanics Apprentice Library (established by their
employers) achieved 1,500 volumes of the most solid nature for free
use of the artisan, whose freedom had not yet won a ten-hour day for
journeyman mechanics or carpenters. In short, learning was a popular
thing. Everyone bowed down to the Athenaeum, which in a few years
after its founding had won the awesome respect of the country at
large. As a repository of all genteel knowledge it was principally a
library, immediately commanding an impressive reputation. The most
glorious days of the Athenaeum were to come in the years following,
but its founding in 1815 was blessed by a modern Ptolemy Phila-
delphus, and 25,000 rare volumes poured into its confines within a
decade; eventually it had a collection of Canova statues which could
have received no more attention had they been sculptured by Michel-
angelo.

Among the literary and philosophical clubs, many of them leaving
no record, was the Anthology Club, which helped to give Boston its
reputation as a seat of literary productivity and refinement. "Phi-
lena," the authoress of Beacon Hill, and Robert Treat Paine, the
writer of odes, carried on, as Schouler relates, some well-bred cooing
together upon one another's verses, but the *Monthly Anthologie* is
best forgotten as a literary document. The American Antiquarian
Society, likewise born of the desire on the part of Isaiah Thomas to
preserve the sources of our national development and fostered by
others whose vision saw no further than an impressive result of
accumulation, came into being in 1812 and dedicated its building in
1820. Boston citizens sponsored organizations for the improvement
of the individual and of the group—here, in the vast hereafter, and
at a great distance from home, all were remembered. The merits of
most of these organizations reveal the saneness of the ideas direct-
ing them and the cultural alertness which called them into being. The
American Academy of Arts and Sciences (1780), the Massachusetts
Medical Society (1781), the Boston Library Society (1794), the
Massachusetts Historical Society (1797), the Massachusetts Agri-
cultural Society (1796), together with the Athenaeum (1815) and
the Antiquarian Society (1812) mark a few of the most important;
all the above, it may be noted, recognized the prestige of a fine
library as basis for growth.

There were other societies no less ardent in the purpose of alleviating human misfortune, as the titles reveal. Among them were the Berkshire Society for the Suppression of Vice and the Promotion of Good Morals, a Society for Apprehending Horse Thieves in Dedham, the Boston Female Asylum, the Massachusetts Charitable Fire Society (1794), and the Penitent Females Refuge Society, an institution "formed with the hope of reclaiming, from the paths of vice and ruin, a portion of those unhappy women, whose false steps have blasted their prospects of enjoying a reputable standing in life." To which the writer of the time suggestively adds: "The institution has been remembered on the dying beds of some eminent men in this city, and is worthy the attention and patronage of the living." [8]

In advance of the lyceum movement, public lectures on all subjects designed to improve the lot of man found ready audience among all classes of society. Lectures on chemistry, and orations on oratory, a course in French readings, including recitations in that polite tongue, lectures on singing and the use of the voice, and Mr. Gleason's public course in astronomy, these entertained and uplifted all, aided and abetted by evening schools in reading and writing, accomplishments in which no class of society was entirely proficient. Probably the mechanic had little use for the French lessons and lectures by M. Artiguenave, but he more than likely found occasion to seek instruction in German from Frederick Gustavus Primker, a native of that learned country who settled in Boston in 1824. New England's philosophical and theological unrest was not uninfluenced by the introduction of Carlyle and through him the German metaphysicians, a study given impetus by Frisbie at Harvard and by the genial President Kirkland. Most of the New England thinkers of a generation later learned of them through translation, but scores of systematic young men must have decided that the right way was to begin with a mastery of the language, and if they seem to have taken the long way 'round it may be recalled that Latin and Greek and Hebrew, not to mention Aramaic and other tongues, were read by a surprisingly large number. Parker's mastery of twenty tongues was a generation later, but, on the other hand, Dr. Bentley's fluency in reading eight was already two decades past. Who should stop at another language when all New England was speaking with a new tongue! Ticknor

[8] Caleb Hopkins Snow, *History of Boston* (1825), p. 253.

had not found a single German grammar in Boston in 1818 when he was preparing for his *Wanderjahr*,[9] but his return brought much enlightenment, together with a great many books which awoke the slumbering Cantabrigian mind and gave encouragement to many New Englanders who were already better prepared for progress than the faculty of Harvard College.

Magazines came pouring forth, but the uninspired scholarship of the Cambridge theologians and upholders of passing literary fashions gave little satisfaction to the lay mind, which perceived the brightness of a new era. The *Monthly Anthologie* (1803–1811) offers little of importance, either in self-contained merit, or as reflection of the life of the time, although it fairly bursts with local poetry and a high literary ideal. In a verse by Mrs. Morton it asks for one thing which was never granted:

> No glory I covet, no riches I want,
>   Ambition is nothing to me,
> The one thing I beg a kind Heaven to grant
> Is a mind independent and free.[10]

The fact that the most able wielders of pen and pencil were of the clergy mitigated against unbiased consideration of secular matters, and the moralizing tendency, stamped on every page, while good for the ethical tone of the magazine, made for dull reading among those whose virtue was beyond reasonable question.

The *North American Review*, established in 1815, had Jared Sparks as editor and some notable contributors, among them William Tudor, Walter and Ellery T. Channing, Edward Everett, Theodore Lyman, Ex-President John Adams, William Cullen Bryant, Mrs. Sigourney of Hartford, Wendell Phillips, and James T. Austin, but in spite of this array the *Review* soon outlived its promise and left New England's livelier minds chafing under the lack of a truly representative means of expression for new ideas. They must perforce rely on reviews from other parts of the country and from England, but it must be admitted that there were none with sufficient command to hold the fort until the period of "the Newness" and the appearance of the

[9] There may not have been a grammar, but there were hundreds of volumes in German, as Dr. Harold Jantz has shown in his "German Thought and Literature in New England, 1620–1820," *Journal of English and German Philology,* Vol. XLI, No. 1, Jan. 1942.
[10] Page 374.

Dial—a long wait, indeed, from the days of our concern. New England, as well as all parts of the country partaking in any measure of the intellectual ferment, was so greatly occupied in the assimilation of the rich heritage suddenly revealed by the European literature of old and new times that the digestive process was hardly begun; a native literature could not free itself from the overwhelming weight of a powerful tradition. It was as though America's keenest minds had suddenly emerged from a darkened room, and the glory of the scene so completely overawed them that original expression on a mature level was, for a time, impossible. Even those who would try found themselves uttering imitative or distressingly crude words and second-hand ideas. The notion of a native literature was early conceived and many earnest souls tried to add their mite, but the charge to break away from a foreign tradition was not clearly voiced until Emerson quietly propounded revolution in "The American Scholar" address of 1837, making very many enemies by his words. Meanwhile the trials and failures of the earlier day strewed the path throughout the first quarter of the century, for there were no very persuasive utterances in print to denote any single arrival of native genius until William Cullen Bryant's time. Typical, if not shining, examples of the subject matter conceived by the literary mind when not occupied by matters of the soul are Alexis Eustaphieve's "Demetrius, the Hero of the Don" and Robert Treat Paine's stream of effusions which show a classical basis, even when the actual subject matter is concerned with the American scene. No, New England was thinking hard and reading with avidity, but the pen was not put to paper with great advantage either to author or public.

The religious opinions of the people were undergoing in these years more marked a change than had occurred in the two previous centuries since the first settlers arrived. That which became change within a quarter of a century seemed like gradual broadening of view at the time, but the powerful impetus of enlarged cultural life, extending the borders of a narrow theological dogma, carried the well-prepared minds of the populace to a new concept of faith and works, quite remote in many respects from that which characterized the early history of New England. The material aspects of a prosperous era were greatly responsible for the change, but by themselves they would

have had a destructive effect had they not been subservient to the
high principles of the spiritual ideal held by the best minds of the
time. The broadening of cultural vistas and the natural extension
of classic literary and philosophic ideals into recognized forms of
art helped to maintain the high level of purpose cherished by the
Christian believer. These brought about a true flowering of a sturdy
but not especially beautiful plant.

Before the turn of the century Calvinism very generally prevailed
among New Englanders, and the emphasis was on salvation reserved
for the afterlife. Present existence was of small consequence in so far
as organized secular enjoyment was concerned, although the increasing prosperity following the effects of the Revolution brought about
conditions of ease which were certainly not unwelcome to those who
enjoyed them, or unworthy of emulation by the larger citizenry
which comprised the "have not" class. New England's landscape was
sprinkled with meeting houses of many denominations and with many
edifices dedicated to the same denominations. In these years many of
the beautiful spired structures, now treasured as landmarks of the
countryside, were consecrated to the service of God by communities
which felt their nearness to the Divine Being. Harvard College prepared a large portion of the ministers occupying these small but
pleasant benefices, with Yale and a few other colleges adding a substantial number, but the Presbyterian complexion of the Princetonian
did not meet with approval in New England. The clergy was often
young and usually forthright in conviction; it was deeply educated
in the classics and ably instructed in the finer points of doctrine,
which, indeed, often constituted its chief rallying point. More often
than the surviving legend hints it was liberal, but liberality of outlook often depended on the parish and, directly, on the connection
of the townspeople with the trend of thought in the outside world.
For instance, the clergy of Salem was notably broad both in interests
and in viewpoint toward other faiths and toward contributing arts
and cultures. In Newburyport and Portland a similar broadness was
noticeable, but within other denominations and other districts the
strength of a faith often lay in its narrowness. Boston, then as
today, was center of the broadest and of the narrowest faiths, with
Dr. Channing paving the way for a period of "the Newness," though
hardly recognizing it in the later day, and the Baptist and Methodists

holding to an extremely literal interpretation of the letter of scriptural authority.

The Unitarian body, as an independent movement, did not declare itself until 1819 when, once convinced that the conception of God as a jealous Being, mankind as conceived in iniquity, and salvation only by special grace did not partake of scriptural authority, Dr. Channing regretfully perceived the necessity of withdrawing from the Congregational conference and threw his whole weight on the side of new and warmer articles of faith. He found, and preached, a humane spirit teaching the goodness of God, the essential virtue and perfectability of man, and freedom of the will with its individual responsibility for action. Here was a liberalizing doctrine for the not inconsiderable number of malcontents among the old Congregationalists. The response was overwhelming, with fellow clergymen leaving their pulpits and many of the worshippers following them to new and sunnier regions where the soul dwelt in peaceful contemplation of a world fairer to the sight than the one they had known.

As Dr. Channing's thought was liberated, religion became integrated with daily life and work and with recreation. He denied the distinction between cultural and vocational studies, insisting on the possibility of attaining culture by means of one's vocation intelligently pursued. He advocated improvements in hygiene, food, recreation. If, in the long run, his thought inclined to lose immediate connection with God's part in the plan of human improvement, the reaction soon caused the Concord group to turn once again to the metaphysical. Not until the 'thirties did the strong and vigorous doctrine of this new order, with its implications of social and cultural betterment, appear so weakened by the successive dilutings of Unitarianism that some of its leaders, among them Emerson, Ripley, J. S. Dwight, and an host of others, turned away in disappointment. President Dwight of Yale, staunch believer in the old order of militant theology, wrote that Unitarianism appeared to be the predominating system but added: "It is believed that neither ministers nor people have had any reason to congratulate themselves on this change." Dwight, however, belonged to the previous century, as remote a time in matters of theology and culture as though it were two centuries past.

Outside the church, the theater, literary life, and art movements of the new day drew the attention of parishioners with non-denomi-

national and interdenominational interests. Within the sacred confines
the music was changing from the old style of Billings-inspired psalmody to the new hymns of Watts and the tunes inspired by Mozart,
Beethoven, and the English hymnodists. Some of the worst offenses
against a loving God, whose true nature was certainly not discerned
in this verse, were purged from the hymn-books:

> Ye monsters of the bubbling deep,
>   Your Maker's praises shout;
> Up from the sands, ye codlings, peep,
>   And wag your tails about.[11]

Brattle Street Church had installed an organ as early as 1745,
and replaced it in 1774, the latter remaining until 1874 when the
building was demolished. The Old South organ, built by Edward Brom-
field, was the first organ of American make in a Boston church, while
the first Boston organ factory, owned by William Goodrich (Good-
ridge), made an installation in the Catholic Cathedral in 1805.[12] By
1815 there were five organs in Boston churches, it is said, in King's
Chapel, Christ, Brattle Street, Trinity, and the Cathedral; within
two years two more were added, in the First Universalist and Federal
Street, and after a few years more new and expensive organs replaced
the primitive boxlike creations then current, while the recalcitrant
parishes of Boston and elsewhere continued to rely on the serpent,
clarionet, and bass for doleful accompaniment to even more doleful
sentiments. With the installation of adequate organs, the standard
of church music was subject to improvement; professional organists
were added to the singing leader, whose power and authority de-
creased accordingly. From Trinity Church, Boston, one of the leading churches in so far as its expenditure for music was concerned, we
may deduce some conclusions applicable in reduced measure to other
congregations. In 1800 the parish paid one hundred dollars to its
organist, fifteen to the bellows-blower, and fifty to the singing leader.
With the advent of the accomplished Peter Von Hagen, who served

[11] The Rev. W. S. Christopher's *Poets of Methodism;* this is not a typical example,
fortunately.
[12] "There are said to have been fewer than twenty church organs in all New England as late as 1800, and probably a not much larger number in other parts of the
country in proportion to the population. As late as 1814 singing in the Park Street
Church, Boston, was supported only by a flute, a bassoon, and bass viol, and in
1845 the Hanover Street Church was still using only a clarinet, an ophicleide, and a
double bass." Henry Wilder Foote, *Three Centuries of American Hymnody,* p. 85.

during the first decade, the salary progressively increased to two
hundred, and the church fathers voted a special letter of appreciation to Major Higginson, J. R. Parker, and the Rev. Mr. Gardiner
for their efforts on behalf of the choir. Through a succession of distinguished ministrations on the organ by James Hewitt and the thrice-
eminent Dr. Jackson the salary remained the same, but the choir
regularly received votes of thanks through the brothers J. R. and
Matthew S. Parker "for their long continued zeal & attention to the
music of the church & also that the same be extended to the gentlemen
of the choir." [13]

The choir at Trinity, be it known, was not a heterologous assemblage of vain parishioners with new hats, but a properly organized
body enrolled in a singing school; there were about eighty-five members about equally divided between men and women. In 1820 about
four hundred dollars each year was spent for employing a singing
master of "first rate talents and respectability," to whom upwards of
one hundred persons came regularly for instruction. This zeal was but
typical of other congregations and explains, in part, the inevitability
of the Handel and Haydn Society, organized in 1815, which brought
together singers of many denominations whose enthusiasm for the
great composers was equal to the test of many laborious rehearsals.
Solo singing was not permitted in churches until the works of Händel
and Haydn had revealed instances of lofty strain possible of presentation without theatrical affectation. Mrs. Graupner and Mr. Stockwell
were among the earliest and bravest proponents of the sacred solo,
which remains today a doubtful acquisition to the ornaments of sacred
worship. The revolution in style of music sung in churches created a
major disturbance in ecclesiastical realms, and not without reason.
All the benefits claimed for the new method were not immediately
forthcoming, and the transition period was a difficult one indeed for
adherents both to the new and to the old styles. The *North American
Review* summed up the matter fairly in a review of Thomas Hastings's
Dissertation on Musical Taste:

There was general recognition that the old music, represented by Billings
and his "fugueing" tunes was poor stuff and that the best music should—at
that time—come from the recognized masters of Europe. The break, however, had been too sudden in many cases, for the singers were incapable of

13 *Columbian Centinel,* April 12, 1819.

properly representing the new music and made such a bad job that many wished for the return of the old music which at least received performance worthy of its mettle. "Tear away, brother Martin, never mind, so you do but tear away," is the maxim on which they often proceed. Something like this has been the case in the change which, within a few years has taken place in the character of our music. The attempt was a laudable one; at the same time it must be allowed that the knowledge and good judgment of those who were active in the measure, were outstripped by their zeal. The community needed more preparation for so great a change, and to the no small astonishment of the reformers, the anticipated result was not realized. The tune was changed, but the manner of singing was unaltered, and of course the effect was much the same.[14]

Few types of publication poured forth from the press in greater number than the collections of sacred anthems, each labeled with the name of a specific parish, as *First Church Collection, Bridgewater Collection, Old Colony Collection*, or, the greatest of them all, *The Handel and Haydn Collection*. The Harvard University Choir owned *Thirty Anthems*, selected by John Hubbard, "late Professor of Mathematics and Natural Philosophy in the University of Dartmouth," published in 1814, a collection boasting works by Händel, Purcell, Croft, Clark, "Bird," and other respected authors, all of them moderately difficult. If the Harvard Choir, which sang at Commencement Exercises in company with the Pierian Sodality, founded in 1808, did them justice, it must have been a good choir indeed. Every congregation with pretensions to leadership in the new and fashionable style of church music caused its name to be conspicuously emblazoned on a collection of church music; the custom, for the most part limited to New England, proved to be one with astonishing business advantages and the various collections spread among the states with rapidity.

Boston found the visual arts quite within the range of early comprehension, once the prejudice against sacred representations, as smacking of Papist leanings or pagan idolatry, was overcome. Prominent New England burghers had for generations suffered their likenesses to be rendered by such as Copley and Stuart and a group of lesser men who did not develop into painters of first rank. Miniaturists, wax-figure artists, and silhouette cutters flourished from time unknown, many of the first worthy of greater recognition as artists

14 Vol. XV, Oct., 1822.

than they received. With the increased consciousness of society's obligation to preserve and display the culture of all times, these artists found increasing recognition in a community taking its ease and its pleasure among worldly refinements.

Museums are not far removed from peep shows and have a history deriving from the circus. At this period they were the repositories of the strange and the rare, giving preference to "the only one of its kind" rather than to a "typical specimen"; they were designed to cause amazement and wonder, excite curiosity over nature's mistakes at home and in the most distant parts of the earth. The era of classification and sub-classification evoked by the German scientific mind had not yet arrived, and each museum remained a law unto itself, stooping or rising to any attraction, living or dead, which would separate the citizen from twenty-five cents. Needless to say, they were assembled with the thought of providing amusement, and many of them were dedicated to the "believe it or not" school of thought, drawing a public which profited by the stirrings of the imagination caused by a lively array of curiosities. Boston early had its quota of museums, which changed hands, exhibitions, and locations, but constantly improved in purpose and scope until they were superseded by such august institutions as the galleries of the Athenaeum when the separation of the scientific, the fine art, and the freak—if they are ever completely separable—was finally arrived at.

The first museum in Boston was owned by Daniel Bowen at the American Coffee House, State Street, about 1791, but moved to a hall over a schoolhouse in 1795 when it became the Columbian Museum, flourishing under that name for many years. Mr. Bowen in 1798 held an ambitious exhibit which excited some comment by reason of its quantity and novelty, if not by its quality. The usual array of wax figures included John Adams, George Washington (both of these gentlemen still among the living), Dr. Franklin sitting with Dr. Stiles "late President of Yale College, Connecticut," and the guillotine with a man beheaded. The paintings, 123 in number, ran the gamut from ancient times to the very present, while offering no discernible organization of subject matter. These titles indicate the range of the exhibition:

> Mr. Garrick speaking the Ode to Shakespeare
> Mrs. Yates in the character of Medea

Scene in the 4th act of Hamlet
Scene in the 3rd Act of King Lear
Mr. Lowndes and family of Maryland
A beautiful Grecian Lady
Garrick resigning the State
Boadecia, an ancient British Queen
Canute
the Four seasons
Mr. Sterrett and family of Maryland
An elegant fruit piece
Col. Alexander Hamilton
Baron Stuben
A house and Garden in England
Contemplation
A mad woman in Prison [15]

To these should be added a live rattlesnake, alligator, and eagle—in the gallery with the Presidents.

Fire often endangered the permanency of these collections, and the Columbian Museum suffered conflagration which several times completely demolished this panorama of history. The first disaster, in 1803, resulted in the immediate assembling of other exhibit material for installation at Milk and Oliver Streets; Bowen was joined by William S. Doyle, the miniaturist, in 1806 when a new five-story building was erected near Stone Chapel, only to be ravaged within seven weeks of its opening. Another was built and opened on June 2, 1807, the third attempt surviving until 1825 when it was sold for about five thousand dollars to the New England Museum. Travelers —and it must be remembered that New England's extensive commerce took her citizenry to distant parts—took pride in returning with offerings for the local museum, while the seemingly endless series of calamities which attended each step of its progress elicited much goodwill from the populace, which contributed in its several capacities toward rebuilding the exhibitions. Mr. Bowen was a respected citizen who edited a valuable guide-book history of Boston after his retirement.

A competitor during the summer of 1811 was the New York Museum, in Boylston Hall under the direction of Mr. Savage. Here the public was invited to inspect "Quadrupeds, Birds, Reptiles, Insects, Shells, Fossils, Minerals, Coins, Indian Curiosities, Paintings, Prints, Wax Figures, &c. to the number of 15,000. A telescope through which

[15] *Columbian Centinel*, Nov. 28, 1798.

the Moon, Mars, and Saturn may be viewed is available on evenings when the atmosphere is clear." [16] Concerts of music were given regularly on the "Grand Pianoforte" by Peter Dolliver and on other types of instruments from hand to mouth organs. The Columbian Museum showed the same class of exhibition, adding statuary, and offering miniature portrait painting "executed in an elegant and pleasing style" and profiles cut correctly by Doyle and Williams. Many of these are now in the Boston Museum of Fine Arts, including miniatures of Gottlieb Graupner, Boston's leading musician, and Joseph T. Buckingham, the editor and publisher of the *New England Galaxy;* they show a fine skill, deserving a place among the best of American miniature paintings.

A new museum of wax figures, patterned after the famous London palace of entertainment, was opened by James Bishop in 1812 at the Columbian Coffee-House but appears not to have remained for long. The prime attraction was a female elephant, long on exhibition, which finally gave way to an African lion. "The form of the Lion is strikingly majestic, and his figure is respectable, his looks are determined, his gait is steady, and his voice tremendous," quoth the press. Other special attractions at the Columbian Museum included vocal music by a lady and a gentleman and the ascent of an illuminated air balloon. In fact Boston boasted three museums in 1818. The New England Museum showed natural and miscellaneous curiosities and wax figures; the Market Museum had an elephant, camel, moose, a bone weighing 500 pounds, an elephant skeleton; while the superior Gallery of Fine Arts showed paintings, statuary by Canova, prints, and medals. Ever mindful of the patriotic fervor of these ardent times, on significant holidays special attractions were offered, of which the attached is an example: [17]

TRIBUTE OF RESPECT

The Columbian Museum, in Milk-street, will be opened on Monday
Evening Next, in honor of the Birthday of John Adams Esq.
Late President of the United States of America.
Mr. P. Dolliver will, on this occasion, perform a variety
of Patriotic Pieces, &c. on the Grand Piano Forte. . . .

There were famous painters in Boston whose names have lasted to our own day, even though their works are stored in the basement or

[16] Boston *Gazette*, Aug. 12, 1811.   [17] *Columbian Centinel*, Oct. 29, 1803.

relegated to obscure galleries in the present-day museum. Washington Allston, whose pupils were Morse and Leslie, was elected to the Royal Academy of Fine Arts in 1819, a cricumstance which gave his *Jeremiah* added interest for a public which visited it at the Boylston Market House and paid twenty-five cents for the privilege of viewing this frightening figure of huge proportions. At Doggett's Repository another panorama drew throngs for many months during the season of 1823; this was Samuel F. B. Morse's *Representative's Hall at Washington* (properly titled *The Old House of Representatives*) with eighty-eight portraits in the large canvas; this was followed in May— at the customary admission fee—by Thomas Sully's *Washington Crossing the Delaware* and later by Rembrandt Peale's *The Court of Death*. Boston recognized her artists with reasonable pride, and supported them as eminent craftsmen to be called upon for such diverse matters as painting the family portrait or designing a tavern sign. The *North American Review* gave attention to painters long before taking any notice of musicians, mentioning these men with especial pride: Gilbert Stuart, Col. Henry Sargeant, Samuel F. B. Morse, Stuart Newton (his nephew), Penniman and Fisher (pupils of Newton), Tisdale, Corny (a ship painter), Willard (the sculptor), Jones, Greenwood, Coles, and Doyle (the miniaturist). Paintings by Trumbull—his *Signing of the Declaration of Independence* shown in 1818 before permanent hanging in Washington—and others of the New York and Philadelphia schools joined the procession exhibited for an art-conscious public, while West's designs for *Death on the Pale Horse*, painted by William Dunlap on the subject of Revelation: 6, 1–2, deserve special mention.[18] The lesser painters who enjoyed high esteem in the Boston of this era included Chester Harding, Henry Sargent (1770–1845), whose *Dinner Party* (frontispiece) and *Tea Party* were attractions in the galleries for nearly a year; J. R. Penniman, erstwhile scene painter; these were ranked with the architect Bulfinch in merit, if not in social position or civic influence. A glowing tribute ranked Sargeant highly, but the flat, stale, and unprofitable canvases now reposing in one of the lesser American rooms at the Boston Museum do not justify such a tribute as this:

18 "And I saw when the Lamb opened one of the seals, and I heard, as it were the noise of thunder, one of the four beasts saying, Come and see. And I saw, and behold a white horse: and he that sat on him had a bow; and a crown was given unto him: and he went forth conquering, and to conquer."

JOSEPH T. BUCKINGHAM
Miniature by Trumbull

GOTTLIEB GRAUPNER
Miniature by Doyle

We feel confidence in asserting that few if any living artists can paint two interiors more perfectly than the two by Mr. Sargent. We have seen over twenty interiors among a great body of pictures by French painters in a late exposition in the Louvre; and it is hardly extravagent to say that their perspectives were Chinese compared with the two of which we now speak.[19]

By 1827, however, the system of privately sponsored art galleries was inaugurated in Boston, when the Athenaeum opened its first show by American artists; this salon continued for many years. Indeed, by this time the Athenaeum had long since deserved Dwight's tribute that "The institution is prosperous, and is certainly very honorable to the town, and particularly to the gentlemen who have raised it to such a degree of respectability."

Congress had taken cognizance of the importance of certain momentous occasions in the early years of the young democracy and had passed a resolution commissioning the execution of four historical paintings. They were completed in 1824 and sent to Washington after each had enjoyed a triumphal tour of the major cities, while the press of the country praised the measure and the paintings and hoped for a continuance of the custom of marking important national events. In Boston these works were shown, appropriately enough, at Faneuil Hall. The editorials exclaimed: "How much must the United States do to advance the arts and sciences!" and Dr. Channing's prophetic words were coming true:

To rid society of its sordid vices, music should be taught in the common schools. Dancing should be encouraged and festivals fostered, so that old and young might share in sports and pastimes. There should be picture-galleries and halls of sculpture. Boston should develop the sense of beauty by creating beauty.[20]

So had Boston come a long way from the severe Puritanism of Dwight, Jonathan Edwards's grandson, who frowned on "song" and the "arts of the pencil and chisel."

Possibly the righteous objector had been fortified by such an exhibit as that shown in Boston in 1818, one which, if understood, might have given the most broadly cultured Puritan descendent some pause. Inevitably, the "Progress" series must have been included, but some of Hogarth's works, at least, had been shown many times before.

19 *Columbian Centinel,* May 8, 1824.
20 *Life of William Ellery Channing,* American Unitarian Association.

HOGARTH'S WORKS

THE entire works of this inimitable Painter, comprising one hundred and eleven superb Engravings, together with a key and book of explanation, is just placed in

THE GALLERY OF FINE ARTS
At No. 76, Court-Street

Those who have had the pleasure of viewing this great and interesting work, will need no inducement to call and view it again and again. Those who have not seen it should not miss so good an opportunity. Several additions have been recently made to the Gallery.[21]

The same Museum within a few months offered "The Lilliputian Songsters," a pair of dwarfs who sang songs "modern, fashionable, and patriotic"; these minute phenomena attracted very full and fashionable houses by reason of "their very small and beautiful persons, their intelligence and genteel deportment," which were very edifying to an art-loving public.[22]

The art criticism of the day was no better than the music criticism, nor was thoughtful and intelligent comment to find expression until Margaret Fuller's article on the Canova sculptures and Italian paintings appeared in 1841. Local pride and prejudice occasionally ruffled the surface of what would otherwise be a united encouragement of American art. A Major Jackson, aide to Washington, testified that the Philadelphian Peale's portrait was the best likeness he ever had seen of the Father of His Country, but the editor inserted a simple question by inquiring if the venerable Major had ever seen that by Stuart which hung in Faneuil Hall. Stuart, despite his residence in the Quaker city, was jealously considered to be a Bostonian, although Boston did little to justify its claim on the basis of any special affection. Following Stuart's death this tribute was paid to him:

THE 5 PRESIDENTS OF THE UNITED STATES
DOGGETT'S REPOSITORY
No. 16 Market-street

Is opened for the exhibition of the portraits of the five Presidents of the United States by Stuart.
The room will be opened at 9 o'clock and kept warm.
Admittance 25 cents.

[21] *Columbian Centinel*, Sept. 23, 1818.   [22] *Ibid.*, Oct. 16, 1819.

The next month Doggett's exhibited the following masterpieces of art, if we are to believe the announcement:

> Paintings by Raffaello, Guido, Domenichino, Rubens, Titian, Giotto, Paul Potter, Claude Lorraine, Del Sarto, Poussin, Ostade, Corregio, Rembrandt, Murillo, etc.

A rather staggering lot for that time, place, and condition! Either the exhibition failed to include impressive works by these masters or Boston was not ready for an event which might well have marked a new era.

II. THE POLITE ARTS

*It is a circumstance peculiarly fortunate to the temporary
introduction of a Theatre into this town that with respect
to the foregoing characters their theatrical talents are
only to be equalled by their domestic virtues.—Eastern
Herald* (Portland), Oct. 13, 1794.

D R. CHANNING's interest in the dance was not especially shock-
ing in 1815. The persistent legend of the Puritan frown on
this form of entertainment has been over-stressed, for dancing as a polite form of amusement had found wide acceptance in New
England before the turn of the century, as it had long before that
time elsewhere. Dancing was associated with French culture, as indeed it must be, and its popularity was brought about by the influx
of Revolutionary volunteers in the entourage of Lafayette. Not that
the revered general brought his own dancers as entertainment with
him, but as an incidental accomplishment of most young Frenchmen
the dance was developed to a point which seemed professional to the
virtually untutored social grace of the average well-to-do American.
Many of the volunteers remained in the States, or in neighboring colo-
nies, finding employment in the several occupations among which cultural pursuits were liberally represented. Boston received Mr. Mallet,
the actor and singer, a gentleman of much refinement according to
contemporary accounts, while "Mon. Labasse, one of the first dancers
at the Paris Opera," proved his mettle by becoming dancing master
at the Federal Theatre and an orchestral conductor. From the beginning a ballet was conceived of as integral part of the ill-fated Haymarket Theatre.

H. Mann led a cotillion band of ten members for assemblies in
Boston, as did Mr. Porter Tidd, and the dancing teachers numbered
no less than three or four at any time. George Labottiere, Peter
Landrin Duport, and William Turner were active before 1800 as

proprietors of dancing classes, the latter persisting at Concert Hall
for many years; George Schaffer and Vincent Masi both belonged to
artistic families, other members figured prominently as muscians,
barbers, and confectioners; while the names of Mr. Carter, Mrs. P.
Jutau are periodically in the list of dancing teachers, several of
whom gave summer classes with apparent success. "Rural Grace,"
a ballet, was presented at the theater as a special attraction in 1815,
while three years later "Love among the Roses" graced the boards.
"Shelty's Frolic" appeared in 1819, and other evidences of the ballet
form, coupled with pantomime, are to be found in the records of the
Boston stage. The dance was often considered an adjunct to an evening of Shakespeare; at all times it was confined to the theater, or
to the public exhibitions of the teachers, and not integrated with the
concert life. The conventional forms of choreography were adhered
to, if we may accept that concocted by M. Labarre for his pupil's
recital as typical of the time; this exhibition took place in 1823.

GRAND EXHIBITION AND BALL

Messrs. PARKS AND LABASSE have the honor to inform the Ladies and Gentlemen of Boston, and their friends that their GRAND EXHIBITION BALL will
take place on Tuesday Evening, 4th inst. at Concert Hall, where a new
ballet, composed for the occasion, will be danced by Mr. LABASSE and the
pupils. Neither pains nor expense have been spared to make it in every respect satisfactory to all who will honor them with their presence.

1. Entry of the Corps de Ballet, by 60 pupils.
2. Pas de Huit, by 4 young ladies and 4 young gentlemen.
3. Pas de Trois, by 3 young ladies.
4. Pas de Quatre, by 4 young ladies.
5. Gavotte, by three young Ladies.
6. Pas de Huit, by a young Lady.
7. Pas de Trois, by 3 young ladies.
8. Gavotte by 2 young Ladies and 2 young Gentlemen.
9. Pas de Sept, with shawl, garlands, and wreaths by 2 young ladies.
10. Pas de Deux with wreaths, by 2 young Ladies.
11. Folies d'Espagne, by Mons. Labasse, with 2 young Ladies.
12. FINALE, GARDEN DANCE, by 48 pupils.[1]

There were in these early days no individual dancers with attractions
comparable to Fanny Ellsler, on whom Emerson looked with pleasure
and many Boston dowagers with feelings akin to horror.

[1] *Columbian Centinel*, Nov. 1, 1823.

Boston's official conscience—formidable weapon!—was for long at variance with the desires of its populace with respect to the introduction of a theater. The struggle between the two had some amusing incidents before resistance was overcome sufficiently to permit abandoned enjoyment in footlight entertainment; however, a theater by any other name had on occasion delighted a few of the inhabitants of New England, the other name usually being a "Moral Entertainment" on so grave a subject as Hamlet, or a series of recitations interspersed with a variety of miscellaneous matter. When a group of leading citizens of the town of Boston prayed the legislature to permit the repeal of the onerous restrictions on plays and theatrical representations, the opposition surveyed the petition with proper dignity. William Tudor (later editor of the *North American Review*) affirmed that stage exhibits were consonant with the moral life of the people, but Benjamin Austin at length produced a series of essays to prove that Shakespeare had no genius, at least in 1792, and his lengthier judgment carried the day.

In the face of this blow and the consequent denial of the legislature, a group of gentlemen caused a building to be constructed, called the New Exhibition Hall, in which a program of tight-rope walking, hornpipes, tumbling, and minuets by Mr. and Mrs. Placide was installed. The diversion was a pronounced success with the public and the type of entertainment was extended to include the forbidden fruit of acted plays. In the course of a performance of *The School for Scandal*, while Sir Peter and Lady Teazle were on the stage of the little hall in Board Alley, the sheriff arrived and put a summary end to the iniquitous proceedings which were being viewed with satisfaction by some of Boston's leading citizens. Demonstrations by an aroused public within and without the courtroom vindicated Mr. Harper as manager and soon paved the way for the removal of obstructions to legitimate theatrical entertainments. The enlightened citizens of the town speedily pushed their resolve until a theater, called the Federal Street, was formally opened on February 4, 1794, with an Ode written for the occasion by Robert Treat Paine; thereafter regular seasons of dramatic and musical plays became an established and lawful fact.

A second playhouse, the Haymarket, opened in January, 1797, but Boston was not large enough for two institutions and an agreement was made whereby the Federal Theatre would be used for winter and the Haymarket for summer productions. Within a short time, however, the Federal Theatre was burned, an event acclaimed by the Baptists as judgment visited upon the children of darkness. But another and better playhouse was constructed and remained for many years the scene of notable successes, for the great plays of that and other days were produced and the finest actors in America trod its boards. Dunlap writes that "many of our very excellent actors made their first appearance in America on the stage of the Boston theatre."

Hartford and Providence followed suit, enjoying for the most part visits of casts selected from the Boston company, while Salem continued for a time a hospitable town for entertainment of all kinds. The flourishing seaport towns of Salem, Portsmouth, Newburyport, and Portland had not shown Boston's early hostility to the theater, but had early welcomed the drama in makeshift productions, sending its clergy to profit by such cultural opportunities as productions of *The Beaux' Stratagem* and *Thomas and Sally*.

With the backing of leading citizens, and under the management of the Powells, the Federal Theatre immediately took its place among the finest theaters of the country. Not until the turn of the century, or even later, did the great actors of the day visit America, but in the earliest seasons those brought over from England, comprising young talents or secondary favorites from the provincial theaters of Bath and Bristol, were equal to the demands of the American audiences; many of them became popular as professional ladies and gentlemen and esteemed as citizens of the new land. They were familiar with the current London successes and were practiced in the plays of Shakespeare; they possessed moderate vocal accomplishments and could turn a song in the course of an evening's divertissement; also, a factor essential to the complete satisfaction of a Boston audience, they boasted a general respectability, with a few scandalous exceptions who were hustled out of town in short order and with a minimum of publicity.

By the turn of the century the Boston public had reversed Austin's dictum and discovered that Shakespeare had genius. It had seen *As You Like it, The Merchant of Venice, Macbeth, Othello,* and *Hamlet* often enough to appreciate the main outlines of the action and a measure of the wisdom expressed in the lines. The final act of *The*

FEDERAL STREET THEATRE

Positively the last night this season

Miss Field's Benefit

This Evening, May 11, Will be presented (for the 1st time these two years)
Shakespear's celebrated tragedy of Macbeth. With the original Airs, and
Choruses, of Matthew Locke, got up under the direction of Mr. Graupner.

Macbeth,	Mr. Rutley	Assassins,	Parsons and Cory
Banquo,	Mr. Whitlock	Officer,	Mr. Moore
Duncan,	Mr. Kenny	Macduff,	Mr. Jones
Malcolm,	Mr. Downie	Hecate,	Mr. Story
Lenox,	Mr. Dykes	1st Witch,	Mr. Bates
Fleance,	Master Schaffer	2nd Witch,	Mr. Villiers
Messenger,	Mr. Barnes	3rd Witch,	Mrs. Simpson

Lady Macbeth,   Mrs. Whitlock
Lady in Waiting, Miss Bates

Vocal parts—Messrs. Story, Bates, Villiers, Dykes &c.—
Mrs. Jones, Mrs. Graupner, Miss Field, Miss Westray, &c.
After the play, the favorite song of
Crazy Jane, in character, by Miss Field
In the course of the evening, the favorite song of
The Twins of Latona, by Mr. Story

The whole to conclude with a Farce (Never performed in Boston) called
The Spirit of Contradiction. Written by a Gentleman of Cambridge. . . .[2]

Merchant was omitted, and the play was advertised as a comedy;
Jessica, when played by Mrs. Graupner, was "with a song," as was
Patience, the Woman to Queen Katherine, in *King Henry the Eighth*.[3]
In *Othello* the scene where his recall and the ill-timed intervention of
Cassio leads Othello to personal violence on Desdemona was struck
out as too strong for the tastes of refined audiences.[4] In all the
plays the parts were stripped to leading roles with the star's role
remaining head above all. Before long the list of Shakespearian plays
was extended to include both Richards, *King Lear, Coriolanus, Romeo,
Catherine and Petruchio, Henry IV,* and *Much Ado about Nothing.*
Romeo was played by a woman for many years and doubtless other
things were done to the sacred lines and scenes which would horrify
the twentieth-century audience which likes its Shakespeare una-
bridged. The noble lines, however found their way into the vocabu-

2 Boston *Gazette,* May 11, 1801.   3 Performed Jan. 6, 1800, and March 10, 1800.
4 Act IV, Sc. 1.

lary of the time and were apt for quotation, or misquotation,[5] with increasing frequency. *Macbeth* closed the season of 1801, played by Mr. Rutley, Mr. and Mrs. Whitlock, and interpolating the airs and choruses of Matthew Locke, arranged by Mr. Graupner.

Fortunately the lines of Shakespeare were spoken by English actors and not subject to the vagaries of Yankee accent, but their provincial tongue was not free of errors of grammar and a frequent approximation of lines which rendered the dramatic sense but not the beauty of the speech. However, the forte of the majority of the players was farce or comedy and not the elegance of classical English. Classical English, by the by, hardly does justice to the letters furnished the press, which provide an interesting commentary on the public's reaction.

To Readers and Correspondents
Theatrical

. . . We acknowledge the receipt of several theatrical paragraphs, containing strictures on the "Merchant of Venice."—The Piece signed "Ballario," claims much credit. He is just, candid, and at times pointedly severe. His remarks are chiefly occupied with the characters of "Shylock," "Portia," "Bassanio," and "Launcelot." . . . The critic says, that Mrs. Jones's "Jessica" had more interest, strength and vivacity, than the town has before seen in that character. Her song of the "Tuneful Lark" drew forth repeated peals of applause. He then slides into the mention of her Masquerade Song in "My Grandmother"; and after remarking that this song requires as much of grace, volatility and spirit, in acting, as vocal talent in singing, he concludes: "This lady has indeed been called the LITTLE SYREN; but in this character, she exhibited so rare a combination of fantastic elegance and sportive melody, that she seemed rather like the Queen of the Fays, transported with joy, that she had stolen the lyre of Euphrosyne.[6]

With the introduction of the star system the popularity of Shakespeare rested in part on the brilliant actors who essayed the leading roles in the great tragedies. While their names do not survive today as historic figures of the theater, they were mighty men, undoubtedly actors of outstanding merit and important as means of instituting a sound tradition in America. Cooke thrilled Boston audiences each season with eight or ten nights of Shakespeare, according to Garrick's reduced versions, and the theater remained open four nights instead

[5] See p. 181, note.   [6] Boston *Gazette*, Dec. 12, 1803.

of the usual three for his engagement. During his visit of 1811 Gilbert Stuart painted him. About the same time Thomas Cooper began a long American career. Cooper, a handsome young Englishman brought up by Godwin, had come to these shores after experiencing complete failure in the few parts he had essayed in the provincial companies of England. Although always a difficult person temperamentally, he progressed to major roles within a brief time, attracted an enthusiastic following, and repeated his repertory endlessly for thirty-five years of trouping throughout the ever-expanding road of the American hinterland. The second decade of the century marked his fullest talent, but his career extended from 1796 to 1830 and his popularity was constant during most of that period. His daughter by second marriage became the wife of President Tyler's son Robert, and she did the honors of the White House. Within a fortnight in 1815 Cooper impersonated the Moor, the Merchant, Richard III, Hamlet, Macbeth, Petruchio, and Henry IV to a town thoroughly familiar with all these plays; in the next few years it was to have the opportunity of comparing other able impersonations of the leading roles. Cooper and Cooke remained unchallenged, for the most part, until the arrival of Charles Kean.

The great Kean, a sensation of proportions destined to sweep away the memories of his predecessors, arrived in Boston on February 12, 1821, for a gallery of Shakespearian parts, occasionally relieved by other favorite dramatic roles. His personal popularity led to the stupid custom of an actor's appearing before the footlights after the play, and gave encouragment to the ticket brokers, who became such a nuisance that the management warned the public not to buy except at the regular price and reserved one box to a person; all the precautions failed to stem the tide of enthusiasm which demanded tickets at any price. Within five evenings Kean played Richard III, Hamlet, and King Lear (twice) for the regular engagement, adding Othello, Sir Edward Mortimer,[7] Sir Giles Overreach,[8] Brutus, Bertram,[9] Orestes,[10] and Macbeth in a second week. His acting was the most successful event in the theatrical history of nearly a quarter of a century,

[7] Godwin's *Caleb Williams*, dramatized as *The Iron Chest* by Colman in 1796; the music was by Raynor Taylor.
[8] Massinger, *A New Way to Pay Old Debts*.
[9] Scott, *Guy Mannering*.　　　　[10] In *The Distressed Mother*.

and after such brilliance, which could not be maintained by other actors of the day, the theater suffered a setback.

Farces and comedies were on every bill, for theater-going in this
period unfailingly offered something to please all tastes, and to send
the spectators home in a happy frame of mind. A drama or tragedy
opened the proceedings at six o'clock, followed by an interlude of song
or dance, and concluded with a farce. The entire evening's entertainment occupied a little more than three hours, but as the town became
sophisticated and secured such improvements as lights and paved
roads, the curtain was raised at a later hour. From a pit charge of
fifty cents in 1800, admission was gradually increased until one dollar
was the customary fee in 1820 for the pit; the boxes were more, and
the gallery less. At first there were disturbances from the disorderly
elements frequenting the upper reaches, with a disgraceful episode or
two to harm the reputation of the players as peace-loving and order-
inspiring artists. Mr. Powell found it "necessary to ask patrons not
to throw apples, stones, and other missiles into the orchestra," referring particularly to the gallery customers; the following regula-
tion, however, applied to all parts of the house: ON NO ACCOUNT
WHATEVER, WILL THE SMOAKING OF SEGARS BE SUFFERED IN ANY PART
OF THE THEATRE [11]

While the theater was at first conceived entirely on the pattern of
its English prototype, the management gradually gave attention to
the American features of entertainment; comedians showed awareness
of American humor, American music was used even though it was
composed by resident foreigners, and a few plays bore the unmistakable mark of a native inspiration while betraying a native inexpertness
in the requirements of the theater. In redecorating the theater in 1810
the management considered it expedient to mention that the lamps
were of American manufacture.

Theatrical salaries were at first very modest, with the average actor
of leading parts earning from thirty to fifty dollars per week in 1797.
After the establishment of permanent theaters in the several cities and
the increase of popularity for all forms of footlight entertainment,
the stipends increased markedly until the salary list for a company

[11] Nov. 4, 1805.

playing in Boston in 1810 amounted to eleven hundred dollars per week; little wonder the manager ended the season prematurely and with a deficit! It must be remembered, however, that the playhouse was open on only three nights each week, Monday, Wednesday, and Friday, with an occasional extra evening which never fell on Saturday, owing to the imminence of the Sabbath. Actors were entitled to benefits as test of their popularity and as opportunity to receive a share of extra favors at the close of the season; often these benefit evenings would yield about one hundred dollars for the resident player. The star, however, was in quite a different category, since his visit considerably augmented the activity of the booking office and must needs do so to compensate for the large fee which he was able to command. These figures reveal the commercial side of several important engagements in 1818:

Wallack	13 nights	average	$640
Cooper	11 nights	average	675
Phillips (1817)	7 nights	average	804
Incledon	7 nights	average	912

It should be noted that Mr. Cooper was a seasonal visitor, while the last two were making sensational first visits to America.

Farces and comedies were repeated over and over, satisfaction being given by the privilege of seeing different casts in favorite roles; thus *Lock and Key, Agreeable Surprise, The Spoil'd Child, The Poor Soldier,* and *Love in a Village* survived for many years on the playbills, and the playwrights turned out others fashioned in the same pattern. Bickerstaffe, Garrick, O'Keefe, Coleman the younger, Sheridan, and Shakespeare, with banners unfurled, constituted a season to which "fashion, science, and beauty" attended with alacrity.

American audiences were by no means nurtured entirely on the heavy diet of Shakespeare and the star system, although it is possible that the bard put the theater on a paying basis more often than the lesser fare, and that the truly memorable events of the season concerned these works. The resident companies were sufficient unto themselves much of the time, or were visited by singers and comedians whose popularity extended to a moderately wide audience. Few of these stars were of such magnitude as to leave any impression on the records of today. Mr. Williamson, Mrs. Burke, Mrs. Holman, the Misses Westray, Mrs. Poe, Mrs. Jones (who "bore her faculties so meekly, that

the lowest underling in the theatre was more presuming than she"),
Mrs. Graupner (wife of Boston's leading musician),[12] John Howard
Payne (author of "Home, Sweet Home"), and Mrs. Barnes were
steadily applauded as exemplifications of grace and charm, proper-
ties which often covered up a want of great talent. None equaled the
excitement created by Thomas Phillips and Charles Benjamin Incledon, who came in 1817 and 1818, the latter trailing a distinguished
London reputation, but the former making the more lasting impression.

Phillips was a gentleman of refined manners whose forte was the
tender ballad; while desiring to please the public, he refused to introduce "Eveleen's Bower" into a play on artistic grounds and thus gave
slight offense to a public which did not understand the propriety of
such things. The sincerity of the man won the Bostonian's heart, however, as it had the Philadelphian's and the New Yorker's, and his songs
were widely sold for home consumption. His benefit brought thirteen
hundred dollars, added to a salary of twenty-five hundred for eleven
nights. Incledon was no longer at his best, relying upon a tremendous
physical enthusiasm for his success and, after hurrying through dialogue, devoting his energy to the songs which made him famous. Without Phillips's artistic scruples, he willingly introduced "Hail Columbia!" into *The Devil to Pay* and won an ovation from gallery to pit.[13]
Both gentlemen sang with the dignified Handel and Haydn Society,
Phillips finding a true "oratorical stile" for "Every Valley Shall be
Exalted" and "Comfort Ye, My People" and Incledon likewise showing so thorough a knowledge of *The Messiah* that he gave the chorus
impromptu direction which was accepted in good part by director and
chorus.

The music of the theater was by no means neglected. Not only were
the orchestras of presentable quality and numbers, but the music itself
was of acceptable quality. At the opening of the Federal Theatre,
grand symphonies by Signor Charles Stametz (*sic*), Signor Haydn,
and Charles Ditters (Dittersdorf) were played in the course of the
evening. These were doubtless played very often, helping to establish

---

12 See Chap. VI.
13 Story and McFarland showed this same willingness to capitulate to the popular demand. The former arrived on these shores on Oct. 27, 1800, and three days
later sang "Adams and Liberty" at the opening of the theater, reaping a marked
personal success.

a repertory for the music-conscious Bostonian. Each cast included several singers, and each evening's performance had a musical interlude, either between the play and farce or in the course of the play. Mrs. Jones, Mrs. Graupner—for two decades Boston's favorite songstress—Mrs. Holman, or other vocalists were among the most popular features of the season. The prominence of the advertising and the frequency of performance of request numbers denote the affection in which the music and musicians of the day were held. The arrangements of music for the comedies was a thing for commendation as the occasional defection of the players was of condemnation. At times the native composer was recognized, as on the opening night of the 1799 season—a season cut short by the death of Washington—when an overture by Mr. Linley of Boston was performed. The music of Matthew Locke gotten up for *Macbeth* has been mentioned. That for *The Forty Thieves* was of scarcely less moment to the audience of 1811, and Joseph T. Buckingham, who never hesitated, found it not entirely to his liking:

The greater part of the chorusses were omitted—those retained were lamely executed. Mrs. Mills' voice is not unpleasant if she would contrive to get it in unison with Mr. Hewitt's violin, instead of running parallel to it at a distance of a semitone above. Her singing is also rendered harsh and discordant to musical ears by the sudden taking in her breath; which produces a noise that tended to remind one of the heaving of a bellows. Mrs. Mills however is a favorite with her audience, and justly so; for in addition to her genteel figure and pretty appearance on the stage (qualities which in the present hard times are valuable on account of their scarcity) she discovers much good taste in many things and a laudable desire to please in everything she undertakes.

We cannot close this article without paying a compliment to Mr. Hewitt on his judicious and pleasing arrangements in the orchestra; we have heard but one opinion on this subject and that is that his selection of well-known and favorite pieces for interludes, in preference to the sinfonia and "sonata" and his taste in modulation from "gay" to "grave" and from grave to gay is highly desirable of approbation.[14]

From the beginning certain musical works which have a familiar sound to us were included in the repertory. Thus *Follies of a Day*, or *The Marriage of Figaro*, played in 1799 was a mangled version of a familiar work, as was the burlesque opera *Don Giovanni*, or the *Spectre on Horseback* played in the Bishop version in 1825. As Sonneck

[14] The *Comet*, Dec. 7, 1811.

states, "It should be kept in mind that such English pasticcio operas as *Love in a Village, Lionel and Clarissa,* etc. were full of music by Italian opera composers. Thereby American audiences had a taste of many a famous opera composer of the 18th century from Porpora down." [15] Fully half of the popular songs issued from the press of Gottlieb Graupner, Boston's leading publisher, had been heard at the theater many times, and were attributable to favorite musical plays.[16]

A quarter of a century had wrought many changes in the cultural life of Boston, of New England, and of the entire country. The horizon was immeasurably broadened, and awareness of the several arts must now enter into every consideration of the coming of age, or flowering, which began about that time, bringing forth indigenous and mature works. It is difficult to set an exact moment of time for the awakening of any slumbering art form in a community, but it is a fact that at the turn of the century Boston had only the slightest acquaintance with the main currents of the theater, music, or dancing, whereas by 1825 a real achievement had been made along all lines of creative endeavor. Furthermore, another great period of development in European literature was at hand, and as these factors in combination enlarged the prospect of America's receptive thought, even religion itself underwent a cataclysmic change.

The awakening music consciousness of New England and, in particular, Boston, offer an account which, it is intended, may be as lively as the circumstances permit, since the human element, by no means negligible in dealing with the arts, is one replete with fascinating suggestion of interesting personalities. Mr. and Mrs. Graupner, Dr. George K. Jackson, John Rowe Parker, Louis Ostinelli, and his wife, Sophia Hewitt, all declare an influence on the life of their time which can be re-created today only in small part. Their names all warrant more praise and more gratitude than has been given them. These pages can only record a portion of our debt to earnest pioneers.

15 *Early Opera in America,* p. 197n.
16 These are given in detail in Appendix III, in the nearly complete listing of Graupner's publications, while an exhaustive survey of a season's repertory may be found (pp. 220–23) in connection with Mrs. Graupner's participation in the season of 1800–1801. For fuller details of the exact repertory, the reader is referred to the excellent accounts by Seilhamer and Dunlap.

Part II
THE ORGANIZATIONS

III. CONCERT LIFE

*We hope the candid votaries of THESPIS, will always
find us liberal in their cause; and we shall endeavor to
co-operate with them, when we believe their exertions to
be in consonance with the morals, as well as the amusement of the community.—The Euterpeiad, Vol. I, No. 1*

1.

THE INTIMACY and charm of the small town characterized the relationships of Boston's populace at the eventful turn of the
nineteenth century. Notwithstanding the rapidly enlarging
population, spurred by a gratifying upturn of prosperity, the physical aspect of every street and every quiet square reminded one of the
placid life into which arrogant commercialism was entering almost
naïvely. Gracious living befitted the scene, while a quiet conviction
that utopia was geographically not very remote brought forth good
works and a benign satisfaction to every honest New England face.
The outward habits of the urban New Englander were often reminiscent of those customary on the farm, with hearty dinner at eleven
o'clock in the morning, the day's work done at five, or earlier, and
evening amusements commencing at six and concluded before ten
o'clock. The sophistications of indoor culture were perceptibly trans-
forming these simplicities of village life in so far as the hours of observance were concerned, for the flourishing life of a township which
boasted fine theaters and concert halls demanded not daylight saving
but daylight sacrificing. Thus the hours of amusement and labor were
pushed ahead, but rarely did the curtains part or the music commence,
later than seven o'clock precisely, a respectable and socially correct
moment of time.

Boston was a tight little community, as are all New England towns
to this day, with knots of houses set closely against each other, protec-

tion against the severe weather and self-evident testimony to a sensible economy. The compactness of the man-made fortifications, these modest but elegantly appointed houses—inspired by those which Bulfinch knew in London and Edinburgh—provided for fullest cultivation of the finely decorative spirit of the Federal period. The hasty opening and closing of finely-proportioned doors mounted with shining fanlights revealed domains forbidding to the outsider, but dignified and graciously hospitable to the guest. The confident ease in the enjoyment of well-being of the master and his family as they emerged to attend the Sabbath worship (for Boston was generously furnished with churches of every varying shade and color of denomination and belief), the theater, or—last to achieve recognition—the concert might have gratified the distant Pilgrim Fathers had they envisioned the practicability of such a life as this generation had brought to pass among its finer representatives.

Before the family left the home, shrewdly intrigued by thrifty "bargain" rates by which one might "carry one's family for the price of ten dollars" for the season, important adjuncts to performance—singers, instrumentalists, and bustling officials (most of them drawn from the humbler dwellings) hurried to Concert Hall, the "little hall in Pond street" where a scraping and mustering of all the paraphernalia associated with music making was early in progress. Such a terrible earnestness, yet so complete an attendant aura of happiness surrounded these men! Their enthusiasm shines through the years, a definable part of the intangible assets of the Boston Symphony Orchestra and the Handel and Haydn Society. Petty differences, intense jealousies, and—yes—even that old serpent, temperament, filled the bosoms of these players, some of them prosaic bank clerks or dry-goods merchants of the day, but transformed into "les artistes" for a magic twilight hour or two each week.

The audiences were fairly standard, for the musical public of Boston made up in enthusiasm what it lacked in numbers; they comprised a model gathering, in that they were interested in their own orchestra, chorus, or soloists, while those interposing visitors who would attract the Bostonian closed society were expected to enlist the aid of recognized talents if they would achieve a respectable following for themselves. In a later age this would be called "civic pride" and emblazoned on banners sponsored by Kiwanis clubs and chambers of commerce;

it was unforced and entirely natural to the nineteenth-century American, whether in Boston, Philadelphia, New York, or Charleston.

In a community where the narrower aspects of theological dispute throve mightily and the clergy wielded an enormous influence over the beliefs of their denominational constituents, the broadness of outlook shown by the musical public is worthy of comment. It was so open as to be empty of traditional measuring sticks and so avid of culture, so anxious to be present at a fortuitous moment when genius might be unveiled, that the public received Mrs. French's superior vocalism and Mr. Schaffer's spiccato (an instrument made of common nails) with like curiosity and cordial good will, for encouragement, like charity, endured all things. The theater had become a lawful pastime only after a bitter struggle ending flagrant violations by licensed construction of the Federal Theatre and the repeal of the mandate whose provisions had been successfully circumnavigated by devious and unlawful means. "Moral lectures" in which the story of Hamlet was told, or recitations on uplifting and beneficial subjects, were the obvious pretexts for plays without scenery and with only such action as the temper of the immediate audience would stand. Boston and the New England towns were the last fortresses of righteous indignation directed against the theater; even with proper licensing of stage plays opposition was by no means at an end. The Baptist *Christian Watchman* and other denominational newspapers pledged open defiance, and the pulpit of many a Boston church was scene of denunciation of this strangely fascinating never-never-world which must have sent innumerable wavering souls to taste the forbidden fruit and become lost forever in the allurements of Shakespeare and Prince Hoare.

Many of the bitterest enemies of the stage turned readily enough to music as an art having no shame, and it is likely that many whose scruples would not permit them to enter the theater were foremost in their championship of the various musical activities which sprang into renewed success with the turn of the century. Both music and the theater flourished and the artists of the latter were extremely serviceable to the concerts of the former, an association which tended to break down the wall of partition between the two forms of public improvement and amusement—the Siamese twins of middle-class culture.

A single convention seems to have attached to the amusement business of the time, both in England and in America; that concerned the aura of respectability surrounding marriage. Thus the vocal celebrities of the day were Mrs. Graupner, Mrs. French, Mrs. Burke, mature women all who, for the most part, kept their feet on the ground and refrained from describing hypnotic circles while in action; the few damsels unblessed by marriage, like Miss Dellinger, were repeatedly mentioned in connection with accompanying relatives, fathers preferred. By 1823 there were enough single ladies to make a majority; the rapid change of married names unto the third and fourth husband had become too much for the memory of the public. No breath of scandal, however, attached to the public lives of these favorites, their success being attained by the regularity of their conduct rather than through the conspicuous excesses which identify the twentieth-century celebrity, although there are brilliant examples of private excesses, and miscalculations enough to have whetted the popular imagination.

Not all the vocal celebrities were women, of course, and one might derive the impression from all accounts that much of the singing was of reasonably high caliber. The voices were apparenty adequate, with some exceptional ones among them; the good taste which was traditional among the English actors of the time must have been reflected in the singing. There is no doubt but that many of the favorites of these early years would have been considered either second-rate or passé in England, with here and there a refreshing instance of youthful inexperience, but they more than pleased Boston audiences at the turn of the century, and Mr. Story, Mrs. Graupner, and Mr. Mallet sufficed to prepare the way for such impressive talents as Incledon and Phillips, similarly on the decline when they braved the Atlantic in 1818. The principal fault chargeable to the singers, but even more chargeable to the earlier uncultivated audiences, lay in the quality of the music sung. While the orchestras drummed into their hearers' ears innumerable performances of the "Overture to Lodoiska" and movements from Pleyel and Haydn, the singers offered such confections as the program on page 47 illustrates.

The artist attempting a debut in Boston might well have been encouraged by the cordiality shown him could he offer the requisite personal and musical qualifications. In few cities along the American coast—and it is remarkable how steadily the procession of visitors followed the coast line from Charleston to Portland—could he find resident forces more capable of assisting him than in Boston. The theatrical band was small but efficient; moreover the members appear

CONSERVATORY

Mr. Story, respectfully informs his Friends, and the Public, that Tomorrow Evening, Nov. 6, A Concert of Vocal and Instrumental Music Will be given at the Conservatory Hall, Rowe's Lane, For that Night Only.

Part I

1. Overture to Lodoiska,
2. Song, (the Hare Hunt)   Mr. Story
3. Song (Blue Bell of Scotland)   Mrs. Graupner
4. Harmony   Rosetti
5. Song, (Sweet Maid at whose melodious lay)   Mrs. Graupner
6. Duet, (Bid me when forty winters)   Messrs. Story and Mallet
7. Simphonie   Pleyel

Part II

1. Overture de Chemene   Sacchini
2. Song, (The sweet little Girl that I Love)   Mr. Story
3. Solo, Oboe   Mr. Graupner
4. Song, (the Fashions)   Mrs. Graupner
5. Song, (When freedom on the foaming main)   Mr. Story
6. Full piece   Pleyel
7. Triumphant Glee of the Red Cross Knights returning from the Holy
   Land   Mrs. Graupner, Mr. Story and Mr. Mallet [1]

to have been unusually accommodating. Once the Philharmonic Society was established there was an opportunity for collaboration welcomed by both parties, with Mr. Graupner as principal intermediary. The majority of visiting musicians, apart from those connected with the theater, were seeking a place to settle down; hence they were at leisure to remain in a city for a few weeks, exhibit their powers and proclaim themselves available for giving instruction. In a small and decidedly closed community such as Boston one could not easily succeed unless he was temperamentally and socially amenable to the resident group of musicians. The fact that these comprised Germans, Frenchmen, and Englishmen, most of them come to America after some residence in England, seemed to preclude the establishment of several Italians who made a brave attempt to capture the fancy of Boston audiences. Their time had not come, for the programs of the day hewed to a Teutonic line either in origin or derivation until the late eighteen twenties.

The records of concert life in Boston could hardly be interpreted as an unceasing round of pleasure at any time preceding the emer-

[1] Boston *Gazette,* Nov. 5, 1801.

gence of the Handel and Haydn Society in 1815; yet there is abundant evidence of a regular series of "exhibitions" in the several concert halls which must have stimulated the interest of everyone present at the friendly gatherings. The fashionable world of Boston reserved its favor for the theater, and the small musical public adhered to inexpert, though earnest, representations of stock pieces at Concert Hall; the literary population, and those learned minds at Harvard so often celebrated to the neglect of the other arts, are conspicuously absent from the roll of musical personages and, presumably, went in for acting or—just books.

Sonneck has shown in greatest detail the correlation of concert life and theatrical, whereby singing actors stepped from one to the other with entire ease, bringing their ballads and snatches with them, or fitting comfortably into the setting of an oratorio for which their English experience had prepared them with surprising adequacy. This dual personality must have been most effective in wooing the righteous protestant into the wicked temples of make-believe and in destroying the prejudice harbored by the eminent and powerful theologians, both lay and professional.

The day of the concert given entirely by a single individual had not come at the turn of the century; on the contrary, the greatest excitement came with an evening containing both new talents and old friends alternating and combining into a veritable vaudeville with frequent juxtaposition of "Let the Bright Seraphim" by Mrs. Graupner and "The Origin of Common Nails" as sung by Mr. Bernard, low comedian. Either the extreme reticence of the visiting performer for whose benefit the concert was launched or his patent inability to furnish a lengthy entertainment by himself led to the summons of all available hands, who were delighted at the prospect of public performance before a friendly audience. In the majority of instances the routine of arranging a concert is plain. Out of the void an itinerant musician reached Boston, having stopped on the way to undertake a concert in the smaller hamlets; after a few days of friendly intercourse with the musicians of the town, which in Boston would begin with Gottlieb Graupner, or James Hewitt, though seldom with both, he would enlist coöperation for an evening of music at Concert Hall or the Exchange Coffee House. "Communications" would forthwith appear in the paper, attesting the abilities of the visiting artist and coyly announcing a remarkable exhibition of vocal or instrumental powers such as had never been heard in that metropolis, assisted by the leading musicians of the town.

The following "Communication" serves as a proud example of cordiality quite evidently unfathered by any spirit of disinterestedness:

COMMUNICATION

We observe by advertisements in the papers, that two Italian gentlemen of the first eminence in the profession, propose offering a Concert at the Exchange Coffee House, on Tuesday evening next. Of the merit of those gentlemen in the science of music, it would be improper for us to expatiate, particularly as themselves, with becoming modesty, hazard their reputation in a strange land upon the specimens which they have promised to produce. —We therefore, think it only necessary to remark, that as strangers we must "give them welcome;" and where will they receive more support, or a warmer and more cordial reception than in the bosom of the American Republic?

C.[2]

Without appreciable deviation from routine, each concert was preceded by similar announcement to the newspapers and followed by silence.

The public press cannot be relied on to give a complete account of the concerts which occurred through the early decades of the nineteenth century, although very few can have escaped notice of some sort. Those chronicled therein bespeak a liberality of the editors for which we are immensely grateful today, since they not only provided the principal record for our enlightenment but set a precedent for the generous space accorded the arts in the press of today. The concerts given by the short-lived "Conservatorio or Academy of Music" are of special interest, for they not only bridge the turn of the century but mark the early years of Gottlieb Graupner's important influence on the programs of the time.[3] These did not include works for orchestra but were in the nature of faculty concerts with solos and chamber music predominating; they did not include performances by students, a practice which occurred more conspicuously with the dancing masters in advertised recitals. The final concert of the season 1800–1801, given by Mr. Mallet and associates, offered music which was typical of the best standards known to the public of Boston.

[2] *Columbian Centinel,* Aug. 2, 1817.
[3] Programs before 1800 have not been included, since Mr. Sonneck's *Early Concert-Life in America* contains a representative selection.

CONSERVATORY

To the Lovers of Harmony

Last Concert this Season. M. Mallet respectfully informs his friends and the Public generally, that on Tuesday, May 19, a Concert of Vocal and Instrumental Music, will be given at the Conservatory Hall, Rowe's Lane, for his benefit.

Part I

1.	Overture to Chimine	Composed by Sacchini
2.	Air, sung by Fil Trajetta, accompanied on the Oboe, Clarinet, tenor and bass, Messrs. Graupner, Granger, Schaffer and Mallet,	Fil Trajetta
3.	Concerto, Clarinet, Mr. Granger (by desire)	Schaffer of Boston
4.	Song: "My plaint in no one pity moves." Mrs. Graupner, accompanied on the Clarinet by Mr. Granger,	Storace
5.	Concerto, Violin, Fil Trajetta,	Fil Trajetta
6.	Glee, "Come all Noble Souls," Mrs. Jones, Mrs. Graupner, and Mr. Mallet	Fil Trajetta

Part II

1.	Overture, on the Piano Forte, Mr. Mallet, accompanied by Messrs. Graupner and Trajetta,	Haydn
2.	The favorite Song of "The Wolf," Mr. Mallet,	Shield
3.	Concerto Bass, Mr. Mallet	Breval
4.	Song: "The Soldier Tir'd," Mrs. Jones,	Dr. Arne
5.	Concerto Oboe, Mr. Graupner	Le Brun
6.	Song: "Come, sweet Sleep," with accompaniments on the Sistre, by Mr. Mallet,	Gluck
7.	Duet: "Bid me, when forty Winters," Messrs. Story and Mallet,	S. Webbe [4]

J. B. Breval hardly finds mention in the encyclopedias of today, but he was a contemporary of minor note, while Ludwig A. Lebrun's name on a program is helpful since this is one of the very few instances of a composer's name being affixed to the title of one of Graupner's oboe solos, and the building up of his personal repertory is a difficult task. Viewed as a list of names, Sacchini, Haydn, and Gluck, together with

[4] Boston *Gazette,* May 18, 1801.

Shield and Storace in the vocal department, show a commendable taste. Filippo Trajetta [5] inevitably considered himself more important than the composer he elected to perform, but one may suppose that a generous selection of work by his illustrious father and by other noted Italians was included.

The overture to *Lodoiska* by Kreutzer or to *Chimène* [6] by Sacchini, Grand Symphony by Pleyel or Haydn, together with other "Full Piece" or "Harmony within the Instruments" were common enough long before the advent of Graupner. They sufficed, albeit with a reduced or altered instrumentation, for theatrical pieces, one movement from the symphonies admirably serving the purpose of an overture. The identification of Haydn symphonies provides a baffling guessing game to the most initiated, but a plausible surmise favors the endless repetition of the "Surprise," the "Military," a Paris Symphony in B flat, and others of the Salomon set, since Graupner had played in the famous orchestra conducted by Haydn before coming to America, and they were the favorites of the day everywhere.

Mr. Graupner's oboe solos gave much pleasure, duly attested by the newspaper accounts of the time, but he relinquished that instrument in favor of the double bass while yet director of the theater orchestra. The reason may lie in the fact that as director his leadership with the oboe, rather than with the bow of the double bass, too much resembled the Pied Piper leading his errant children on to destruction. A contemporary notice mentions that other oboists had been heard in Boston, none of them comparable to Graupner, but there appear to have been no surfeit of wind instrument players at this time—another plausible explanation for his change. To be sure, there was no double-bass player recorded either. Graupner's talents were indeed unique.

A separate series of student recitals followed in the summer, making a tremendous appeal to the social and musical parts of the community. The First Conservatory Exhibition received this glowing testimony:

FIRST CONSERVATORY EXHIBITION

The Exhibition, at the Conservatory, on Saturday morning last (July 18) attracted a brilliant and fashionable attendance, as well from the novelty

[5] 1777 (Italy)–1854 (Philadelphia).
[6] *Chimène*, originally *Il gran Cid*, was produced in London about 1773 (Paris revision 1783); Sacchini's scores are for small orchestra, with only oboes, horn, and sometimes trumpets and bassoons, added to the string quartet.

of the entertainment, as from the just expectation which had been raised by the known science of the Preceptors of the elegant Academy. Never was the concord of sweet sounds, poured on the listening ear, with more enchanting effect. The extreme youth of most of the performers, their sex, and their beauty, gave to the impression and correctness of their execution, the applause of wonder, as well as of taste. Where all excelled, it would be invidious to distinguish. From the peculiar to the subject, private comment is the proper vehicle of criticism. No one was without a share of applause. If there were any auditors present, "who had not music in their souls," they may rest assured, that their hearts were unassailable through the avenue of the ear. We can not conclude this notice, without sincerely wishing the amplest patronage to the gentlemen who have founded the Conservatory.[7]

In view of Trajetta's famous name it is worth while to give an example of the benefit concert which marked his final appearance before a Boston audience.

Last, and most important, in the concerns of this establishment was that of Graupner, whose benefit followed directly on the heels of those given by his confrères. (See programs on pages 53 and 54.)

The choruses provide a distinct novelty in this program above anything contained in the foregoing lists. One may wonder, however, that Trajetta did not participate in these, and whether his defection was due to temperament or to a plain inability to read the music of the English composers. Very likely the Quartet was by Abt Vogler; Mr. Bonemort must have been a temporary resident in Boston for his name does not occur thereafter. Already one may see the beginnings of a loyal orchestral group which would eventually become a nucleus of the Philharmonic Society.

Citizens of Boston were embarrassingly insistent when bent on bestowing alms. The several societies organized for the purpose were active and generous in matters of fund-raising, and the hand of charity was extended for all to see. Musicians of the town showed their liberality by providing elaborate music for the several anniversaries, such as those of the Charitable Fire Society wherein eight of twelve numbers comprising a church service were musical. Special "odes" were composed, while Mrs. Von Hagen offered voluntaries flanking the prayers, lessons, and address of the attending divine. This particular society doubtless had many calls on its accumulated resources, for its purpose was to relieve individuals or families in distress by

7 Boston *Gazette,* July 20, 1801.

MR. TRAJETTA'S BENEFIT
CONCERT
of Vocal and Instrumental Music

Filippo Trajetta, respectfully informs the ladies and gentlemen of Boston and its vicinity that there will be a concert of music at the Conservatory Hall (formerly Duport's Hall) Rowe's Lane,

Tuesday Evening, April 7th.

Act 1st

1st.	Sinfonia	Composed by Pleyel
2nd.	Song Mr. Story	Mazzinghi
3rd.	Quartet, clarinet, **Messrs. Granger,** Trajetta, Graupner and Mallet	Michel
4th.	Song Mrs. Graupner	Storace
5th.	Quintetto, Messrs. Trajetta, Graupner, Mallet, Schaffer and Bonemort	Pleyel
6th.	Celebrated recitation and serious air, Oh! Elfrida Inquista, Fil Trajetta	Paisiello
7th.	Concerto, Violin **Fil Trajetta**	Paisiello

Act 2d

1st.	Sinfonia	Fil Trajetta
2nd.	Song Mrs. Jones	Dr. Arnold
3rd.	Concerto on the hautboy Mr. Graupner	Le Brun
4th.	Madrigal Fil Trajetta	Fil Trajetta
5th.	Glee Mrs. Jones, Mrs. Graupner and Mallet	
6th.	Armonia, Clarinet, oboe, Corno and Fagotto	Pleyel

Tickets one dollar to be had at the Commercial Gazette office, of Mr. Trajetta or Mr. Mallet, Court street nearly opposite concert hall, and at Mr. Graupners, Sweetser's Alley, Newbury street. Doors open at half past six and the performance to commence promptly at seven o'clock.

reason of fire or carnage. The imperfect protection given by volunteer brigades in a town where the water supply knew nought of street piping caused many unfortunate victims, including the Graupners, to have need of its help in 1799. In view of these circumstances it is not surprising that Mr. Mallet's closing "Ode" at the exercises of May 28, 1802, was "Rule, New England," more suggestive of violent political than charitable or religious sentiment, and that sacred and secular rubbed elbows constantly at these affairs.

Other organizations claimed their share of attention, including the

CONCERT

Mr. Graupner respectfully informs the ladies and gentlemen of Boston and its vicinity that his Benefit Concert will be on Tuesday, May 5th at the Conservatory Hall, Rowe's Lane, and trusts the following selection of vocal and instrumental music will meet with their approbation.

Part I

1. Symphony   Composed by Pleyel
2. Romance Mr. Trajetta   Trajetta
3. Trio, oboe, horn, and bassoon Messrs. Graupner, Mallet and Trajetta
4. Song Mr. Story
5. Quartet, violin, tenor, and bass, Messrs. Trajetta, Graupner, Bonemort, and Mallet   Pleyel
6. Song; "O, Nightingale," Mrs. Graupner, accompanied on the oboe by Mr. Graupner   Shield
7. Grand Chorus from the Shipwreck Mrs. Jones, Mrs. Graupner, Mr. Story, Dickenson, Dykes, and Mallet   Arnold

Part II

1. Harmony, oboe, clarinet, horns, bassoons Messrs. Graupner, Granger, Schaffer, &c. Rosetta (Rossetti)
2. Song, The Traveller Benighted Mrs. Jones Arne
3. Quartet, clarinet, violin, tenor, and bass Messrs. Granger, Graupner, Trajetta, and Mallet   Vogle
4. Song, Waving Willow Mrs. Graupner Shield
5. Concerto, oboe Mr. Graupner   Winter
6. Glee and full chorus Mrs. Jones, Mrs. Graupner, Messrs. Story, Dickenson, Dykes, and Mallet   Arnold

Finale [8]

Female Asylum, the Grand Lodge of Free and Accepted Masons of the Commonwealth, and the Humane Society—all making conspicuous use of musicians and of the clergy, special odes and voluntaries, and—always—a procession. The path from the State House or Concert Hall and the several meetinghouses must have been well worn with the feet of Massachusetts crusaders. Thus five such affairs were recounted in the press within sixteen months from May, 1802, to September, 1803. The "Great credit is also due to the Musical part of the Celebration" [9] refers to the Franklin Musical Society; unfortunately

[8] Boston *Gazette*, May 4, 1801.   [9] Boston *Gazette*, Sept. 26, 1803.

the several programs make no mention of the specific selections used, of the director, or of the number and quality of the singers. The society gave annual exhibitions of "sacred, vocal, and instrumental Music" at the Rev. Dr. West's Meeting House for the benefit of these worthy causes, but the group in all probability comprised the choir of that church, which assumed the title for the purpose of widening the repertory beyond the narrow confines of psalm-tune literature.

The Charitable Fire Society celebrated its tenth anniversary in 1804 and as usual a special ode was composed for the occasion. The effect produced must have substantially aided the collection which followed, while the newspaper commentary furthered the progress of musical criticism:

The performance concluded with an original and appropriate ode, "The Street was a Ruin," written by Mr. Paine. This lyrick composition, which contemplated a scene of touching interest and simplicity, was admirably adapted to Music by Mrs. Jones, and sung by her in a style of taste and execution which has not only been never equalled in the most excellent vocal performances of this town, but was truly and literary [sic] beyond all praise of cursory criticism. The strong sensibility it excited, and the unexampled effect and applause it produced, will remain the most eloquent commentators on her merit and taste. We hope to see this Ode and Music in print.—It should be annually repeated.[10]

One might be more intensively concerned with several musical societies which had a brief career were there evidences of any lasting contribution made by them to the life of the time. The St. Cecelia Society is shrouded in mystery except for the details of this brief announcement, together with subsequent notices of meetings covering less than a twelvemonth.

St. Cecilia Society

The Members of the St. Cecilia Society, are hereby notified to meet this Evening, at Vila's, for the purpose of choosing Officers and preparing for the first Concert.

Agreeable to the 9th Article of the regulations of the Society, one quarter is always to be paid in advance; which present will be six dollars.

Bryant P. Tilden, *Treasurer* [11]

A third concert was announced for March 26, a fourth for April 25, and a fifth for May 9, but no programs are available; in the fall con-

[10] *New England Palladium*, June 5, 1804. [11] Boston *Repertory*, Feb. 5, 1805.

certs were held on October 15 and 29, November 12 and 26, but no further record of the society's existence is to be found. Vila's Hall was part of a coffeehouse, and the treasurer, Bryant P. Tilden, was later active as vice-president of the Philharmonic Society in 1820.

A third society, denominated the Boston Musical Association, was comprised of those who "usually perform Sacred Music in the several Religious Societies in this town," but no evidence of organization is available beyond an invitation to attend the first meeting on June 28, 1805; had the association been productive of public concerts, some notice would certainly have found its way into the sympathetic press.

In 1807 fifteen persons gathered together "for the purpose of forming themselves into a Society for improving the mode of performing sacred music." They met monthly and commenced a library which grew to sizable proportions, with Amasa Winchester as leading spirit. The organization, known as the Massachusetts Musical Society, had a struggling career, attaining a membership of not more than twenty, hardly enough to permit of notable accomplishment within itself, or of great influence on the town; testimony to this effect is contained in the vote of March 21, 1810, to sell the library in order to liquidate accumulated debts. On July 7 of that year the society ceased to exist and the library is now in possession of the Handel and Haydn Society in Boston.

No other organized bodies are reported in the press until 1814 when the Harmonic Society is mentioned as holding a dinner at Massachusetts Hall, Atkinson-street, with James Hewitt in the chair. It does not appear that this is the same group as the Sacred Harmonick Society notified to meet on a May evening in 1813. In either case further details are lacking. Occasional references to the Old Colony Musical Society concerned a psalm-tune assemblage inspired by Bartholomew Brown, but having little interest in the newer type of music. All of these—of which there were a great many—may be dismissed as virtually unrelated to the development of modern musical culture as embodied by the newer and more advanced talents in Boston.

These societies, all doomed to a brief existence, were formed for the purpose of learning the newer type of sacred music represented in its highest estate by Händel and Haydn. Inability to read the difficult passages and lack of proper leadership delayed these noble ends for a few years, but the contribution of such societies was invaluable in the long run. The simpler arias from *The Messiah* were widely known before an adequate hearing of the choruses was possible, but they were sometimes perpetuated in guises which would shock the more exacting Händel enthusiast today. Mr. Mallet, a bass, favored the Massachusetts Charitable Fire Society with his rendition of the tenor aria, "Comfort Ye My People" "with correctness, and in a true Oratorial stile"; Oliver Shaw, a pupil of Boston teachers, delivered himself of "I Know That My Redeemer Liveth" in a manner which drew this rather dubious comment: "The music of this piece is heavy and solemn, and perhaps not calculated to please the airy spirit." It must be admitted, however, that the editions then in use neglected to signify a specific voice for any of the solo parts, and a hearing of the selection as sung by another voice than that for which it was written was less of an offense than a misconception of the fundamental musical intent of the piece as indicated by the comment on Mr. Shaw's performance.

Few visiting soloists appeared in Boston during the first five years of the century, and Boston, in effect, became a self-sufficient community, favored by the rare excursions of Mr. Story from the theater, and the theatrical, but also residential, talents of Mr. and Mrs. Graupner and Mr. Mallet. Mr. Fox's concert, enlisting the principal talents of the town, was not unappreciated:

Mr. Fox's Concert

Mr. Fox's Benefit Concert, which took place at Concert Hall, on Monday evening last, was patronized by the principal inhabitants, and supported by the united exertions of many eminent performers and musicians. The entertainments, consisting of vocal and instrumental music, interspersed with various recitations, were alloted to Mr. and Mrs. Fox; Messrs. Bates, Mallet and Shaw, assisted by the Band of Music, under Mr. Everdell.

In the course of the evening, the audience were gratified with several excellent songs and recitations from Mr. Fox; displaying uncommon talents, and performed in a superior style of excellence.

The vocal powers exhibited by Mrs. Fox entitled her to general approbation; and notwithstanding this was her first appearance in public, her essays were distinguished by that softness, delicacy, and ease, which are frequently wanting in experienced performers, and which are considered as an ornament to the most perfect.

The well established fame of Mr. Bates, renders all comment on his performance superfluous. Nothing but the smile of approbation, is a warrantable eulogium on such superior merit.

Of Messrs. Mallet & Shaw, we can only observe, that they contributed essentially to the entertainment of the audience, and received the great applause due to their meritorious exertions.

The Instrumental music was good,—some parts were particularly excellent.

Considering the performance generally, and the evening as it passed, the whole was regularly conducted, and the time agreeably spent. Mr. Fox is entitled to much credit for his individual assiduity, exertions and particular attentions. Should he be induced to repeat these exercises, we are confident that he would receive the most general and flattering encouragement.[12]

This eulogistic notice referred to such classics as "Wounded Hussar," "The Laughing Song," "The Soldier Tired of War's Alarms," "The Stag through the Forest," "The Wolf," "When Pensive I Thought on My Love," "Dibdin's Country Club," and "The Jealous Don, Won't You Assume When We're Married."

Francis Mallet may be credited with a praiseworthy ambition to leaven the concert life of Boston at the turn of the century, but there is no overwhelming proof that his talents were of a very high order. He sang and he played, very briefly managed a "Musical Repository," and brought forth his young daughter, aged seven, and young son, aged nine, in the best tradition of prodigy baiting; but once Graupner and Hewitt became established as musicians of able parts, and after the wind which was Trajetta had blown away, Mr. Mallet became a distinctly secondary figure. The program of his most ambitious attempt immediately followed his withdrawal from the Conservatory and is of interest since it was given without assistance from Mr. and Mrs. Graupner. Mr. Everdell, leader of the theatrical orchestra, was in charge of the delectable overture by Cimarosa, and the Mr. Shaw in this instance was not Oliver, but one "late from London, and last from Philadelphia"—an evacuation which seems to have been purely personal. Mr. Mallet sponsored another concert the following May.

Mr. Mallet's Concert

The lovers of Music will be highly gratified, this evening at Concert Hall, in hearing the daughter of Mr. Mallet, (a child not 7 years old,) perform a number of the most difficult Sonatas by Nicholai, and Pleyel on the Piano Forte, in the most correct and pleasing manner. We have no doubt but the fostering hand of munificence will cherish this child of genius.

12 *New England Palladium,* June 21, 1805.

CONCERT HALL [13]

M. Mallet, respectfully informs the Subscribers, and the Public, that the Concert of his Daughter, is fixed for This Evening, Sept. 26—at Concert-Hall.

Part I

1. Overture—Del Matrominio Secreto (sic) — Composed by Cimarosa
2. Hunting Song—"Bright Phoebus," &c. Sung by an Amateur
3. A favorite Sonata, on the Pianoforte, Miss Mallet, aged 7 years, with Violin Accompaniments, by Mr. Mallet. — Nicolai
4. Violin Quartette—Messrs. Granger, jr. Everdell, Von Hagen and Mallet. — Pleyel
5. Song—"The Poor Songstress," with Piano Accompaniment, Miss Mallet, — Smith
6. Flute Concerto—Mr. Augier, (lately from Europe) — Pleyel
7. Battle of Prague—for four hands, on the Pianoforte, Miss and Mr. Mallet, — Kotzwaraw
8. A Concerto, on the Bassoon, by Mr. Shaw, from Philadelphia, being his first performance in Boston, — Schoniback [14]

Part II

1. Tenor Concerto—Mr. Von Hagen, — Hofmenster [15]
2. Song—"The Ireful Battle rages," Mr. Mallet, — Mazzinghi
3. Grand Sonatas—the Rondo, a Scotch tune, with variations on the Piano Forte, with Violin Accompaniment, Miss and Mr. Mallet, — Pleyel
4. Duette—"Time has not thin'd thy flowing hair," by an Amateur and Mallet, — Dr. Jackson
5. Andante—with Variation and Rondo on the new patent Flageolet, lately introduced in all the Theatres and Musical Societies in London, Messrs. Augier, Everdell, Shaffer and Mallet, — Hayden
7. A Favorite Glee

* * *

Tickets One Dollar each * * [16]

[13] *Columbian Centinel*, Sept. 25, 1805.   [14] K. S. Schönebeck, 1758–1800.
[15] F. A. Hoffmeister, 1754–1812.   [16] Boston *Gazette*, Sept. 26, 1805.

The period of time between announcement of intention to perform, and the actual event was often somewhat long; concerts were sometimes no more than wishful thinking, while the subscription paper languished in the hands of a bookseller, insurance broker, or music dealer. In the above instances, while Mr. Mallet gathered around him many of the "old guard," Mr. Graupner came forth with an imposing array of names which included Messrs. Hewitt and Mumler of New York, himself, and Messrs. Moffat and Von Hagen of Boston; for vocalists, Mrs. Graupner and Mr. Shapter (of New York) were billed. Exactly three months were required before the subscription promised to "equilibrate the expense" and bring out the program which appears on the opposite page.

For the only time on record, Gottlieb Graupner is registered as a violinist, but there is no reason to question the accuracy of the record, in view of his proficiency on the double bass. It is elsewhere stated that both Mr. and Mrs. Graupner were creditable pianists, a very likely matter since he was popular as a teacher of that instrument and a skilled tuner and repairer. The bassoon concerto ascribed to Mr. Shaw is probably the same one by Schönebeck which he played in Mallet's Concert; "Coloot" doubtless refers to Calcott, and "Spaff" to Spofforth, author of that well-known ballad. "Rossety" is Franz Anton Rössler, or Francesco Antonio Rossetti, the once popular composer of chamber music, operas, and symphonies.

The widow Von Hagen appealed to the charity of her friends and the public for occasional assistance by means of a concert in which the Graupners and other miscellaneous talents, including Peter Von Hagen Jr., a violinist and pianist, invariably assisted; pupils were introduced as partners for four-hand arrangements, thus giving a homelike touch of amateurism to a gathering of those who had reason to consider themselves of professional caliber.

Interest attaches to the concert of Messrs. Everdell and Mumler, violinist and violoncellist respectively, on April 29, 1806, since the latter figures as composer of a trio sonata, accompaniments, and a "duetto violino," and the program lists names of other composers pleasant to contemplate in this benign age. Mr. Everdell was leader of the theatrical orchestra which on this occasion transferred its activities to Mr. LaBottiere's Pantheon and performed works by Haydn, Pleyel, Gluck, Hoffmeister, and the afore-mentioned Mumler, not to

MR. GRAUPNER'S CONCERT

G. Graupner, respectfully informs his friends, and the public, that his Concert will be Tuesday Evening next, the 17th inst. in the large Room, Concert-Hall, when the following Performances will be exhibited. To commence at 6 o'clock.

Part 1st

Overture, full Orchestra,	Pleyel
Song, the ireful battle rages, Mr. Fox.	Moulds
Concerto, Clarinet, Mr. Moffat,	Pleyel
Song, Aeolean Harp, Mrs. Graupner, accompanied on the Clarinet, by Mr. Granger	Shaffer
Sonata, Piano Forte, by a young lady, pupil to Mr. Graupner, and accomp. by him.	Nicolai
Song, Origin of Gunpowder, Mr. Twaits,	Braham
Concerto, Violin, Everdell,	Cramer
Sweet Echo, Mrs. Graupner, accompanied on the Oboe, by Mr. Graupner.	Arne
Glee, Mrs. Graupner, Messrs. Darley, Fox, Twaits and Shaw.	Coloot

Part 2d

Symphonia, full Orchestra,	Hayden
Song, The Beautiful Maid, Mr. Darley,	Braham
Concerto, Bassoon, Shaw,	Shaw
Song, The Auctioneer, Mr. Bernard,	Dibdin
Glee, Mrs. Graupner, Messrs. Darley, Fox, Twaits, and Shaw.	Kelly
Sonata, Piano Forte, by another young lady, Pupil of Mr. Graupner, ac. by him on the Violin	Pleyel
Song, Julia to the Wood Robin, Miss Graupner	Spaff
Concerto, Oboe, Mr. Graupner,	Rossety
Song, A Soldier to his Fireside, Miss Graupner,	Granger
Symphonia, full Orchestra,	Hayden

Tickets of admission, at one Dollar, may be had of G. Graupner, at his house in Franklin-street, at Mr. Burley's Insurance-Office, of Mr. Whitcomb, at Concert-Hall, and of Russel and Cutler.[17]

[17] Boston *Gazette,* Dec. 16, 1805. The *New England Palladium* gives the program on Dec. 17th, differing from the above in these respects:
In Part 1st—"Full Band" is given instead of Orchestra.
"The Negro Boy," sung by Mr. Fox, is given as second number.
In Part 2d—Mr. Bernard's Song "The Auctioneer" is omitted.
Ascribes the two songs to Mrs. Graupner which in the above are given to Miss Graupner.

mention one or two names scarcely known by the most expert musicologist of today. The program, although it contained most of the works in constant use in these years, is as musicianly a program as it is possible to discover.

CONCERT. *April 29*

Messrs. Everdell & Mumler respectfully inform their Friends and the Public, that their Concert is fixed for Tuesday Evening next, at Mr. La Bottiere's Pantheon. The following is the Order of Performance—

Act I

Grand Overture,	Haydn
Quartetto, Violin,	Pleyel
Song, in Benault & Armil de [*sic!*] [18]	Gluck
Duetto, Violin, Mr. Everdell and Son, being only 11 years of age, and his first appearance	Pleyel
Polacca, a favorite song, Mrs. Graupner. ("Be mine the tender passion")	Braham
Concerto Clarinet, Mr. Moffat,	La Feaver [19]
A favorite Song, Mr. Fox	
A patriotic Glee, Messrs. Mallet, Shaw, and Fox, with accompaniments for a full band.	Mumler

Act II

Violin Concerto, Mr. Everdell,	Fodor [20]
A favorite Song, by Mrs. Graupner.	
Sonata Piano Forte, Miss Mallet, accompanied by Messrs. Mumler and Mallet.	Mumler
Glee, Sailor Boy, Mrs. Graupner, Messrs. Shaw and Mallet.	Kelly
Concerto, Violincelo, Mr. Mumler	Hoffmeister
Duetto Violino, Messrs. Everdell & Mumler.	Mumler
Romance au Fontenai, followed by the Rondo, Visitandines, La Bottiere.	
Finale,	Haydn [21]

Performance to begin at 7 o'clock. Tickets one dollar each.

Mrs. Graupner's appearance in this event served to enlist the good will and the services of the other participants in her own forthcoming benefit, an "all-star" program which must have lasted far into the night. Reprinting of her program in these pages is hardly necessary,

[18] Renault et Armide, better known as Armide (1777 Paris).
[19] J. Lefebvre, (1763–1829), clarinetist at Paris Conservatoire; compiled official Tutor, published in 1802.
[20] J. L. Fodor, 1752–1828.   [21] *New England Palladium*, April 25, 1809.

since every major work performed in recent years was heard once more in honor of Boston's leading female vocalist. Only the name of Mallet is absent from the roll. It is difficult to imagine that the audience was of less than capacity proportions and of fashionable mien. The woman described as "a beautiful blonde with regular features and a sweet voice" enjoyed remarkable popularity in this first decade of the century, and though her powers may have declined thereafter, her usefulness in the development of Boston's musical taste did not greatly diminish. In addition to professional duties, both Graupners were liberal in support of charitable causes and the benefit concerts of needy or "decayed" musicians, where they joined with others in performances which "exhibited science, judgement and ability."

Many of the artists familiar to Boston audiences were friends of days gone by when they had shared triumphs in the theaters and amusement gardens of New York and Philadelphia. George Everdell had conducted for Mrs. Oldmixon at the Columbia Garden in New York in 1799, following the directorship of James Hewitt; the Von Hagens had been active in the New York field until 1796 and knew more of the celebrities from those days than they had occasion to associate with in Boston; Mallet had come to Boston after a theatrical engagement in Philadelphia in 1793 and remained in Boston as musical jack-of-all-trades, while James Hewitt's career took him in and out of every orchestra pit on the Atlantic coast before he descended on Boston and proceeded to distribute his sons to the several corners of the new world. Boston audiences awaited some of the most celebrated singers with utmost patience, waited, in all probability, until some of them were well past their prime. No reasonable explanation is at hand for the exceptionally late advent of Mrs. Oldmixon, whose reputation had preceded her by more than a decade. She had been prominently occupied in every other major city on the coast since 1794 as actress and oratorio singer. Boston had not been so well furnished with vocalists as to neglect her with good reason, and one can therefore understand the enthusiasm which greeted her stay. Her major concert on June 1, 1807, once the Fire Society benefit was over, brought her before the astonished public nine times, including glees, during the long program which listed most of the favorite arias and ballads of the day, some of them of the most difficult nature.[22] Her

22 *Independent Chronicle*, June 1, 1807.

battle horse "The Soldier Tir'd of War's Alarums" was omitted from the printed program but possibly added "by request." The reporter, or editor, of the Boston *Gazette* found that "Her execution not only astounded by its rapidity and force, but captivated by its variety of inflection and clearness of tone," observations similar to those made elsewhere during a long and distinguished career. In other words, Mrs. Oldmixon lived up to expectations before a public already wise enough not to accept first-rate reputations at second hand.

The cult of Händel was furthered by the presence of a great vocalist who obliged with several airs when the occasion warranted this type of music. Secured as guest for the thirteenth anniversary of the Fire Society, she sang "Angels Ever Bright and Fair," immediately succeeded by Mrs. Graupner, who sang "Let the Bright Seraphim." Mr. Mallet already had "The Trumpet Shall Sound" in his constant repertory, and any group of vocalists could "put over" the "Hallelujah" chorus by main strength. There is a suggestion that Mrs. Graupner was not greatly inferior to Mrs. Oldmixon in the notice that "We are persuaded the Musical Powers of Mrs. Oldmixon and Mrs. Graupner, together with the oration, will give them [the audiences] satisfaction.[23] Mrs. Graupner also sang "O Had I Jubal's Lyre" in a true oratorical style, and adhered to these selections with far greater constancy than other singers, a tribute to the musicianship which unfailingly characterized the careers of her entire family.

Summer amusement parks in the manner of the Vauxhall or Columbia Gardens fared less well in the uncertain and changeful climate of New England than in the cosmopolitan New York or sultry Philadelphia, Baltimore, or Charlestown. "Father" Schaffer was proprietor of such an institution, but Mr. Bowen's indoor Columbian Museum, on Tremont Street near the Stone Chapel, served the purpose, and to the collections of miscellaneous objects installed there the management added Mr. and Mrs. Graupner for weekly concerts of vocal and instrumental music. The Proprietors wished to "render it a pleasing and rational resort for the public, as well on account of its collection of rare and valuable articles, as to gratify the lovers of music." Plainly the Museum functioned as purveyor of warm-weather entertainment with less regularity than its counterparts in the less inhibited cities. On these occasions Mrs. Graupner "plugged"—to use that

[23] *New England Palladium*, May 29, 1807.

For One Night Only,

MRS. OLDMIXON'S CONCERT

Will be presented at the Theatre, This Evening, June 1, 1807
Consisting of Vocal and Instrumental Music, Divided into Three Parts.

Mr. Everdell—Leader of the Band

Part I

Overture	Lodoiska
Song, The Willow,	Mr. Vining
Song, Each coming day,	Mrs. Oldmixon
Glee, Oh Lady Fair, Mrs. Oldmixon, Mrs. Graupner, and Mr. Caulfield	
—accompaniments, by Mr. Granger	
Song, The Mode,	Mr. Dykes
Song, Oh, how hapless is the Maiden,	Mrs. Oldmixon
From the Opera of the Spanish Barber,	B. Carr

Part II

Symphony,	Pleyel
Song, Oh had I Jubal's Lyre (Handel)	Mrs. Graupner
Duet, Eve's Morning Hymn, (Milton) Sweet is the Morn,	Mrs. Graupner
	and Mrs. Oldmixon
Song, (From Handel)	Mr. Caulfield
Song, (by desire) Angels ever bright and fair,	Mrs. Oldmixon
Glee, Oh stay sweet Fair, Mrs. Graupner, Mr. Caulfield, and Mrs. Old-	
mixon. Sir John Stevenson; Accompaniments by Mr. Granger	

Part III

Song, Sweet Echo, from Milton, accompanied on the	
Hautboy, by Mr. Graupner	Mrs. Oldmixon
Song, The Ireful Battle Rages,	Mr. Fox
Ballad,	Mrs. Graupner
Song, (by desire) The Beggar Girl.	Miss Fox
Glee, The Red Cross Knights, Mrs. Oldmixon, Mr. Fox, and Mr. Caul-	
	field
Song, (by desire) The Auctioneer,	Mr. Bernard
Song, (by desire) Mad Bess,	Mrs. Oldmixon
Glee, The Harp of Bragels, Mrs. Oldmixon, Mr. Dykes, & Mr. Caulfield	
Song, (from the serious Opera of Didona Abandoneta)	Mrs. Oldmixon

Box Tickets 1 dollar—Green Box 75 cts. Pit, 50 cts. and
Gallery 37½—Curtain will rise quarter before 8 o'clock

extremely professional term of the present day—those compositions
recently published by her husband; these included "I Canna Munna
Marry Yet," "Sweet Echo," "Tally Ho," and so forth. Her name was

as indelibly associated with those works as it would have been had the sheet music been published with a cover bearing her benign visage. Resident musicians assisted in these Museum concerts, and the standard of instrumental music was again far higher than the vocal; on one interesting program for July 29, 1807, there occurs a "Trio, violin, tenor and bass, Messrs. Everdell, Von Hagen and Graupner, Mozart," [24] a work and a composer, unmentioned in Boston since the turn of the century. It was repeated on August 10, with Schaffer replacing Everdell. To Graupner may be given the credit for introducing the work, but it is not known whether or not the violoncello part was played on the double bass, a somewhat grim prospect but quite possible by reason of the simplicity of that composer's bass parts in slow movements and by the skill of this player who might have transposed them up an octave. My assumption would be that Graupner played them on the 'cello. Whether or not this may be the reason for so long an absence of works by Mozart from the concert programs, the fact remains that his music was conspicuously avoided until the thirties.

Passing events during the summer of 1807 included two concerts by Mr. Webster of the Theatre Royal, Dublin, worthy of note only in so far as they concern the presence of an orchestra, which opened both programs with an "Overture" by Haydn, later played an "Andante," and again a "Sinfoni," a continuity of interest not common to the programs of the day and here interpreted as indicating three movements of a single symphony; at the conclusion the usual "Finale" is indicated, without composer's name; perhaps this provided the rondo to a complete symphonic performance. As for Mr. Webster, he played in America but one season, became involved in a disgraceful business, and took French leave. Otherwise Messrs. Vining and Caulfield, singer and reciter, respectively, from the theater, gave performances in Charlestown at Massachusetts Hall, listing selections which hardly offer a claim for association with music.

The advent of "Signior" Comvoglio (or Comoglio) "a celebrated vocal performer of the first Theatres of Europe, and lately from Havana," was cause for the welcome introduction of new scores on the evening of September 23, 1808:

[24] Dr. Smith suggests that this may have been the Divertimento for violin, viola, and 'cello (K. 563).

CONCERT

Signior Comvoglio informs the Public, that in consequence of Mr. Mallet's relinquishing his Concert, (for the reasons already made known in yesterday's papers) begs leave to inform them that the same Concert advertised by him will be given This evening, Sept. 23.

Part 1st

1. Overture—Del Matrimonio Secreto, composed by   Cimarosa
2. An Italian Song, with grand Recitative, called the Will, from the favorite Opera of Papa Mosca, by Sig'r Comvoglio, lately from Europe.—   Sarti
3. Song—"Softly waft ye southern breezes," by Mrs. Graupner, with Obligate Hoboy by Mr. Graupner.   Hook
4. Grand Sonata on the Piano Forte—by Miss Mallet, aged 10 years, with Violin and Bass accompaniments.   Pleyel
5. Song—The Wolf, (by desire)—by Mr. Mallet.   Shield
6. Italian Duet, from the Opera La Belle Mulinara—by Mrs. Graupner and Sig'r Comvoglio.   Haydan [25]

Part 2d

1. Symphony,   Pleyel
2. An Italian Song, with grand Recitative, called the Dream from the Opera of Il Fanatico per il Lotto, Sig. Comvoglio,   Hayden [25]
3. Aid me Venus, a much admired new Pollaca—by Mrs. Graupner, with Obligate Hoboy by Mr. Graupner—   Shield
4. Grand Concerto, called La Chasse, on the Piano Forte, —by Miss Mallet, accompanied by full orchestra.   Steibelt
5. Italian Duet, from the Opera of Del Matrimonio Secreto—by Sig'r Comvoglio and Mr. Mallet.   Cimarosa
6. Glee, "Oh Lady Fair," by Mrs. Graupner, Miss O. Graupner, and Mr. Mallet   Moore

Tickets one Dollar each, * * [26]

"Signior" Comvoglio remained in Boston long enough to participate in another concert on October first in which he perpetrated "a Grand arioso Recitative and Air and a Duet between a Mother and a Son" together with "a comic Recitative & Air to conclude with a Duet in which will be given an imitation of the Quail and a Turkey."

[25] Operas by these names are unknown as productions of either Joseph or Michael Haydn.
[26] *Repertory,* Sept. 23, 1808.

That James Hewitt was a personage of some consequence to the life of his time has been established by John Tasker Howard. His wide experience as orchestral conductor in England and in America had given him a flair for colorful public relations and his Boston concert on May 16, 1809, was preceded by numerous communications to the newspapers of a most flattering nature. It is likely that he wrote them himself. Although "Mr. Hewitt's residence among us has done much towards the improvement of musical taste," there is no evidence to show that he had been a long time in Boston; in fact his last public appearance was announced for September, 1805, but the concert—a Graupner benefit—was postponed until December, and Mr. Hewitt was no longer at hand; at that time he was billed as "of New York." I can discover no single instance of Mr. Hewitt's having appeared outside the theater in Boston up to that time; this concert was given on the eve of his departure for New York, a return, one may assume, after a visit. He was orchestra leader at the beginning of the season, on September 26, 1808. By June, 1810, he was in Boston again—from New York—and his presence there in August, October, and December as teacher, publisher, and conductor suggests that residence was established at that time and not, as Mr. Howard states, in 1812.

The very handsome eulogy written for him, or by him, however, is probably correct, for Hewitt was an excellent musician of wide experience and one of the half-dozen first figures of his time. "His disinterested services have conferred favours on several societies instituted to cultivate this social accomplishment; their influence, it is to be presumed, will not be wanting on this occasion." [27] Despite these protestations of elevated musical taste, the program offered at the concert mentioned above, which was given in the Exchange Coffee House,[28] liberated no masterpieces other than the overture to *Demas-boon* (Demophon) by "Vosel," [29] a trio by Viotti, and a solo by himself which introduced some Scottish airs. The Graupners repeated famil-

[27] *Republican,* May 5, 1809.
[28] The Exchange Coffee House, under the management of Mr. Barnum, was "the pride and boast of our metropolis," and was universally admitted to be the finest in the United States. It covered 12,753 feet of ground, measured 132 by 84 feet, and was seven stories in height; the building contained extensive reading rooms, Masonic Hall, offices, headquarters for various organizations and for insurance brokers, exchange brokers, and merchants, all comprising a total equipment valued at nearly $600,000. In a spectacular blaze the structure burned to the ground on Nov. 3, 1818.
[29] J. C. Vogel.

iar songs, and Mrs. Poe [30] participated in several glees and sang two
songs, "The Lass of the Lake," and the bravura song, "On the Rock
Where Hangs the Willow." A trumpet concerto, hailed as a novelty,
suggests the emergence of Mr. Rowson as a useful member of the community, for he functioned as assistant to soloists from this time forth.

The trumpet, singularly absent from the lists of the day as a solo
instrument, came into its own with a vengeance in a program given
by Mr. Graupner on September 14, 1809, as obbligato to a song by
Mrs. Graupner, in a concerto, and as glad participant in the "Battle
of Prague" together with kettledrums, cannons, and so forth. In this
concert Miss Catherine Graupner came before the public as pianist,
assisted by her step-father, and Mrs. Graupner sang for the first time
a composition by Mr. Hewitt, "How Cold and Piercing Blows the
Wind" written to words by Mrs. Rowson.

A long interval occurs between the concert mentioned above and the
next one on May 24, 1810; it is inconceivable that no single musical
event occurred during the interim, but the record is singularly blank.
Notice to the press, which constituted advertising for the public,
would seem essential to the success of any concert, but there is neither
political nor social circumstance sufficiently apparent to explain an
entire winter's silence, other than the fact that Mr. Graupner was conductor of the theater orchestra once again and his time well occupied
with the routine business of the day. If this is the reason, it is a tribute
to the leadership of Mr. and Mrs. Graupner that no concert activities
were advisable without their participation and support.

Mr. Graupner's concert at the Exchange Coffee House [31] on June
13, 1810, a month after the closing of the theater for the season, introduced younger talents to Boston audiences, whereas concertos on
the clarinet, oboe, and bassoon spoke well for the capabilities of the
town musicians, who had recently banded together into an orchestra,
called the Philharmonic, for concert purposes; these, together with
the aforementioned trumpet and kettledrums, bespoke sheer volume
of sound as well.

30 Mrs. Poe, the former Elizabeth Arnold, appeared as a child actress, nine years
of age, in Portland in 1796; the audiences were charmed by her voice and ability.
In fact, "Miss Arnold, in Miss Biddy, exceeded all praise." Her mother had played
at the Theatre Royal, Covent Garden, and arrived in America less than a year
before.
31 Boston *Gazette,* June 7, 1810. It was strange that Mr. Graupner's concert should
be held there instead of in the familiar hall in Pond Street.

MR. GRAUPNER'S CONCERT

At the Coffee Exchange, June 8

Part First

Overture to Media and Jason,	by Gluck
Song—Old Towler	Mr. Darley
Concerto Clarionet,	Mr. Turner
Song,—The Soldier Tired,	Miss C. Graupner
(Accompanied by the Trumpet.)	
Trumpet Concerto, in which will be introduced Pleyel's celebrated German Hymn	
Ballad—The Linet's Nest,	Mrs. Graupner
Glee	Mrs. Graupner, Mr. Darley &c.
Quartetto Violino, (Pleyel)	T. Granger, Dalaru, &c.

Part Second

Overture to Lodoiska,	Kreutzer
The Laughing Song	Mr. Bates
Glee—The Red Cross Knights,	Mrs. Graupner, Mr. Darley &c.
Oboe Concerto	Mr. Graupner
Song,—The Rose and the Lilly,	Mr. Darley
Bassoon Divertimento,	Mr. Wood
Song—Let the Bright Seraphims, (by Handel),	Mrs. Graupner, accompanied by the Trumpet

Finale

The celebrated Grand Sonata, the Battle of Prague, with Double Bassos—Cymbals—French Horns—Kettle Drums—Trumpets—Cannon etc.[32]

The celebrated Grand Sonata, "The Battle of Prague," [33] by Kotzwara, now became indispensable to climax every concert in Boston, and

[32] The concert was postponed to June 13 because of the weather.

[33] A delightful commentary on the music of the day is contained in *Vanity Fair,* Chap. XXI:

"The sisters began to play the 'Battle of Prague.' 'Stop that d—— thing,' George howled out in a fury from the sofa. 'It makes me mad. *You* play us something, Miss Swartz, do. Sing something, anything but the "Battle of Prague." '

'Shall I sing "Blue-Eyed Mary," or the air from the Cabinet?' Miss Swartz asked. 'That sweet thing from the Cabinet,' the sisters said.

'We've had that,' replied the misanthrope on the sofa.

'I can sing "Fluvy du Tajy," ' Swartz said, in a meek voice, 'if I had the words.' It was the last of the worthy young woman's collection.

'Oh, "Fleuve du Tage," ' Miss Maria cried; 'we have the song,' and went to fetch the book in which it was."

And this classic description by Mark Twain in *A Tramp Abroad,* Chap. III:

"There was a small piano in the room, a clattery, wheezy, asthmatic thing, certainly the very worst miscarriage in the way of a piano that the world has ever

the next two concerts sponsored by Francis Mallet advertise it "as performed at Mr. Graupner's Concert."

Mr. Mallet's programs listed a grand resume of all existing pieces known to the Bostonian public, but there was some novelty in the presence of Messrs. Hewitt, Graupner, and Mallet in one hall at the same moment. Mr. Mallet invited the public to attend his second concert on June 26, 1810, at the Exchange Coffee House, "assisted by Mr. G. Graupner and all the Musicians of the Town; also Mr. Hewitt from N. York, and a gentleman amateur from Europe," yclept Yonge; the Mallet children sang, played, and for all one may know, collected tickets, for Mallet concerts were family affairs. Pleyel, Kreutzer, Kotzwara, and Viotti were indulged with some intensity during these years, if not with great variety in the choice of numbers, but the name of Händel as a composer of instrumental music remained unknown to this generation of concert goers.

Meanwhile the battles raged, for the "Grand Battle of Wagram" and a "Grand Military Overture—The Battle of Austerlitz, or the Three Emperors" by J. Hewitt figured intermittently, while the publishers catered to the household trade by assorted overtures such as "The Battle of New Orleans," "The Battle of the Nile," and "The Battle of Maringo" for pianoforte. To these should be added also

---

seen. In turn, five or six dejected and homesick ladies approached it doubtingly, gave it a single inquiring thump, and retired with the lockjaw. But the boss of that instrument was yet to come nevertheless; and from my own country—from Arkansaw.

"The bride fetched a swoop with her fingers from one end of the keyboard to the other, just to get her bearing, as it were, and you could see the congregation set their teeth with the agony of it. Then, without any more preliminaries, she turned on all the horrors of the "Battle of Prague," that venerable shivaree, and waded chin-deep in the blood of the slain. She made a fair and honorable average of two false notes in every five, but her soul was in arms and she never stopped to correct. The audience stood it with pretty fair grit for a while, but when the cannonade waxed hotter and fiercer, and the discord average rose to four in five, the procession began to move. A few stragglers held their ground ten minutes longer, but when the girl began to wring the true inwardness out of the "cries of the wounded," they struck their colors and retired in a kind of panic.

"There never was a completer victory; I was the only non-combatant left on the field. . . . None of us like mediocrity, but we all reverence perfection. This girl's music was perfection in its way; it was the worst music that had ever been achieved on our planet by a mere human being.

"I moved up close, and never lost a strain. When she got through, I asked her to play it again. She did it with a pleased alacrity and a heightened enthusiasm. She made it all discords this time. She got an amount of anguish into the cries of the wounded that shed a new light on human suffering. She was on the war path all the evening."

the "Battle Overture to Henry the Fourth," occasionally performed.

Mr. Hewitt celebrated his return to Boston by enlisting the forces of the town on October second and bringing forth his daughter Sophia, destined to become an able pianist, in a sonata by Pleyel.[34] The program is notable for Mr. Graupner's performance as a flutist, a single instance of his public execution of any piece on that instrument, and further evidence of his virtuosity.

CONCERT

J. Hewitt, respectfully informs his friends and the Public, that his Concert will be Tomorrow Oct. 2 at the Exchange Coffee-House.

Act 1

Symphony.	Gyrowetz
Comick Bravura Song (Composed by J. Hewitt)	Mr. Stockwell
Grand Sonata Piano Forte (Pleyel)	Miss Hewitt
Song (The Tuneful Lark) accompanied on the Flute by Mr. Graupner, Miss Dellinger, pupil of Mr. Hewitt	
Andante,	Pleyel
Song,	Mrs. Graupner
Duet (Now at moon-light fairy hour) Miss Dellinger and Mr. Stockwell, accompanied on the Piano Forte by Mr. Hewitt.	
Concerto, Violin (Viotti)	Mr. Hewitt

Act 2

Grand Military Overture—The Battle of Austerlitz, or the Three Emperors—composed by J. Hewitt. No. 1—sunrise—2. movements of the army —3. grand march—4. battle—5. cries of the wounded—6. battle renewed—7. lamentations of the soldiers over their slain comrades—8. grand march of victory—9. rejoicings.

Song (Vive la Bagatelle)	Miss Dellinger
Overture (Demophon)	Vogel
Song,	Mrs. Graupner
Andante	Haydn
Song, (Love sounds the Trumpet of Joy) accompanied on the Trumpet by an Amateur.	Miss Dellinger
Glee, (The Pilgrims) Miss Dellinger, Messrs. Stockwell and Mallet.	
Full Piece,	Haydn [35]

[34] Four daughters of leading musicians showed remarkable talent as pianists at this time: they were the Misses Catherine Graupner, Hewitt, Mallet, and Eustaphieve.

[35] *Repertory* Sept. 28, 1810.

At his next concert on December 27, Mr. Hewitt presented his pupil, Miss Dellinger, but apart from Mr. Labottiere and his daughter, included neither orchestra nor other Boston musician as performer. Miss Dellinger was pianist as well, however, in one selection—"duetto" by Mozart, with Mr. Hewitt as the other half.

Much of this new and scientific music met with stubborn resistance from the loyal adherents of the older styles. The new terminology, much of it utilizing foreign terms, seemed like affectation to those who took their Billings straight, while Händel's high-flown counterpoint amounted to direct negation of the often plodding style laboriously practiced since Puritan times.[36] A conscientious objector unburdened himself in the *Centinel*: [37]

I think they stand no test at all . . . I have heard a great deal said about *expression, proper modulation, true partumento,* with *affettuoso, condolero,* and *ditonios,* and *chromaties,* and *enharmonics,* with an abundance more of such nonsense, which no body understands, and none but fools make use of. No, Sir, away with all such stuff, and other flummery about the *science* of Musick. 'Tis all mere chips and porridge. I know it is not such a mighty difficult thing to compose tunes; for a cousin of mine in the country, in the course of three weeks, made enough to fill a large book—and all of the first stamp many of which I have heard performed in the meeting house to admiration. Every tune had four parts to it, and my cousin has often told me he could make one with five; and yet perhaps he never spent the amount of a week in the close study of Musick in all his life. 'Tis all a hum then, to talk about the mighty labours of the European composers . . . shame on such ninny-hammers as Handel, Croft, Purcel, Arne, Arnold, &c.

Despite the air of a tongue-in-cheek, leg-pulling correspondent attaching to the article, I believe its sincerity, particularly when the writer recommends an Address to the Legislature asking for a ban on late collections—*Lock Hospital, Essex* and *Middlesex Harmonies, Bridgewater Collection,* "and especially a little pestiferous Pamphlet lately published for the use of the *Brattle-Street Society.*" "When this business is completed, let us adopt the old tunes—place suitable leaders over each Singing Society, and keep out every *scientific* in-

---

[36] It should be noted, however, that some of the sacred music was so lively that the term "Geneva jigs" was applied; one of Billings' most attractive features was the rhythmic impetus given to his fuguing tunes. Note the refrain to "A Virgin Unspotted" as an example of his liveliness.

[37] Jan. 5, 1811.

truder. We may then hope to have the true, rational, and genuine
Musick once more heard in our Churches." A gentleman with so much
thrust to his writing deserves a mission more hopeful of success, but
his was a cause already lost beyond hope of recovery.

The fact that Mr. Moffat gave a concert on the 25th of July, 1811,
was no guarantee that that gentleman would figure prominently in the
music of the evening; actually the star was Mr. McFarland, from the
theaters of London and New York who sang the usual popular songs
while the sponsor performed en solo *once*, on the clarinet "in which
will be introduced a favorite air." Notable in these years were the
political songs which secured a foothold in the concert hall, even as
"Adams and Liberty" had done a decade before. Mr. McFarland had
been in this country long enough to shake off his loyalty to the king
and remaining empire whenever the interests of personal success were
in the balance, and he achieved that treasured desideratum with the
song, "Arise, Arise, Columbia's Sons Arise," accompanied by trumpets and kettledrums; later he added "Columbia, Land of Liberty,"
written by Mr. Barker of Philadelphia, to his repertory of patriotic
songs. The press acclaimed both him and it, but cautioned: "Should
Mr. M'FARLAND repeat Mr. PAINE's Ode, we think he would produce
greater effect by singing it ad libetum [*sic*]. The nature of the ode and
the music, demand it."

An unaccustomed tendency to levity is shown in a program wherein
Mr. McFarland and Mr. Moffat produced "In Ireland So Frisky, with
Sweet Girls and Whiskey," and "The Glasses Sparkle on the Board,"
subjects not common to the circumspect audiences of that day; Mr.
McFarland remembered his native heath by adding "The Land of
Sweet Erin's the land of Delight" and "The Sprig of Shillalagh, and
Shamrock So Green." [38]

The majority of theatrical singers forsook the stage for an occasional concert in the less profane quarters of Concert Hall, Boylston
Hall, or the Coffee House, but their programs benefited by far less
change than any opera singer's concert appearances today differ
from the familiar repertory of the opera house. The theatrical
orchestra, the conductor, and local singers combined to make an evening which had variety and some music of merit, but that latter quality was generally added by the instrumentalists. A list of names, pre-

38 See Boston *Gazette,* July 22, 1811.

sumably containing the majority of members of the theater ensemble, is appended to the announcement of a Masonic Charitable Anniversary Meeting on May 6, 1812; these were: Mallet, Drake, Wood, Gayetano, Granger Sr., Stockwell, Boquet, Drake Jr., Pilkington,[39] Granger jun., Schaffer, and Mallet, jun., who were, collectively, equal to Winter's Overture to *Zaide,* a medley Overture by Mr. Hewitt, and the pestiferous "Battle of Prague"; Mr. Stockwell here functioned as pianist, and the proceeds, if not the pieces, were destined to alleviate the distresses of widows and orphans in Boston. Mr. Graupner's absence may be charged to the fact that the concert was under the direction of Mr. Hewitt.

A discussion of the music found on the programs of this period affords less reward than might be expected, since repetition rather than variety characterized them. The symphonies of Haydn, found entire but most often played in dismembered parts, are those most familiar to us today; description of them or essays on their historical value is hardly necessary to any one who is even remotely conversant with the standard repertory. The remaining works of symphonic character have long since been banished from the list of performed works; they comprised entirely overtures and battle pieces, the latter not to be tolerated today, and the former replaced by those of sturdier nature than the thinly orchestrated ones then current. Possibly some of them are of sufficient charm to deserve a hearing, but such a missionary purpose is hardly a part of this writing. With few exceptions the overtures were scored for strings and three or four woodwinds, two horns, and possibly drums. The sudden popularity of "battle pieces" was probably due to the fact that they included "trumpets, drums, cymbals, double basses, French horns, cannon, etc." and were constructed with a larger sense of melodramatic effect than the typical theatrical overture. That the special instrumentation was often advertised suggests that these were new sounds to the concert audience, with the exception, of course, of double basses. Had the old-fashioned overture of the time not employed them, it is unlikely that French horns would have been available in the Boston ensemble of 1810.

Something must be said, however, for the selections to be found on the programs for every concert under the title of "Glees." Their per-

---

[39] Mr. Pilkington's name was "announced for the first time on this Continent" on Oct. 10, 1811, as assistant in a concert by Messrs. Hewitt and Chambers.

sistence denotes a special fondness for the delightful rhythms and bright harmonies of a form now undeservedly neglected, but then in the heydey of popularity. Many collections were current in the households of all "cultivated amateurs," and a touch of the familiar was here united with the skill of all members of a concert company. These, in essence, were a reflowering of the madrigal but were doomed to disappear whenever the informality of the concert gave way to professionalism and star guest performers. The visiting celebrity did not often deign to line up in a row with local talent and submerge his voice in "The Red Cross Knights," "Life's a Bumper" by Wainwright (one of the finest of glees), or "Glorious Apollo" by Samuel Webbe. Soon the amateurs were to join choruses where nothing less than the mighty oratorios sufficed for study, as they had in Boston on a few occasions in the nineties under William Selby. Serious business that, with no time allowed for the frivolous playthings of wine, women, and song. If any aspects of the concert program can be used to cite the passing of one phase of development to another, it must be the tradition of extensive glee singing in public concerts. The custom flourished through the first decade of the century, wavered in the succeeding five years, and had entirely vanished by the end of the quarter century.

Glees, it will be remembered, were in the nature of popular songs, or at least, songs of the day, if there be any real distinction. Many of their authors were still living as the collections fairly poured from the presses. More often than not, the title of the piece was unmentioned, "a favorite glee" giving the cue, with the names of the singers. Invariably glees came at the end of the first part of the concert and next to the end of the second part, giving way to the "Battle of Prague" which eventually became as unavoidable as a benediction. Stevenson's "O Stay Sweet Fair," and Kelly's "Sailor Boy," together with Moore's "Oh Lady Fair," were the larger part of the limited repertory sung over and over again. Mr. Hewitt composed one glee, at least, "When Is the Glad'ning Beam."

On occasion, dramatic recitations were alternated with musical selections at a concert given by some gentleman of the theater. Such a one was Mr. Cleary, who employed an orchestra, allowed three songs, and quoted Shakespeare, Scott, and Sterne, a triumvirate possibly considered at that time equivalent to the three B's in music, or the three R's in education.

READINGS AND RECITATIONS

Mr. CLEARY respectfully informs his Friends and the Public, that from the occurrence of several unforseen circumstances, his Readings and Recitations are postponed until TO-MORROW EVENING. The following is a list of the Pieces to be Read and Recited.

Part I

Overture,	Haydn
Reading, Sterne's Story of Le Fevre	
Harmony, for Wind Instruments, Messrs. Hart, Wood, &c. &c.	
Recitation, Hamlet's Soliloquy on Death	
Minuetto,	Pleyel
Reading, R. T. Paine's Monody on the Death of Gen. Moore	
Song,	Mr. Stockwell
Recitation Cato's Soliloquy on the immortality of the Soul	

Part II

Overture,	Picha
Recitation, Dagger Scene, (from Macbeth)	
Song, (accompanied on the Guitar)	by an Amateur
Reading—Combat (from Walter Scot's Lady of the Lake)	
Andante	Garovety
Recitation, Octavian's Soliloquy, (from the Mountaineers)	
Song,	Mr. Stockwell
Recitation, Macbeth's Soliloquy previous to the murder of Duncan.	
Full Piece,	Echner

To commence precisely at half-past 7 o'clock. Admittance 1 dollar. Children half price. Tickets to be had of MR. CLEARY, at the Exchange Coffee House, and at the Bar of the Exchange Coffee House.[40]

This seminar on death and immortality was grievously treated by the typesetter, for the Overture to Part II was by Pichl, the Andante by Gyrowetz and the full piece by Eichner.

The increasing competence of the soloists and the rapid enlargement of the musical audience permitted the convergence of interest on the individual, whose development as a personality reached new

[40] *New England Palladium*, July 14, 1812.

heights; simultaneously, in many instances, the festival aspect of a
June pupil's recital was overcome and the modern concept of a solo
recital established. Mr. McFarland was one of the more independent
members of his profession, joining with Mr. Hewitt and an orchestra
in presenting several concerts before audiences in outlying town-
ships. Boston artists, and those temporarily resident in that metropolis, frequently visited near-by towns for brief engagements of one
night or longer; these often came at the close of the Boston season,
but sometimes occurred during the winter months. Salem, Newburyport, and Charlestown were nearest at hand, but the list was not a
long one, for some towns had never heard a concert by skilled amateurs
or professional talent. Concord, a town yet unaware of its budding
destiny as cradle of America's finest minds in other fields than music,
claims attention by the signal importance of this brief notice:

GRAND CONCERT
OF VOCAL AND INSTRUMENTAL MUSIC
AT CONCORD, MASS.

THIS EVENING, Sept. 16, will be performed at Concord, a Grand CONCERT of
VOCAL and INSTRUMENTAL MUSIC, consisting of Songs, Glees, Duetts, Concertos for Clarionet, Flute, Bassoon, &c. &c. by a select band of Professors
and Amateurs from Boston.

N. B.—As there never has been any thing like a full Concert performed
at Concord; it is presumed the musical Amateurs and lovers of harmony in
that town and vicinity, will eagerly embrace this opportunity of encouraging merit, pleasing themselves, and publickly evincing their own musical
taste, by patronizing scientific musical compositions, performed by not a
few of the best Professors in the U. States.

* * *Admittance*—Box tickets, or first seats, 75 cents, Gallery 37 cents—
Children half price;—to be had at Messrs. Pritchard & Burr's store, and at
Mr. Buttrick's Tavern. To commence at 7 o'clock.[41]

2.

The aspect of the formidable Dr. George K. Jackson, Mus. D.,
now gives us pause. He did not, in the larger sense, precipitate a war,
but his advent nearly coincided with that historic titanomachy, and
the hostilities began at once; they culminated in the retreat of the
good Doctor to Northampton some five months later at the height of
the fray, but not until he had displayed a sample of his quality by or-

41 *Columbian Centinel,* Sept. 16, 1812.

ganizing several concerts of memorable importance. The Graupners welcomed so distinguished a veteran with cordiality and coöperated with him to the utmost, paying deference to an enthusiasm for the music of Händel which was the center and circumference of his artistic and professional being. The first oratorio under his capable direction was the immediate predecessor, more than any other single event, of the Handel and Haydn Society.

Grand Sacred Oratorio at the Stone Chapel

G. K. JACKSON, Doctor of Music, respectfully informs the Ladies and Gentlemen of this Metropolis and its Vicinity, that his ORATORIO is now in a state of great forwardness, and will be publicly performed next week—The Evening of Performance, and other particulars, will be announced in future advertisements.

> Organ—by DOCTOR JACKSON
> Leader of the Band—Mr. GRAUPNER
> * * * Mr. Hewitt has declined.[42]

The further particulars were issued without delay.[42]

Dr. Jackson's debut as an impresario entailed "considerable expense, and much trouble, in arranging and getting up the above selections; He will be assisted in the performance, by the Theatrical Band, (Mr. Graupner, leader) by Mrs. Graupner, and a large number of the first vocal and instrumental amateurs of both sexes in this place.

"These select votaries of Apollo, with Dr. Jackson as grand leader on the organ, we hope and trust, will do justice to their beatified composer Handel!

> "Now strike the golden lyre again;
> A louder yet, and yet a louder strain."

In all probability the last line was more effective than any other in attracting a numerous auditory.

The sudden flowering of the repertory of Mrs. Graupner and Mr. Mallet to include the more intricate airs of Händel suggests considerable coaching of these singers by Dr. Jackson, while the success of Mrs. Graupner in the concert hall, following her retirement from the theater, may be attributed with confidence to the inspiration of one whose enthusiasm for these sacred works was companioned by a thorough musicianship in imparting the principles of oratorio style to the

42 *New England Palladium*, Oct. 20, 1812.

A GRAND SACRED ORATORIO,

WILL BE PERFORMED AT THE

STONE CHAPEL,

On Thursday Evening, Oct. 29th,

UNDER the direction of Dr. G. K. JACKSON, assisted by the Theatrical Band
and many respectable Vocal and Instrumental Amateurs of this town.
Leader of the Band, Mr. GRAUPNER.

Part I

Overture	Occasional Oratorio
Recitation, Comfort Ye, Messiah	Mrs. Graupner
Air, Every Valley Messiah	Mrs. Graupner
Chorus, And the Glory	Messiah
Duetto, O lovely Peace, Judas Maccabeas—	by Amateurs
Song, Why do the nations, Messiah—	Mr. Mallet
Chorus, Lift up your Heads,	Messiah
Song, Arm, arm ye brave, Judas Maccabeas—	By an Amateur
Chorus, Break forth into Joy,	Messiah

Part II

Overture	Sampson
Song, Angels ever bright and fair, Jeptha	Mrs. Graupner
Celebrated Bell Chorus, Welcome mighty King,	
Accompanied on the Carilons, by Dr. Jackson	Saul
Song, Honor and Arms, Sampson	Mr. Mallett
Chorus, Happy we the Star, &c.	
Song, O Thou tellest,	Messiah
Song, The Trumpet shall sound, Messiah	Mr. Stockwell
Chorus, Hallelujah (with Trumpet and Kettle	
Drums)	Messiah

Doors to be opened at half past 4—Performance to commence precisely
at half past 5 o'clock.

A single Ticket, $1—A Ticket to admit a lady and gentleman, $1 50—
Childrens' Tickets, 50 cents each to be had at Dr. JACKSON's. No. 18 Pinkney-street, and at Messrs. GRAUPNER & MALLET's Music Stores.[43]

willing talents at hand. Dr. Jackson's worldly goods were not extensive, but he owned a full set of Händel's works as edited by his friend
Dr. Arnold, a set now in possession of the Handel and Haydn Society of Boston which purchased them after Dr. Jackson's death. Unfortunately there are no marks in the owner's hand anywhere in the

[43] Boston *Gazette*, Oct. 26, 1812.

several scores. The good doctor knew *Samson* especially well, and his introduction of that score was a novelty to Bostonians.

A "Communication" [44] observes that "there has not been an Oratorio performed in this town, since the year 1783," reference to the notable concert directed by Selby on January 10, 1786, and fully chronicled by Mr. Sonneck.[45] Indeed, the Communication states, "Heroes may be forgotten; nations may become extinct; but the fame of Handel is IMMORTAL!!!" High praise indeed, even for Händel, and doubtless encouraging to the populace which joined the venture with enthusiasm, making this the most important musical event of the century thus far. A repetition of the concert, with the chorus ranks considerably depleted, was given in Salem a month later, but the sentient emotions of the Boston performance were not duplicated, at least in the breast of Dr. Bentley who recorded the evening in his diary with these words:

(Dec. 1, 1812) This evening we had as it was called an Oratorio of sacred music. The organ of the First Church was preferred to that of the North Church because of its tones. The celebrated Dr. Jackson, an Englishman, performed on the organ with great power and pure touch. Mr. Graupner led the violins & Mr. Granger the Clarinet. Mr. Mallet had the tenor viol & good Father Shaffer assisted at the drum. Mrs. Graupner was at the head of the female singers which were seven in number & the whole company exceeded 20 in all parts. The instrumental music transcended the vocal which had nothing extraordinary about it to fulfil our expectations. Mr. Jackson's voluntaries were beyond anything I had heard, and the best music was before the second Chorus when the organ was the accompaniment with only the violins. However upon the whole it was a rich entertainment & if not all we wished more than we ever before enjoyed. Mallet sings harsh. Mrs. Graupner had one pathetic strain with her natural voice, at all other times she strained.

Dr. Bentley's detailed account is valuable, for it is the first commentary on the talents of Mrs. Graupner by a disinterested person unfettered by personal admiration. Either the lady was not at her best, or the encomiums indulged her by the Boston press were exaggerated. As for the gentleman himself, Dr. Bentley was one of the most cultivated amateurs of music known to us at this remove. For many years minister in Salem, he kept a diary in which he recorded his every interest for more than twenty years. Unusually alert to music

[44] Boston *Gazette,* Oct. 29, 1812. See also p. 206.   [45] *Concert Life,* p. 275f.

wherever he went, he made careful note of the quality of the scores and of the performance. His own tastes were excellent, as this entry signifies: "I had my principal singing girls with me to dine as a testimony to their good performance on Thanksgiving day. . . . We then turned to Bach Church music. Then turned to Bach's Symphonies & Himmel's airs." [46] A man of strong self-discipline, yet of kindly disposition, he read French on Tuesday, Latin on Wednesday, Spanish and Italian on Thursday, German and Dutch, etc. Friday, and on Saturday, philology in relation to versions of the texts of the Hebrew and Greek scriptures. Monday was devoted to Greek. It has been said that Thomas Jefferson offered Dr. Bentley the presidency of the University of Virginia, an offer refused on account of advancing age.[47]

The saga of Dr. Jackson at this period is by no means complete. Success of the first venture encouraged preparations for another concert, intended for Christmas Day, 1812,[48] but it was not "sufficiently mature" to bring forth at that time—fateful misfortune—and the date was finally set for January 29, 1813. An ambitious all-Händel program was planned, to begin at five-thirty o'clock, but the arm of the law intervened and whisked the reluctant figure of Dr. Jackson away on the very eve of the event.[49] The performers, numbering nearly two hundred persons, bereft of their chief support and direction, postponed the concert until late in March, at which time the music was sung with electrifying effect and the proceeds given to the Russians rather than to the English.

Excitement preceding the declaration of war was nowhere more keenly felt than in New England, where connections with the mother country had been affectionately maintained, and where sympathies with the Federal administration had at times wavered vastly in accordance with the sectional influences at work in the capitol city. A visitor wrote: "You have only to travel to Boston to find that our best citizens consider the interests of the United States interwoven with those of Great Britain, and that our safety depends on hers." [50] The press and the clergy denounced the Federal administration with enjoyable vehemence, the former with sarcasm and journalistic—odd

[46] Dec., 1810.   [47] *Diary,* published by the Essex Institute of Salem in 1907.
[48] It will be noted that the first Handel and Haydn Society concert was on Christmas Day, 1815.
[49] The details of Dr. Jackson's collision with the law may be found in Chapter VII.
[50] Schouler, *History of the United States,* II, 202.

word for the time, but suitable in this instance—misrepresentation, the latter by political brimstone and hell fire, freely enjoining scriptural passages as applying to Thomas Jefferson, or other traitor to the ideal of democracy, New England style.[51] President Dwight of Yale preached a sermon on the text "Wherefore, come out from among them, and be ye separate, saith the Lord," a veiled encouragement to the secessionists who advocated separation of the New England states from the Union; meanwhile, open flagrancy of the national laws was practiced to such an extent that New England suffered less economic inconvenience than some of those sections which observed the law with greater faithfulness. The undercurrent activities of certain respected senators and representatives were sufficient for a first-rate scandal; the embargo was resisted, and New England Federalism made much tangible profit by opposing the new national policy, while the Massachusetts legislature, advised by a committee, took extreme British ground in 1809, justifying England against France, and pressing Congress to repeal the embargo and annul the present treaty with France.

The one administration, the single hero, on which the entire country was agreed was George Washington; around him odes and popular songs of wide variety were composed to celebrate the annual birthday of this illustrious patriot. It is not surprising, therefore, to find this notice which unites musical and political interests:

THE BIRTH DAY OF WASHINGTON

Was celebrated by the Washington Benevolent Society of Charlestown, with all those mingled emotions, which the political aspect of the times is calculated to excite. . . .

A patriotic Ode, which was composed for the occasion by a member of the Society, was received with high approbation. The music was excellent, and the whole of the exercises were suited to warm the patriot's heart, and nerve his arm to defend the invaluable rights of New-England.[52]

Passing events, less related to the restrictive term of "music" than to the all-inclusive designation of "entertainment" include programs

51 While not related to this particular problem of national policy, a hymn "Chester" by William Billings, suggests the same intensity of feeling:
> "Let tyrants shake their iron rods,
> & Slavery clank her galling chains,
> We see them not, we trust in God,
> New England's God forever reigns."

52 Boston *Gazette,* Feb. 24, 1814.

by Mr. Bernard in which "Songs, stories and Recitations from rare Mss." were grouped into a comic lecture on July 5, 1813, in Concert Hall, and a rather more formidable entertainment by Mr. Spiller, Mr. McFarland, and Mrs. Wheatley, together with orchestra directed by Mr. Hewitt at the Exchange Coffee House on January 27, 1814. The Graupners had no part in the latter enterprise and the cleavage of the two houses is plain to all who read the tell-tale "**Mr. Hewitt has declined" note on the occasion of Dr. Jackson's mighty concert. Tickets for Hewitt's concerts were *not* obtainable at 6 Franklin Street. Miss Hewitt and the Graupners, however, were frequent associates. Mr. McFarland, as was his custom, took to the provinces and arrived in Hamilton Hall, Salem, on April 7 with other company, including a new song "Huzza for the Gallant Constitution" in the repertory of his American group. This type of song suggests that made popular by Incledon in England in so far as the forthright ballad style is concerned; one may judge Mr. McFarland to have been a dramatic baritone with sentimental overtones reserved for the Irish melodies.

Miss Hewitt's reappearance before the public as a mature pianist may be said to date from 1814, when she played Steibelt's concerto, "The Storm," on the grand piano forte in the course of her father's concert. The *Repertory* felt constrained to add these words of praise for Miss Hewitt: [53]

We cannot refrain from expressing our admiration of the Concerto by Steibelt and the performance of it by Miss HEWITT; it is far beyond our ability to do her ample justice, and the impression on every person present, and the spontaneous burst of applause which followed are the best tribute of praise. We never witnessed a performance on the Piano Forte which could compare with it.

Steibelt was generally admired as a composer, and his works were often played; Miss Catherine Graupner played a concerto by him at a concert for Mr. Hupfeld on August 22, 1814, wherein the name of J. P. Rode was added to the list of favored composers. Mr. Hupfeld was a competent German violinist who joined Benjamin Carr and Raynor Taylor the following year in Philadelphia as an active influence in promoting chamber and orchestral music in the Musical Fund Society, but his Boston career was confined to this single concert.

[53] May 12, 1814.

Among the lesser events of the season may be included Signor Pucci, from Italy, who aroused some interest by his concerts on King David's pedal harp and on the Spanish guitar; the established musicians of the town had no traffic with him, even though his success warranted a second performance "interspersed with songs." The Pucci programs were never given in detail but comprised a string of dance forms and street songs with an occasional attempt to graft English words to an Italian tune, or Italian words to an American tune. Given at the Exchange Coffee House, they had no support from either theatrical group or resident musicians.

Brief mention has been made of the summer gardens occasionally engaged for the months of July and August. By no means can the idea be interpreted as having arrived at such popularity as did the celebrated ones of New York and Philadelphia in these very years, or as they flourished before the turn of the century when Mr. Darley was at his best. Father Schaffer, timid innovator in 1807, reaped greater rewards in 1815 with his Grand Gala Vauxhall, brilliantly illuminated for outdoor concerts under the direction of Mr. Hewitt. The place was called the Washington Gardens on Common Street and the program on page 86 is typical except for the extra inclusion of patriotic songs since the concert was being given on the evening of July 4; some of these show the enthusiasm and conviction of the Bostonian mind.

During the summer of 1816 Mr. Graupner was in charge of the music and some measure of brilliance may be discerned in the engagement of Mrs. Burke from New York. The Gardens were splendidly illuminated with variegated lamps and a brilliant display of fireworks, with several wheels, pots of blue lights, rockets, and other familiar paraphernalia appropriate to the setting. Popular songs of the season included the Polauca (!) "Let Me Borrow for a While," "Just Like Love," "The Jealous Don," and "O Joyous Day." Science and invention went hand in hand with Mr. Schaffer's progress, for in the following year he breathlessly announced "a wonderful and ingenious invention."

The Gass Lights

Which will give a brilliancy of scene, for its
kind unparalleled in the town before.[54]

54 *New England Palladium,* May 28, 1817.

INDEPENDENCE EVENING

GRAND GALA—Vauxhall

Brilliant Illumination

MR. SCHAFFER

respectfully acquaints the public that there will be a GRAND CONCERT of Vocal and Instrumental music at the Washington Gardens THIS EVENING JULY 4th under the direction of Mr. Hewitt.

·Act I ·

Overture	Kozeluch
Ode Wreaths for the Chieftain we Honor	
written by L. M. Sargent Esq.	Mr. McFarland
Minuetto	Pleyel
Song Little Sue (Hook)	Miss Trenor
Harmony Messrs. Granger, Turner, Hart, Norbaur (Neibuhr), Wood, &c.	
Comic Song William and Jonathan	Mr. Stockwell
Song Advice to the Ladies	Miss Stockwell
Song Old Towser	Mr. McFarland

Act II

Overture Lodoiska	Kreutzer
Patriotic Ode with Chorus Live Triumphant, or Contending Die written by T. W. Brackett Esq. for the 4th of July Music composed by T. Hewitt to be sung by Mr. Stockwell	
Andange	Pleyel
Echo Duett	Mr. and Mrs. Stockwell
Allegro	Gyrowetz
Song When a Shepherd asks my hand Sir	Miss Trenor
Minuetto	Vauxhall
Patriotic Song Arouse, Arouse, Columbia's Sons, Arouse written by the late R. T. Paine Esq.	Mr. Stockwell
Full Piece	Gyrowetz [55]

Throughout these recent years the career of the Philharmonic Society was becoming increasingly important, a career recounted in detail in Chapter IV. But apart from the evenings of music sponsored by this organization, the concert life of Boston was not distinguished, and the unpardonable lapse from standard on the occasion of Father Schaffer's concert, when the new instrument called "spiccato" was demonstrated—"the music being produced from common nails,"—

[55] *New England Palladium*, July 4, 1815.

suggests the need for organized music-making on a higher level.[56] To the level of the "spiccato," the programs of Signor Pucci, and the "canned" noises of the Panharmonicon, the town had descended when the announcement of the first concert by the newly formed Handel and Haydn Society was issued, an event justly famed in the annals of America's musical life, and recorded in the History of the Society written by Perkins and Dwight. To that excellent record incidental items may be added and occasional corrections noted.

The Handel and Haydn Society came into being after many predecessors had tried and failed, but the day had arrived when the public mind was sufficiently prepared for the imposing works selected as basis for the repertory. In these pages we have passed lightly over several predecessors of a private nature, and over church choirs which turned increasingly away from the old style of "lining out" hymns to a "new style" of hymnody and to the inspired works of the immortal Händel. The most ambitious organization preceding the Handel and Haydn Society was the Massachusetts Musical Society, founded by fifteen gentlemen, which purchased Händel's *Messiah, Judas Maccabeus*, and *Acis and Galatea;* Prang's Twenty Anthems; Stephens' *Cathedral Music* and Mozart's six anthems as nucleus of a musical library. They soon found the music quite beyond their capabilities and reverted to hymns from the *Worcester Collection of Psalmody* (1779), with its contents of St. Anne, Old Hundredth, Pleyel's Hymn, some of these none too easy for the inexperienced members. No public concert was ever given during the three years of existence of the society which held twenty-three meetings at Vila's Hall, Boston, Sumner's in Roxbury, or Hovey's Hall in Cambridgeport. The great choruses of Händel and Haydn were not for these humble and unskilled amateurs. Of the members given by name, William Bennett was the only one known in other musical circles of the time; he joined the Philharmonic Society.

Among the church choirs, that of Park Church was the most influential under the direction of Elnathan Duren. The dedication in 1812 was the occasion for an impressive musical service, and several of the singers became active in the Great Society. The detailed researches made by Perkins and Dwight omit mention of Dr. Jackson and the

---

56 The spiccato was Schaffer's own invention (See Sonneck, *Concert Life,* p. 307) but it may have been patterned on one of the many other instruments enjoying a brief popularity, some of them described in Chap. X.

impressive musical event sponsored by him on October 29, 1812, and
the enthusiasm resulting therefrom; had the war not intervened, it is
possible that future concerts (of which only one was given, and that
without the presence of Dr. Jackson) would have resulted in the earlier establishment of a great musical body. Another concert given on
Washington's Birthday, 1815, contained many of the same works and
solos as that of the first notable event on Christmas Evening, 1815,
and many of the same soloists were at hand; they may be credited with
inspiring the ultimate aim of a perpetual organization. Mr. Cushing
states that immediate steps were taken following a cloak-room meeting of the Philharmonic Orchestra wherein the low state of church
music was the subject of discussion. He claims to have suggested action
rather than words, and a call for those interested to meet, probably
on March 24, in Mr. Graupner's hall. It is interesting, and perhaps
obscurely significant, that Dr. Jackson had at that very moment returned from his retirement in Northampton to take up teaching once
more in Boston. His part in the society, however, remained advisory,
although he was at one time considered for leadership, and at another
time for organist; there must have been those who agitated securing
his skilled services from the beginning. Dr. Jackson's circle of warm
supporters was equaled only by the insistence of those who strongly
disapproved of his participation in any public affairs.

Sixteen members enrolled at the second meeting, March 30, but
these appear to have been leaders of groups representing a potentially
large chorus.[57] "The association contemplates digesting a plan, embracing all the musical talent in the town, for the purpose of sacred
oratorio performances, towards establishing a fund to carry so laudable and praiseworthy an undertaking into full operation," the Advertiser reported. The plan was digested, and within a month forty-
four persons signed the constitution, these including the controlling
(or original) sixteen in addition to other persons whom they saw fit
to select. Nine churches furnished members of their choirs for the
chorus of ninety-odd participating in the first concert. Meetings of
the trustees were held in Mr. Withington's house, rehearsals on Thursday (changed to Tuesday after 1816) evenings at the "little hall in
Pond street." S. Richardson was elected secretary with the duties of

[57] *History of the Handel and Haydn Society* Boston (Alfred Mudge, 1883–1934)
Vol. I (1815–90), p. 37n.

attending all meetings, providing suitable attendants, fire, and lights, and caring for the music. Col. T. S. Webb became president and, by virtue of his office, the conductor of the society, a principal adhered to with varying success for nearly fifteen years. Rehearsals became more intensive as preparations for the first oratorio were made, eight occurring in the seventeen days preceding December 25; the Philharmonic Society attended one of them. However discouraging the final preparations may have been—the president ordered a special rehearsal on the afternoon of the concert—the event itself was the most overpowering cultural exhibition of the generation in Boston and stirred echoes in distant parts for years to come. The newspapers tossed critical hats in air while the jubilation of so great an achievement was furthered by still more concerts. There was no lack of appreciation of their own accomplishment.

Other successes by the Handel and Haydn Society followed immediately, since the attentions of the town revolved around this organization and the Philharmonic Society as the two powerful musical influences. A calmer atmosphere attended the concerts of the following season, owing to the endless repetitions of the same works and the necessity for much rehearsing until the inexperienced singers could master that which special enthusiasm had carried through in rough outline. New works were introduced slowly; other choruses from *The Messiah,* the complete *Creation,* selected works from the various collections of anthems and miscellaneous works from American and British composers occupied the chorus. As the chorus became an accepted fact, attention was drawn to visiting soloists. Whatever the means, the Society waxed in power and influence, being the factor which, more than any other, stimulated the increase of musical understanding in Boston and throughout the country. The trustees wrought well in every department of their activity.

Membership soon totaled one hundred and fifty singers, including a few tenors, male and female sopranos, male altos, and a large number of basses; the first concert had included five women, while twenty were included in this large total. To this day actual membership is held only by the male of the species, but the chorus is equally balanced between men and women. The orchestra was placed at the rear, next the organ. Under these circumstances, no imagination is required to estimate the difficulties arising from such arrangements, the straggling orchestral

will perform an ORATORIO, consisting of a selection of pieces of Sacred Music, chiefly from the works of Handel and Haydn, on MONDAY EVENING, the 25th inst. in the Stone Chapel, in School-street, to commence at six o'clock.

ORDER OF PERFORMANCES

Part First

From the CREATION, by Haydn.

RECITATIVE, In the beginning God created the heavens and the earth, &c.

CHORUS. And the Spirit of God moved upon the face of the waters, and God said, let there be light, and there was light.

RECITATIVE. And God saw the light, that it was Good, &c.

AIR. Now vanish before the holy beams &c.

CHORUS. A new created world springs up at God's command.

RECITATIVE. And God made the firmament, &c.

CHORUS. The marvelous work beholds amaz'd, &c.

RECITATIVE. And God said, Let the waters under the heaven be gathered together, &c.

AIR. Rolling in foaming billows, &c.

RECITATIVE. And God said, Let the earth bring forth grass, &c.

AIR. With verdure clad the fields appear, &c.

RECITATIVE. And the heavenly host proclaimed the third day, &c.

CHORUS. Awake the Harp, &c.

RECITATIVE. And God said, Let there be light in the firmament, &c.

RECITATIVE and AIR. In splendour bright is rising now the sun, &c.

CHORUS. The heavens are telling the glory of God &c.

Part Second

CHORUS. They played in air, &c.

AIR. I know that my Redeemer liveth.

CHORUS. Sing ye unto the Lord our God &c.

AIR. He shall feed his flock &c.

CHORUS. Lift up your heads &c.

AIR. Let the bright Seraphim &c.

DUET & CHORUS. By Thee with bliss &c.

Part Third

DUET. The Lord is a man of war.

CHORUS. He gave them hailstones for rain.

AIR. 'Tis liberty, dear liberty alone &c.

DUET. Come, ever-smiling liberty.

CHORUS. When winds breathe soft, &c. (Webbe)

AIR. O had I Jubal's lyre.

CHORUS. The Lord shall reign for ever and ever.

CHORUS. Hallelujah! For the Lord God Omnipotent reigneth.[58]

[58] *New England Palladium*, Dec. 22, 1815.

parts, the overwhelming drums, the incomplete harmonic and tonal balance, the effects of Yankee diction on the sublime roulades of certain chorus parts, the stentorian enthusiasms of leading members whose faith in God was second only to faith in their own mastery of every interval in the gamut. Little wonder the press's desire to be at one with Händel and Haydn had frequent recourse to harsh words in describing the sounds, vocal and instrumental, which purported to represent these immortals.

A decided improvement in the quality of many visiting artists was noticeable by this time, and the tendency to acclaim each vocalist as superior to any heard before indicates a development of theater and concert life which justified profitable tours by some of the leading singing actors from England. Furthermore, Americans were achieving note, for example, Mrs. Burke, who became known as the finest American singer of her day, a lady "with experience in the sweetly pathetic as well as rich and varied warblings," and one "who is amiable and worthy in domestic life as she is justly admired in her public calling for the vocal powers with which she is endowed by nature." [59] Heralded as the "American Catalani," Mrs. Burke came to the Washington Gardens during July with a repertory which added not one whit to the progressive musical understanding of the populace; favorite songs by the celebrated Henry Rowley Bishop larded her programs, and though she stepped indoors to sing at Concert Hall under the direction of Mr. Graupner and "at the request of a number of respectable families of Boston," the songs continued to run the range of "Let Me Borrow for a While," "Just like Love," "Whilst with Village Maids I Stray," and the favorite "Echo Song." Mr. Graupner was conductor of the Washington Gardens and Mrs. Graupner the featured soloist, each receiving the customary benefit at the close of the season with all hands contributing to the miscellaneous program, but nothing of the slightest musical consequence occurred during these evenings of innocent amusement.

Messrs. Gilles and Etienne arrived in Boston briefly for a pair of concerts at Concert Hall early in September, 1816. Both were composers of such eminence, if one accepts the evidence of the program, that the selection of music other than their own was merely sketched

[59] *New England Palladium*, July 2, 1816.

in without reference to its creator; hence their programs contain nothing identifiable except an omnipresent Battle Piece and a motley assortment of Romances, Fantasias, and Variations. Mr. Gilles later became a leading figure in the musical life of Philadelphia, while Etienne settled in New York.

Besides these frail offerings, the town was invited to hear the Panharmonicon, set up in the Columbian Museum and opened to the public several evenings weekly; only a few selections were available but those at hand were rearranged in every possible way to give the effect of novelty. After an engagement of nearly a year, the Panharmonicon was packed up and shipped elsewhere.

Part First

1.	Overture la Clemenza di Tito	Mozart
2.	March and Rondo	Marchand
3.	Waltzes	Maelzel
4.	Three Military Marches	Naderman
5.	Finale	Hadyn

Part Second

6.	Overture to the triumphal entry of Constantine the Great into Rome	Stiebelt
7.	Andante	Hadyn
8.	Military and Pastoral	Rigel
9.	Creation of the World	Hadyn
10.	Military Symphony	Hadyn

Lyceum and Chautauqua movements were yet afar off, nor were the famous Hutchinsons or Bakers making the rounds of town halls or "opry" houses, but a few family groups toured as concert attractions, unacceptable either to the theater or to the choral societies, but providing satisfactory entertainment in their own way. Such an aggregation was the Lewis family—P. Lewis (from England) and children three. It is apparent that Mr. Lewis was seeking a place to remain as teacher and practitioner of an art in which there is no reason to suppose he was especially well qualified. His Boston experience commenced in January, 1817, as teacher of piano forte "according to the latest and most approved system of fingering," of singing "with the piano forte," and of violin; instruction given either at home, 14 Charles street, or on the wing, with piano tuning added as service. Subsequent events suggest that Mr. Lewis was busier teaching his own children than those of others. His first venture before the public took place at the Exchange Coffee House in company with Mrs. Wheatley, Mr. Williams (late of the Boston Theatre), and Mrs. Allen of the Philadelphia Theatre; a Concerto by Viotti and unnamed pieces by the band set off a worthless set of comic songs and tender effusions ranging from "Booby" to "Fly from the World, O Bessy, to Me," composers unknown and unlamented.

Immediately afterward Mr. Lewis disappeared from the Boston scene but in 1819 he was heard as organist in a severely classical program held in Portland, Maine, thereafter touring again with his three children, Master P., eight years of age; Master James, seven; and Miss Ann, four; these aspired to a concert in the manner announced on March 24, 1819:

EXTRAORDINARY CONCERT

P. LEWIS, Professor of Music, respectfully informs his friends and the public, that he intends giving a CONCERT, with his three Children, on Tuesday, the 6th of April, at Boylston Hall, the youngest only four years of age, the oldest eight, when those who may favor him with their attendance will have an opportunity of witnessing to what an astonishing degree of excellence Children at that early period of life may attain with proper instruction and attention. The different Instruments on which the Children will perform will be the Organ, Piano Forte, Violin and Pedal Harp. The particular mode of P. Lewis' instruction by which they have exclusively profitted is the same which he adopts with all of his pupils, and is too well known to need explanation.

March 24.[60]

The program lists two works by Mozart, arranged for four hands, and concludes with a rendition of the Hallelujah Chorus on the organ by the eldest scion of the family. Once again thereafter Mr. Lewis announced his profession as teacher, adding the pedal harp, "that most elegant of all instruments," for females, and having in his rooms a complete set of the various instruments for the use of pupils who were given the privilege of receiving lessons on any two of them alternately, without an additional charge. This complicated but generous arrangement seemed no more calculated to attract a large clientele than the previous one, and no more is heard from Mr. Lewis as a teacher. He enjoyed the favor of Graupner enough to secure a small amount of

[60] *Columbian Centinel.*

work copying parts for the Handel and Haydn Society orchestra but did not play an instrument at any time in public. The Lewis ménage was frequently disposed to give concerts in Boston and environs at which symphonies by Haydn and Mozart, Dussek and Ries, were performed in four-hand arrangements, but the ambition to amaze was often more apparent than the wish to gratify by sign artistic, and the net result made a very slight contribution indeed to the musical culture of the time. A typical Lewis program is given on page 95.

America entertained prodigies with kindly concern and no little delight at juvenile precocity. Boston had the resident Miss Eustaphieve about this time, Miss Hewitt and Miss Graupner having grown to maturity, and on May 14, 1818, Master George Smith, a child of five years, aided and abetted by his father gave a concert under the patronage of the Philharmonic and the Handel and Haydn Societies at which the child performed a "solo on the Violin," introducing Grammachree and Patrick's Day. Mr. Granger led the band, Mr. Smith Sr. performed on the violoncello, and Mr. Graupner officiated at the double bass, all as featured performers at the new Boylston Hall, while the sponsorship of the leading musical organizations was guarantee of the child's talents.

Once assured of its place—an assurance gained without delay—the Handel and Haydn Society set about systematic mastery of the two great works chosen as most representative of the composers honored in its title. After two years of study, the feat of complete performance (according to the editions of the time) was attempted, together with other anthems and incidental works, in three evenings within the week. The first performance, April 1, 1818, consisted of the first part of *The Messiah* and the third part of *The Creation*, together with an intermediate selection; while the second performance, two days later, consisted of the second part of *The Creation* and the second part of *The Messiah*, with an intermediate selection; the third performance, on the following evening, offered the third part of both works, and miscellany. The Philharmonic Society assisted, and special books of words were printed. This undertaking marks one of the earliest festivals in this country devoted to so noble a purpose as the sacred works of eminent composers. With so much ambition and so little experience on the part of the performers, there is room for

EXTRAORDINARY CONCERT

P. Lewis, respectfully informs his friends and the public, that his Children's Concert will take place at Boylston Hall, On THURSDAY next, the 8th inst.

Their respective ages are as follows:—Master P. Lewis, 8 years of age—Master James Lewis, 7, and Miss Ann Lewis, 4

ORDER OF THE CONCERT

Part I

The Hailstone Chorus, arranged as a Duet, Organ—
    Masters P. & J. Lewis,   Handel
Duet—Dulce Concerto, Piano Forte, do. do.   Mozart
Lesson—Piano Forte, Miss Ann Lewis.   Challoner
Duet—Violins, Master P. & J. Lewis.   Pleyel
Sonata—Pedal Harp, Master P. Lewis, after only seven
    week's practice on that difficult instrument.   Barthelmor
Duet March—Piano Forte, Master P. and Miss A. Lewis.
Sonata—Piano Forte, Master J. Lewis   Stiebelt
Battle of Prague—arranged as a Duet—Piano Forte—
    Masters P. & J. Lewis—   Kotswara

Part II

The Horse and his rider—arranged as a Duet, Organ,
    Master P. & J. Lewis,   Handel
Duet March—Piano Forte, Master P. & Miss A. Lewis.
Concerto—do. do. Master P. Lewis   Cramer
Duet—Violins, Masters P. & J. Lewis. ~   Pleyel
Sonatina—Pedal Harp, in which are introduced the fa-
    vorite airs of blue-eyed Mary and the Copenhagen
    Waltz
Lesson—Piano Forte, Miss Ann Lewis   Challoner
Solo—Violin, Master P. Lewis   Kreutzer
Overture—arranged as a Duet, Piano Forte, Masters P.
    & J. Lewis,   Mozart
Finale—Grand Hallelujah Chorus, Organ, Master P.
    Lewis,   Handel

Tickets of admission at one dollar each to be had at the Franklin Music Warehouse, No. 6 Milk-street; at Mr. Parker's Circulating Library, No. 12 Cornhill; at Mr. Lewis', No. 15, Carver street; and at Boylston Hall, on the Evening of Performance.

Concert to commence at 7 o'clock.[61]

[61] *Columbian Centinel,* April 3, 1819.

admission of the several doubts expressed in the press as to the complete success of all parts of the affair; furthermore, there was some diversity of opinion regarding the merits of the two works, a healthy discussion, if not one to settle the question for all time. The assignment so willingly undertaken required more time than the two and a quarter years allowed for complete assimilation, and the following seasons were marked by a continued absorption in these two compositions, sung over and over again, and rehearsed constantly; in fact, seventeen concerts had been given in the two years since its founding and the number continued apace. Audiences heard concert after concert without any apparent sign of weariness, while the various projects for publishing and importing scores confirm the enthusiasm of a public which desired to study them more intensively.[62]

Example of the incidental scorn poured on the old-fashioned pre-Händel and Haydn harmony is shown in an article preceding a concert:

The Harmonic and Handel Societyes sustain a character too well known to require eulogy—Their efforts have nearly produced a revolution in our musical world; they have roused an emulation, whose consequences have been of infinite importance, not only in establishing a relish for genuine harmony but of doing away with the drowsy moments of that up-and-down monotony, whose dolorous creak has so often agonized the nerves of the stoutest Christian and

Whet his teeth on barbarous gritting edge.

To vary the fare, soloists of note were engaged to assist the Society at fees ranging from one to four hundred dollars, while the subtle emanation of social importance attached to all the activities of the Handel and Haydn Society. Oliver Shaw, the blind singer and composer of Providence, became a prime favorite with his songs, "There's Nothing True but Heaven" and "Mary's Tears"; ere long, by this means, such notables as Incledon and Phillips came before the public of Boston. To further charge the pride of the musical public, a special celebration in behalf of the visiting President of the United States included a performance in Chauncy Place Church on July 5, 1817; on this occasion there was given to "the citizens of Boston and vicinity, particularly the Ladies, a better opportunity than they would otherwise have had, of being gratified by a sight of the Chief Magistrate of the Union," and "Gentlemen who intend to carry Ladies," were re-

62 See p. 239 for subscription editions of Händel and of Haydn.

quested to respond with alacrity. Exceptional to the "ephemeral
puffers" of the day was the sane and convincing "Communication"
written for the *Palladium* and published on April 1, 1818:

COMMUNICATIONS

The lovers of Sacred Harmony anticipate to-morrow evening a renewal
of the delight which they have so often experienced from the performances of the Handel and Haydn Society. The high approbation of amateurs and professors, and the liberal patronage of the public have long
shown the estimation in which their Oratorios are held. And we are gratified to observe, that their exhibitions have advanced not only in celebrity
but in merit. We know that there is a fashion in admiration, but the exertions of these gentlemen have continually presented us with something
more and more worthy to be admired. It is doubtless to them that we must
ascribe in a great measure the improved taste in Sacred Music that is
prevailing among us. The revival of this taste within a few years led to
the formation of the Society; and they in turn have promoted and we hope
will perpetuate the impulse. We feel a confidence that they will continue to
receive the encouragement which they have so well deserved, and be able
not only to meet the exigencies of the establishment, but to add to it a
library that shall contain the works of the most eminent composers.

The warmth and cordiality expressed to visiting artists throughout the history of public amusements in Boston is in direct contradiction to the tradition of coldness and inhospitality associated with
that city; through the accumulating dust of more than a century an
enthusiasm shines over the record of all these organized activities devoted to the arts; the theatrical life, the open-house evenings of the
Columbian Museum, the Saturday musicales of the Philharmonic Society, and the fashionable oratorios of the Handel and Haydn Society
bear ample evidences of an exciting cultural life in circles warmed by
music's radiant beam. Boston was still a town, with town government,
but in its quiet way the forces of national policies were felt by the
individual and group, and the importance of the New England capital
in all respects of culture and manners was a matter of intense pride
to every member of the community. To the stranger within the gates
a discreet reserve was maintained unless he came well recommended or
immediately proved his mettle; this attitude, held to with great consistency, was a selective method in so far as the musician was concerned, gently repelling the incompetent candidate for permanent
residence, but cordially welcoming and providing for the useful talent.

This latter cordiality is frequently shown in the public press, for the effusions appearing there are often forced to the point of ridiculousness, but the effect must have been often spoiled by common knowledge that such publicity releases were more often than not written by the performer himself.[63]

The striking influence of the Handel and Haydn Society is shown in the concert life, for independent concerts nearly vanish from the seasonal lists and the few individuals who make an attempt—an attempt which might have been successful before 1816—now receive slight encouragement unless properly sponsored. A novel program, in so far as the first half is concerned, and deserving of success, is that announced by Mr. R. A. Taylor, on August 13, 1817:

CONCERT OF VOCAL MUSIC

Mr. R. A. TAYLOR from New-York, and recently from England, respectfully informs the inhabitants of Boston that he intends giving a VOCAL CONCERT, THIS EVENING, at the Exchange Coffee-House. Mr. T. flatters himself that the selections he has made for this occasion cannot fail to please the lovers of Vocal Melody.

Part I

1. Recitative—"Comfort ye my people."   Handel
2. Song—"Holy, holy Lord."   Handel
3. Song—"In native worth and honor clad."   Haydn
4. Song—"Lord remember David."   Handel
5. Song—"Pleasure my former ways resigning."   Handel
6. Recitative and Air—"Deeper still."—"Waft her
   Angels."   Handel

Part II

1. Song—"Said a smile to a tear."   Braham
2. Song—"To the brook and the willow."   Stevenson
3. Song—"Death of Nelson."   Braham
4. Recitative and Song—"Ye gloomy caves."—"On this
   cold flinty rock."   Braham
5. Song—"The Thorn."   Shield
6. Song—"Death of Abercrombie."   Braham

Tickets One Dollar each, to be had at the Bookstore of Mr. Greenleaf, Court-street; Mr. Parker's Library, corner of Water-street, and at the Bar of the Coffee House.[64]

[63] See page 49.
[64] *Columbian Centinel.* This was not the seventy-year-old Raynor Taylor or S. P. Taylor who came to Boston in the same year.

No orchestra assisted, and no support was forthcoming from the Graupners; all told it was a novelty, as the prospectus promised:

MR. TAYLOR'S CONCERT

A novelty is announced for this evening;—A Concert to be sustained by an individual, without the aid of other noises or an orchestra.

This last circumstance proved to be no handicap, for the sweet word "success" was applied to Mr. Taylor's efforts, and a second concert was immediately announced, in which he was generously assisted by Miss Hewitt, Mr. Mocenig, and Mr. Hart; Mr. Taylor relaxed the severity of his offerings on this occasion, relaxed them considerably, in fact, and admitted other noises. Mr. Taylor's first recital is a very early example, indeed, of its kind, for not even in Europe had the custom of solo performance gained headway, nor was it customary for at least a decade until Liszt established, if he did not inaugurate, the general practice.

Miss Hewitt, nothing daunted by the heat of summer, came before the public on August 28, assisted by various talents from theater and town, to play in a Trio by Taskin [65] and Pleyel's German Hymn with Variations by Latour for piano and flute, with Mr. Norton at the flute; Miss Hewitt also sang a song by her father, "Rest Thee, Babe," with words from *Guy Mannering*, and in glees. The program is more interesting for the names of the performers, several of them new to these pages, than for the music.

The advantage of good violinists is apparent where an orchestra is concerned, but it does not appear that Signor R. Giovanni Mascarelli, from Sicily, remained long enough in Boston to assist any of the permanent organizations; he gave two concerts and left a testimonial, "sensible for the encouragement received, begs leave to say, that in his efforts to please he hopes to evince that he is not a stranger to the sentiment of gratitude though a stranger in this land." [66] Within the same fortnight Mr. Mocenig, lately from Trieste, spent two evenings in the leading halls of the town and advertised in a "Particular Notice" that he intended to remain in Boston if sufficient scholars favored him with their commands; there is reason to suppose that he did not succeed, for his name is not in any directory or in future bills of the day.

[65] Henri Joseph Taskin, 1779–1852.   [66] *Columbian Centinel,* Aug. 30, 1817.

CONCERT

Miss Hewitt respectfully informs her friends & the public, that her Concert will take place TO-MORROW EVENING, Aug. 28, at

Concert-Hall

Leader of the Band, Mr. Lewis

Part I

Sinfonia—Full Band,	Haydn
Song—"The Girl of my heart," . . .	Mr. McFarland
Song—"One Kind Kiss" . . .	Mrs. W. Clark
Pleyel's German Hymn, with Variations by Latour for Piano and Flute	Miss Hewitt and Mr. Norton
Comic Song—"Capt. Wattle & Miss Roe"—	Mr. Bray
Glee—"Shepherds Tell me" (Mazzinghi)	
Song—"Here's the Bower"—Miss Hewitt, Mr. Bray, and Mr. Hart	
	words by T. Moore
Trio—PianoForte, Violin, Violincello, (Taskin) by Miss Hewitt, &c.	

Part II

Quartette—Clarionet Principal (Duvernoy)	Mr. Hart
Song—"Where shall the Lover rest" . . .	Mr. McFarland
Tyrolese Airs, with Variations (Gelineck)	Miss Hewitt
Song—"Rest thee, babe" (words from Guy Mannering, composed by Mr. Hewitt)	Miss Hewitt
Air—"The Ploughboy," with variations, composed and to be performed on the Clarionet by Mr. Norton—his third appearance in Boston	
Comic Song	Mr. Bray
Glee—"The Nightingale" (King) Miss Hewitt, Mr. Bray, and Mr. Hart	
Finale	Full Band

Tickets at $1 each, to be had at Concert-Hall; Mr. Parker's Library, corner of Water-street; Mr. Callender's Library, School-street, Mr. Graupner's No. 6, Franklin-street, and of Miss Hewitt, No. 52, Marlboro-street. The Concert to commence at a quarter before 8 o'clock, precisely.

Thomas (Irish) Phillips first visited Boston in April, 1818, and caught the public fancy, for his vocal method was an excellent one and his knowledge of the true oratorio style was greatly appreciated by the singers who knew the notes but here experienced for the first time the finer subtleties of technical accomplishment; his manners were similarly of so refined a nature as to entirely captivate the comparative crudities of the New England gentry. The Great Society welcomed him in a manner befitting a twentieth-century celebrity, while the public bought his songs in quantity and showed other evidences of affection and esteem.[67]

Phillips came as a singing-actor, of course, at the Federal Theatre, making his first appearance as Count Bellino in *The Devil's Bridge*, always his most celebrated role. He received $2,500 for eleven nights, a very large salary for the time. The favorable impression, attested by similar successes in New York and Philadelphia, was made without delay, while his Philadelphia benefit netted the amazing sum of $1,300 and the average intake, according to W. B. Wood, was $804 nightly for seven nights, a figure exceeded only by Incledon. In England he had apparently been a useful rather than a brilliant artist in the several first and second-rate theaters, including the English Opera House (the Lyceum); Michael Kelly, however, mentions him, a pupil of Dr. Arnold, as the most accomplished singing-actor in England. In Dublin he had lectured on the art of singing, with illustrations, and attracted much attention by this means; wherever he went publication of his repertory intensified interest in him; his songs were "sung or played during his absence by almost every real or pretended amateur in music, by professional men on the stage, by every girl who could finger a piano, by every boy who could whistle, and by about every fifer who could play a march before a company of militia.[68] The reigning favorite featured these songs:

Mr. Phillips' Songs

For sale at the Franklin Musical Warehouse, No. 6, Milk-street.

>Ah Give a pair
>Behold in his soft expressive face
>Braham's Polacca—Beautiful Maid
>Come tell me where the maid is found
>Dear Erin—Eveleen's Bower
>Robin's Adair.
>In vain may that bosom—a Bravoura
>I'll love thee dearly
>Is there a heart that never lov'd
>Love's Young Dream

[67] In the *Columbian Centinel* of May 13, 1818, there is given this interesting notice: "The Arts—The elegant full length portrait of Mr. Phillips painted by our townsman Penniman, mentioned in our last, is now placed for public inspection at the Franklin Music Warehouse, Milk street. Judges speak of it as a chef d'ouvre." Earnest search has failed to locate this portrait, if it still exists.
[68] *History of the Handel and Haydn Society,* Vol. I, p. 84.

Let fame sound the Trumpet
Loud roared the dreadful—(Bay Biscay O)
My early day what joy
My heart with love is beating
Tis but fancies sketch
This blooming rose—The Hunter's Horn
The Death of Abercrombie
Together let us range
The last words of Marmion.
Sigh not for love—The Bird Duet
Said a Smile to a Tear
Love among the Roses
The Death of Nelson
Together with the Songs in the "Cabinet" and "Siege of
    Belgrade," and "Maid of the Mill." [69]

The Handel and Haydn Society captured the star of the day, paying him $200 each for two concerts, and he sang suitable selections
from Händel and related authors. There were many who failed to
share the majority's enthusiasm, but the net result of Mr. Phillips'
visit seems to have been an elevation of taste by reason of the refinement of his style and purity of his diction. Vocally he was undistin-
guished, but he made skillful use of his talents. He was grateful to the
Society for giving him the opportunity to come before a Boston audience as a singer in oratorios, showing his appreciation by presenting it with an original duet, "Here Shall Soft Charity." After his second visit he sent a manuscript anthem, "O Lord! Our Governor,"
composed by Sir John Stevenson and dedicated to the society at his
request.

After an absence of three years Phillips returned to America for
Christmas Day, 1821, receiving much the same attention, but acquiring far less popularity than before; his new songs failed to please and
the old ones were worn threadbare; his voice had declined markedly,
and the novelty of his appearance, together with the intervening appearance of the sensational Incledon, robbed the visit of its novel
characteristics. He lectured to fashionable audiences in Boston, however, and published a *Method of Singing* which seems to have escaped
survival. The press was uniformly cordial, exhibiting the unfailing
kindness of Boston audiences to those who had been admired in the
past. But both parties recognized the diminishing success of this en-

[69] *Columbian Centinel*, April 8, 1818.

gagement, and President Winchester wrote a finely expressed letter of appreciation which must have further cemented the cordial relations already established between the two:

My regret that the most finished specimens of vocal talent which have ever been exhibited among us should have met with so disproportionate a reception is increased, when I reflect that the improvement of the vocal art resulting from your visit to this place will be a source of delight to the lovers of music for ages; and this consideration will be your best remuneration. It was but little that the Handel and Haydn Society were able to contribute to your happiness, but that little flowed from hearts sensible of the benefits received from your precepts and example.[70]

After his return to England Phillips became leading tenor in Elliston's troupe at the Surrey Theatre, London, and lived until 1841.

The highly refined art of Mr. Phillips had hardly faded from the scene when another of the great English vocalists visited the Federal Theatre and likewise participated in concerts of the Handel and Haydn Society. Charles Benjamin Incledon, well past his prime, made his first American tour through a considerable part of the United States, where he was received with unanimous favor; less subtle, but more forthrightly vocal in his interpretations, he was invited to join in an oratorio program, his last appearance before a Boston audience; lacking the traditions of his dignified predecessor he nevertheless sang some of the tenor parts of *The Messiah* with success, but preferred the histrionics of the song "Total Eclipse," for Incledon had a robust and manly style best suited to naval songs and declamatory pieces. There is no record of Bostonian objection to his burly manner, or to a slight deterioration perceived by any who may have heard him in earlier days. He retained his high spirits in performance and filled the house for every play which permitted him to hurry through dialogue in order to arrive at the songs. Despite his lack of scientific approach to the art of singing, and his ridicule of the Italian methods, his voice was a notable one, ranging from A to C in falsetto, in which latter voice there was much power.[71] He would not study and could not read the simplest melody but learned all his roles by rote, finding greatest success in sea songs. "The Storm" by G. A. Stevens and "Black-Ey'd Susan" were among his favorites. In so far as the public

[70] *History of the Handel and Haydn Society,* Vol. I, p. 84.
[71] T. Williams, *A Treatise on Singing; an Analysis of the Vocal Powers of Incledon and Braham,* (1834).

was concerned, Incledon thoroughly duplicated the success of Phillips and surpassed him at the box office; his visit almost immediately followed that of the earlier artist and came at the end of his association with Covent Garden at the age of fifty-five years. There was a breath of scandal in connection with his eventual departure from these shores, but the sensational qualities of his delivery lingered in the memory of all who heard him and caused his name to be enrolled among those who early made a deep impression on the theatrical and concert life of the country. After a phenomenal Boston engagement he traveled in Colman's "Wandering Minstrels" to Salem, Newburyport, Portsmouth, and Portland. Once returned to London, he was quoted as saying: "With regard to musical science in America, I must say that I was agreeably surprised in finding it, in every State, in such high cultivation."

·The wonderful impetus given to the musical life of Boston, and to other leading cities up and down the coastal plain was owing in some part to the general facilitation of means of travel, social progress along many lines, and the up-turn of business after the War of 1812. Commercial relations with England, less affected by the subtle resistance of New England's attitude than they were elsewhere to the southward, were once again strengthened with a full tide of commerce flowing in both directions. The theater was accepted as a permament and useful institution, enjoying regular seasons, while signs of lasting influence attended each concert by the Handel and Haydn Society. The Philharmonic Orchestra was in the course of a new tide of prosperity, enjoying, in fact, its greatest esteem in these very years.

Boston's population grew apace, and the time was ripe for graduation from the status of township to the rank of city; already the potent influence of great movements destined to elevate Boston and its environs to world-wide importance were showing themselves. The literary figures of a great day were in their youth, training for a mighty adventure in the realm of the mind and preparing to give America her mature literary heritage as well as a substantial musical and artistic flowering. Emerson, Hawthorne, Margaret Fuller, Alcott, Ripley, and Thoreau were enjoying normal childhood within the outposts of Boston's influence, warmed by the gentle stimulus of an awakening age and taught by the thrilling words of Dr. Channing,

ORATORIO

TO BE PERFORMED THIS EVENING

AT BOYLSTON-HALL

By the

HANDEL AND HAYDN SOCIETY

assisted by

MR. INCLEDON

And positively the last time the lovers of music will be delighted with the extraordinary powers of this eminent vocal performer in this town.

ORDER OF PERFORMANCE
IN TWO PARTS

Part I

Song—Now heaven in fullest glory shone, &c.
Chorus—Achieved is the glorious work, &c.
Air—Great God, what do I see and hear; &c.—Mr. Incledon
Chorus—Great God, &c.
Air
Air—The Marvellous work, &c.
Chorus—And to the etherial vaults, &c.
Duet—Ode to Charity—Messrs. Incledon and Taylor
Chorus—The horse and his rider, &c.

Part II

Recit.—Comfort ye my people—Mr. Incledon
Air—Every valley shall be exalted—Mr. Incledon
Chorus—And the glory of the Lord, &c.
Air
Chorus—The heavens are telling, &c.
Air—Total eclipse—Mr. Incledon
Chorus—He gave them hailstones for rain.
Chorus—HALLELUJAH

Tickets of admission may be had at One Dollar each, at the stores of No. 6 Franklin-street, J. R. Parker, Agent; No. 12 Cornhill, S. H. PARKER's Circulating Library; and at G. GRAUPNER & Co.'s Music Store, Marlboro-street. Performance to commence precisely at 8 o'clock.

(*Columbian Centinel,* July 1, 1818)

Ticknor, Prescott, and an host of keen minds whose world reached across the sea to the comparative cultures of England, Germany, Italy, and Spain. As in Europe, the individual was becoming a figure of concern apart from the group; America was soon to feel the stress of one man's thinking, often set against another man's in that free and happy community of active minds, fostered by a liberal social and political tradition. The striking, independent challenge of Emerson's "Self Reliance" had its roots in the new freedom of that day when, weary of the stultifying theological classifications and glimpsing a new world in the ideas from abroad, New England minds were spurred on to a challenging expression of individual thinking and acting. "I hope in these days we have heard the last of conformity and consistency," the man of Concord later wrote. "Let the words be gazetted and ridiculous henceforward. . . . I will stand here for humanity, and though I would make it kind, I would make it true. . . . Let us affront and reprimand the smooth mediocrity and squalid contentment of the times, and hurl in the face of custom and trade and office, the fact which is the upshot of all history, that there is a great responsible Thinker and Actor working wherever a man works; that a true man belongs to no other time or place, but is the centre of things." [72]

These thoughts were seed planted in the young mind of New England's intellectual awakening at a time when the innumerable aspects of civilized culture were finding renaissance in the new world. The force of attraction brought seekers for truth from distant lands where they were tested by invisible but infinitely wise hands; selected, distributed, or rejected as their talents were required, the chosen were speedily welded into a new social fabric. Two centuries had labored to provide a background for the genius now appearing from the humblest origins. Here great men were seconded by a host of original men throughout the structure of society; here each man in his rightful place thought and expressed grand and noble verities, no less deserving to be heard were they only constituted of ideas expressed by the ancients with slightly differing emphasis. These were challenging times when the muddy river bed of thought became stirred, for the age had not arrived when able men were content to resign their thinking to others.

Thus the years were filled with a new alertness to every aspect of human society. Horizons were widened with such suddenness that a generation or more was required to comprehend the entire view placed before it. New faces hopefully disembarked from the ships in the har-

72 Emerson, *The American Scholar.*

bors and from the stage coaches at the hotels; some strange visitations indeed were made by opportunists whose sudden arrival was matched only by speed of departure. Boston looked serenely on, for outward expression was not an inherent means of communication in this section of the country; those who could see no more deeply went away unsatisfied, but those who felt and thought, who stopped to listen to the inner voice, found the wisdom of their coming explained them and acted accordingly. The strains of Haydn's "A New-Created World," resoundingly sung by the Great Society, was a song of the day, containing as much timeliness as the semi-weekly newspaper.

The advent of Louis Ostinelli added much to the musical advantage of Boston, following his debut on September 7, 1818, and a second concert the next week. The program of that evening's music included a work by Beethoven,[73] the first known instance of a work by this composer performed in Boston.[74] The name of Beethoven became further known to the inhabitants by the singing of a recitative "Now the Work of Man's Redemption" and chorus, "Hallelujah to the Father and to the Son" from *The Mount of Olives* on November 24 at Boylston Hall; it was repeated on Thanksgiving Day evening with orchestral accompaniments composed and adapted by Mr. Granger Sr. The works of the now obscure Samuel Chapple likewise entered the repertory at this time.[75] Mr. Graupner's one published selection deriving from Beethoven ("The Bonny Boat") belongs to a considerably later time.

The announcement of a concert by Mr. Keene, sometime member of the theatrical company, struck an original, if not entirely conclusive note, in these words:

[73] The program is given in full on p. 134. W. T. Upton has made the magnificent coup of publishing a program displaying a Beethoven work played in Lexington, Ky., under A. P. Heinrich on Nov. 12, 1817. (*Anthony Philip Heinrich, 1939.*)

[74] Dr. Kinkeldey speculates with his usual foresight and accuracy on this subject as follows: "There must have been many of the younger Germans who came to America in these early years who knew of Beethoven at first-hand and who played some of his variations for the piano or his early sonatas or even some of the chamber-music or arrangements of larger works, in the privacy of their own homes." Miss Hewitt's performance of a piano forte sonata is mentioned on p. 144; copies of "2 Beethoven Symphony duets" appear on a bill from Clementi, Banger, Collard, Davis & Collard in 1817 and addressed to Graupner. (*Musical Quarterly,* April, 1927.)

[75] This blind composer was an English contemporary, pupil of a blind teacher whose mentor had suffered a like infirmity; his works included anthems, glees, and pianoforte sonatas; many of the former were in the most popular vocal collections of the time.

As a *stranger,* young and inexperienced, of amiable disposition, of liberal feelings, far from his kindred and his home, remote from paternal protection, and looking forward for indulgence, we hope Mr. Keene will be greeted with a portion of that hospitality which commemorates the land of genius and of sympathy—*his own native Erin!* May her harp ne'er waken the chords of lamentation, nor echo the tones of despondency.—May its melodies ever ring the halls of the banquet, and reverberate to the touch of festivity;—and its *minstrel,* alive with sympathy and emotion, may be sheltered by the wings of benevolence, and grow warm in the sunshine of the charities that foster him.—There is something here closely associated, which should inspire the heart of sensibility, and excite the latent feelings of humanity.

April 14.[76]

Mr. Keene deserved all the loyalty of his fellow countrymen (how much better he would do now!) for he ripened into an artist of first rank during the next few years, embodying many of those talents shared jointly by Incledon and Phillips. He sang in the first performance in America of *Der Freischütz* on March 2, 1825.

Mr. Holland offered himself as an object of much-needed charity, if we are to believe the implications sounded in the introductory notice, for the assisting friends, the Philharmonic and the Handel and Haydn Societies, are eulogized to the complete neglect of the beneficiary. We may credit this to the traditional impersonality of the news columns, and remind ourselves that it was this same gentleman who inspired the following editorial comment two years afterwards in *The Euterpeiad:*

The Philo Harmonic and Handel and Haydn Societies intend patronizing the concert of Mr. Holland on Tuesday next. Mr. Holland's talents for singing are principally confined to a clear and distinct verbal articulation. . . . he has a numerous young progeny.

But Mr. Holland's need was apparently great, for he took another benefit in "the little hall in Pond-street," enlisting the formidable talents of Dr. Jackson to play the pianoforte accompaniments and the carillon, which instrument had of late become a resounding plaything for the latter gentleman. Mr. Holland lifted up his voice *once,* in a song "The Sea Fight" (by desire).

During the winter of 1819, besides the Lewis family, the two solidly

[76] *Columbian Centinel.*

organized societies were the only purveyors of musical evenings wherein the merits lay in the music itself. How much forbearance is invoked in praise of sweet charity! It is worthy of note, however, that Miss Jane, a fourth child of Mr. Lewis, joined the act on her third birthday, November 18, 1819.

Of the winsome visitors to the Boston metropolis, Mrs. French was the most attractive to the public; she was announced as "the most scientific and charming female vocalist in the U.S." and was important enough to enlist the services of Dr. Jackson at the pianoforte on May 25, 1819. The attraction must have been in her personality and womanly virtue, for her music was not scientific in the accepted sense; however, it was enough to hold Dr. Jackson for the entire series of concerts, four in number, which listed not one single aria, but specialized in ballads by Moore, Clarke, Stevenson, Braham, Storace, and Bishop's celebrated "Echo Song," "the echo being entirely performed by herself." The lady's appreciation is attested by a charity concert for the benefit of the Female Orphan Asylum. Thereafter she was engaged for an evening in which she essays five of the more familiar arias by Händel "with the aid and assistance of that useful institution, the Handel and Haydn Society."

When Mrs. French returned to Boston in August, 1820, she gave three concerts a fortnight apart, with Miss Hewitt as accompanist; there was some change, but little improvement, in the repertory of "fashionable" songs. Neither Mrs. French nor Mrs. Burke were connected with the Federal Theatre, and they may be considered only as concert artists. Both Phillips and Incledon had considered Mrs. Burke as the most able vocalist in America prior to Mrs. French; the press, never hesitating to make comparisons, considered Mrs. French superior in every respect. This charming vocalist was a pupil of Benjamin Carr of Philadelphia, and the wife of a dry-goods merchant in that city. She enjoyed a very great reputation, owing to her charm of manner, and to her genuinely fine voice which enabled her to sing up to F. Fine diction, and a bell-like quality were combined with a sense of style, a virtue which Mrs. Burke seems to have lacked. Bostonians quite took the lady to heart, and wrote poems in her honor, some of them reaching a rather higher level than is customary with such effusions.

When not overawed by the proficiency of juvenile entertainers who preyed on a gullible public, Boston audiences attended the novel programs of Mr. and Mrs. Bartley, which, if well done, must have provided a cultural oasis in this sea of mediocrity.

CONCERT HALL

Second, and positively the Last Night but Two

———

MR. AND MRS. BARTLEY

will give the following

READINGS AND RECITATIONS

on Tuesday Evening, Nov. 23

Part I

Selections from the 4th Book of Paradise Lost, by——	Mrs. Bartley
Shakespeare's King Henry 5th, by	Mr. Bartley
Selections from the 2, 3rd, and 4th Acts.	

Part II

The 3d Act of Julius Caesar, (including the Orations of	
Brutus and Antony) by	Mr. Bartley

Recitations

"May the Maid of the Inn," by	Mrs. Bartley
Comic Tale, "The New-Castle Apothecary" by	Mr. Bartley
Moore's Melologue (written expressly for her) by	Mrs. Bartley

Description of the effects of National Music on National Character, in which will be introduced the airs of Greece, Switzerland, Spain, Ireland, and America.

To commence precisely at 7 o'clock.

Tickets one Dollar each, to be had at Wells & Lilly's, and O. C. Greenleaf's Circulating Library, Cornhill; and at Concert Hall, on the evening of performance.

The Third Performance will take place on Friday the 26th, and the Fourth on Tuesday the 30th, being positively the last night.[77]

The organization of the Handel and Haydn Society was surprisingly efficient from the beginning, and few changes of policy were made in the succeeding years. The most constant names were those of the composers inscribed in the title, but the interpreters also remained

77 *Columbian Centinel,* Nov. 20, 1819.

faithful for many years, devoting an ardent zeal to the society's conduct and sharing in its mighty triumphs. New names appear to give a glimpse of future days, as those older ones pass from the scene. Mrs. Graupner did not sing solo parts after the first season, but confined herself to the Philharmonic concerts; she had been prominently before the public of Boston for more than twenty years, and the importance of her services can hardly be over-estimated. In September, 1817, a new name was entered on the rolls, that of Jonas Chickering, who was to prosper mightily in the succeeding years as he furthered the construction and merchandising of the pianoforte. Miss Hewitt declined the position of organist for the society, and Dr. Jackson's terms were considered outrageous; with lavish hand, S. P. Taylor of New York, who had played for a few concerts, was engaged as regular organist. This act gave strength to the assertion that at this time there were not a half dozen professional organists in Boston; it is a question, for that matter, whether any city had a half dozen organists of the caliber of Taylor, or with sufficient understanding to play the repertory of the society with requisite skill. Miss Bennett (Mrs. Martin), Mrs. Withington, Mrs. French, Oliver Shaw, Phillips, and Incledon passed in review as soloists, each bringing some new quality to the understanding of the works at hand. In 1820 the society brought out the first of the *Collections* bearing its name, an undertaking destined to increase its influence afar, and establish its financial well-being at home. Following Mr. Taylor's term, cut short by the desire for retrenchment of expenses, Miss Hewitt, then Mrs. Ostinelli, assumed the position and held it for a decade, until the appointment of Charles Zeuner. Within the programs there was nothing of especial interest beyond the solid worth of selections already known, or elsewhere mentioned in these pages.

The summer, then as now, brought certain attractions of the sideshow variety which have no place in the record of concert life; mere mention will suffice to show the nature of those things which purported to be music, and in some measure at least, were accepted as such. First in the order of appearance during the summer of 1819 was Signor Helene "being the only person in the U. States who can play on *five* instruments at once." These included the Italian violin, Pandean pipes, Chinese bells, Turkish cymbals, and tenor drum—the latter with no specific national connotation. Moreover Signor Helene would also

CONCERT

Mr. Christiani, respectfully announces his Third concert on Tuesday Evening next, Aug. 29, at the Marlboro' Hotel.

Part I

1.	Overture—del Vingrero (Vinagrero?), composed by	Christiani
2.	French Song—le Troubadour (by particular desire)	do.
3.	Los Companas—Spanish Volero	do.
4.	Duet—of secret marriage, matrimonio secreto,—	Cimarosa

Part II

1. Mr. Artiguenave having offered to Mr. Christiani his friendly assistance for that evening, he will declaim a Hymn to Peace the Chorus of Which has been set to music in Boston by Christiani, and he will sing it.
2. Mr. Artiguenave will read the first act of the Misanthrope of Moliere; the scene between Philinte and Alceste and the scene between Alceste, Philinte and Orente, reading of the Sonnet.

Part III

1.	Overture to Tankred	Rossini
2.	A National Hymn, in honor of America, composed in Boston, by	Christiani
3.	Italian Song—(Nannetta Amabile)	do.
4.	A Comic Trio	do.

The doors will be open at half past seven o'clock. Tickets 1 dollar—Children half price—may be obtained at the Bar of the Marlboro' Hotel, and of West, Richardson & Lord, Cornhill.[78]

occasionally accompany the Italian violin with his mouth, in imitation of the mocking bird; the latter anatomical feature was not counted among the bona fide instrumentation. This exhibition was confined to the New England Museum and was not permitted at one of the leading concert halls; hence it may be dismissed as truly a side show, but one which delighted the town for more than two weeks.

Later in the summer, the Lilliputian Songsters entertained for a fortnight; as the name signifies, these were midgets, so small as to require little of our attention at this remove. By name they were Miss Caroline and Master Edward Clarke.

Mr. Christiani, "first Musician of his Catholic Majesty of Spain,

[78] *Columbian Centinel*, Aug. 26, 1820.

Compositor of Music to the Theatres of the Courts of Spain, and member of the Philo-Harmonic Academy of Bologna," arrived in July, 1820, to give concerts and teach pianoforte and singing during his stay in Boston, a stay confined to a few months, at the most, and consisting of two concerts at the Amphitheatre, or Washington Gardens. His program of Italian, Spanish, and French songs and pianoforte pieces was of his own composition, and apparently not very numerously attended. A third evening at the Marlboro' Hotel, however, contained some interesting works. (See program on page 112.)

No program is available for his fourth, and last concert, on September 14, but Mr. Christiani was so far encouraged that he proposed tarrying for a year, opening a school for teaching the art of singing in the true Italian style as taught by him in Europe, in Washington, and in Philadelphia, but not—for very long, at least—in Boston.

The Italian gentleman was succeeded by Ramo Samee an entertainer so elusive that we are unable to identify his instrument or means of communication to an audience; the attached is as much information as the newspapers show:

AMUSEMENTS

CONCERT-HALL

Ramo Samee, greateful for the unexpected and very flattering manner in which his Exhibitions have been received, during his visit to this Metropolis respectfully informs the inhabitants of Boston, that being persuaded that many persons have not yet witnessed his *Entirely Novel and unrivalled Performances*—he will continue here ANOTHER WEEK, and exhibit in Concert Hall, This and Friday Evenings, that every one, may have an opportunity of visiting him before he takes his departure.[79]

Boston's musical life, stabilized by the two permanent organizations, was a smoothly running organization of unfailing interest. Kindly thought was given to the older members of the musical community by means of benefit concerts. Mr. Schaffer, in particular, was favored by several of these. The soloist, Eckhardt, does not figure in the life of Boston other than on this occasion.

Miss Sophia Hewitt was, for the most part, the outstanding pianist of the town, and Mr. Ostinelli immediately became the favorite violin-

[79] *Ibid.,* Oct. 6, 1819,

F. C. SCHAFFER'S CONCERT

A GRAND CONCERT of Vocal and Instrumental Music will be given at Boylston Hall on TUESDAY EVENING NEXT by the Professional Gentlemen of the Orchestra and Amateurs, for the benefit of Mr. F. C. SCHAFFER, an infirm, aged, and decayed Musician.

Part I

Sinfonia, Lachasse	Pleyel
Song, Diana, Amateur	Shield
Variations, Piano Forte, by Mr. Eckhardt,	
Duet, "Sweet is the vale," Miss Schaffer and Amateur—Eckhardt	
Concerto, Clarionet, Mr. Hart,	F. C. Schaffer

Part II

Sinfonia	Haydn
Song, Amateur	
Sonata, Pianoforte, Mr. Eckhardt, accompanied on the	
Violin, Ostinelli—	Mozart
Song, "Trumpet of Victory," amateur,—	Braham
Minuetto,—	Krommer
Glee, Amateurs.	
Finale, full Orchestra.	

By particular desire, a Voluntary on the Organ will be performed by Mr. Eckhardt, between the first and second parts.

Tickets to admit a Lady and Gentleman, at one dollar, may be had of Mr. G. Graupner, No. 6, Franklin-street, Mr. Sam. H. Parker, No. 12, Cornhill, at the Franklin Music Warehouse, No. 6, Milk-street, and at the Door, Boylston Hall, on Tuesday evening, Performance to begin at eight o'clock precisely.

The Professional Gentlemen of the Orchestra, and those Amateurs who intend to offer their services for F. C. Schaffer's Concert on Tuesday next, at Boylston Hall, are requested to meet at the above Hall THIS EVENING, at 8 o'clock.[80]

ist; both were socially attractive. Prosperity gave them constant employment as teachers and recitalists, and Miss Hewitt played the organ; after their marriage they made tours to other cities in New England and built up an enviable reputation. A typical program, probably the last Boston instance of their appearance in joint recital before marriage, shows some changes in the taste of the selections made, but little improvement as to the introduction of works by

[80] *Columbian Centinel,* Aug. 12, 1820.

Haydn, Mozart, or Beethoven, or those of like rank in the history of music. Kalkbrenner, Lafont,[81] Rosetti, and Woelfl were favored in their stead.

CONCERT

Miss HEWITT, respectfully informs her Friends and the Public, that with the kind assistance of the Philharmonic and the Handel and Haydn Societies, her Concert of Vocal and instrumental Music, will be given in Boylston Hall, on TUESDAY, the 14th inst.

Part I

Symphony—Full Orchestra	Haydn
Song—(The Last Words of Marmion,)	Clarke
Fantasie—With Variations on Roy's Wife, Piano Forte, Miss Hewitt	Kalkbrenner
Song,—Love has Eyes,	Bishop
Solo Violin,—Mr. Ostinelli,	Lafont
Duett—When thy bosom Heaves the Sigh, Miss Hewitt and Amateur	Braham
Concerto—Piano Forte, Miss Hewitt,	Rosetti

Part II

Battle of Wagram—Full Orchestra,	Hewitt
Song—The Minstrel's Harp,	Clarke
Russian Air—Var. Violin, Mr. Ostinelli,	Lafont
Duett—The Butterfly, Amateurs.	Amateurs
Non Plus Ultra—Piano Forte, Miss Hewitt	Woelfl
Glee—Love wakes and weeps, (Words taken from the Pirate,) Miss Hewitt and Amateurs	Clifton
Finale—Full Orchestra	

Tickets, one dollar each, to be had at Messrs. Graupner's, Dickson's and Jackson's Music Stores—at Messrs. Parker's, Callender's and Richardson & Lord's, Greenleaf's, and of Miss Hewitt, No. 32, Federal-street.[82]

Mr. Graupner, on the other hand, was less prominent than heretofore, for his business was practically non-existent, and the passing of Mrs. Graupner in 1820 caused him to withdraw from public life for a time. Of the visitors, Mrs. Holman and Mr. R. A. Taylor were the favorites, the latter reappearing in 1823 after an absence of seven

[81] Charles Philippe Lafont (1781–1839), eminent violinist, pupil of Kreutzer and Rode; played in a competition with Paganini in 1816. His compositions are of little value but include fantasias, seven concertos, rondos, two operas, and 200 ballads which were popular in their day.
[82] *New England Palladium,* May 10, 1822.

years. The description of "his delicate, chaste, and instructive performances" suggest a comparison with Mr. Phillips, while the "great
musical improvement of the last few years" enabled Boston "lovers
of music the more justly to appreciate the exalted taste and style of
Mr. Taylor." Mrs. Holman's concerts brought together the most
fashionable audiences ever assembled for such events, guarantee that
this lady's charms were apparent to the eye, and that her program
did not rise above the popular conception of entertaining balladry.
The singer was well-known elsewhere, and must be ranked in the succession of Mrs. Oldmixon, Mrs. Burke, and Mrs. French as leading
concert artist of her day. No program of her concerts survives in
newspaper or periodical, but we may accept without hesitation the
verdict of the time as to her very considerable vocal talents.

Miss Davis visited Boston in January, 1822, bringing a freshness
to the repertory by means of two arias by Rossini, and Dr. Jackson
came before the public for the last time as accompanist to this singer.

The most striking personality of these years was Anthony Philip
Heinrich, whose travels brought him to Boston in May, 1823. He was
not unknown by reputation, and the musical societies of the town
hastened to welcome his arrival by giving a concert; the *Columbian
Centinel* proffered a brief notice which complimented both the visitor
and the community:

A. P. Heinrich's Concert.—If there be a real pleasure in rewarding genius
and merit, the above Concert offers more than ordinary inducement to
taste of this pleasure. It can scarcely be doubted but the discerning public
will second the laudable efforts of professors and amateurs to rescue worth
from the darkness of solitude, and place it in the broad sunshine of a pop-
ulous and enlightened community.[83]

Heinrich found the standards of musical development rather higher
in Boston than in Kentucky, but his initial concert necessitated his
being director, composer, pianist, and organist. He numbered the
leading talents of Boston in his wake, including Mr. Graupner. The
native wood-notes wild of this accomplished musician must have succeeded in stirring the Bostonians out of their enjoyment of such old-
style mediocrities as those represented on the programs of a quarter
of a century. Ries, Kalkbrenner, Stiebelt, Kotzwara, and their ilk

---

[83] May 28, 1823. This is one day earlier than the paragraph quoted by Mr. Upton
in *Anthony Philip Heinrich*, but it is less comprehensive as an introduction to a
new personality.

were soon to be replaced by Weber, Rossini, Mozart, and an accompanying array of latter-day mediocrities. All things considered, Boston was kind to Heinrich, and he reaped his share of publicity and, doubtless, of glory. The first concert offered this program:

CONCERT

By the unanimous desire of Professors and Amateurs, and under the immediate Patronage of "The Philo-Harmonic and Handel and Haydn Societies," as a tribute of respect to private worth and eminent professional talents, there will be given

This Evening, May 29,
in Boylston-Hall,

A GRAND CONCERT, CONSISTING OF THE FOLLOWING
VOCAL AND INSTRUMENTAL SELECTIONS

Part I

Symphony, No. 8,	Haydn
Song—"From thee, Eliza, I must go." The words by Robert Burns.—Amateur,	A. P. Heinrich
Duetto on the Piano Forte,—Mrs. Ostinelli and A. P. Heinrich,	Rossini
Glee—"Love wakes and weeps." The words from "The Pirate." Mrs. Ostinelli and Amateurs,	Clifton
An *Extempore* interlude on the Organ	A. P. Heinrich

Part II

The Celebrated Bolero Overture.	Kauphner
Song—"At an early dawn the hunters rise," Amateur.	Rimbault
Solo on the Violin, Mr. Ostinelli	Ostinelli
A Glee,—Amateurs.	

Finale

The whole being for the benefit of A. P. HEINRICH.

Leader of the Band, A. P. Heinrich, and the Double Bass by Mr. Graupner.

☞ Tickets at $1 each, admitting a Lady and Gentleman, may be obtained at all the public Music Stores, and at the door of the Hall. The Concerto to commence precisely at eight o'clock.[84]

Heinrich's immediate appointment as organist to the Old South Church was probably owing to "An Extempore interlude on the Organ" given as a part of his benefit concert which Dr. Jackson did not

[84] *Daily Advertiser*, May 29, 1823. Kauphner was doubtless Joseph Küffner (1776–1856).

hear, having departed this world. His term at the Old South lasted one quarter and ended with his resignation, not unforeseen or unhoped for by an organized band of captious objectors. From Heinrich's letter it may be inferred that objection was made to his use of "fancy" registrations, overuse of the pedals, and excessive tendency to key modulation, all intimate reflections of the man's individual style. Nothing daunted by a deficit from his first concert, Heinrich continued to give benefits until April 29, 1826, when a colossal program rounded up all the known talents, plus a few strangers, and including "last, altho' not least, Mr. GRAUPNER, of this City, the Veteran Professor and American Dragonetti!" The last named, after many years of silence on the oboe, played a concerto by Winter.[85]

Heinrich's stay in Boston lasted three years and was full of trouble, for his temperament often led him into excesses in speech comparable to those excesses found in his scores. James Hewitt, much the older but little the wiser, was on hand as foil for a part of the time, and J. T. Buckingham, whose pen was often more powerful than any baton, labored on. Heinrich and Buckingham immediately came to pens' points, interpolating a vindictive spirit quite without precedent in the placid musical life of Boston; but it must be admitted that the editor showed less temper than the "scientific and eccentric Heinrich" whose letters to the *Centinel* must have caused many a well-disposed citizen to rub his eyes.

A CARD

A musician takes the liberty briefly and bluntly to inform Mr. Buckingham that he is a total ignoramus in the science of music. Were he not such he could never have introduced into his Galaxy of November 12 so senseless and barbarous an editorial criticism on Miss Kelly. This fair stranger was certainly entitled to better courtesy and gallantry from the mighty champion of the milky paper. But as it declares so truly galaxian that Miss Kelly sung "wretchedly" and that her voice is as "inflexible as the trumpet of a mail carrier" he is most fortissimo entreated if his ears are not totally cracked to continue and exercise them a little better before he ever attempts again to divert the public with his musical Capriccios. It may be somewhat sympathetic for the editor of the Courier and Galaxy to take his musical similies from the mail carriers as they accompany a trumpet by grand

[85] Mr. Upton's statement that the Philharmonic Society had disbanded a couple of years earlier must be amended, but it is true that, as Snow states, its existence was for the most part confined to annual election of officers. Mr. Granger, leader of the orchestra at the Federal Street Theatre, was a violinist rather than a clarinetist.

flourishes. But the humble writer of these cursory remarks assures him most confidently that a little beyond the circulation of his papers he would not be able to comprehend a portion of the tunes of a common postillion. . . . Miss Kelly has done herself great credit in the judgment of every liberal and competent professor for having executed to the very note elegant passages and difficult intonations of the most eminent operatic composers the beauty of whose works are finely expressed and exemplified by the very essence of musical articulation. Whether the learned editor understood this is a matter of great doubt. We will however in charity not doubt of the competency of his judgment on squeaking of coach wheels and the blasts of the stage-drivers trumpet.

A. P. HEINRICH [86]

In fairness to Mr. Buckingham's bold challenger it must be said that Miss Lydia Kelly became a very popular singer, gaining particular fame for her Agatha in the first performance of *Der Freischütz* in 1825.

With the passing of James Hewitt in suffering and poverty, the virtual retirement of Mr. Graupner, the disappearance of nearly every fixture of the old days, and the emergence of many new talents, musical life of Boston experienced a great change. The musicians and the composers—excepting the immortal Händel and Haydn—who had been leaders for two decades now found themselves out-of-date and often reactionary; life in the new world speeded on at an uncomfortable rate, while the older generation desired to be left alone with those things which they had loved and cherished for so long a time. For the most part, the musical life of Boston changed so completely in the five years following 1823 that little remained to identify the few survivors of those gracious days securely locked in memory. Thereafter begins another chapter, one filled with equally great things, but one which owed much to those men and events gone before.

[86] *Columbian Centinel,* Nov. 17, 1824.

IV. PHILHARMONIC SOCIETY

To say anything in praise of Musick, to the citizens of Boston, is unnecessary; that correctness of taste, which has always distinguished them, makes it wholly superfluous.[1]

1.

THE CAREER of the Philharmonic Society was of sufficient duration to make a lasting impression on the musical tastes of Boston. By reason of frequent performance of certain established works of undisputed merit a basic familiarity with the classic tradition was gained, while the fact that these works were performed by resident musicians whose prime concern, in many instances, was not with music as a profession, but as a necessary factor of their cultural existence, added to the value of this experience in shaping the interests and traditions of succeeding generations. On the other hand, the leadership of men who had gained training in several European capitals gave a highly desirable professional aspect to the musical development of Boston during the first quarter of the nineteenth century. This combination of amateurism and professionalism lent a telling enthusiasm to the notable contributions of this orchestra in shaping musical habits during a formative period of national growth.

No phase of musical life in Boston—and indirectly throughout the country—is complete without the inclusion of Gottlieb Graupner as the leading figure. It is conceivable that the extensive business of publishing and selling music might have been undertaken by others, that the Handel and Haydn Society would have been formed without the participation of Graupner, that the music of the Federal Theatre might have pleased the patrons without the sound of his oboe or double bass, and that other musicians would have carried on his teaching employment by individuals and academies; by no means, however,

[1] Boston *Gazette,* April 15, 1802.

could the Philharmonic Orchestra have found a leader possessed of the inner fire, the outward patience, and the practical wisdom for carrying on a career so useful to the awakening musical intelligence of Boston's populace.

J. R. Parker wrote in *The Euterpeiad:* "Until the formation of the Philo-Harmonic for Instrumental, and the Institution of the Handel and Haydn Societies, for vocal performances, regular concerts have never succeeded in this metropolis." [2] The record, gained primarily from the newspapers of the day, plainly bears out the correctness of his statement, and Mr. Sonneck's detailed analysis, while noting some interesting concerts, by no means reveals an established tradition of concert-going among Bostonians. There were few resident musicians capable of giving a concert by themselves, nor did custom then sanction concerts in the modern manner of solo performances. Visiting performers rarely possessed sufficient competence to attract attention unless they were connected with the theater, although a number of them tried to stake a claim to popular affection. Only the enlisting of all available talents, including singers, "reciters," and instrumental soloists, insured sympathetic reception by an audience, and an orchestra was essential to fullest enjoyment of any program.

The precise date of formation of the Philharmonic Society is not to be determined with absolute finality. It is likely that a group of amateurs and professionals, assembled for the pleasure of playing together, eventually found themselves prepared for an audience, and that the success of their endeavors led to the creation of rules, regulations, a plan of subscription, and—in short—a society. The public press was unfailingly sympathetic to the arts, and the *Columbian Centinel* under Mr. Russell, and the *New England Palladium* showed a deep and sometimes extravagent pride in the productions of native genius. These semi-weekly newspapers ardently championed the various movements designed to further exhibitions of painting, the drama, and music. Notices of the Philharmonic Society rehearsals were carried with great regularity in the form of brief advertisements; thus one may accept the first of these public announcements, appearing on October 4, 1809, where members were "notified to meet at the Society room Franklin street on Saturday evening next. Samuel Stockwell, Sec'y." as heralding an early meeting, and possibly the first, since the

2 *Euterpeiad,* April 8, 1820.

members continued to assemble early in the same month until October 6, 1827. According to the notice, some preparation had been made before this meeting, for a room was duly assigned the members, but whether the reference is to the previous season, or the previous week, must be left to conjecture. In the earliest notices the society is referred to as the "Philoharmonica," [3] but the title was soon changed. The two principal orchestras of the town—those of the Federal Theatre and the Philharmonic—had many members in common; the latter group held meetings on Saturday evenings, for there were no theatrical performances on the eve of the New England Sabbath.

The orchestra which had functioned in connection with concerts earlier than 1809 bore no particular designation and quite apparently had no organization apart from its connection with the theater; invariably it played fewer numbers and gave small assistance in concertos, trios for two violins and bass appearing on the programs more often than orchestral works. On a few occasions the players were referred to as the "Band," reasonable proof that the theatrical musicians were intended, without aid of amateurs.

Graupner had severed his connection with the theatrical band some years before, owing, one may assume, to other activities which greatly enhanced his prestige in the community; these included teaching, publishing, retailing, and conducting, all features of a distinguished career treated elsewhere in these pages. Directors of stage music were invariably violinists; consequently Graupner's place as oboist or double bass was a humble one in comparison with other occupations which enabled him to function as an individual and as a leader. Without doubt, his usefulness to the profession and his own financial well-being were increased by an independent career, which took him back to the theater but rarely and on occasions enabled him to play obbligati to his wife's songs.

The limitations of the pit are apparent, although Graupner had

[3] Sonneck (*Concert Life,* p. 309) raises the question as to the relationship between this society and one with a similar name mentioned in the *Columbian Centinel,* April 6, 1799. I see no reason to suppose that the two were identical, for the interval of ten years would surely have brought to light some mention of the organization beyond the single notice. As to Graupner's place in it, it is quite within the bounds of supposition that he was one of the founders, although in 1799 Graupner's career in Boston had not brought him an influence by any means comparable to that achieved in the succeeding years. The secretary, W. H. M'Neill, cannot be further identified.

frequently introduced sinfonias, overtures, and occasional pieces of a quality not often associated with places of amusement, and his careful supervision of the music to *Comus* and *Macbeth* in 1801 had won him the respect of many discerning individuals, and of the press. He had played in Haydn's orchestra during the introduction of the "Salomon" Symphonies in 1791–1792 and earlier had learned his profession in the military bands of Hanover; presumably these memories were not greatly dimmed through successive experiences in the comparatively poor orchestras of the Charlestown and Boston theaters; rather were they sharpened by the treasured memory of so remarkable an experience, inculcating in him a love of Haydn and Pleyel which made him an ardent champion of their works. When Graupner reached Boston and sensed the sincere musical interest about him, an interest benefiting by his own quiet enthusiasm, he must have discovered that his early training provided precisely those elements so much needed by these resident musicians. He was familiar with the standard musical literature of the time, sufficiently understanding to make a compromise between their abilities and their ambitions, and he was thoroughgoing enough to offer such suggestions as would improve their technique. By the commencement of the season 1810–1811 Graupner's residence of fifteen years in Boston, his cordial relations as dealer and publisher with the professional members of the community, and his high standing as a teacher combined to establish him as the proper leader of the permanent organization which he envisioned.

A round of public concerts marked the return of James Hewitt to Boston in the late spring of 1810, with the fiery director as chief protagonist; he had been in New York, active as publisher, composer, and conductor. Neither Graupner's name, nor that of the Philharmonic Society appeared among those assisting at Hewitt's managerial efforts, although the two played together for the only time on record at the second of two concerts given for the sufferers by fire at Newburyport. On that occasion, September 13, 1811, four instrumentalists, including Graupner and Hewitt, "accompanied" Miss Mallet in "The Grand Overture on the Piano, called, the Queen of France, of Hayden." [4] There are few intimations of cordiality be-

---

[4] This symphony is one of the famous "Paris" set of 1784, with an instrumentation of 4 wood winds, 2 horns, and strings; it is in B flat major and has a charming romanza for second movement.

tween the two leading conductors of the town; each pursued his way successfully, and managed to avoid the other in the course of professional conduct. Concerts directed by Mr. Hewitt were invariably held at the Exchange Coffee House,[5] whereas those involving Mr. Graupner's direction of the theatrical band were given in his own Concert Hall,[6] in Pond Street, or in Stone Chapel;[7] furthermore, tickets for Hewitt's concerts were not sold at Graupner's music store. The thrice-starred notice " ***Mr. Hewitt has declined," affixed to the announcement of Dr. Jackson's momentous concert of October 29, 1812, would seem to bring matters to a head and preclude further discussion of this point; ergo, Mr. Graupner led the band.

Public "exertions" of the Philharmonic Society are not apparent for several years, for the orchestra which functioned in the various concerts given each season was either the theatrical "Band," or a group of individuals made up of these players, and amateurs. Mr. Graupner often conducted them, for it is plain that his relations with all the musical talents were most cordial; since the members were probably paid for their services, the matter of leadership was of secondary importance in a day free of union domination. There appear to be no records concerning the early seasons of the Philharmonic Society beyond periodic notices of meetings and other lesser matters which, although interesting, are poor substitutes for programmatic documentation.

The first meeting of the season 1812–1813 was held on October by order of "Wm. Coffin Jr.," the new secretary, who filled that office henceforth for many years—in fact, until the final trump was sounded. With the season of rehearsals beginning on September 29, 1813, at which a punctual attendance was requested, the time of meeting was changed from six to seven o'clock; all meetings were held in Concert Hall. An embarrassing loss incurred during the previous season was exposed in the press, with a touching plea for aid of amateurs in recovering so necessary an item.

[5] A concert for "Father" Schaffer on Sept. 27, 1815, was an exception.
[6] The little hall in Pond street, formerly Rowe's lane, referred to as Concert Hall, or Mr. Graupner's Hall, was built in the late nineties; and it had been used by Peter Landrin Duport, the dancing master. There was a house adjoining which was offered for rent either with or without the hall in April, 1799, and described as "capacious and elegant," attributes which should have been reasonably true when Messrs. Mallet, Graupner, and Trajetta took over the premises for the purpose of founding a Conservatorio, or Musical Academy, early in 1801.
[7] King's Chapel.

To the Amateurs of Music

DURING the last season of the Philo-harmonic Society, was lost or mislaid, the BOOK containing the Tenor Part of a large and valuable collection of Symphonies, the property of the Society—Amateurs are respectfully requested to examine their Music, and if found, to send the Book to Mr. Graupner's, in Franklin Place—or if it should have fallen into the hands of any person careless about Music, and indifferent as to its value, Notice is hereby given, that a reward of Five Dollars will be paid for the Book, on receipt at the above address.

The Members of the above Society are requested to meet on SATURDAY evening next, at half-past 6 o'clock, precisely, on business of importance.[8]

Oct. 20

The date is not known when invitations to the Saturday rehearsals were instituted; but with improved forces at the disposal of the Society in the season 1813–1814 requests for admission were flatteringly large, owing, in part, to the advent of several new talents, more or less uncertain of tenure, and—a fact not to be overlooked— to the increasing capacities of the regular members. Each member of the society was entitled to a stated number of tickets, transferable at will. Beginning with the last concert of the season, advertised April 16, 1814, notices were frequently given, of interest to the favored few, as to the place of meeting and precise hour at which the music might be expected to commence.

Showing due regard for the business aspect of organization, notice is given to all persons having demands against the society "to leave their Accounts immediately at Mr. Graupner's Music Store." "Those indebted, are requested to make payment at the same place without delay, to enable the committee to ascertain what amount can be appropriated for New Music." [9] Mr. Graupner will forthwith select the new scores, order them during the summer from London, and have them on hand for the commencement of the new season! Unfortunately no program for the first concert on November 2, 1814, is available, but it must have been an attractive one since the growing demand for admission is shown by the fair warning that "Members are particularly requested to notice, that no one will be admitted without a Ticket." With the new and improved fortunes of the Handel and Haydn Society, energies of the accompanying orchestra were directed toward mastering the accompaniments for *The Messiah* and *The*

[8] *Columbian Centinel,* Oct. 20, 1813.   [9] *Ibid.,* May 21, 1814.

Creation, and there appear to have been fewer orchestral concerts, although they were by no means abandoned. The Philharmonic Society achieved its greatest celebrity between 1817 and 1822. For this period we have a fairly comprehensive list of the Handel and Haydn Society orchestra, which comprised, without doubt, the majority of available players in the town; most of them, we know, also belonged to the Philharmonic Society. They were, according to the Englishman Sharp: [10]

Thomas Granger,	1st violin
Louis Ostinelli,	2nd violin
A. P. Heinrich,	2nd violin
Asa Warren,	2nd violin
W. Bennett,	2nd violin or viola
A. Passage,	2nd violin or viola
G. Graupner,	double-bass
G. Pollock,	1st flute
Asa Fillebrown,	2nd clarinet or oboe
J. Hart,	clarinet [11]
Simeon Wood,	bassoon
Frederick Granger,	clarinet
Henry Niebuhr,	1st horn
S. Wetherbee,	2nd horn

We know from other sources that Wm. Turner and one member of the Loring family played, but their instruments are unknown. It is likely that several inaccuracies exist in properly allocating the string players, for they must have been placed with greater equality among the two sections than is indicated here, and Ostinelli, who received the highest pay, ultimately became concertmaster. Niebuhr is elsewhere referred to as "single bass"; probably he "doubled" violoncello and horn as required. "Father" Schaffer appears to have had a monopoly of the violoncello section, and it is unthinkable that he was not included in the Philharmonic ranks whenever his health permitted, or his duties as owner of the Washington Gardens left him free of an evening. Both Grangers [12] and Niebuhr are known to have been in long

---

[10] *History of the Handel and Haydn Society,* Vol. I, p. 50.

[11] John B. Derby, the Salem merchant, writes of Hart that he became "the finest clarionet player in the country with the softest tone, most brilliant in execution."

[12] Little can be said of the pretensions of the Grangers, father and son, as composers. The records of the Pierian Sodality of Harvard University, however, show that Granger composed music for it in 1819; this does not give any clue to which of the two was called on, whether the music was newly written, or one of several

service at the theater; George Cushing had been flutist at least during earlier seasons of the orchestra, and one Boquet, whom Sharp omits, played in the Handel and Haydn orchestra, but was not a member of the Philharmonic. Anthony Philip Heinrich should not be included in a list of players available at this time, for he did not return to Boston until 1823.

The amateurs came from various, and respectable, walks of life. Pollock, the flute player, was engaged in dry goods, Bennett was a stonecutter; Hart was at one time an usher at civil court; Boquet was probably Louis Boquet the hairdresser, but his instrument—once the clippers were laid by—is unknown; George Cushing had been a bank cashier, and for one brief and unpropitious year took over the business of G. Graupner & Co; Asa Warren was in dry goods. The remainder were professional musicians, for the most part associated with the theater; A. Passage does not appear in the directories or other records of the time.[13]

To the above should most emphatically be added William Rowson, husband of the noted Susanna, who won, despite his wayward habits, blessed assurance from his wife on the day of their twenty-fifth anniversary that she had no regrets in having joined her life with his. Rowson had been leader of the band attached to the Royal Guards in London and subsequently became an actor, but gave up the stage when his wife retired to become proprietess of a school and author of successful novels; he played in the theater orchestra, however, and may be supposed to have functioned elsewhere as time and opportunity permitted; eventually he achieved an influential post as clerk in the Custom House, serving in his leisure time on boards of the several musical societies in the town. His participation in the early concerts of the Handel and Haydn Society is amusingly chronicled in the *History*:

The gravity of the Society was also to my own knowledge severely put to proof at times, by the vagaries of a trumpet-player named Rowson, who

pieces already heard on programs in the town of Boston. Quite possibly it was merely a job of copying parts or arrangements. The Pierian orchestra—if an ill-assorted collection of instruments, mainly flutes, may be called such—played the "Air" from Händel's *Water Music* and a "Gavot" by the same composer, but conviviality was more earnestly entertained than the desire for masterful performance.
[13] Directories are among the most unreliable of reference works, of course, but often served a useful purpose as corroborative evidence; in all cases herein the newspapers are taken as authoritative.

usually sat on the upper most tier of seats, apart from the orchestra. He had learned early in life to play on an old-fashioned instrument without valves, on which, for the production of many top notes, the action of the lips and tongue was necessary; and his attempts to execute with his thickened and rugged lips, the long runs of semi-quavers in the obligato accompaniment to "Let the bright Seraphim," were so uncertain in pitch and frolicsome in movement that, with the utmost self-command, it was difficult to control the temptation to laughter.[14]

Rowson had his moments, however, if we may trust the mellow Buckingham, when his performances ravished the ears of his hearers:

There are probably many persons who recollect (for no one who heard can ever forget) the sublime and spirit-stirring tones of this gentleman's trumpet, when he played, for the Boston Handel and Haydn Society, the accompaniment to that magnificent air in the Messiah,—"The trumpet shall sound and the dead shall be raised.[15]

Some anxiety may be felt for the regular habits of Mr. Wood, the bassoonist, for within a year his instrument, minus crook, was lost between Hingham and Boston on a cold winter's morning, dismembered and tied in a kerchief, while later the bassoon part of a set of symphonies, lettered on the cover "Fagotto Philo. H. Society," was similarly mislaid. Graupner acted as intermediary, offering suitable rewards for the return of either, or both, but the orchestra functioned meanwhile as best it could, and we may never know whether the mellow tones of the clown of instruments were thereafter rendered according to Haydn or Wood.

Only Graupner, Francis Mallet, Granger Sr., and Louis Schaffer were in Boston before 1800; they represent the old guard, a dependable support, though failing, on which the new order was built. These four belong to the busy days of the Von Hagen family, of William Selby, and Hans Gram, three important figures whose names briefly surviving the turn of the century, became dimmer as the new order arose. Graupner settled in Boston in 1797, although he had been there before; Francis Mallet is believed to have been one of the numerous attachés of Lafayette who remained after the Revolution, arriving in Boston about 1793; the histories of the ancients Frederick Granger and Francis Schaffer are unknown other than that they appear in the records cited by Sonneck as early as 1793 and 1796 respectively.

The officers of the Philharmonic Society played no instrument with

14 p. 72.   15 Joseph Buckingham, *Personal Memoirs,* (1852), p. 83n.

sufficient skill to justify the honor of their office on that account. They were the admiring hangers-on who knew not how but probably would awfully like to try; they came from business and meaner occupations, finding outlet for their cultural enthusiasms and serving loyally with admiring devotion all the works of skill and genius set before them. Several professions bred music lovers, with bank cashiers and dry-goods merchants in the predominance. Coffin, the secretary, was teller at the Branch Bank; Eben Frothingham, a director, was cashier at the New England Bank, and M. S. Parker a cashier at the Suffolk Bank. President Tilden was a merchant, and Trustee Allan Pollock, the sealer of weights and measures; John Dodd was Elliot Simon & Co., snuff and paper store, Amasa Winchester, who had been president of the short-lived Massachusetts Musical Society (1809–1810), was in the provision business and, like Parker and Dodd, acquired some local reputation as a singer. Thus are the directorate established as business men with reputable connections, a fair comparison with the governing boards of today's leading symphonic organizations.

Other regular members whose names survive are remembered for their vocal talents; these include Miss Hewitt, Mrs. Graupner, and Chester Stebbins. The latter was a printer by trade, who had completed an apprenticeship with Isaiah Thomas; on his own account he printed a pocket edition of Milton's *Paradise Lost*, and as junior member of Greenough & Stebbins was responsible for two editions of the Bible about 1812. "His voice was a rich tenor, of great sweetness, power, and flexibility, and whether exercised in the church, the parlor, or the concert-room, it never failed to command admiration. One of his favorite songs, was the 'Crazy Jane' of M. G. Lewis, which he sung with a tenderness and pathos, that touched the heart of every one who heard it." [16] Stebbins died in 1818.

Visiting musicians were invited to attend these Saturday gatherings and participate informally in the music of the evening and there are many reasons to suppose that they welcomed such an opportunity. In these years of uncentralized management of concert artists, custom demanded that the visiting performer desirous of giving a concert should seek assistance from the leading performers in the town for, failing in his own exertions to please an audience, the resident talent could carry the evening to success and possibly bear him along.

16 J. T. Buckingham, *Personal Memoirs*, p. 48n.

Incidentally, this was an age which recognized merit in the local performer and was willing to patronize his concerts.

Among the passing events which gave impetus to the season of 1815–1816 was a concert by Mr. Lefolle, unknown in Boston, who is referred to in a "Communication" as "the greatest performer that ever appeared in America." "No one who has heard him or who has not been in Europe can form an accurate judgement on the wonderful compass of the violin." Mr. Lefolle also won his hearers by the "sweetness and richness of his tones and neatness and rapidity of his execution." That the visit was successful from the performer's standpoint is certain, for the Philharmonic Society assisted him in two public concerts, further enhanced by the combined abilities of Mrs. Graupner, Mr. Stockwell,[17] and Miss Catherine Graupner. The program, though disconcertingly incomplete, is of interest for it provides the first mention of works played by the orchestra, works which were retained in repertory for so many years that John Rowe Parker may have held them in mind when he complained, in 1822, that no new works were added to the repertory and that the same things were played over and over again.[18]

Part I

Overture—full band	Haydn
Song—by Mr. Stockwell	
Harmony within the instruments	
Song—Ye streams by Mrs. Graupner	
Concerto violin by Mr. Lefolle	Kreutzer
Song—The origin of old bachelors—	Mr. Bray

Part II

Symphony Concertante—by Mr. Lefolle and Ribes—	Kreutzer
Song	Mr. Bray
Song	Miss Graupner
Air varie violin	
Overture to Lodoiska [19]	

With the rise of the Handel and Haydn Society to a leading place in the cultural life of Boston, the close and cordial relations with the Philharmonic Society are maintained without a break. The original letter, calling for the first meeting, bears the signature of Graupner,

[17] A bass with powerful but untrained voice.   [18] *Euterpeiad,* 1821
[19] *New England Palladium and Commercial Advertiser,* June 20, 1815.

among others, and the directorship of the two major organizations contains several names common to both, as Eben Frothingham, William Rowson, and John Dodd, trustees. Wm. Coffin was secretary of the one and trustee of the other; Matthew S. Parker was treasurer of the Orchestra and secretary of the choral society, and Amasa Winchester was trustee of the former, and vice-president of the latter. Professionally, none of these, with the partial exception of Rowson, was a musician.[20]

Moreover, both societies shared the same place of meeting for a time, the new and elegant Boylston Hall (thus making that pleasant place an established musical center), alternating with the little old hall in Pond Street for orchestra rehearsals and smaller events. Boylston Hall occupied the entire third story, forming one of the most spacious rooms in town, a truly "noble apartment," 100 feet long by 48 feet in breadth, with an arched ceiling 24 feet high. At the west end an orchestra was constructed, commodious enough to seat 150 vocal and instrumental performers; at the extreme westerly end, a handsome organ, built by Mr. Appleton, was encased in an imposing receptacle which nearly grazed the ceiling. The orchestra chairs were in semi-circular form, with a central desk from which the president conducted. The audience occupied settees, accommodating about 800 persons, including a gallery.[21]

Boylston Hall was too large for the semi-professional needs of the orchestra, however, and after a special meeting to consider the matter, a return was made to the Pond Street meeting place; meetings were scheduled for the earlier hour of six o'clock and the roll was called precisely at quarter past six.

Few notices regarding the season of 1816–1817 found their way into the columns of the newspapers: there are announcements of date and place of meeting, but neither program nor names of the performers. During this year the Handel and Haydn Society flourished exceedingly with the aid of the celebrated organist from New York, Samuel Priestly Taylor, and the mastery of the whole of the two oratorios by the two celebrated composers from whom the society's

[20] The memoirs of George Cushing suggest that the Handel and Haydn Society was conceived as a result of frequent conversations on the low state of church music during intervals of the performances by the Philharmonic Society. *History of the Handel and Haydn Society*, Vol. I, p. 37.

[21] The description of Boylston Hall is taken from Bowen's edition of Snow's *History of Boston* (1825).

title was derived. The Philharmonic Society aided in certain rehearsals and at the performances, no small task, but one designed to make for a busy season for the professional and amateur musicians, if one accounts for the evenings of the week. Rehearsals were held on Sunday and Tuesday evenings, the theater was open on Monday, Wednesday, and Friday, while Saturday was sacred to the Philharmonic Society.

The final concert of the season occurred on the last Saturday of April, 1817, in accordance with established custom, but the work of the Society was by no means ended; an impending visit of the President of the United States called forth all the available talent for an extra evening at the little hall in Pond Street, and early in July His Excellency James Monroe was favored with a lengthy program given by the combined forces of the Handel and Haydn and Philharmonic Societies. A very comprehensive sampling of the Society's repertory may be found in the program given on page 133.

Our chief executives have been men of varied accomplishments, but music has seldom been one of them, and a concert of music even in the best tradition of the Great Society in the flush of initial honor by the nation's highest officer must have been a very trying experience for the worthy gentleman.[22] Adams' letters more often describe the ladies' towering headdresses and manners than the music.

The commencement of the season 1818–1819 was notable for the advent of Louis Ostinelli, who arrived in September to give a concert in company with one Thibault. Both Thibault and Ostinelli boasted achievement of the Grand Premium at the Royal Conservatoire of France, the former on the pianoforte, the latter on the violin, and stated that they had "already exhibited their talents in different Capital Cities of America with universal applause." [23] Mr. Thibault thereafter disappeared from the scene but Mr. Ostinelli secured the good-will of the resident instrumentalists of Boston immediately following his initial concert and arranged a program which featured

[22] It is on record that Hartford had an orchestra in 1816 known as the Euterpian Society, and that 36 members attended the first meeting on June 5. Officers were elected as follows: Jeremiah Wadsworth, president; David Isham, and George Bolles, vice-presidents; Hezekiah Huntington, treasurer; and James S. Bigelow, collector; Orin Fay was clerk. Six concerts were given before Dec. 15, 1818, the first on Jan. 24, 1817, the programs containing 29 pieces including six by Händel; otherwise marches were in the majority. (W. H. Allen in the *Connecticut Quarterly*, Vol. III, No. 3, 1897.)

[23] A letter addressed to the Paris Conservatory in 1940 has not been answered.

SELECT ORATORIO

Performed in Chauncy Place, Boston, Saturday, July 5, 1817
by the
HANDEL AND HAYDN SOCIETY
in the presence of James Monroe, President of the United States.

ORDER OF PERFORMANCE
Military movement composed by F. Granger called
President Monroe's March.

Part I.—Handel

1   Duet: "Hail, Judea, happy land."
     Chorus, do.
2   Solo: (Haydn) "Now heaven etc. (Creation)
3   Chorus (from Israel in Egypt): "Moses and the Children of Israel"
4   Recitative: "For the house of Pharaoh"
5   Chorus: "The Lord Shall Reign"
6   Recitative: "And Miriam," etc.
7   Air: "Sing Ye to the Lord"
8   Chorus: "The Lord Shall Reign"
9   Trio: "Desolate is the Dwelling" (Calcott)
10   Solo: "There rest the sinful Mary's tears" (Shaw)
11   Chorus: "He gave them hailstones," etc. (Israel)
12   Solo: "In splendor bright" (Creation)
13   Chorus: "The heavens are telling"

Part II

1   Welcome, welcome, Semi-Chorus from Solomon
2   David his ten thousands slew.
3   Ode: "Wreaths for the Chieftain" Sung at Peace Jubilee
4   Chorus: "Achieved is" etc. (Creation)
5   Solo: " 'Tis Liberty, dear Liberty"
6   Duet: "Come, ever-smiling Liberty"
7   Trio and Chorus: "Sound the loud timbrel" Avison
8   Solo and Chorus: "The marvellous work"
9   Aria and Chorus: "Strike the Cymbal" Pucitta
10   Chorus: "Hallelujah"

Granger Jr. as leader of the orchestra and Mr. Graupner as double bass. The program deserves reprinting in full.

Many of Boston's leading musicians arrived after an experimental residence in Charleston, Philadelphia, Baltimore, or New York; Graupner had trod that path, for the most part, as had the prodigious figure of Dr. Jackson; it is likely that Ostinelli's case was a similar

Act I

Leader of the Orchestra . . . . Mr. Granger, Jr.
Double Bass, ... Mr. Graupner

Grand Symphony—Full Orchestra—	Haydn
Song—"Great Booby"—	Mr. Williams
Air with Variations—Piano Forte—Mr. Willson	Gelinek
Solo—on the Oboe—	Mr. Graupner
Song	Mr. Bray
Grand Violin Concerto—Ostinelli	Viotti
Minuetto—Full Orchestra	Beethoven

Act II

Overture—Lodoiska—Full Orchestra	Kreutzer
Air with Variations—Piano Forte	Mr. Willson
Song—"Nothing at all"	Mr. Williams.
Catalani's Favorite Air, with Variations on the Violin— Ostinelli	Ostinelli
Song	Mr. Bray
Fantasia, on the Violin—Ostinelli,	Ostinelli
Finale—	

Tickets One Dollar each, may be had at the Franklin Music Warehouse, No. 6 Milk-street, at Mr. Graupner's Music Store; at Mr. S. H. Parker's Circulating Library, Cornhill, and at the Bar of the Exchange Coffee-House.[24]

one. Certainly he had no reason to complain of the flattering reception accorded him by the handful of musicians then residing in Boston, and their extreme cordiality may have betrayed the fact that they sorely needed him. Following the concert reported above, the Philharmonic Society was called for a meeting at Mr. Graupner's "on particular business"; the outcome, if one may read between the lines of the public announcements, was a concert by the society for the benefit of Mr. Ostinelli in Boylston Hall on October 10. The program repeated some selections already heard, but brought forth a Concerto by Kreutzer, "Sul margine de Puo" (!) and "La Chasse Symphony" by Pleyel, with the solo parts performed by Mr. Ostinelli. Inclement weather necessitated a week's postponement. Mr. Russell of the *Co-*

24 *Columbian Centinel,* Sept. 19, 1818. Mr. William Treat Upton has brought to light a program in which "Simfonia con Minuetto . . . Beethoven" was performed on Nov. 12, 1817, in Lexington, Kentucky, under the direction of Anthony Philip . Heinrich.

lumbian Centinel, or his henchman, seemed well pleased with Mr. Ostinelli, whose "execution of the Violin, and Mr. Graupner's on the Oboe, drew repeated applause from the Company." Praise was equally divided between the two, for it was particularly "gratifying" that "this latter gentleman has resumed the oboe, which he had long since laid by; his skill does not seem to have forsaken him by disuse, as he is universally admitted to perform better on it than any one who has been before heard in Boston." [25]

The flattering attentions of the musical public were well bestowed, for, whereas Mr. Lefolle had slipped through their fingers, Mr. Ostinelli remained in Boston to become the town's leading violinist and to prove himself a musician of parts. The talented pianist who was to become Mrs. Ostinelli was the daughter of James Hewitt; she had been in New York from 1812 to 1816, but returned to Boston as organist and teacher. Miss Hewitt played often at the Philharmonic meetings, and one may accordingly assume that those Saturday conclaves were the scene of romantic attachments, which, in this instance at least, resulted in matrimony. In 1822 Mr. and Mrs. Ostinelli removed to Portland, where they became leaders of an enthusiastic coterie; a man of some temperament, Mr. Ostinelli was reputedly jealous of his celebrity and became exceedingly annoyed if anyone referred to his instrument as a "fiddle." [26]

Membership in the Philharmonic Society was renewable each season, for the notice was issued that those who considered themselves a part of the orchestra must inform "the president or Secretary that it may be ascertained how many the Society consists of that a suitable place to meet at may be selected." [27] Opportunities and responsibilities, often extensive enough to tax the abilities of the players, necessitated a semblance of discipline if standards of improvement were to be upheld. The social aspect of the weekly meetings was attracting more attention, while the presence of several talented musicians increased the pleasure to be derived from hearing works of greater variety than those laboriously mastered by the plodding mediocrities who constituted the rank and file. Among the entertainments for the evening of December 26, 1818, may be noted "Dusseck's Grand Con-

25 Oct. 17, 1818.
26 George Thornton Edwards, *Music and Musicians of Maine* (Southworth Press, 1928).
27 *Columbian Centinel,* Oct. 31, 1818.

certo for the Piano Forte, Opera 49, and Cramer's La Chasse Quartette on the Violin, by Mr. Ostinelli, several songs by Professors and Amateurs, Symphonies, with a full Orchestra." [28]

The position of the Handel and Haydn Society as an amateur organization of immense importance to the growing musical consciousness of Boston and New England and its far-flung influence elsewhere are generally understood, but certain aspects of its organization and operation as a factor in the life of the professional musician resident in Boston have not hitherto been utilized by the historian. The kindness of the present trustees of that estimable Society now enables us to examine certain private matters dealing principally with the pecuniary aspects of these early years. The evidence of the success of concerts from 1815 onward is satisfyingly complete; vouchers remain, approved by officers and receipted by the performers, concerning virtually every expenditure in connection with the conduct of the society. They are written in careful hand by Mr. Webb, the president, on small slips neatly folded to uniform size like billets-doux. From them we learn that the rental of Pythian Hall, and subsequently Boylston Hall, was three dollars per night, and that the cost of moving an organ from Mr. Spear's to the Hall averaged twenty dollars each concert. We are here interested in a society gracious enough to send a hack for Mr. and Mrs. Graupner, a token of respect conferred on no others, and learn that the charge was nominal. We discover that part of the

---

[28] Dr. Otto Kinkeldey, in his article on "Beginnings of Beethoven in America" (*Musical Quarterly,* April, 1927), writes: "We know very little about the activity of Gottlieb Graupner's Philharmonic Society in Boston in the early decades of the "nineteenth" century. Graupner belonged to the generation for whom Haydn and Mozart were the culmination of musical art. It would not surprise me to learn that he and his organization fought shy of Beethoven." With his usual perspicacity Dr. Kinkeldey's surmise is correct, for only two Beethoven works appear on the programs of the Philharmonic Society; in view of the very special mention given to this composer in the years following 1818, it would seem that, had Beethoven been introduced into these programs, his name would have been set forth with especial care. In any event, Bostonians did not have a real opportunity to become acquainted with Beethoven symphonies until 1840–42, after the formation of the Academy of Music Orchestra. As Dr. Kinkeldey has pointed out, William Gardiner was the first Beethoven enthusiast in England whose works were published in America; these several editions of *The Music of Nature* were first issued in 1812 and 1815, but they do not appear in Boston advertisements before 1818 at least. Furthermore, the garbling of Beethoven tunes, transference of string quartet melodies to hymns, etc. were hardly complimentary to the composer, nor can they be taken into account as inculcating a love of the composer's music. Oliver Shaw's "Sacred Melodies," printed by Miller & Hutchins in 1818, contained two Beethoven tunes fairly rendered.

attraction of the frequent rehearsals came under the bookkeeping head of "Brandy, Gin, and spirits" to the tune of two hundred dollars during the first year alone, and that heating arrangements were thus partially offset by this item which must have amply provided for all. President T. S. Webb approved the bills which concerts of selections from *The Messiah* and *The Creation* made possible of payment. Mr. Perkins, historian of the society, suggests that this custom was the cause of an occasional problem during rehearsals, and the disappearance of vouchers in payment for convivial enhancements suggests that the custom was dropped, as a regular feature, at least after the second or third year of organization.

To President Webb much credit was due, for he shared that genial disposition and talent for administration also associated with Amasa Winchester. In addition to a creditable term as vice-president of the Philharmonic Society, he was the admired first president of the Handel and Haydn Society. Born in Boston in 1771, he was "endowed by the bountiful Creator, with a mind above the common rank, the sweetness of his disposition, and the amiableness of his manners, while they procured for him the esteem of his instructors, and young associates, riveted also the parental affections, and strengthened the hope, that he would one day become both an ornament and a blessing to society." His friend, J. R. Parker, reports that he played the fife and flute, and sang, and that in his several offices, he "possessed the faculty of surmounting difficulties, of removing objections, allaying jealousies not unfrequent among musical men."

The fact that nine hundred dollars was taken in during the first weeks of the society's career brings to question the purpose for which the funds were used. Expenditures were freely made, and the organizers were promptly, if not extravagantly, reimbursed for their efforts on behalf of the movement. Mr. Graupner's house was the scene of directors' meetings and he was accordingly paid for his cordiality, as "3 meetings at my house and sundry articles, $5.50" in 1815. The Graupner music warehouse supplied much of the music from stock, rented the pianofortes and other instruments, keeping them in tune and repair, but others, such as James Loring, shared the business. The earliest copies of "The Creation, 40 copies bass, 25 tenor, 20 soprano, 5 alto" were purchased of Graupner on October 5, 1815, but the uneven distribution of parts indicated in this bill is due, in part, to the fact that some copies were already on hand, as well as to the constitution of the chorus, which was comprised of ninety male and five female voices, the latter augmented by a few falsettos.[29]

The collaboration of the Philharmonic and the Handel and Haydn Societies in carrying out these concerts was not a simple matter. Instrumental parts were not readily available and much copying was done of all parts by the Grangers, Schaffer and Philip Lewis, with the first two, possibly by right of prior residence, sharing the major portion of the work. They were paid at the rate of twenty to twenty-five cents per page, and quantities of their carefully transcribed scores are now in the Society's library.[30] Thus, in 1817 T. Granger received $65; F. Granger, $79.95; Schaffer, $4; and Lewis $25.40. These figures represented the orchestration of solo songs which were done with full accompaniment rather than with pianoforte. The figures are considerably more than the yearly average, since, once at hand, the material was available for frequent repetition.

What would be an unwonted luxury in these days of unionized musicians, was the presence of all, or part, of the orchestra during rehearsals. It is impossible to determine the rate per evening paid to each member, excepting Ostinelli, who received two dollars and attended nineteen rehearsals for four oratorios in 1819, but the respective abilities of the members are approximated by fees at different levels, with Graupner and Ostinelli receiving the highest. The bill on page 139 is for the first concert of the society.

One thousand programs were printed by Chester Stebbins for thirty dollars, and the advertising in the *Centinel* which regularly conveyed news of the forthcoming rehearsals cost ten dollars for six months.

It would appear that the majority of the players received about twenty dollars quarterly, but by 1823 notice is given that the orchestral benefit constitutes the only reimbursement received during the entire season. Catherine Graupner was given ten dollars for her services at the organ for the second concert on January 18, 1816, and other players were allowed these amounts: Graupner, $20; Stockwell, $10; Warren, Niebuhr, Wetherbee, Loring, Turner, each $5; Mrs.

29 *The Creation* was published by T. Badger, Jr., in 1818 after the Clementi edition.
30 String parts for Handel's songs (Walsh) were owned by the Philharmonic; these gave a six-part accompaniment for the majority of solos used in the concerts. It is interesting to note that Graupner's name appears in the second violin part.

To Nathaniel Tucker
    Treas. Handel and Haydn Society

Dear Sir:
    Please to pay the following, viz:
to Messrs.   G. Graupner $30
             S. Stockwell   20
             F. Granger   20 and for writing music
             T. Granger   20
             Warren   10
             Niebuhr   10
             Bennet   10
             Wetherbee, S.   10
             Boquet   5
                                ————
                                $135.

for the services at & prior to the oratorio performed
on the 25th December. 1815
             By direction of the Society
                    T. S. WEBB
                        Prest.

Bennett, $5 (presumably on behalf of her husband) ; T. Granger, $15 ;
F. Granger, $12. Mr. Ostinelli had not yet arrived in Boston and
Thomas Granger was concertmaster. In 1817 fifty dollars was given
"to the Philharmonic Society for an orchestra at Boylston Hall"
and in May, 1818, $212 for the same purpose. As an index of Mr.
Graupner's charges to the society, these entries are made:

    Graupner: $68   "services" Jan. to May 1823
                104   1819, May
                 18   —also use of kettle drums
                 25   1818
                 30   1817 June

Oliver Shaw, the blind singer of Providence, received $25 in 1817 for
a first appearance and $50 and expenses of $20 for a later concert;
his note of thanks is on file with the Society, a casual sheet of tiny
paper, reminder that ornately embossed stationary was unknown to
the middle classes of those days. The importation of S. P. Taylor took
on the glamour of a soloist, in so far as the problem of reimbursement
was concerned. These payments give a partial indication of his success:

S. P. Taylor $285 in full, April 11, 1817, including
expenses to New York
  100 Dec. 5, 1818
    20 Dec. 12, 1818
    20 June 1819
   87.50 Quarter salary as organist, April 1819

When Taylor was succeeded in 1820 by Miss Sophia Hewitt, the salary was reduced to $62.50 "one quarter" and later to $50. It may be supposed that these were the more resplendent days of the society's income, for rising costs, and a diminishing attendance, in so far as the concerts were concerned, soon caused readjustment of the instrumentalist's fees; the resort to annual "Benefit" concerts for the players has been mentioned; in May, 1823, the rewards were distributed as follows:

Proportions of Benefit concert, May 1823, for Orchestra
Th. Granger —$40
A. Warren   — 32
Ostinelli   — 40
Niebuhr   — 25
J. Hart   — 18
S. Wetherbee— 20
W. Bennett — 20
A. Lapage   — 25

Throughout the period the Philharmonic Society and its members had remained closely connected with the choral body, but quite sufficiently apart from it to maintain a professional relationship. In 1829 Graupner was made an honorary member of the Handel and Haydn Society, and in 1843 Mr. Ostinelli was likewise favored, his address being entered as "Italy." Throughout the many years of its distinguished career, this society has been organized on a sound business basis.

These were fruitful years in Boston, following the brief strain of interrupted relations with the mother country. Peace and prosperity were reflected on every hand, and the arts were in the first flush of successful beginnings; the enthusiasm which marked each activity was undimmed by any shadow of doubt as to the future development of them all. While the initial inspiration generated untold enthusiasm, it

was the calm assurance that those hopes were well founded which gave
permanence to ideals, and the stirrings which brought forth the Handel and Haydn Society and established a complimentary orchestra by
their very infectiousness caught up a host of contributory factors on
every hand. The presence of New England statesmen in the high coun-
cils of the Federal government dispelled any as yet unmerited suspi-
cions of a diminishing influence in national affairs, and the steady
attraction of Boston as metropolis of wide fame gave her citizens a
gratifying sense of superiority not without its accompanying effect
on self-confidence. The disunity of purpose so darkly hinted by the
conflicting loyalties to the mother country and to the independent
union was now healed; to be sure, little inconvenience was experienced
by the parleying of economic strategy during the late war, but the
consequent mutual distrust was overcome, and the cultural activities
of the town, at least, felt the benefit of wholehearted support by the
several classes and nationalities.

It was as though Boston felt the significance of certain omens
destined to bear fine fruit during the next generation and determined
to prepare the way. Concord and its environs had not yet become
renowned as a fountainhead of American literature, while the arts
were never to recognize there even the remotest relationship. Lexington, having achieved its eternal fame, was the more notable site in that
direction, while to the North, Bostonians looked with affectionate regard toward Salem and Newburyport as cultural influences worthy
of inclusion in their own sphere.

In Boston the Athenaeum was not named with any sense of modesty as to its scope and purpose, and New England was so termed with
careful recognition of the difference implied in the use of that adjec-
tive over a possible alternative of "Little" England. The Athenaeum
met the challenge by girding its loins for a career which in a few brief
years assumed a leadership of many literary and artistic movements,
—excepting those of music—, cultivated under the aegis of leading
citizens whose forebears were of ancient lineage.

Yes, 1818 was a worthy year, one in which the world of Europe and
America might pause ever so briefly and utter thanks for the blessing
of peace and prosperity. Thus did the *Columbian Centinel*, in the last
issue of the year, survey the world, and find it good:

CLOSE OF THE YEAR

The year now drawing to its final close will probably be marked in the great kalendar, as the most auspicious to the World of any of its predecessors for a long period of time.

During this year, by the withdrawal of the allied troops from France, the last act of the Drama which for more than a quarter of a century has astonished, bewildered, and affrighted mankind has been brought to a close. The World may now be said to be at Peace, and left to pursue the things of Peace. The affairs occurring in India and Ceylon are but corrections of disobedience and family disloyalty; and those in Spanish America if stripped of the falsehood and bombast given them in the gazettes, would scarcely be considered exceptions to our general rule.

Let us then hope, that this may be succeeded by many similar years; and that during them there be no other contest among nations, than which shall best advance Agriculture, Commerce, Industry, and Science, which shall diffuse the most solid Knowledge; which best secure Liberty & Law and which is the most efficacious in succoring misfortune.

2.

Conveying the air of a successfully managed and important cultural institution, the first concert of the year 1819, given on the second evening of January, brought forth this varied program:

THE PHILO-HARMONIC SOCIETY,

WILL meet at six o'clock THIS EVENING. Music to commence at 7 o'clock precisely. Rice's (Ries) second grand Concerto, allowed to be the greatest piece that has yet been composed for the Piano Forte, will be among the performances—Gillineck's Queen of Prussia's Waltz with variations—Several songs—Chorusses from Haydn's Creation—Quartette, violin by Mr. Ostinelli—Symphonies, by a full Orchestra, &c.

Members can bring their friends every Saturday evening agreeable to the Bye Laws of said Society.

WM. COFFIN, Jr. Sec'y [31]

Precisely three weeks later another concert offered certain works which were there undoubtedly through the spell of Mr. Ostinelli's ascending favor. No additional names are available to show the changing constitution of the orchestra, but the presence of several new resident performers may be assumed to have manifestly improved the fortunes of the Philharmonic Society; in all likelihood students of Mr. Graupner took their place in the orchestra and, in time, those of Mr.

[31] *Columbian Centinel*, Jan. 2, 1819.

Ostinelli; furthermore Miss Hewitt had become an able pianist with an enlarged repertory of concertos by Cramer, Gelinek, Steibelt, and others.

So great was the popularity of these events during the month following the liberal invitation to bring friends that further regulations became immediately necessary for a stricter enforcement of order and decorum.

Philo-Harmonic Society

The "Standing Committee," while they congratulate the Members and their visiting friends, on the increase and unprecedented popularity of the Society, are fully impressed with the necessity of making such further arrangements in regard to their accommodation and matters of administration, as will justify and keep pace with that popularity. Liberality, precision and a strict enforcement of the Laws, being the most obvious means to obtaining this desirable object. The Committee take this method of making known, the following regulations, the observance of which, they strongly recommend in all cases.

1st. No person can be admitted without a card of introduction.

2nd. Each Member shall have a special Ticket for himself, which is not transferable.

3d. Members heretofore privileged to bring their families gratis, shall, besides their own Ticket, be entitled to two cards of admission for every Saturday evening.

4th. Order of the performance shall be printed, for the accommodation of the company.

The Committee inform the members, that their own special tickets and family cards of admission, can be obtained of the Secretary, and also that a plank walk will be made on the north side of Pond street to render the access of the Hall convenient at all times.[32]

Concerts were given weekly during the height of the season with Mr. Ostinelli and Miss Hewitt providing the principal solos and various amateurs singing the ever-popular glees. There was a renewed interest in the performance of quartets, but exact titles, or opus numbers, are not given in the newspaper announcements. Murmurs of praise may be heard here and there for the execution of a choice movement, as in the case of a previously unknown gentleman: "We were particularly pleased with the really chaste and truly delightful first attempt of Mr. Warren in a Violin Quartetto, which, exceeded our expectations and impressed us with a due sense of this gentleman's

32 *Columbian Centinel*, Jan. 2, 1819.

modest merit." [33] In Salem bound volumes of parts are found containing Pleyel's edition of Haydn, Mozart, Kreutzer, and Foulls [34] quartets, and Dr. Oliver refers to concerts by the Salem Glee Club which were "occasionally varied by the introduction of instrumental quartet and quintet playing" of "music by Mozart and Haydn" with two violins, viola, and violoncello. [35] One may assume that substantially the same works were current in Boston musical circles. During the season of 1818–1819 Kotzwara's "Battle of Prague," Pleyel's most celebrated symphony, "La Chasse," Variations for violin by Rode, Ballet-Air with variations on the pianoforte by Gelinek, "Sul margine di dio" (*sic*), Variations by Latour, and by Kalkbrenner, and other works of like caliber were given, adding a genial recognition of native talent by the "celebrated Cossack Song" with accompaniments composed by Mr. Granger Sr.

Of greatest importance, however, was the inclusion on February 27, 1819, of another work by Beethoven in the course of this program:

PHILO-HARMONIC SOCIETY'S CONCERT

THIS EVENING

at the Hall . . . Pond Street,

GRAND Symphony (Pleyel); Song; celebrated Grand Sonata, for the Pianoforte, with the funeral march (Beethoven); Glee; Finale. [36]

No performer is mentioned, but since Miss Hewitt was the principal pianist at these occasions, the theory is tenable that this young lady was responsible for the initial performance of a Beethoven pianoforte work before a Boston audience. The sonata, Opus 26, was composed in 1801; the third movement is the Funeral March. It was not played again, nor did Miss Hewitt play other works by Beethoven in the course of her long career. Other sonatas, had they reached her, would have been more suitable for the tastes of the Philharmonic circle than this particular one.

Following the introduction of seasonal novelties, no attempts were made to quote the detailed programs in the papers; the announcements were principally concerned with soliciting punctual attendance of the performers and with giving a rough sketch of the order, as:

[33] *Euterpeiad*, March 3, 1821.
[34] One "Foulis" is mentioned as second violinist in the Handel Commemoration orchestra, but I find no record of him as a composer. Possibly "Filtz" is intended.
[35] Salem *Gazette*, Dec. 15, 1868.   [36] *Columbian Centinel*, Feb. 27, 1819.

Part I—Symphony, Song, Glee, Rondo, Song, Concerto, Clarionet

Part II—Symphony, Song, Solo Violin, Duetto, Minuetto, Glee

After a remarkably successful season extending well into May, the members concluded with a fishing party; a packet was chartered early in July to carry the band complete, and the day was spent in what we may hope was a wholesome round of innocent amusement.

It may be ascertained from the foregoing account that the Philharmonic Society was extremely popular during the season of 1818–1819; this was a popularity which brought its own special problems, mainly those of finance, and raised fond hopes on the part of the membership and on the part of the leader who envisioned the formation of an orchestra on a more substantial basis than that in effect at the time. Accordingly, petition was made to the state legislature, with a response which must have been evidence of the good-will felt toward the organization by the leading citizens and lawmakers. Occurring precisely ten years after the founding of the Philharmonic Society, the move was made in all likelihood in celebration of the first decade, and consequently was made as the result of careful planning for the future development of orchestral music in Boston.

Chapter 50

AN ACT TO INCORPORATE THE PHILHARMONIC SOCIETY [37]

SECT. 1. BE it enacted by the Senate & House of Representatives, in General Court assembled, and by the authority of the same, That Gottlieb Graupner, Thomas Smith Webb, William Coffin, junior, Matthew S. Parker, John Dodd, and Bryant P. Tilden, together with such as may become associated with them and their successors be and are hereby incorporated and made a body politic and corporate for the purpose of extending and enlarging and improving the style of performance of vocal and instrumental music by the name of the Philharmonic Society; and by that name they may sue and be sued, have a common seal and the same, at pleasure, alter; and be entitled to all the powers and privileges incident to aggregate corporations.

Sect. 2. relative to choosing officers and making rules.

Sect. 3. relative to holding real estate not exceeding $5000.

Sect. 4. That Gottlieb Graupner have full power to call the first meeting of said corporation.

June 19, 1819

[37] Massachusetts Special Laws, p. 324.

In accordance with Section 4 Graupner caused the following to be inserted in the *Centinel:*

Notice
To the Petitioners for an act to incorporate the
"Philo-Harmonic Society"

The subscriber, being authorized and directed by the said Act to call the first meeting of the Petitioners, hereby notifies and requests them to meet at his Music Hall, No. 6, Franklin-street, This EVENING, 14th inst. at 8 o'clock precisely, to choose a President, Treasurer, and such other officers as they may deem necessary and to act on such other business as may come before them." [38]

Such a notice suggests a greater effect on the fortunes of the society than is apparent from any subsequent events; in all probability the changes, actual or contemplated, were designed to improve the business affairs of the individual members by offering them payment for their services. The Handel and Haydn Society had become a comparatively wealthy organization in a short time, owing to ticket sales and to publishing ventures. There was no reason why the good-will of the public should not be tested by asking friends and guests of the Philharmonic Society to purchase tickets in a similar manner; receipts of this kind, augmenting the seasonal membership fees paid by the more ardent devotees, would vastly benefit the cause of orchestral music in Boston and further establish the dignity of the professional musician, whose sources of income were unpredictable to an uncomfortable degree.

Five weeks later the members met in the same hall to receive the report of the committee appointed to draft the constitution. Regrettably, no copy of the constitution or of the bye-laws is extant, and only one portion has been discovered in the newspapers.

Extract from the Bye-Laws

Any persons having been a member of the *Philo-Harmonic Society*, at the close of the last season, may have the privilege of subscribing to the New Constitution without being ballotted for, any time previous to the first meeting in November, on complying with the terms prescribed.

By order of the Trustees,
WM. COFFIN, JR. SECR'RY.[39]

[38] *Columbian Centinel,* Aug. 14, 1819.   [39] *Columbian Centinel,* Oct. 9, 1819.

No further effect on the conduct of the society is shown through the Act of Incorporation, unless it is a decision to keep its affairs from the public press. Whereas the former season had been reported with gratifying completeness, the season of 1819–1820 affords no news until the occasion of a benefit concert for Mr. Granger Sr. the veteran who had suffered a stroke of palsy. The society generously resolved annually to appropriate an evening's entertainment for his benefit and, although regulations forbade the sale of tickets, occasions of this kind were always excepted. The program contained Haydn's "Surprise" and Pleyel's "La Chasse" symphonies and the latter's Concertante in E Flat.

The orchestra which assisted the Handel and Haydn Society was virtually that of the Philharmonic Society, but there were exceptions among those employed at the Federal Theatre, or the City Theatre, who had commitments not to be laid aside even for the great oratorios. These circumstances often deprived the choral society of professional services, and may account for the dissatisfaction often expressed with the orchestral accompaniment to *The Messiah* or *The Creation;* occasionally the Philharmonic Society omitted its rehearsals in order to permit members to assist in the final rehearsals of the projected oratorios, for which they were duly paid. The records show a total of $382 paid to musicians during the season of 1822–1823, but before that time they were reimbursed through annual concerts, "The proceeds of which will be applied to the Benefit of the Professional Gentlemen who have so generously come forward to the assistance of the Society in the present season." In February, 1823, Matthew Peter King's *Intercession* was presented for the benefit of the professional gentlemen of the orchestra, "being their only compensation for the season's work."

Benefit concerts were the accepted manner of showing compassion for the unfortunate, but were also considered the just due of favorite members of the theatrical company; all hands joined to promote the success of these special events which, in a way, attested to the popularity of the individual. The receipts were often quite handsome, or "bumper," as they were described, but at other times they were discouragingly small; both conditions were often told in the press with an invocation for better luck next time.

The spirit of benevolence was extended to old "Father" Schaffer, "the infirm, aged, and decayed Musician" during August, 1820; an orchestra, not designated by title, contributed the very familiar Pleyel and Haydn symphonies, and Mr. Ostinelli played a violin sonata by Mozart. While it is extremely likely that more than one symphony by Haydn was played during these years, the lure of the "Surprise" is certain to have guaranteed its favor above all others, and the fact that Graupner was in the orchestra when it received first performance under the direction of the composer testifies to his predilection for the work.

The weekly or fortnightly concerts of the Philharmonic Society were excellent training ground for the young musicians of Boston who contributed their services with great regularity. Enthusiasm attended the development of Miss Eustaphieve, daughter of the Russian consul, who showed a remarkable childhood talent; she had studied Pleyel's sonatas with various local teachers, including the transient Etienne, in Boston during the autumn of 1816, making such progress that her father took her to St. Petersburg with the intention of placing her under Steibelt and John Field. They remained in Russia only two months, hence intensive study was not feasible before returning to Boston. Thereafter the child played before the Philharmonic Society such pieces as have little relation to her Russian sojourn; these included "The Battle of New Orleans," by D. Etienne, "dedicated to the American nation" and copyright in 1816.[40] "The Conflagration of Moscow," Steibelt's "Storm" rondo, and "the like compositions," according to her enthusiastic biographer Parker, were in her repertory; this baptism of fire and water gone through, Miss Eustaphieve "passed with the same success to the master pieces of Kalkbrenner, Ries, and the gigantic Beethoven himself," until in 1824 she was declared to own the largest private collection of music in the United States, "perhaps"!

Miss Eustaphieve suffered an unusually quiet press, but her particular champion Parker unflinchingly asks this rhetorical question and promptly answers it: "The proper question, then, is, was Mozart, as performer on the piano, equal at the age of twelve, to the young lady of the same age, whom we are describing? We answer without hesitation, no"! Heinrich dedicated an extravagently Lisztian

[40] "Published for the author" by G. Graupner; it is a work of 20 pages.

piece to the young lady entitled "Fair Pupil of the Tuneful Muse." [41]

Alexis Eustaphieve, the child's father, was a violinist of no small talent, and a great help to the Philharmonic Society during those years in which he was a member. Nourishing a classical taste, he was a prolific writer to the newspapers on such varied subjects as politics, international relations, literature, law—in fact, every subject that newspaper discussion is heir to—even in Boston's pre-*Transcript* days. He was celebrated for lengthy criticisms on the drama, on concerts, and music, was a writer of several poetic dramas founded on incidents in Russian history, and was proud of his superiority as violinist and of his proficiency in the favorite amusement of fishing. "In brief, he was, or supposed himself to be, the autocrat of the fashionable world of Boston; and, of course, *that* world was not without individuals who sometimes doubted the correctness of his decisions, and became restive under his assumed supremacy," wrote Joseph T. Buckingham, one of the most egregious deflaters in American letters. [42] The Great Society, however, found him a "polished gentleman from a European Capital" and in acknowledgment of his services invited him to become a member.

The personnel of the Philharmonic Society shows no conspicuous change during the years, a fact which testifies to the harmony of relations maintained between the players and the conductor. In October, 1820, Graupner was president; Bryant P. Tilden, vice-president; Wm. Coffin, jun., secretary; and Matthew S. Parker, treasurer. The trustees remained the same with the addition of Allan Pollock (sealer of weights and measures) and Thomas Granger. Applications for membership in the Society were balloted for at the commencement of the season; presumably these were lay members as well as participating instrumentalists.

After a decade characterized by steady growth, but fundamentally unaltered policy, the seasons progressed with order and assurance and with constant evidences of success in all quarters, including that of performance; it was, in effect, a permanent orchestra with a permanent conductor. Rehearsals always began early in October, but few

---

[41] This selection, not mentioned by Mr. Upton, was brought to my attention by Mr. Burkat of the Boston Public Library.
[42] J. T. Buckingham, *Personal Memoirs*.

public notices were issued until January, a procedure that suggests adequate preparation before public hearing of the works to be performed. In 1821 an overture composed by Dr. Wiesenthal, a symphony by Winter, and an unidentified overture by Mozart were among the novelties; the disconcertingly incomplete programs given in the papers suggest that the remainder of the works were already known to the audiences and that Mr. Hart, Mr. and Mrs. Graupner, and Mr. Mallet were given to continual repetition of their favorite selections; as for Mr. Ostinelli and Miss Hewitt, it would seem that the frequency of their appearances would hardly allow for a new work each time. The society occupied a new hall, the Pantheon, on October 20 of this year, a spacious room, midway in size between the little hall in Pond Street and Boylston Hall; the dimensions given by Bowen are 72 feet by 22 feet.

Gottlieb Graupner was a busy man, beset too by various personal difficulties. He conducted the Neponset Sacred Music Society in Dorchester in several concerts, and was the object of various expressions of gratitude in the press, all flavored by "a lively sense of favors to come." The impression is inescapable that Graupner preferred conducting to any other professional activity.

It must be held in mind that an audience for the semi-public concerts of the Philharmonic Society was a very limited one indeed when compared with those courted by the Handel and Haydn Society at Boylston Hall; the orchestra of 15 to 20 players functioned on a much smaller scale than a chorus of one hundred or 150. Complaint was made that the orchestra played the same works repeatedly, but the programs of the choral society show an endless repetition of standard choruses to a greater extent. The inevitable result in both cases was an eventual relaxing of interest on the part of the public; this was especially disastrous to the larger society, owing to the suddenly inflated pride in its initial accomplishment and to the brief taste of extraordinary financial success, but the real reason for its limited repertory undoubtedly is to be found in the inexpert standards of performance. The candid J. R. Parker wrote,

There have been many instances where a deficiency of patronage has been manifested, but it may with propriety be observed, that the encouragement given, has always been fully adequate to the claims, and it cannot be too evident that this deficiency, was more owing to the deficiencies in genius and in practice, than any unwillingness on the part of the public, to award the meed of excellence.[43]

The private nature of the Philharmonic Society, together with its lack of pretension, may have spared it from similar outspoken estimation of its talents, and the esteem felt for Mr. Graupner may have softened the critical blow, in so far as Parker was concerned, for the orchestra was completely the expression of the founder's thought, whereas the choral society revolved around no single outstanding individuality. Buckingham, unmellowed friend, professed no particular allegiance to either and let the axe fall with this devastating remark: "The orchestra was lamentably deficient in numbers or power, perhaps in both."

The season 1822–1823 is devoid of special event, excepting for a single concert given under the patronage of the two societies for the benefit of Miss Hewitt on May 14; the young lady played works by Kalkbrenner, Rosetti, and Woelfl, and the orchestra paid compliment to her eminent father by performing the "Battle of Wagram"—full orchestra, that is with trumpets and kettledrums. Mr. and Mrs. Ostinelli—the former Miss Hewitt—moved to Portland shortly after for a brief residence.

The loss of these two able performers was a body blow to the fortunes of the Philharmonic Society and to the musical life of Boston; there were new members listed for the season 1823–1824, but neither Mr. Dixon, the British consul,[44] nor John Henry Howard Graupner, the conductor's son, was sufficiently talented to hide the need of another performer of the rank of the eminent Louis Ostinelli. Anthony Philip Heinrich had arrived in Boston in May, 1823, and was received with great courtesy by the two major organizations, but there is no evidence that he became a member of the Philharmonic Society, although he played in the Handel and Haydn Society orchestra. His talents were spectacular enough but this German-American Berlioz had not the qualities equal to those of the gracious Italian. Warren, Wood, Rowson, and the two Grangers are identifiable as charter members, but some of these had lost their cunning. All told, approximately sixteen pieces are accounted for as constituting the orchestra of the Philharmonic Society, with few local additions during the thirteen

43 *Euterpeiad*, May 20, 1820, editorial.
44 *History of the Handel and Haydn Society*, Vol. I, p. 34.

years of its career.[45] The officers remained substantially the same, but four new trustees were added about this time; these were O. Everett, A. Whitman, N. Ford, and one Hall. Tympani were acquired to assist in the popular overtures and battle pieces. Yet, all was not well.

The growth of all musical activities during the preceding decade had been rapid; an amazing number of instruments were imported from England and the Continent, quantities of music were received and quantities more published in America. The manufacture of pianofortes was a lucrative business in Boston, and the mark of fashion attached to the possession of them. The ventures of the Handel and Haydn Society, both in respect to concert giving and publishing, had opened up a new field of enthusiasm; to all these belongs credit for an astonishing growth of public interest and a rapidly improving taste. Whereas the concerts of the Philharmonic Society had seemed wonderful in 1818, the defects of performance must have been woefully apparent by 1824, particularly when the same pieces were repeated ad infinitum by players technically incapable of mastering every measure put before them. Possibly not every composer, flattered by regular performance, could maintain so fully the respect of the listener on close acquaintance, while further exploration of the works of Mozart and Beethoven was more to be desired than attempted under existing conditions.

The final program carrying the patronage of the Philharmonic Society was given in aid of Mr. Williamson, the singer, on May 1, 1824; the orchestra played three overtures: to "Henry the Fourth," "Lodoiska," and "A Conversation Overture"; two of these appear to be new to the repertory; there was but one concerto requiring aid of the orchestra, which had an easy time of it. Thereafter the players again functioned as individuals rather than as the familiar unit denominated "Philharmonic Society."

These illustrations are provided as partial explanation of the conditions, not in all respects plain, which resulted in the sudden decline of the society. The usual announcement of the first concert was made

45 The directories are of small assistance in filling out the changes in orchestral personnel; the greater number of persons connected with music are listed as manufacturers or dealers, while the practicing instrumentalists are identified merely as "musician," or "teacher of music"; these include pianists and organists in increasing number, particularly since the removal of prejudice allowed for installation of organs in churches, thus replacing the bass viol, clarionet, or serpent.

on October 29, 1825, and was twice repeated,[46] but no further mention is made of that event, or of any ensuing concert. Annual meetings were called for October 7, 1826, and October 6, 1827, for the choice of officers, but the statement made by Abel Bowen in 1828 that "Latterly, however, the meetings of this society have been limited to their annual convention for choice of officers, and for occasional purposes" must be taken to signify the termination of active seasons. Rowson had passed on; Hart was leader of the Boston Brigade Band; Thomas Granger Jr., was leader of the Federal Theatre Orchestra; and Louis Ostinelli, returned to Boston, had become "Maestro di Capello" of the Apollo Orchestra; eventually he became conductor of the Italian operas. All had gone on to higher, or more remunerative occupations. The two theaters, the City and the Federal Street, were open four or five evenings each week, while the body of wind and brass players that functioned on public holidays had become organized into a noted ensemble with a nation-wide fame. There was now little time for the amateur and professional to function together on so uncertain and so unprofitable a basis as that underlying the Philharmonic Society; possibly avoidance of these very circumstances was contemplated by Graupner in his act of incorporation.

This little amateur band, containing his best friends and concerned with a love for informal music-making, comprised Gottlieb Graupner's most treasured interest. He devoted himself unselfishly to its continuance, and suffered through its trials, relieved by occasional rejoicing at a surprising triumph when all things worked together for good intonation, unison of attack, and smooth execution—all in the face of apparent incapacity. At times his ambition unquestionably exceeded the abilities which faced him from the players' desks. His it was to reconcile these limitations among his humble followers with the temperaments of experienced travelers like Mr. Eustaphieve; without a doubt, he imparted sound instruction to the players, joined with a quiet friendliness and an unvarying patience. Had Graupner lacked any of these virtues, the Philharmonic Society would have perished much sooner.

Whereas the orchestra ceased to function under its own name, these "occasional purposes," mentioned by Bowen, included several concerts given by Graupner for his own benefit; in one of them Haydn's "Mili-

46 It is commonly stated that the last concert occurred on Nov. 24, 1824.

tary" Symphony is identified for the first time, but it is probable that it was already in the repertory of the orchestra, as was the Overture to "Lodoiska" played in the same concert. Mr. Graupner advertises for pupils in the fall of 1829, "having for the present relinquished his connection with the public orchestras," but in May, 1831, he is at work again as conductor of the Music Professional Society, announced to give the first of ten regular concerts. The fine hand of the sixty-four-year-old conductor can be detected in the arrangements of this new society, but the officers were entirely new to Boston, and of several generation's remoteness. They were: Charles Zeuner, president; G. J. Webb, vice-president; E. R. Hansen, leader; Charles Geitner, assistant-leader; Gottlieb Graupner, conductor; William M. Pray, treasurer. Season tickets admitting one gentleman and two ladies for one year cost ten dollars, or four dollars for an individual. The society was open to "all respectable Professors," and such amateurs as were capable of assisting in the performances were invited to join as honorary members. Verily, a rebirth of the Philharmonic with only the conductor as survivor! The fate of the Music Professional Society remains undisclosed, but one interesting item concerns a brief note in the *Columbian Centinel* of March 20, 1833, indicating that "Bills to incorporate the Boston Musical Professional Society, etc." were passed to be enacted by the General Court. It is significant that this action occurred in precisely the same week as the incorporation of the Boston Academy of Music.

The days of the parent society, the Philharmonic, were well past, and the brief career of the orchestral resurgence of which Gottlieb Graupner was a strange figure from a seemingly distant past, belongs to another story chronicling the second phase of musical development in the nineteenth century.

Part III

THE PERSONALITIES

V. THE VON HAGEN FAMILY

O F THE INDIVIDUALS claiming a secure place in the forefront of
Boston's musical life, the several Von Hagens are first in point
of time. They were energetic and industrious, and their cease-
less activity must have made more than a fleeting impression on the
minds of New England's casual audience, which considered music
either as confined to crude psalmody, on the one hand, or as accompanied by all the accessories of the theater, on the other. It was inevitable that the Von Hagens labored under difficulties, for music
making in the home on a scientific basis was a comparatively new idea,
and the small number of harpsichords or pianos owned by Boston's
gentry at the turn of the century suggests that the taking of music
lessons often entailed the procuring of an instrument of distant manufacture and of music imported from across the seas. One must be merchant as well as musician. All told, the efforts of the Von Hagens were
like a curtain raiser to the longer and more brilliant successes of the
Graupners, but there is no mistaking the terrible earnestness with
which they brought forward each new enterprise.

The Van Hagen [1] family came to Boston in 1796 and immediately
made their presence known; at once embracing every aspect of the
profession, they acquired potential control for a short time. This ambitious trio became the first important publishers of music in Boston,
the most competent teachers, and organists of talent; father and son
were experienced conductors and were composers and arrangers of
theatrical music to boot. Other minor accomplishments were displayed
with gracious good will in due season.

The precise reason for the removal of the Van Hagens to Boston
cannot be determined, although a guess may be hazarded that places
in the theatrical orchestra were promised them. Boston must have appealed to them as an auspicious location for an active family of mu-

[1] The change in the spelling of the name is explained on p. 159.

sicians, while a survey of their decade in New York shows a declining return in business and in concert management. In Boston the Federal Theatre had opened with a grand flourish, and a company of actors had speedily come to fame as an extraordinarily competent body, if not quite equal to "The Americans" in New York. The Van Hagen family had tried other cities along the coast, treading out the same march of northerly progress which was followed by a long line of fellow musicians in the next two decades. In a sense they were rugged pioneers.

Sonneck first discovered that Peter Van Hagen (then Jr.) was in Charleston in 1774, at which time he must have been about twenty years of age and, possibly, a bridegroom. He traces the family back to Rotterdam and a noted family of organists in that culturally enlightened city, quoting Burney:

> M. Van Hagen, a German, who is the principal organist here, is likewise an excellent performer on the violin, of which he convinced me by playing one of his own solos. He was a scholar of Geminiani, and he not only plays, but writes very much in the style of that great master of harmony.
> His daughter has a fine voice, and sings with much taste and expression.[2]

The family had sojourned in London, possibly returning there from Charleston and thus explaining their whereabouts between the Charleston experience and that in New York, for Van Hagen Sr. is described as "recently from London" in 1792. By 1789 he was a dealer and teacher in New York, playing at concerts and occasionally conducting, notably the successful French opera company which visited that city in 1791. He still employed the designation "late Director of concerts in Holland," furthering that aspect of his career by engaging with Henri Capron and George Edward Saliment in several series of subscription concerts in New York. At one time James Hewitt was competitor, at another, partner, and then—as associations generally proved in the case of the latter gentleman—once again and indefinitely, competitor. These New York concerts brought before the public the celebrities of the day, including Benjamin Carr, Mrs. Pownall,[3] Mrs. Hodgkinson, and—most often—the three Van Ha-

[2] Charles Burney. *Present State of Music in Germany, the Netherlands, and United Provinces* (1773). The name does not appear in London directories of the time. Hereafter "Von" is used, since they were known in Boston only by that name, and the change was apparently made with a purpose.
[3] Died in Boston, Sept. 15, 1798.

gens. "Master" Peter was continually featured as violinist, varied by
an occasional session with the "tenor"; father and mother played the
piano in concertos. "Miss Van Hagen," "about" thirteen years of age
in 1792, rarely appeared, and John E., another son, is not mentioned,
either on account of extreme infancy or because he did not share the
family's musical talent.

Whatever the immediate urgency, the Van Hagens arrived in Boston early in 1796, exchanged the "Van" for "Von," and settled down
to an intensive conquest of the new metropolis, which duplicated their
New York experience with uncertain results. They did not take up
concert management on an elaborate subscription basis. Sonneck describes the low state of concert life in Boston during the last five years
of the old century; even such experienced hands as this family took
no steps to enter the field on a large scale.[4] The apparent severity of
this condition may be partially excused if one remembers that Boston
had just made the theater a legitimate enterprise, and the novelty of
that experience was rather overwhelming; not only were the wonders
of the Federal Theatre repertory at hand to claim attention, but the
competitor Haymarket opened its doors, providing an embarrassment
of riches which the burning of the one and the closing of the other
made somewhat more readily digestible. Furthermore, those persons
without exception most likely to make concerts a success were engaged at the theater and constantly occupied there. To alleviate this
distress, however, there were exhibitions of an elephant, Mr. Pinch-
beck's learned pig, and the continuing waxworks installed in the Columbian Museum.

Peter Von Hagen Sr. conducted on one occasion, at least, in the pit
of the Haymarket Theatre. This was in December, 1796, but should
not be construed as affording him a regular means of support, for the
Haymarket was experiencing a difficult time, and before its recovery
Von Hagen had transferred to the Federal Theatre, where he succeeded Trille Labarre. Labarre and Leaumont [5] had contributed accompaniments for the operas, but the former was the principal director; his death, at the age of thirty-nine, was announced in the *Gazette*
of January 1, 1798. It would appear that Von Hagen conducted from
January, 1797, until the close of the season of 1800, to be followed

[4] *Early Concert Life in America*, p. 306.
[5] Later became active in Charleston, S. C. Burned out in the Jarvis Buildings fire
in Boston, June, 1796.

the next year by Gottlieb Graupner, who had risen from his post as oboe player to leadership and the double bass. During Von Hagen's incumbency three works, at least, were composed by him: "Columbus," performed February 17, 1800; [6] accompaniments for "The Battle of Hexham"; *Adopted Child*, "music entirely new and composed by P. A. Von Hagen," March 15, 1797.

There is also mention of an "Overture to be played at the Haymarket Theatre, Oct. 25, 1797, composed by Peter Von Hagen Jr.," but the newspapers indicate that the theater was not opened regularly at that time. A "Federal Overture" was performed on June 11, 1798, at the Federal Theatre; possibly this was the same piece. Another "Federal Overture" for the 1799 season is advertised as published (see Appendix I).

Outside the theater, the family established itself as "P. A. Von Hagen jun. & Co." in May, 1798, or earlier, entering into partnership with Benjamin Crehore of Milton for the purpose of importing instruments from London and Amsterdam. Despite Crehore's later fame as a maker of pianos, there is no mention at this time of American-made instruments as having any special virtue. The firm included father Von Hagen as well, and future references combine the Sr. and Jr. members without discernible system, although the senior member would appear to be the controlling factor. No details of the Von Hagen stock are available, but the frequent removals suggest that it was not boundless, while a survey of sheet music of that time reveals no extensive selection of imported songs or instrumental works for sale anywhere in the States. Having few publications from abroad, they were encouraged to publish for themselves, as the bibliography appended makes plain. [7] The firm was severally referred to as "Musical Magazine and Warehouse," "P. A. Von Hagen's Musical Magazine," or "P. A. Von Hagen and Son." From their first address at 62 Newbury Street the proprietors removed to 65 Marlborough Street (at the head of the Mall) by March 13, 1799, and to No. 3 Cornhill by July of the same year, when the partnership with Crehore was dissolved as of June 28 (see Chapter IX, page 270). At all these addresses the entire family was available for instruction of pupils on

---

[6] James Hewitt also wrote music to this subject.

[7] The John Carter Brown Library, Providence, has the largest number of their imprints.

the harpsichord, piano, organ, and singing, also "theoretical knowledge of music."

An interesting side light in connection with early publishing concerns this announcement:

> Songs in the musical drama of the Adopted Child this
> day published and for sale at the ticket office State Street
> and at Ede's Office in Kirby Street. price 4½.
> These songs will be sung at the theatre this evening.

The *Adopted Child* was by Attwood, and the accompaniments for
this production were arranged by Von Hagen. It is possible that these
marked the beginning of Von Hagen's enterprise in the publishing
field, although the music was sold at the office of the Boston *Gazette*
(Ede's Office), which advertised the above on April 9, 1797, and at
the theater box office. Sometime during this year—or early in the next
—the Von Hagens established their business. No copies of these songs
have survived, and it cannot be known whether their titles correspond
to some of those advertised by Von Hagen but not located. Again, it
is possible that only the words were published.

Oddly enough, the reputation of Peter Jr. as violinist was not appreciably furthered in Boston. He probably served for many years in
the orchestra of the theater (he was there in 1806, since he mentions
the fact in an advertisement of June 1), but he made no reputation as
a soloist there or in the concert hall, a rather perplexing lapse since
the theater offered frequent opportunity for the obbligatos of Mr.
Graupner, and there is no reason to suppose that Von Hagen would
have lacked for some celebrity as a performer had he possessed the
necessary skill. Good violinists were not common in Boston, even by
stretch of the imagination, until at least 1815; the odds are definitely
against Peter Von Hagen's having lived up to the promise of his youth
or, perchance, the encomiums penned by his ambitious father. His few
solo appearances in family benefits were received with the utmost lack
of enthusiasm in so far as the popular record is concerned.

The family made some attempt to describe their joint efforts as a
school, or "Musical Academy," but there is no consistency in the use
of the terms, and the results do not detract from the glory of the
Graupner-Mallet-Trajetta institution as the first "Conservatorio or
Musical Academy" in Boston and, in all likelihood, in the country.

This increase of teaching load, however, was carefully regulated. Peter Jr. journeyed on the road to Salem each week, while the elder made "weekly trips to Dorchester, Milton, Dedham, Newton, Watertown, Waltham and Cambridge." Their first concert of vocal and instrumental music was advertised to take place in Salem in 1798, but it was not given until February 5, 1799; [8] by this time visits of the male members of the family had been made in connection with field trips by the theatrical entourage, while Mrs. Von Hagen's talents were proclaimed by this flattering "Communication" in the Salem *Gazette* of June 25, 1800: Mrs. Von Hagen "whose taste and talents procured her, when in Holland, admiration of the great at the Hague, as they have since in America commanded the applause of all who have heard her perform." The family sponsored no repetition of this concert in Boston.

Peter Jr. greeted the new century with a bride, the former Lucy Ballard, on January 12; he was then between nineteen and twenty-one years of age. He also became organist in 1800 at Trinity Church (then Episcopal), whose records show payments until 1809, when he was succeeded by Mr. Cooper. His frequent assistance at the organ of King's Chapel suggests that he followed his mother in that post, possibly holding both positions at the same time; in these later years his performances were confined to voluntaries for charitable societies. Mrs. Von Hagen's final benefit evening was held on March 6, 1806, when she was assisted by an able corps of singing-actors from the Theatre. (Program on page 163.)

With the passing of the elder Von Hagen on August 20, 1803, [9] the fortunes of the mother and son apparently suffered a sharp decline. The publishing of music ceased, and the Musical Magazine and Warehouse maintained a feeble existence for only a brief time. In 1806 Peter (now Sr.) purchased the stock of Paff, but in 1809 the address is given in the directory as 6 Franklin Street, the site of Graupner's home and business. This was probably a mailing address for Von Hagen, who now had no regular means of support in Boston or, in so far as may be discovered, in the surrounding towns. Thus the extent of the older man's influence on the fortunes of the family may be

[8] The program is given in Sonneck, *Early Concert Life in America*, p. 315.
[9] "In this town . . . M. Peter Von Hagen, professor of music, aged 48, an accomplished, scientific musician, and a worthy man." Boston *Gazette*, Aug. 24.

ARRANGEMENT OF MRS. E. VON HAGEN'S CONCERT,
AT CONCERT HALL, 6TH INST.

Part 1st

Overture,	Haydn.
Song, Mr. Darley	
Sonata for four hands, Mrs. Von Hagen & her pupil,	Pleyel.
Song, Ala Polaca, No more by sorrow chased,	
Mrs. Graupner,	Braham.
Concerto Oboe, Mr. Graupner.	
Song, Mr. Bernard.	
Concerto, Piano Forte, Mrs. Von Hagen,	Fodor.
Glee, by Mrs. Graupner, Messrs. Darley,	
Bernard, Twaits and Fox	
Concerto, Violin, Mr. Von Hagen.	Gordani.

Part 2d

The Battle of Prague, A Sonata for four hands, by Mr.	
and Mrs. Von Hagen,	Kotzwara.
Song, Be my tender Passion, Mrs. Graupner.	Storace.
Sonata, for four hands, Mrs. Von Hagen & her Pupil,	Haydn.
Song, The origin of Gun powder, Mr. Twaits.	
Duetto for 2 clarinets, Messrs. Granger & Moffat	Mitchell.
Song, The ireful Battle rages, Mr. Fox.	
Finale,	Pleyel.

ascertained through the vanishing prosperity on the part of the son. Peter Jr. rarely participated in the concerns of the newer lights of the Boston scene, Mallet, Graupner, or Trajetta, nor did he acquire a prominent place in this musical life by dint of his own efforts. Mrs. Elizabeth Von Hagen continued bravely to teach privately, to play the organ, and to give occasional benefits—occasions when the hand asking for charity was rather obviously extended. She also continued as music mistress in private schools but was succeeded at Mrs. Rowson's by Mr. Graupner. The last mention of her participation in a concert was contained in the program of a Graupner benefit for July 2, 1806, when she was announced: "Concerto on the Piano Forte by Mrs. Von Hagen." Peter played a "Concerto on the Tenor by the late P. A. Von Hagen" and took the tenor part in a quartet. Lucy Von Hagen [10] was listed as a schoolmistress in 1816, while John E. Von

10 This assumes that she was a daughter of Peter Jr. and Lucy Ballard, and not the Lucy Von Hagen mentioned by Sonneck. That lady, I would suppose, was

Hagen's blank-book manufactory led a very quiet existence if it survived 1809.

The conclusion devolving upon the sudden decline of an active family is not entirely based on a sense of their incapability as practitioners of their art. Within these few years influences proclaiming a new day had made their appearance. The "old-fashioned" repertory of the harpsichord was rapidly passing, the new importations by way of the theater brought a sudden intensity of activity in the realm of published music, and the domination of so towering a figure as Graupner was quite enough to banish the frail shadows cast by the older Dutch family. There is, furthermore, no reason to suppose that Peter Jr.'s musical accomplishments were in any sense masterful. One senses that it was the circumstances of the time quite as much as any deficiencies that they may or may not have shown which denied them a long-continued and more considerable influence on the musical life of Boston. Certainly it was Peter Sr. who possessed the energy and the genius for organization; while he survived, the family occupied a reasonably prominent place in the professional, if not the social, life of the Boston circle.

An unexplained coincidence occurred in 1833, when a Von Hagen was listed as playing viola in the orchestra of the Tremont Theatre. Surely this was Peter, still at his "tenor," humble member of the pit orchestra! Where had he been these twenty-four years? Not in Boston proper, or the Directory would have recorded him. Still in his fifties, the last of a line of musicians, he was but a dim shadow of that which was bright with a Mozartian brightness in the gay 1790's. He died in Boston on September 10, 1837.

While a modest warmth and friendliness shines through the recorded personal and business affairs of the Graupners, no single glint of individuality enlightens our way as we try to capture some vision of the Von Hagen family. No word, likeness, or memoir bears witness to any of them as living beings; even the special mention that "Mr. Von Hagen has recovered from his late indisposition," or that "Mrs. Von Hagen, respectfully informs That she has returned from New York," conveys a sense of personality. The biographer may err in failing to discern more, but is it not a commentary on the careers of

---

Peter's aunt, though it would not surprise me if Burney's statement was wrong and that she was Mrs. Elizabeth Von Hagen.

the two musical families treated in this volume, that the one which seems most alive was also immeasurably successful when compared with the brief candle which was Von Hagen? [11]

[11] Von Hagen Sr. published his own compositions with few exceptions. They are listed, therefore, in Appendix I.

VI. MR. AND MRS. GRAUPNER

SOLID VIRTUES and the impress of uncommon talents exercised in a musically primitive society are more characteristic of Gottlieb and Catherine Graupner than any recoverable trace of the spectacular or the glamorous. Yet, when surveyed in the mellow glow of a candlelight era, a vision of more than ordinary radiance is generated by the memory of Mrs. Graupner as she trod the magic carpet which was the Federal Theatre stage or appeared, always as featured guest, in the concert halls of Boston and Salem. The rather severe and imposing bearing of her husband was fit counterpart, while together, reflecting an impression of kindly benevolence and dignified unaffectedness, they were as engaging a couple as one might meet in Boston's plain and dignified society. Much of the social life of their class remains unrecorded, for the Channings, Ticknors, Everetts, and others of the tight literary hierarchy seldom mingled with the essentially middle-class majority, while the mere names and facts attending the professional record of the theater or concert hall affords slight glimpse into the real lives of these active and influential persons.

A large portion of the factual material regarding Gottlieb Graupner is contained in a brochure compiled by Catherine Graupner Stone, granddaughter of the subject, and presented to the Boston Public Library in 1906.[1] Some of the statements have been questioned, but there is very little evidence to discount their authenticity, while the general accuracy of the statements made by Mrs. Stone is clearly substantiated by documents which she has painstakingly assembled.

Johann Christian Gottlieb Graupner was born between two and three o'clock in the afternoon of October 6, 1767, to Johann Georg and Anna Maria Agnesa (Schoenhagen) Graupner of Hanover. The family name is asserted to have been "Graubner," but birth records

[1] Copies were presented to the Library of Congress and to the New York Public Library. The work is in typescript and has never been published.

in the parish go back only to 1708, according to the superintendent, and further research into the family is therefore impossible, a regrettable fact since there is justifiable curiosity as to the possible distant connection of this branch of the Graupner family with that of the more famous Christoph Graupner, of Darmstadt, born in 1683. The father received his training as apprentice to the city musician of Hanover from 1743 to 1748 and was honorably dismissed; marriage followed in 1752 and Gottlieb was the third son, seventh of eight children, born between 1753 and 1771. It was virtually decided at the baptismal font three days later that the child would be an oboist, for two of the witnesses were accomplished oboists; they were Surgeon Johann Gottlieb Bohloke of the regiment and Gate-Secretary Christian Heinrich Wilde, the former dignitary contributing two of the Christian names.

With so excellent a musical background, the young man's talent soon warranted a post in the Hanoverian band, and he, too, received an honorable discharge in 1788. The reasons for the young man's departure from his native town are not clear, but it is known that there was an influx of Germans to England in these years, drawn there for various reasons, among them the increasing fame of Händel and the continuing Hanoverian character of the English court. The slender young man, free of obligations at home and companioned by a slender oboe, arrived in London before 1791. John Sullivan Dwight states [2] that Graupner played in the orchestra directed by Josef Haydn which introduced the "Salomon" Symphonies in 1791–1792; a very likely matter, since Haydn was at a London concert on March 2, 1791, with thirty-five or forty performers, and left in June, 1792. There is no official program of these events by which one may check the names of the orchestra members [3] as there is in the case of the great Händel Commemoration of 1784, but the legend that the intense admiration which Graupner constantly affirmed for Haydn was owing to his association with the venerable composer is plausible on every count. If the reader is willing to grant this premise, there is the added consideration that his direction of that master's works in Boston was authoritative, for Graupner's thoroughness in every department of his career would guarantee a meticulous execution of tempi and all other factors

[2] Winsor, *Memorial History of Boston* (1880–81).
[3] The British Museum knows of none.

entering into a faithful interpretation of such momentous works.

Graupner's stay in England lasted no more than four or five years, and at no time did he attain sufficient permanency of address to warrant inclusion in the city directories. His employment was for the most part with the theatrical orchestras, where he became well acquainted with the popular works of the day by Arne, Reeve, Mazzinghi, Arnold, Shield, Storace, Attwood, and others. From the life of A. P. Heinrich [4] some picture of the life of the theater musician in England may be derived, particularly at a later date, but it is a dull tale sufficient to prove that the ambitious and talented musician possessed of a strong business ability would not long be satisfied to remain as an obscure member of the pit orchestra in any English theater. The musicians who came to America in these decades were unusually talented, including among them George Gillingham, Alexander Reinagle, Henry Niebuhr, Dr. Jackson, James Hewitt, Jean Gehot, B. Bergmann, William Young, some of them of the "Hanover-Square and professional Concerts under the direction of Haydn, Pleyel, etc., London." Many of these were drawn here by the reputed excellence of theatrical companies engaged by new-world impressarios for the opening of important theaters in leading cities.[5]

Dwight writes, probably basing his account on the statement of Parker, that Graupner arrived at Prince Edward Island but found his way almost immediately to Charleston, South Carolina, where he speedily became a member of the City Theatre orchestra. The cultivation of music in this charming and enlightened city was not confined to the theater but gave scope to the presentation of concerts and balls, and in one of these we find the following entry to denote a first recorded solo appearance in this country:

Concerto on the Hautboy, by Mr. Graupner . . . Fischer

The concert was given by Messrs. Petit and Villars on March 21, 1795, for their benefit,[6] and was of full measure running over; Mr. Graupner was given a favorable place, as second item in Act II. The excellent Mrs. Pownall performed three times in public before dying of a broken heart, but the remaining performers have no subsequent connection with the career of Graupner. On the opening night of the

4 William Treat Upton *Anthony Philip Heinrich* (1939).
5 Sonneck has made much of this subject in his *Early Opera in America.*
6 Sonneck, *Early Concert Life in America,* p. 33.

following season, Nov. 9, he also played a concerto between the play
and the farce.

Mrs. Catherine (Comerford) Hillier was born in England, but of
her early life or first marriage nothing is known. Her father, according to Mrs. Stone, was an attorney at law, but the name of Hillier, or
any of its variations, is not given in the incomplete directories of
London. A reasonably exhaustive search into the theatrical bills of
the early nineties was unsuccessful in bringing to light any mention of
Mrs. Heelyer, Hellyer, or Hillier (as she was known professionally) in
London, but some of her early theatrical efforts were in very small
parts in Bath. Mr. Sonneck has cited the excellence of the theaters
at Bath, Salisbury, and at Bristol, and has suggested that many
of the players who came to America were from those towns. He also
cites a remark in the *Columbian Centinel* to the effect that much
pleasure was expected from the performance of Mrs. Hellyer "when
she can get the better of those palpitations which have been visible
every time she has appeared," and that her "elegant voice wants only
professional experience to make it captivating—study and a little
stage degagée will render highly agreeable." [7] This plainly suggests
that Mrs. Hellyer's experience on the stage had not been long, if Bostonians in the first year of their professional theater going were able
to detect these things. In fact, Mrs. Graupner never acquired a very
remarkable ability as actress, as numerous accounts testify, and her
chief talents were her handsome appearance, her good-natured charm,
and the sweet and powerful quality of her voice. These were—and remain today—adequate for a prosperous course in the theater, and
Mrs. Graupner did not lack for plentiful opportunities at the Federal
playhouse to cultivate a large and appreciative audience. At this time
she was but twenty-five years of age, according to the least conserva-
tive account which is contained in the notice of her passing; other
accounts would have her but twenty-one years old in 1794.

Mrs. Hellyer made her American debut in Boston at the Federal
Street Theatre on December 15, 1794, the opening night of the second
season at that playhouse. The company had been recruited for the
occasion by the manager, Charles Stuart Powell, who had been to England for the specific purpose of engaging English actors. Possibly

[7] Sonneck, *Early Opera in America*, p. 143.

Mrs. Graupner was one of his acquisitions from the Theatre Royal, Drury Lane; she remained for the entire season which closed towards the end of June, 1795. The management was nearly bankrupt, but the company was of good quality and Mr. Powell's direction marked by good taste; Mrs. Hellyer was the only one of their number to hold a Boston following for many subsequent seasons, and the remainder of the company do not figure large in the dramatic or operatic history of Boston. According to custom, Mrs. Hellyer sang in concerts during the spring; the first, on April 15, was a patience-exhausting program at which she was featured performer, for numbers at the end of the second and third parts are considered very favorable "spots." Mr. Mallet, already established in Boston although not one of the theatrical assemblage, was impresario, and Mr. Granger Sr.[8] was one of the soloists; therefore, two of Boston's then leading musicians became acquainted with the future spouse of their mentor and leader, Gottlieb Graupner. The second program occurred on June 18 for the benefit of Messrs. Jones and Mallet, with the leading male members of the theatrical troupe participating; Mrs. Hellyer represented the distaff side.

All these point to a successful season, and Mrs. Hellyer left for Charleston and the City Theatre, a transference of the Boston company nearly intact, but under the management of Mr. John Solee (or Sollee); to these were added others from New York and the famous company known as the "Old Americans." The orchestra, which included Graupner, was on hand to receive them. The company played regularly from November 9, 1795, to May, 1796, and thereafter intermittently through the last few days of June and early in July. Mrs. Hellyer's first role was that of Madge in *Love in a Village* on November 21. She was given singing roles for the most part, particularly those requiring the warmly feminine touch; never did she step before an audience to march, perform military drills, or other unladylike acrobatics as certain other singers were expected to do in the course of a performance.

Mr. Graupner's presence in the City Theatre orchestra has been noted; there he had made a name for himself as oboist and occasional conductor before the new recruits from the north arrived, including

[8] Frederick Granger and Jane Hughes were married Dec. 1, 1785. Granger may have been one of the many Hessian soldiers who remained in this country, but I have no evidence to prove it.

Mrs. Hellyer. Had they known each other in London, and was it love
at first sight? Both had a background of English experience and must
have accounted mutual friends in the theatrical profession. Mr.
Graupner's American sojourn had been extended a few months longer
than hers, and had ranged a little more widely. More definitely certain, however, are we of the musical ties effecting mutual interests
and leading the way to speedy courtship; the powerful voice and
promising musicianship, added to the quiet charm of the woman, answered to qualities in Gottlieb Graupner, for he is described as tall and
austere, with precise speech and manner. The quality of his musicianship surpassed hers but the fraternity of musically sensitive persons
was not a large one in any American city. Mrs. Hellyer is described
as "a beautiful blond with blue eyes and regular features," characteristics only partially borne out by the later wax likenesses in the Boston Museum of Fine Arts. A fine miniature of Mr. Graupner by William S. Doyle, made in 1807 and now in the same museum, presents a
pleasing appearance, however, and shows him prematurely gray in
accord with Parker's description. (See plate facing p. 24.)

Mr. and Mrs. Graupner were married in Charleston on April 6,
1796 during the City Theatre engagement. On her wedding day she
played Melinda in *The Recruiting Officer* and Betty in *The Irish
Tailor*. Thereafter, under the different management of West and Big-
nall's circuit, the company went to Norfolk for a period which began
in July and extended until late September; the last program of the
Charleston engagement on April 19 listed "Mrs. Hellyer" in the first
play and "Mrs. Graupner" in the second, an amusing slip of memory
on the manager's part, since they were not married between the acts.
Mr. Graupner's oboe solos, deferred through the winter, were resumed
the day before his marriage. In Norfolk Mrs. Graupner took a benefit
in *Doctor and Apothecary* with incidental numbers by her husband,
and from Norfolk the company moved briefly to Portsmouth. There,
on October 7 Messrs. Decker and Graupner announced a benefit concert "to their friends in Norfolk and Portsmouth" with a program
containing the Fischer Rondo (by desire). The entire program is interesting since it records the first concert following their marriage,
precursor of many others to come. The evening was a combination of
straight concert and afterpiece, for "The Wedding Ring" was an old
favorite.

Part I

A Grand Overture   Stamitz
A Favorite Song 'The Poor little Negro'
    by Mr. Prigmore.
A Sonata on the Pianoforte, by Mr. Letuz.
Sweet Nightingale, by Mrs. Graupner, accompanied
    by Mr. Graupner on the hautboy
A Violin Duet (Pleyel) by Messrs. Decker and Graupner
Finale   Le Duc

Part II

Concerto on the hautboy, by Mr. Graupner.
Bright Chanticler, a favorite Hunting Song,
    by Mr. Prigmore.
A French Song, by Mons. Doubillier.
(By desire) Fisher's Rondo with variations
    on the hautboy, by Mr. Graupner.
A Favorite Song by Mrs. Graupner.
What is Love? a favorite Duet, by Mrs. Graupner
    and Mr. Prigmore
The Concert to conclude with the Federal Overture.
To which will be added a Musical Entertainment, in two acts, called The
    Wedding Ring (not performed here these four years) . . .[9]

The company returned briefly to Charleston, where there were
changes in the personnel before starting a second season in Norfolk.
Both must have held the North affectionately in mind, for they soon
turned their steps toward Boston and arrived in time for Mrs. Graupner to join the Federal Theatre company as Laurette in *Richard
Coeur de Lion*. This was billed as "her first appearance these two
years" and took place on Jan. 23, 1797. The newspapers gave no
inkling of her improvement over the palpitations of former times, but
remarked on the musical portions of this work with music by Gretry,
and orchestral accompaniments by Mon. Labarre, that the choruses
were well done with plenty of volume and that the orchestra was improved. No names of performers were mentioned, so overwhelming was
the musical effect. This occasion, therefore, marks the return of Mrs.
Graupner and the engagement of Mr. Graupner in the city destined
to become their home for many years. They did not settle down at
once, however.

9 Sonneck, *Early Concert Life in America*, p. 60.

Salem, as Mr. Sonneck remarks, was virtually a suburb of Boston in these years, and showed mild interest in the stage. From June 21 to July 28 Mr. and Mrs. Graupner played in Washington Hall, "fitted up like a theatre" and gave the inhabitants a selection of musical pieces during and between the acts of the play. Here Mr. Graupner's oboe was raised in plaintive accompaniment to his wife's rendition of "Sweet Echo" and "How d'ye do" and other jejune ballads. Neither before nor since have audiences in the theater paid so much willing attention to the lovely strains of the oboe, and the pleasing spectacle of a handsome couple motivated by such sweet compulsion must have done much to dispel the opprobrium associated with the stage. In smaller hamlets boasting no real theater the importance of these concert items loomed far larger than in the principal cities.

Mrs. Graupner joined Solee's company headed for Philadelphia, playing two nights at the John Street Theatre in New York, but these appearances were her first and only ones in that city. The date of the engagement was August 18 and next performance, 1797. She returned to the Federal Theatre exactly a year and a day after her last debut in that company, joining a distinguished cast that included Mr. and Mrs. Harper, Mr. and Mrs. Pownall, Mr. and Mrs. Barrett. The role was that of Melinda in *The Recruiting Officer* by Farquar, a play never before seen in Boston, although Mrs. Graupner had played it in the South. Her roles during the next weeks included Sjisigambis, a vocal part, in *Alexander the Great; or, Rival Queens;* Lady Kinnegad in *The True Born Irishman* on the same evening, and Lady Grace in *Provoked Husband; Or, a Journey to London.*[10] The fateful and historic conflagration occurred on February 2 and a successful season was summarily interrupted, for the theater was burned to the ground. The company later moved to "Mr. Dearborn's Exhibition Room" to give a very few performances and then broke up, some of the members opening at the Haymarket Theatre on March third.

Deprived of his main source of income, Mr. Graupner turned to the several ways of his profession offering temporary promise of remuneration. He announced a concert by his wife for the 14th of March and at the same time advertised himself as available for instruction on the oboe, German flute, violin, and so forth in this manner:

[10] The biographical data in the footnote to p. 306 Sonneck's *Early Concert Life in America* has since become amended in several respects.

MR. GRAUPNER

most respectfully offers his services to the ladies and gentlemen of Boston to teach

VOCAL AND INSTRUMENTAL MUSIC

Having devoted his life to acquire knowledge in his profession, he flatters himself with giving entire satisfaction to those who honor him with their commands. He will wait on those who prefer taking lessons at their own houses, at such hours as suite their convenience or at his lodgings at Mrs. Granger's, Orange-Tree Lane.

Mr. Graupner also makes and repairs all kinds of musical instruments.[11]

This test of Boston's cordiality was happily met and Mr. Graupner was soon in great demand. Without delay he became the most accomplished professor in town. As the advertisements make plain, the pair were then lodging in rooms at the home of Frederick Granger, fellow musician. In the spring of 1799 Mr. Graupner had an address at No. 10 Jarvis' Buildings, opposite the "Sign of the Lamb," Newbury Street, and later the couple lived in Sweetser's Alley before taking a house of their own.

The promise of immediate occupation with a large school of pupils was temporarily delayed, however, by an engagement in Salem. Mrs. Graupner had meanwhile played a few roles at the make-shift Haymarket, but both arrived in Salem for the entire duration of the engagement which began on May 4 and closed on Independence Day. So busy was the popular actress, however, that she appears to have played in both cities during these months, for she opened in Boston in *The Agreeable Surprise* on April 16 and played occasionally through the first week of June; both newspapers and existing programs attest this extraordinary activity.

The busy town of Salem, far more concerned with commerce and shipping than with music and the theater, must have been embarrassed with the unaccustomed riches of a full cast and orchestra at their service. Boston's finest musicians, all members of the theater band, included Von Hagen, Frederick Granger, old Father Schaffer, and Mr. Graupner; each in his way sought a clientele, the latter gentlemen announcing a benefit concert at the New Concert Hall, Market Street, for the evening of May 15. This concert was designed to excite sympathy for the Graupners, who had been burned out by a melancholy fire in Boston, and the benefit was repeated in Boston at the Colum-

11 *Columbian Centinel,* March 3, 13, 17, 1798.

bian Museum on the twentieth.[12] With the return to Boston, the Graupners settled down, with no further departures; success attended the business and theatrical ventures of both and made for them an ever widening sphere of influence within the community. They ceased to be traveling Thespians, subject to the uncertainties and, at best, brief triumphs of the footlights, preferring to live as abiding members of a simple, prosperous town. Their choice was well-founded and the important years of Graupner's career as an American musician began at this point, those fruitful years that won him such tributes as "the pioneer of classical music in America," "educated professional musician sure of his elevated, artistic ground, incessantly preaching the gospel of true art," and "father of American orchestral music," all fair estimates of his career and his influence on the music of New England and, indirectly, of the country.

Mr. Sonneck has proved that concert life was at a low ebb in Boston, despite the lively presence of the Von Hagens, and that a concert by Mrs. Graupner was both a rare occasion for the public and a gamble on the part of the givers. The first concert at Bowen's Columbian Museum commenced an association which lasted for many years, Mrs. Graupner's final recital taking place there about 1818. A respectable auditory attended her concert in March, 1798, and the latent talent of the town hastily scrambled together to arrange other performances without the aid of the gifted visitors. Other concerts independent of the Graupners followed until Mr. Mallet enlisted both professionals and amateurs for a sacred concert in which Mrs. Graupner sang, for the first of many times, "Bright Seraphim" by Händel, and the gentlemen joined in a quintet for French horn, hautboys, and undivulged instruments in a work by an unnamed composer. Mr. Graupner's next benefit occurred on May 20 of the following year and thus the long tradition was founded.

Concurrently Salem audiences were cultivated but with appreciably

12 On Saturday, May 11, 1799, this item was printed in the *Columbian Centinel:* "This morning about five minutes past two a fire took in some out-buildings in the vicinity of Newbury street which in the course of three hours consumed thirteen dwelling-houses, a number of other buildings, beside damaging others. Mr. Graupner, among those whose names we have not at this early period been able to ascertain, were occupants of Mr. Jarvis' buildings. The loss in furniture and clothes is very considerable. . . . Mr. Jarvis' houses, we learn, were not insured, as reported. Many of the sufferers have claims on the beneficence of the public." The damage was later reported at $30,000.

less ardor after the restoration of the Boston theater, a segment of the current troupe giving a season in Salem from May 28, 1799, to the end of June; according to Sonneck interest waned and as an outlet for "between seasons" Salem was proven unsatisfactory. In all these benefit affairs the music was of a similar type, with the ballads sung in the theater serving again and again. Mr. Graupner repeated the Fischer concerto,[13] and one by Lebrun,[14] neither work a stranger to him; apparently few works were in his repertory, obbligatos to his wife's ballads excepted.[15] No oboe concerto by Händel or Haydn served him in all his long career.

One of the most persistent legends relating to Graupner concerns the introduction of a Negro song in blackface, alleged to have been sung by him in Boston on December 30, 1799. Unfortunately Graupner has become famous for this alleged novelty among persons who know no more about him. The fact is that Mrs. Graupner, not Mr. Graupner, sang the popular ballad "I Sold a Guiltless Negro Boy" as this notice indicates:

"End of Act 2d. the Song of 'The Negro Boy' by Mrs. Graupner."

The text of the song follows:

I Sold a Guiltless Negro Boy

The thirst of gold enslaves the mind
And selfish view alone bears sway,
Man turns a savage to his kind,
And blood and rapine mark his sway.

[13] Johann Christian Fischer (1732–1800), distinguished oboist. For some years at Dresden and in the service of Frederick the Great, he ventured to London and gave a concert at which J. C. Bach played the "pianoforte" for the first time. Fischer became a member of the Queen's band and a popular performer at all concerts, winning the King's special praise with Händel's fourth oboe concerto at the celebrated Commemoration in 1784. Mozart as a boy was enchanted with his playing but later criticized him severely both for his tone and for his compositions, which are so original that they introduce whimsical and extravagant passages. He married Gainsborough's daughter. Mozart wrote a set of variations to a minuet theme by Fischer.

[14] Ludwig August Lebrun, (1746–1790), one of the greatest of oboe virtuosi of the eighteenth century, a member of the Mannheim court orchestra. With his wife, the singer Francesca, he toured all over Europe and met with triumphant success, especially in London (1779) and Paris. He composed 7 oboe concerti, 12 trios for oboe, violin and bass, and other music for the flute.

[15] There is no evidence to substantiate the statement of John Tasker Howard that "No doubt he (Graupner) wrote some of the oboe concertos that he performed at concerts . . ." (p. 136).

Alas! for this poor simple toy,
    I sold a guiltless Negro boy.

His father's hope, his mother's pride,
    Tho' black, yet comely to the view;
I tore him helpless from their side,
    And gave him to a ruffian crew,
Alas! for this poor simple toy,
    I sold a guiltless Negro boy.

In isles that deck the western main
    Th' unhappy youth was doom'd to dwell,
A poor, forlorn, insulted slave,
    A beast, that Christians buy and sell.
To friends, that Africk's coast annoy,
    I sold a guiltless Negro boy.

May he, who walks upon the wind,
    Whose voice in thunders heard on high,
Who does the raging tempest bind,
    And wing the lightning thro' the sky,
Forgive the wretch, that for a toy,
    Could sell a helpless Negro boy!
            (*American Musical Miscellany,*
               Northampton, 1798)

Since the singer's point of view is that of a white person, there is no reason to suppose that Mrs. Graupner donned blackface for the occasion; she was not a comedian at any time in her career, and no example of blackface is to be found in the history of her subsequent theatrical experience. In "Gil Blas" (pantomine) immediately following this song, she played a country girl (white) and sang a song. Furthermore, the theater was hung with black in tribute to the Father of his Country and the whole entertainment concluded with a Monody on the Death of General Washington. The same bill, without the Monody, was given on Dec. 23, 1799, and on Jan. 1, 1800 "Gil Blas" was added to "The Roman Father" and the Monody. Oroonoko, Aphra Behn's tragedy dealing with a stolen African prince, was performed in Salem on May 16, 1798 but neither Mr. nor Mrs. Graupner are listed in the cast of this piece, although Mrs. Graupner performed in *The Romp*, which followed. On this occasion the incidental music was provided by Mr. Villiers who introduced "Sailor's Hobby, the Soldier's do. Scolds do. Lawyers do. Beaus do. Ladies do. and Ameri-

cans do. After the song a Hornpipe by Mrs. Solomon." It is to be
hoped, therefore, that the error will be henceforth corrected and that
the honor of introducing the blackface song will be given to the person who really merits it after these many years of misunderstanding.

As a composer, Mr. Graupner's few works belong to this period;
they are not very distinguished and do not entitle him to an honored
place on that score. Of the number and extent of his arrangements
we have no knowledge; none, at least, exist in the library of the Handel
and Haydn Society with his own copies of orchestral scores and parts.
These slender works survive:

Attic Bower, music composed by Gottlieb Graupner   Published 1802
Governor Brooks favourite Scotch March, engraved and composed by
                           G. Graupner
The new Ode, written by Thomas Paine, Esq. and music composed by
                           G. Graupner

These were all published by the firm, and the second one was copyrighted in a later edition "as sung at the Female Academy" (advertisement, Boston *Gazette* Nov. 30, 1802). To the above should be
added "Columbia's Bold Eagle," "a patriotic song, words by a gentleman of Salem—music by Mr. Graupner" on the program of a concert in Salem in 1799 and mentioned by Mr. Sonneck.[16] This does not
appear to have reached a wider public. There are references to other
music composed by him for special occasions, but it is most likely that
he chose well-known tunes to companion the verses of his contemporaries. In his pianoforte preceptor there are a half dozen examples by
Graupner but they are merely exercise pieces. Quite unlike his fellow
publishers in other cities, he did not compose as freely as did Benjamin Carr and James Hewitt.

An account of the benefit concerts which enlisted the services of the
Graupners is better treated in the chapter on "Concert Life" since
the most important musicales always concerned them directly. Suffice it to record that the spring of the year was regularly favored for
the purpose and that Mr. and Mrs. Graupner assisted the Von Hagens
on June 25, 1799, presumably in return for their aid in Boston on
May 20, and previously in Salem. Mrs. Graupner also sang on March
20, 1800, in Boston, and apart from the concert evenings there were
annual benefits at the theater. Thus the benefit taken on April 21 of

16 *Early Concert life in America*, p. 316.

that year is of interest to us for two things; the principal attraction of the evening was *The Spanish Barber*, in which the featured player sang Rosina in a setting reminiscent of Seville. The music to the Colman play was by Samuel Arnold, partly adapted and partly composed, first performed in 1777 and published in 1783. Secondly, in the afterpiece the two Misses Graupner, Olivia and Catherine, had small parts, and from this time forth these two children appear in spectacles and as child actresses. Mrs. Graupner made no further appearances that year in either concert or theater, for the first child of this marriage, Charles William, was born in the fall.

Teaching became a congenial occupation for Mr. Graupner since he was infinitely patient and properly dignified; he was on the job early in the day, ready for pupils at six in the morning. For many years he retained an association with the private academies in and around Boston, teaching at Mrs. Rowson's, Mrs. Haswell's, and Stearn's in the towns of Medford, Newton, and Charlestown, but seems to have stopped after 1809. The record of the Philharmonic Society is conclusive in suggesting the relationship of the conductor-teacher and his group of willing learners; without his particular talent all would have been lost. So greatly did he prosper that he envisioned the formation of a school with Mallet as fellow teacher and the recently immigrated Filippo Trajetta as head of the vocal department. Mallet had been in Boston for several years and had achieved some measure of success as organist and concert impresario; [17] the combination of French, Italian, and German-English talents in a single musical conservatory held promise of all-inclusiveness. In theory it worked excellently; in practice this was a disastrous embarkation and foundered without delay.

Graupner did not lack in vision and he was shrewd and cautious, as Mallet and Trajetta probably were not. Moreover he was steady of habit and faithful to duty throughout his years, but the other two were more noted for their eccentricities than for regularity of conduct, as a subsequent public notice implies with respect to Mallet.

---

[17] Mr. Sonneck believes that Mallet came to the States from Hispaneola about 1793, arriving in Philadelphia, where he played briefly in Wignell and Reinagle's company, in the same year. He settled in Boston in 1793. Colonel Oliver's remark that he was a "French gentleman of much respectability" might be placed beside a rather pointed notice which Mallet published in 1802 to the effect that "he shall at all times be assiduous to merit their esteem, by the regularity of his conduct" (*Gazette,* Nov. 15, 1802).

Early in 1801 these gentlemen, acclaiming themselves "Professors of Music," appended this notice to that regarding the circulating library:

N. B. The Musical Academy continues to open on Thursdays and Saturdays, and for the convenience of the young Ladies, the hours of instruction in the morning department are from 8 to 11 o'clock. The number of pupils of each department is restricted to eighteen.

> F. Mallet,
> G. Graupner,   } Professors of Music.[18]
> F. Trajetta.

The two days specified were free of theatrical performances, for at the time Graupner was a member of the Federal Theatre Orchestra. By this time, too, the Graupners had taken a house and hall at Rowe's Lane which they denominated the Musical Academy, and later the Musical Conservatory. So remarkable was the sudden prosperity of the newly formed institution that rearrangement of schedules was necessary to accommodate the numbers desiring instruction.

CONSERVATORY

The Subscribers most respectfully return their grateful thanks for the patronage and support which they have received in the Institution of their Musical Conservatory. Conceiving their attempt to be laudable, and the joint exercise of their professional skill to be conducive to the embellishment of female education, they flattered themselves with the hope of success; their hope is now happily realized; and they now with much satisfaction inform their friends, and the public, they are therefore obliged to open a second School for Young Ladies, and to alter the time of instruction for Young Gentlemen, viz. The new school for ladies will be on Mondays and Wednesdays from 3 to 6 P. M.; and gentlemen for wind instruments Tuesday and Friday evenings, same hours; the two other schools as usual.

They have for sale, at the Hall, several excellent Piano Fortes, Violin Strings, &c.

MALLET, GRAUPNER and TRAJETTA [19]

Boston, June 1, 1801
Conservatory, Rowe's Lane

A third school was opened the following April, but Trajetta had departed New England, eventually to find his place in Philadelphia, and a forthcoming change in aim and direction of the partnership may be perceived. The circulating library was given up, if, indeed, it ever

[18] *New England Palladium,* Feb. 3, 1801.   [19] Boston *Gazette,* June 1, 1801.

truly functioned, and a music press was installed. Here was the secret of Mr. Graupner's future success, together with the retailing of instruments undertaken according to the announcement of the previous June. An evening school for flute and clarionet was begun at three dollars entrance fee and eight dollars a quarter as special accommodation to young men. The effect of music on the New England breast was proclaimed in an editorial puff quoted from Shakespeare and immediately applied to Messrs. Mallet and Graupner: [20]

> Musick's sweet power can soften steel and stone,
> Make tygers tame and huge leviathans
> Forsake unsounded deeps, and dance, on sands.[21]

Here the imagination of the researcher must enter, for the firm foundered in short order, Mallet was cast off, and Graupner emerged master of his own fate and subject to no close affiliation until 1812 when another brief and unhappy partnership repeated the situation. The conviction is inevitable that Graupner was better off alone than in association with another. Had he been satisfied with his position as orchestra musician, occasional soloist, or arranger, his career as recorded thus far would not have come to pass. Obviously these were all preparations for an opportunity which he found and discharged amid conditions ripe for exploitation in Boston at the turn of the century. Even teaching was not a complete satisfaction to him, for leadership —without obvious showmanship—and an unchallenged competency in every task were his most conspicuous virtues. Mr. Mallet, on the other hand, was a gentleman of many talents, none of them conspicuously notable, and without any pronounced ability as leader or man of business. His knowledge of music could not be compared to that of Graupner, and without shrewd business acumen or all-round musicianship he could not long keep up with his partner. Furthermore, there is no evidence to show that Mr. Mallet possessed any share of the capital necessary to launch a business requiring expensive imported stock. The generalization is not too far-fetched that Mallet wished to emphasize the instructional aspect of the partnership, pos-

---

[20] *Ibid.,* April 15, 1801.
[21] The correct lines read:
> "For Orpheus' lute was strung with poet's sinews,
> Whose golden touch could soften steel and stones,
> Make tygers tame and huge leviathans
> Forsake unbounded deeps to dance on sands."

sibly after the pattern of the Paris Conservatory, while Graupner was increasingly concerned with the wholesale, retail, and publishing opportunities spread before them. He looked toward the London musician-merchants Clementi, Corri, and others as examples for his own salvation in Boston.

The separation of the two brought forth no explanations in the newspapers. Their notices were similar in style, appearing during the middle of November; Mallet had removed to Congress Street, and Mr. Graupner to 6 Franklin Street, an address which served him for a quarter of a century. Mr. Mallet went so far in a second notice as to state that "the Ladies are absolutely free to re-engage with either of the later partners they may prefer," [22] the deduction from subsequent events being that Mr. Mallet was *not* the preferred partner.

Boston's musical life was not very exciting for obvious reasons, among them the uninspired qualities of local artists. Late in developing an independent musical life apart from church affiliations, the town plunged headlong with increasing momentum until, within twenty years after the balance of power had shifted to favor secular entertainment, Boston was one of the most cultivated theatrical and musical centers in the States, absolute leader and prime influence in the realm of choral singing, although this too, it must be admitted, was preponderately of sacred cast. Mr. and Mrs. Graupner appeared at the opportune moment while the odds and ends of talent then at hand, or arriving later, turned toward this attractive pair of experienced leaders as naturally as flowers turn to the sun. Within six years of their arrival in Boston both had become ornaments to the theatrical and leaders in the concert life, while Mr. Graupner established himself as the town's first publisher and dealer in all departments of the music business and its most capable teacher. With all due credit to his business acumen, one primary factor was responsible for the continuance of his leadership in all these—his talent, his training, and his experience.

To the twentieth-century purist to whom a drama is literature for declaiming and an opera music for singing, without a middle ground in the realm of artistic production, it will be a shock to learn of the musical settings of certain ancient efforts by one Shakespeare. The celebrated tragedy of *Macbeth* was produced at the Federal Street

[22] *Independent Chronicle,* Dec. 13, 1802.

Theatre "with the original Airs, and Choruses of Matthew Locke, got up under the direction of Mr. Graupner." [23] The production concluded the season of 1800–1801, but frequent repetition in other seasons is evidence that the "four singing witches," including the director's charming wife, were a sensation. Mr. Graupner was not responsible for the later stagings of this, or of Dr. Arne's *Comus*, but the initial production under his direction was considered to be the finest of all. With a musician of such refined tastes in the earlier company, the special productions of this nature were turned over to him, since neither Mr. Von Hagen nor, presumably his predecessor, Mr. Trille Labarre, were competent to justify both Locke and Shakespeare in the same evening.

Mrs. Graupner's benefits never failed to inspire the newspapers with respect for the literary and musical worth of her selections. Perhaps too consciously literary are the cream puffs published in the *Gazette*:

The operatic entertainment, of the Prisoner, is also a production, ranking in the first class of scenic merit; and is with appropriate taste prepared for the benefit of an approved musical performer. But the sweet and powerful tones of Mrs. G. create an attraction beyond these adventitious claims; for melody increases in interest and allurement by the same repetition, which takes from comedy its charm and effect. [24]

These were the years of Mrs. Graupner's greatest successes in leading roles; while never a great actress, she had become assured and routined enough to sing such parts as "Rosina" in the *Spanish Barber*, and her "Sweet Echo," or "How d'ye do" had served her for several years. That they did not now fail her is attested in the editorial notice of April 13, 1803:

THEATRICAL

Mrs. Graupner's Benefit presents a respectable claim on the patrons useful and unobtrusive talent, and a powerful attraction to the Musical amateur.—The Comedy of "Secrets worth Knowing," was performed at Mr. Dickinson's benefit with distinguished applause. . . . The entertainment of the "Farmer" and the Musical Interlude, are calculated to display the powers of the Operatic performers. In "Sweet Echo," Mrs. Graupner has, on a former occasion, very highly distinguished the force and variety

[23] The *Macbeth* music is attributed to Locke, produced for Davenant's production in 1672.

[24] *New England Palladium*, April 22, 1802.

of her tones, and the correctioness of her science. In these requisites, she very much resembles the late Miss Broadhurst; and is certainly not her inferior. There is a liquid sweetness in some of her notes, which is peculiarly characteristic of both voices . . .

Sweet Echo is Mrs. G.'s chef d'oeuvre; and with the accompaniment of Mrs. Darley, it must afford a fine treat to the taste of a respectable audience.

As an index to the popular singing-actress's repertory it will be of interest to record a complete season at the Federal Theatre.

ROLES PLAYED BY MRS. GRAUPNER
FEDERAL THEATRE
SEASON 1800–1801

PLAY	ROLE	FIRST PERFORMANCE
Speed the Plough (Morton), Opening night Nov. 14	Lady Handy	Oct. 27
Rosina, or The Reapers (Mrs. Brooks–Shield, 1782), Opening night Dec. 12	Phoebe	Oct. 27
The Poor Soldier (O'Keefe–Shield, 1782)	Norah	Oct. 30, Jan. 16
School for Scandal (Sheridan)	Lady Sneerwell[a]	Nov. 3
The Adopted Child (Birch–Attwood or Von Hagen)	Clara	Nov. 3
Highland Reel (O'Keefe–Shield, 1790)	Jenny	Nov. 5, Mar. 11
Village Lawyer	Mrs. Scout	Nov. 7
Sighs, or The Daughter (Kotzebue, trans. by Prince Hoare)	Ellen	Nov. 10, May 6
Agreeable Surprise (O'Keefe–Arnold, 1781)	Laura[b]	Nov. 10
The Stranger (Sheridan)	Savoyard	Nov. 17, Nov. 21, Feb. 4
Castle Spectre (M. G. Lewis–Kelly)	Vocal part	Nov. 19, Nov. 28, Mar. 6, May 15

[a] Also played Mrs. Candour in other seasons.   [b] Played Cowslip in other seasons.

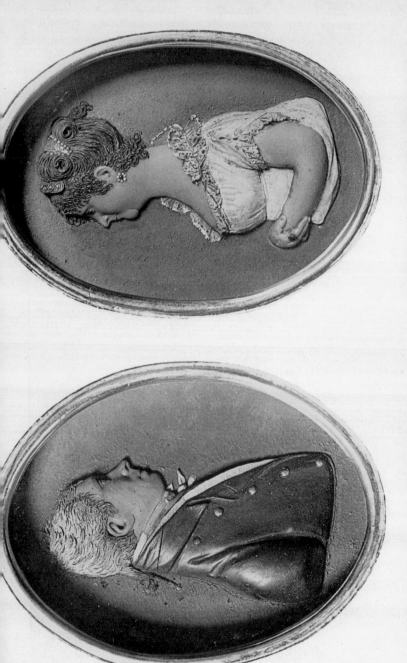

GOTTLIEB GRAUPNER
Wax on Glass Miniature by Rauschner

CATHERINE HILLIER GRAUPNER
Wax on Glass Miniature by Rauschner

PLAY	ROLE	FIRST PERFORMANCE
Preparations for the Cruise, or The Boston Sailor	Polly	Nov. 24
The Waterman, or The First of August (Dibdin–Dibdin, 1783)	Wilhelmina	Nov. 24, Feb. 18
The Purse, or The American Tar (adapted from Reeve by Hodgkinson, 1795)	Sally	Nov. 26, Jan. 14
Aurelio and Miranda (James Boaden–? 1798)	Zingarella	Dec. 1
The Padlock (Bickerstaffe–Dibdin, 1768)	Ursula	Dec. 3
Romeo and Juliet (Shakespeare) Solemn dirge at monument of Capulets, Act V.	Vocal part	Dec. 10
The Spoiled Child (Bickerstaffe–?)	Maria	Dec. 10, Apr. 13
The Votary of Wealth (T. G. Hofman)	Gangica	Dec. 12
Comus (Milton–Arne 179–) "with the song of 'Sweet Echo' accompanied on the hautboy by Mr. Graupner; music by Dr. Arne"	1st Bacchant	Jan. 21, 23
Maid of the Oaks (Burgoyne–Philidor, 1774)	Maria	Jan. 28
Zorinski (Morton–Arnold, 1795)	Winnifred	Jan. 30
Lock and Key (Hoare–Shield, 1790)	Fanny	Feb. 2, 4, 13
Every One Has His Fault	Mrs. Placid	Feb. 9, 27
Retaliation	Lucy	Feb. 11, 16, 23
Pizzaro in Peru, or The death of Rolla (Kotzebue, trans. by Sheridan–Kelly, 1799)	Virgin of the Sun	Feb. 18, 20, 23, March 2, 6, 23
Clandestine Marriage (Colman–Garrick, 1799)	Miss Sterling	Feb. 25
The Farmer (O'Keefe–Shield, 1789–92)	Betty Blackbury	March 4, 6, May 15
West Indian	Mrs. Fulmer	March 4

PLAY	ROLE	FIRST PERFORMANCE
Paul and Virginia (Kreutzer? 1791; Mazzinghi, 1800)	Jacintha	March 18, 25, Apr. 3
Way to Keep Him (Murphy)	Muslin	March 27
Obi, or Three-fingered Jack ("most of the music by Dr. Arnold," 1800)	Quathee's Wife	March 30, Apr. 22
Richard the Third (Shakespeare) Followed by Ode: The Passions by Collins	Duchess of York[c]	Apr. 6
He Would Be a Soldier (Philidor)	Mrs. Wilkins	Apr. 10
Castle of Sorrento (from Le Prisonier—Attwood, 1799)	Widow Belmant	Apr. 13
Cure for the Heart Ache (Morton)	Miss Vortex [d]	Apr. 15
Children in the Wood (Morton–Arnold, 1793[e])	Josephine	Apr. 15, 24
Garden of Love (afterpiece)	Hymen	Apr. 15
My Grandmother	Charlotte	Apr. 20
L'Abbe de l'épée (Boullay–Kemble)	Marianne	Apr. 22
Blue Beard (Colman–Kelly, Reeve, Paesiello, 1791, 1798)	Beda	Apr. 27, May 4
The Times, or A Scarcity of Cash (by a Gentleman of Boston)	Katy	May 8
Oscar and Malvina, or The Hall of Fingal (taken from the Poems of Ossian) (Reeve–Shield, 1791)	Shepherdess [f]	May 8, 13
Macbeth (Shakespeare—"orginal music got up under the direction of Mr. Graupner," by Matthew Locke)	Singing Witch	May 11
Alexander the Great, or The Rival Queens (?–Arne)	Vocal part	May 13

[c] Miss Graupner played the Duke of York.   [d] Mrs. Graupner's benefit.
[e] Benjamin Carr also wrote music to this opera.
[f] The Graupner children also in the cast.
Note: Mrs. Graupner did not appear between Dec. 12 and Jan. 21.

Further detail regarding the estimable place occupied by Mrs. Graupner in the company at the Boston Theatre [25] is unnecessary in view

[25] Called the Boston Theatre after 1803, when the Haymarket was demolished.

of the unvarying repetition of a constant repertory in standard roles. Many of her special moments have value only in relation to the occasion, which moments are duly mentioned in the chapter devoted to the theater. At the end of the season, April 18, 1805, Mrs. Graupner took leave of the company, returning two seasons afterward, but without attaining so great a distinction in featured roles. She returned on August 14, 1807 (the opening night) in *Love in a Village,* but the notice that this was "Her first appearance these four years" was not accurate.

Mr. Graupner's new musical warehouse prospered from the first, and a constant line of publications came from his press. Demands for his teaching led to hours, early and late, beyond the ordinary workman's day, while several afternoons were engaged by ladies' seminaries. In 1809 the Philharmonic Society was formed and the first permanent musical organization added to the civic life of Boston; the history of that struggling band is treated as exhaustively as researches permit in another chapter, and, as Graupner's favorite activity, is closely bound up with his career in these fruitful years. Here his leadership of the musical life in Boston was most clearly evinced, warranting this tribute in the press at the time of a benefit concert: "It should be added in justice, that the husband of this lady, has done more to improve the musical taste of this town, than any other person of his profession." [26]

The ladylike qualities of Mrs. Graupner were subject to public comment in a day when the strictest ideas were cherished in relation to female behavior and were not generally applied to actresses in the theater. Mrs. Graupner's benefits were "annually attended by the most brilliant and respectable circles of the community." [27] The esteem in which the pair was held is indicated by the fact that the officers of the Handel and Haydn Society had the thoughtfulness to send a cab for them on the evening of their first concert.

As the years of ripe maturity came to the celebrated lady, her excursions into the theater became briefer and she turned to the concert halls; it would appear that at times the theaters were turned into concert halls for her benefits. In 1810 her special evening had a concert interlude while the orchestra was augmented by additional members of the Philharmonic Society. Arias by Händel, newer ballads, and

26 Boston *Gazette,* April 26, 1810.   27 *Ibid.,* April 26, 1810.

the ever popular songs of olden times were on the program. I have suggested elsewhere that the removal of Dr. George K. Jackson to Boston, and his acquaintance with the resident musicians, was prima facie evidence for the sudden improvement in Mrs. Graupner's musicianship, for her repertory was immediately broadened to include some of the most sublime arias of the time, and she emerged from the theater to take her place as the leading vocalist in those struggling choral groups which soon found permanent organization in the Great Society. Dr. Jackson had few intimates, owing to the Olympian cast of his person which must have curtailed his sprightliness in getting around, and of his personality, which was acidic to a remarkable— and unpredictable—degree. But he found an intelligent musicianship equal to his own in that of the Graupners, who were the only ones in town worthy to approach him on equal terms and not suffer unceremonious humbling. Even Mr. Hewitt was unable to attain a continuously friendly association with them, owing in part to the strictly theatrical qualities of his musicianship which, it must be admitted, was ample, in contra-distinction to the broader knowledge of the others. The concerts given under the combined direction of Dr. Jackson and the Graupners in Boston and in Salem during the year 1812 must have been sensational, for no assemblage in Boston before that time—with a passing remembrance of the days of William Selby —had approached the efficiency of these. With Graupner in charge of the orchestra, the mighty Jackson at the organ, and Mrs. Graupner at the head of the vocalists, each department was capably managed and the music by Händel and Haydn would not fail them if given half a chance.

Mrs. Hellyer had three children before her second marriage, according to Mrs. Stone, who states that two, a boy and a girl, were left in England with her parents when she first came to America. Question may be raised, however, as to the complete accuracy of the statement, unless it can be explained that the girl later came to America, for on April 21, 1800, the Misses Olivia and Catherine were in a benefit with Mrs. Graupner. Olivia Hillier was the older of the two; she never married, but adopted the name of her stepfather and lived until 1872. Catherine's age is likewise uncertain, but she was the first organist for the Handel and Haydn Society during the rehearsals of

1815 and was at that time organist at Stone Chapel. She married George Cushing on November 14, 1818, in Trinity Church against the desires of her parents, for Cushing, born in Hingham in 1789,[28] was a morbid individual, of morose and sarcastic disposition; moreover he was ten years older than his bride, according to Mrs. Stone. This statement is open to question, however, for the programs surviving from a benefit performance at the theater for "Misses O. & C. Graupner" on April 21, 1800, and again in 1802 at a similar occasion, list the children as singing "Sailor Boy" and "He Pipes so Sweet," a feat unlikely to be undertaken by a child of three even in our own day of cradle-snatching stage mothers. Furthermore Mrs. Stone's record would have Catherine but fifteen years old when she played at Stone Chapel. The newspapers, with traditional New England devotion to the afterlife, carry no lists of births, but concentrate on the marriages and deaths, and there are no existing birth records for these years. Mrs. Graupner was busy in the theater most of the season, and Charles William was born the next year. It is fair to assume, therefore, that Mrs. Stone's statement that Cushing was ten years older than Catherine is incorrect, and that Catherine was a Hellyer, thereby accounting for two of the children originally left in England.

Charles William was born in 1800 and showed some promise as a musician; he played the violin and joined the Philharmonic Society, remaining among its members until his untimely passing at the end of November, 1824. Only rarely as a child does he figure in the theatrical notices of the day in company with his mother at annual benefits. Many of this numerous family passed on before maturity, among them the next two children, Samuel John George, born February 13, 1803, who failed to survive infancy, and Samuel Smith, baptized August 25, 1805, who died in Valparaiso, Chile, in the course of a futile attempt to regain his broken health. Frederick Lewis, named after Frederick Granger, also died in infancy.

John Henry Howard was born on June 17, 1810, and early showed interest in music. He practiced four hours a day, including holidays, under the strict supervision of his father and mother, both of them creditable pianists. A sudden change of interest, however, caused him

28 A statement in the *History of the Handel and Haydn Society* that "Mr. Cushing died in 1880 at the age of 94" would alter this to 1784, of course (Vol. I, p. 30n).

to attend the Episcopal theological school and then go to sea; eventually he settled in Boston as a music engraver for Ditson and enlisted in the Unitarian movement as an ardent disciple of the new faith. Since it is his daughter who wrote the life of Gottlieb Graupner quoted here at such length we may accept the facts regarding this member of the family without hesitation. John Henry Howard Graupner lived until 1886.

Frank (or Frederick) Lewis, born on December 8, 1811, went to sea but died on land in 1842, while the last child of this marriage, Charlotte Elizabeth Rowson, was baptized on December 26, 1813. Named after a close friend of the family, the author of *Charlotte Temple*, she became a noted pianist and organist in Boston; she was buried in the Graupner family lot. Three more children, born of Graupner's second marriage, will be mentioned in due course.

Mr. Graupner was naturalized in 1807, a simple process in those days. He visited the nearest police station, signed a book and obtained a certificate on the first Tuesday of October. The even temperament and constant progress of Graupner as merchant, conductor, and teacher in a rapidly growing community afford no remarkable personal instances on which we may profitably dwell, and the complete lack of autobiographical materials defeat any honest desire to add color and romance to a musician's career. This singularly unselfish gentleman is best explained in relation to his activities, manifold and varied enough in themselves. As his publications came steadily forth from the press, the inventories of stock mounted, the number of concerts increased and, after 1815, the conducting of the Philharmonic Society took much time and concentrated interest in connection with the Handel and Haydn Society. There is a court record of Graupner as successful plaintiff in cases involving the collection of funds for musical instruments. In October, 1816, the case of *Graupner* vs. *Thomas Savage* in the Court of Common Pleas was decided in his favor for the amount of $450, and similar cases were entered against Jane L. Jackson and George S. Jackson. Business grew steadily, reaching a culmination in 1818, but suffering a distinct setback in the less than a year when George Cushing was partner. Thereupon, for reasons not entirely clear, he sold much of his stock and virtually retired from active selling. There was no perceptible diminishing of public life for a while, since concerts were given in the Columbian

Museum where Mr. Bowen offered the Graupners as added attraction in a morbid setting of plaster statuary, old bones, and minerals. In fairness, Mr. Bowen's place of resort must be described as having a hall in the lower part of the building which separated the living from the dead, but one admission price covered all. Hardly a week passed without an opportunity for singing or playing either at the Saturday meetings of the Philharmonic Society, at the oratorio of the great choral society, or other concert in Boylston or Pond Street halls. There are doubtless instances of concerts given in surrounding towns of which we know nothing at this time, for the reputation of this favorite pair was widespread. Mrs. Graupner's name often occurs as participating in the concerts of the Female Orphan Society (her favorite charity), the Charitable Fire Society, or other humanitarian undertaking. Mr. Graupner did not describe as large a circle in the course of his peregrinations as the Von Hagens, who ranged the countryside in a weekly tour of the provinces, but he was surprisingly active at the various seminaries and academies about town and in the immediate suburbs. At various times he was advertised to teach at Medford Academy, then under Mr. Angier's direction, and, of course, in the Young Ladies' Academy which Susanna Rowson conducted as the most polite school in Boston.

For twenty-five years, or the first quarter of the century, Graupner remained the unquestioned leader of all musical forces, and the most esteemed musical scholar of the town. He organized and conducted the first permanent orchestra in this country, forming by his constant, and insistent, concentration on Haydn and the early Viennese classicists, the standards of taste which have remained foundational to all subsequent musical development in Boston. He was among the group which called together the Handel and Haydn Society, although he remained apart from its directorship throughout the years, preferring to restrict his support to the orchestra which functioned at rehearsals and in performances from the first concert onward. His attitude was strictly that of a professional musician whose services were to be engaged and paid for, and the records of the society show the value in which his particular contribution was held. His concern for his fellow musicians in the course of their professional round reveals him as aware of the fairness of an attitude which views the laborer as worthy of hire. Charity was another thing, and neither Mr.

nor Mrs. Graupner were lacking in support of organizations or individuals in need of assistance. In later years his own record on behalf of others availed him much, for the public turned to aid him in his
distresses. Thus the years passed without great change but not without many events occurring each season to further the musical development of the town and to establish the musical standing of professional
and amateur musicianship among its citizens.

These years, however, brought their sorrows, and Mrs. Graupner
passed on in 1821 as this notice attests:

DIED

In this town, on Saturday evening last, Mrs. Catherine, consort of Gottlieb
Graupner, in the 52nd year of her age.[29]

The stone now marking her last resting place gives her age as forty-
nine years, but the church records give fifty-two years. Mrs. Graupner had not sung often after the year 1818, when success enabled the
Handel and Haydn Society to import singers of first rank, and the
theater had immeasureably improved its standards. It is not unlikely
that her voice had lost much of its earlier attraction.

A eulogy on the merits of Mrs. Graupner derived from all available
sources could in no wise better the sentiments expressed with deep
feeling in *The Euterpeiad* of June 9, 1821:

OBITUARY

It is not within our original design to notice the demise of any individual.—We are however constrained to remark, that the usefulness and talents of one who has filled so conspicuous a station in the musical world,
demands a record of those services which have on all occasions contributed
so essentially to endear her memory to a very numerous and much extended
acquaintance.

MRS. CATHERINE GRAUPNER for many years was the only female vocalist this metropolis possessed. Of the deceased, it may be truly said, Her
urbanity of manners, obliging and hospitable disposition, was a general
theme of observation. Her memory will be dearly cherished by those Orphans and friendless children, whom she so readily received under her
kind care, and to whom she was so constant in her protection.—She was
an affectionate wife, a kind mother, a sincere friend, and a true believer in
the merits of our blessed Redeemer.

The Grave has closed over all that was mortal, of this truly benevolent,
and sincerely penitent Christian. Her friends, and the musical part of the

29 *Columbian Centinel.*

community in particular, whom she has so often charmed with her earthly
song, hope, she is now imploring with heavenly fervour,

"Angels ever bright and fair
To take, take her to their care."
Where,
"The bright Seraphims in burning row
Their uplifted Trumpets blow;"
And where
"The Cherubic host, in tuneful choirs
Touch their immortal harps with golden wires."

After this time, marked by his partial retirement from public life,
attention was given Mr. Graupner in recognition of his services to the
cultural life of Boston, and in the fall of the same year a benefit concert was given with copious notices appearing in the paper to testify
the esteem in which he was held. Of the several notices these are typical,
reflecting in their sentiments the same approbation lately bestowed
on the memory of his wife.

Mr. Graupner's Benefit Concert

Upon the suggestion from several of the most particular friends of Mr.
Graupner seconded by an official communication from one of the principal
institutions in this metropolis, the public concert is announced for the
evening of the 20th inst. at Boylston Hall in compliment to the long tried
and much proved services which Mr. Graupner has on all occasions rendered the community. We hope this attempt to reward distinguished talents
will receive proper attention from the parents of the pupils of Mr.
Graupner.

Sat. Intelligencer [30]

For the Palladium.
Messrs. Editors.

I am highly gratified that Mr. Graupner has complied with the solicitations of his friends to give a concert this evening in Boylston hall; and
that there is so much interest excited in the public feelings in favor of a
proposition which will afford to a large number of gentlemen and ladies
of this metropolis an opportunity to testify their high sense of superior
talents and merit by continuing performance.

As Mr. Graupner is well known to the citizens of Boston it is scarcely
necessary to say that for fifteen or 20 years he has not only been constantly
considered an industrious, able, and successful instructor in music and
uniformly maintained the character of a gentleman but to the knowledge of
the writer of this article oftentimes readily, cheerfully, and gratuitously

[30] *New England Palladium*, Nov. 16, 1821.

proferred his consummate talents in celebrating the anniversaries of various charitable, religious, and other societies in this town; has taken a distinguished part at the various concerts or exhibitions of music performed in Boston or vicinity; has given sufficient aid to the many ordinations and has been conspicuously useful in the musical activities at almost all our public festivals. It is therefore readily and generally granted by all who are acquainted with Mr. Graupner's talents and services that his claims upon the public are much greater than those of any other gentlemen of his profession in this town and vicinity. And I conceive it would be an impeachment of good feeling and good sense for Bostonians to suppose for a moment that they will suffer for an opportunity so favourable to expressing their deep sense of appreciation and gratitude and their respect for a worthy citizen to pass unimproved.[31]

The Philharmonic Society assisted in a program comprised of numbers chosen and rehearsed by the beneficiary and augmented by many visiting talents headed by the majestic Dr. George K. Jackson, himself not long destined for this world. The recipient of so flattering a benefit must have been vastly comforted by so sympathetic a recognition of his influence.

Mr. Graupner's grief was not long observed, however. His business had suffered a decline before this and was virtually at a standstill, while, other than in connection with the above-mentioned benefit concert, his name does not figure in the public prints and no publications appear to have been issued. Even the Philharmonic Society ceased to attract press notices and my deduction would be that a series of personal misfortunes visited him with overwhelming results. The curtain need not be long down, however, for his mourning was relieved by courtship, and he married with a minimum of delay as this notice briefly reports:

MARRIED

In Providence, Gottlieb Graupner, Esq. to Miss Mary Hills, only daughter of the late Capt. John H. all of Boston.[32]

The second Mrs. Graupner had no claim to popular favor and was known, if known at all, for her private and domestic virtues.

Three children were born of this marriage—the first, Harriet Hills Graupner, on December 15, 1823. She became the "finest woman pianist in America" according to Mrs. Stone, but never played in public. Her modesty, and disdain of a public career, limited her audience; she

31 *New England Palladium,* Nov. 20, 1821.   32 *Ibid.,* Oct. 4, 1822.

is said to have received as much as five dollars an hour for playing to individuals in their homes. The second child, Stephen Hills, married into the well-to-do Loring family of Boston, and the third, Charles, died while very young.[33]

The quiet disposition of this gentleman was the more pronounced in the years following his second marriage, and he retired from those phases of active life—with one exception—which had kept his name prominently before the public in earlier years. A slight evidence of his participation in the cultural life of the community, other than that connected with his own major interest, is shown in the exhibition of contemporary painting held at the Athenaeum in 1827, in which a painting of "Miss Graupner" was hung. As conductor he had acquired a standing sufficient to give him occupation among amateur groups of instrumentalists other than the Philharmonic, and in 1823 another benefit concert was elaborately prepared for him by his enthusiastic followers at Neponset where he directed, apparently without remuneration, for some time. The attached notice promises a repetition of works by Händel, Haydn, and the lesser Englishmen already in the repertory of the coöperating societies.

ORATORIO

A public oratorio will be performed by the Neponset Sacred Music Society at Rev. Dr. Harris' meeting house in Dorchester on Sunday evening, 12th inst. The pieces to be performed have been selected from the most celebrated composers. Members of the Handel and Haydn Society and of the orchestra have politely tendered their services on this occasion.

The performance of this oratorio is intended for the benefit of Mr. G. Graupner. The services and talents of this gentleman have been gratuitously rendered to the Society from its formation to the present time. To evince the estimation and regard for his personal services and endeavors in the diffusion of the science of music the society proposes to give this oratorio.

M. MANDELL, Sec'ry.[34]

33 "Yesterday morning, Charles E. Graupner, son of the late Gottlieb G. 13½ yrs. Funeral from Trinity Church tomorrow afternoon immediately following Divine service. The friends and schoolmates of the deceased are respectfully requested to attend." Boston *Transcript,* Oct. 23, 1841.

Mr. Henry L. Mason has a letter written by Lowell Mason to his son, then in school in Kentucky, stating that "all the boys went" to the funeral. "The boys" were pupils at Mr. Thayer's school, now Chauncy Hall.

34 *Columbian Centinal,* Oct. 8, 1823. Mandell, proprietor of a private school at this date, turns up the next year as a teacher of music in Boston and Charlestown. The Neponset Society had other concerts on Nov. 16, 1823, and Feb. 29, 1824.

Worthy of note is the attendance of the Governor and his family "among the numerous and respectable auditory."

The career of the Philharmonic Society came to a regrettable end during the latter part of the decade. Another generation was at the helm, and the theater was a going concern nearly every evening of the week, affording fewer free evenings for social and musical pleasures of a non-professional nature. Moreover tastes had changed—although Mr. Graupner would be unlikely to have considered them improved—and the tuneful overtures and arias of the lesser Italians were arousing no end of enthusiasm. The symphonies of Haydn were no longer sufficient to interest the public, and the scores of Mozart were still too exacting and too refined for audiences or orchestras. Moreover, the scores of Mozart's operas were known only through garbled versions by Henry Rowley Bishop. Mr. Graupner's interests did not markedly develop with the years; he held on to that which he could hold, and the remainder slipped from under his feet while other conductors set the style and pace. Overtones of financial embarrassment are to be found in the announcement of his benefit in 1825, for a newspaper editorial comments: "Such artists have a claim upon society and patronage should be extended to keep them above the exigencies of life. They should never appeal in vain. It belongs to the public to see them well bestowed." The customary tone of warmth is evident, however, and the notice further states that the good man's scholars, "not a few in number" are solicitous of his welfare and desirous of a general attendance. Mr. Graupner's own notice is brief and modestly to the point, but a subsequent panegyric notes that he has "troops of friends," and that a full orchestra, together with a number of gentlemen amateurs have volunteered their services to the end that "a rich repast may be anticipated by the musical literati and tasteful lovers of song." [35]

The program is interesting for the participation of Miss Graupner (presumably Charlotte Elizabeth Rowson), who played variations by Latour, and Miss and Master Graupner (probably John Henry Howard), who played a duet by Ries and a "Duett, vocal" by Beethoven, further particulars unrecorded. The orchestral numbers show no progress over those played nearly twenty years before; Kreutzer's "Lodoiska" Overture, and Haydn's "Military" Symphony still led the field. Tickets were available at Mr. Graupner's store, Franklin Street,

[35] *Columbian Centinel,* April 30, 1825.

which address was also his residence. This was the last instance of his address being given as Franklin Street, and in 1827 he was at No. 1 Province House Court, established in an Academy.

MR. GRAUPNER

Intends to give instruction in music on Thursday and Saturday afternoons in addition to his regular school of Monday and Thursday mornings for the accommodation of young ladies who do not wish to interfere with their school hours. His afternoon school will commence on Thursday at half past two o'clock P. M. Apply at his Academy, No. 1 Province House Court.[36]

At this address publishing once more became an important factor in his work, approximately twenty pieces being issued. Still there is the impression to be gained from yearly benefits that Graupner's prosperity was well around the corner and headed in another direction. He had played in many benefits for others in his day, but usually in aid of individuals or institutions known to him and not for utter strangers. The monumental respect due him in Boston must have inspired this program given by the French opera company from New Orleans at Concert Hall on August 23, 1828. The company was about to open a season in a city to which French music and culture was unknown, or under suspicion, and a benefit to so worthy and circumspect a gentleman as Mr. Graupner might easily have created a salutary effect on the commercial aspects of the engagement. While doubtless appreciative, Mr. Graupner must have felt very strange indeed in the company of these artists and composers, except for the very welcome Haydn:

Overture to La Fete da (!) Village	Boildieu (!)
Song by Miss Gillingham—"Adieu thou lovely youth"	
Variations, clarinet, Mr. Schott—	Cramer
Duett—Ah se di mali miei—Miss Gillingham and Mr. Paddon	
Concerto, flute, Mr. Jandot	Drouet
Grand symphony full orchestra	Haydn
Solo, horn,	Mr. Proerchel
Song, Miss Gillingham, Sommo Cielo with violin obligato, acc. by Mr. Elie	
Variations flute, Mr. Jandot [37]	
Overture Delia et Verdikan, full orchestra	Berton

The orchestra under the direction of Mr. Paradol of the French Theatre.

36 *Columbian Centinel*, Sept. 12, 1827.
37 The copy of this program in the Boston Public Library bears the notation that this number was omitted.

Mr. Graupner as an avowed object of charity is not to the taste of those who, having followed with respect the dignity of his career, would rather see him well disposed in later years. The rather pathetic concerts, preceded by well-intentioned but obviously plain messages in the press, were evidence enough in themselves that only humble necessity could direct such affairs. Mr. Graupner several times presented his daughter Harriet Hills as child prodigy and on occasion his son Henry Howard, both pianists. Works by Haydn, and the forgotten "Battle of Prague" (stripped of its trappings and rendered with violin and violoncello accompaniment) [38] were reminders of the olden days before Rossini succeeded to his greater glory, while Weber's modern Overture seemed out-of-place in a Graupner program, even though the date was 1830. The concluding paragraph of an announcement was crowning indignity to one who had lived as shield and defender to all his kind. "A very efficient and Full Orchestra, composed for first rate performers, will assist on this occasion, and every exertion will be used to make it interesting to those disposed to patronize the object." Mr. Graupner as *object of patronage!*

Mr. Graupner was content to resume his place as humble player of the double bass in the theater orchestra on occasion, but probably not with great regularity. The last mention of his name in this capacity was in 1832 when the theater augmented the regular players for special performances of Italian operas. The year before, however, he resumed his favorite occupation, that of conducting the Music Professional Society in ten regular concerts, and so earnestly followed this calling that he envisioned a permanent organization and introduced a bill before the state legislature to incorporate the new orchestra. The bill was speedily approved, but the project seems not to have been established.

The Boston of 1835 was a remarkably different city from that of 1797, or of 1820, for that matter. The limited and tentative gestures toward introducing music into the life of the town had met with gratifying success; as enthusiasm was engendered by the small, ever-growing circles, confidence was gained, a public was wooed and won far beyond the aptitude of certain of the founders to keep up with the

38 "The Battle of Prague" was originally written for piano, with optional parts for violin and violoncello, with trumpets and kettledrums indicated, but Boston had been accustomed to hear it full panoplied.

progress which their own efforts had stimulated. A glance at the development of music in Europe, particularly in Germany and Italy, is sufficient to show the impact of a new order from the days of Haydn to that of Schumann, Wagner, and Berlioz. Beethoven, Schubert, and Weber had all finished their work; Rossini, Spohr, Marschner were in their prime; all of these, with rare exceptions, bespeaking a circle unknown to Graupner and his ardent music-loving friends. The growth of music was not an isolated or forced growth. All the arts, many of them native, had progressed with equal rapidity. From the longer view of the present time we may say that America did not have a literature in 1800, but that in 1835 the names of Bryant, Irving, Hawthorne, Cooper, and even Emerson and Thoreau had begun to lay a firm foundation of national heritage. And so the comparisons run in the subjects of economics, politics, and education. Thirty years in the history of nineteenth-century America—particularly the first thirty years, provide a wide panorama, and another decade in the history of music in America brings us through the introduction of Beethoven's nine symphonies.

None of Graupner's old-time friends were present to companion him during the last decade of his life. Dr. Jackson had passed on the year after the first Mrs. Graupner had broken the firm bond of musical leadership; the old musicians of the Philharmonic group were long since departed, while the brilliant newcomers, like Louis Ostinelli, had gone their several ways. Kendall was the only remaining name listed in an orchestral program of 1833, and he had never enjoyed the privileges of the inner circle of Graupner's friendships. One senses the older fashion represented by Graupner's tastes in music, his mild disapproval of the romantic elements in this "modern" idiom, his grave perplexity as to the future of an art so hotly pursued, wherein the professional view became so extreme as to endanger the dignity and respect due it. In spite of the increasing prosperity of music as a business and profession, Graupner was unable to find a great measure of success in the midst of so much bustle and activity. His estate amounted to less than one thousand dollars—less than the profits of two Handel and Haydn Society concerts given twenty years before! His name must have occurred to the minds of the musicians of Boston frequently, as an afterthought but not as a present reality, and the young men must have privately questioned whether this man really knew much anyway. Even the public lamentations tendered his estimable wife were omitted in 1836 when a simple record dispensed this information, not in all respects correct:

DIED

In this city on Friday, Mr. Gottlieb Graupner, Professor and teacher of music, about 70. Mr. Graupner was a native of Germany but has resided upwards of 30 years in this city where he was equally well known for his musical skill and acquirements as for his private virtues.[39]

The funeral was held in Trinity Church, Summer Street on April 20, and he was buried under St. Matthew's Church, South Boston; when that building was demolished in 1866, his body was removed with others of his family to 630 Heber Walk, Mt. Hope Cemetery, West Roxbury. Here also rests one of the closest friends of the Graupner family, the noted Susanna Haswell Rowson.

[39] *Independent Chronicle & Boston Patriot,* April 20, 1836.

VII. DR. JACKSON

IT WOULD BE EASY to portray Dr. George K. Jackson, Doctor of
Music, as a ripe combination of Dr. Johnson and Mr. Micawber,
a blend of genius, unction, and avoirdupois—all contributing in
liberal measure to the very full stature of this man of parts. Of his
words we have but the briefest surviving memorial, but there is no
mistaking his tone, which was indubitably imperious to all and sundry.
For all his monumental person, and with due consideration for the
profundity of his wisdom and knowledge—a combined musical genius
the like of which had never before been seen upon these shores—his
manner under threat of extreme duress could be described as astonishingly fleet. Surveying the man all in all, no better description fits the
picture as it forms in mind than that applied to a major public exhibit placed in the Columbian Museum in these very years: "The form
of the Lion is strikingly majestic, and his figure is respectable, his
looks are determined, his gait is steady, and his voice tremendous."

Dr. Jackson was undoubtedly too big for the primitive state represented by Boston's musical life, nor could he have been completely at
home in any other city than the London where he spent his early years
and from whose precincts he fled for reasons which, be they simple or
complex, remain undisclosed. His best talents were unused in America,
for condescend he would not to the general level about him, and there
were none to approach his measure of understanding in the practice
of those grand and solemn works of the immortal Händel, or to share
the exactitudes of the sacred chant as revealed at such a fountainhead
of the Church of England, as Westminster Abbey. Boston's church
organs, respectable in themselves, were not to be compared with the
mighty instruments commonly found abroad, and in despair at their
limitations, the good Doctor took to playing the carillon as joint
effort to the mighty utterance demanding expression in his own soul.

This Falstaffian colossus of three hundred pounds—"this very in-

carnation of obesity," as Colonel Oliver explained him—leavened the
musical life wherever he deigned to make brief repose. Inevitably the
multitude parted to make way for his imposing musicality as it appeared briefly in a half-dozen cities along the Atlantic coastline from
Alexandria, Virginia, to Boston, Massachusetts, arriving in 1812. As
a dragonet he was almost—but not quite—captured by the unstable
lines of the professional web in these cities, but he broke away, urged
on by feeble promises of greater opportunity and understanding in
the next, northward metropolis to come. Tired, discouraged, but with
the flame still waiting to be fanned into usefulness, he arrived in Boston, only to be persecuted and driven posthaste from its horrified
confines for the duration of the war. But rising above the temporal influences of political intrigue he returned to Boston, spending his declining years there and leaving several memorials of his benevolent
interest, of editorial prowess, teaching abilities, and of personal idio-
syncrasies. Although he had neither led nor controlled any organized
band, his passing created a mighty void, for his survivors seemed like
a race of little men by comparison with his unapproachable eminence.

The early part of Dr. Jackson's earthly career must be taken on
the word of John Rowe Parker, a word which may be supposed to be
accurate as far as it goes. He reviews the career of our hero in his
Musical Biography, published in 1824, a work containing reprints of
several parts of *The Euterpeiad* and adding other miscellaneous accounts incidental to the musical life of Boston. Parker, as an ardent
admirer of the great Doctor and, in all probability, as one of the few
to share his confidence in friendship, may be relied on to provide a satisfactory resume. Ergo, Dr. Jackson was born in the university city
of Oxford, England, in 1745. At nine years of age he was placed under
the superintendence of the celebrated Dr. Nares (appointed to the
Chapel Royal in 1756), with Dr. Arnold,[1] Dupuis,[2] and Raynor Taylor [3] as fellow students. He remained with Nares until 1773, when he
was appointed a surplice boy at the King's Chapel Royal. In the
course of long continuance in that post, he served as a tenor singer at
the grand commemoration of Händel in 1784. This fact is substantiated interestingly in the records of that memorable event,[4] for Jackson's associates included other celebrated names frequently occurring

[1] Samuel Arnold, born 1740.   [2] Thomas Sanders Dupuis, 1733–1796.
[3] Born 1747, came to Philadelphia 1792, died there 1825.
[4] Program in the British Museum.

in these pages. Calcott, Shield, Samuel Webbe, and Watts were among
the singers, as was one J. Wheatley, possibly the actor who visited
America early in the new century. The orchestra listed "Mallet" as
bassoon, and "Neibuker" as trombone. This was certainly Francis
Mallet who came to America early in the nineties and settled eventually in Boston. The other is surely Neibuhr, long resident of Boston,
member of the Federal Theatre orchestra and of the Philharmonic
Society. Since Mallet's talents knew no limitation—he performed on
the bass, on the sistre, pianoforte, violin, and on the voice, as occasion demanded or opportunity afforded—it is not unlikely that an
assignment on the bassoon offered no unsurmountable problem to so
well-rounded a musician, while the immediate cordiality established
between him and Graupner, on the latter's arrival in Boston, points to
a previous acquaintance with each other, or with similar associations,
in London.[5] The orchestra of the Handel Commemoration furthermore included Mazzingy (Mazzinghi) and Gillingham as violins, and
Reinagle as violoncellist. The two latter gentlemen became leading
figures in the development of Philadelphia's brilliant theatrical and
musical life. None of these appear in London directories during the
period 1780–1795, nor are the names of Jackson, Graupner, or Van
Hagen entered there, a reflection on the incompleteness of the directories rather than on the fact that all these men were present in the
capital at some time during that period.

Dr. Jackson received his diploma from St. Andrew's College in
1791, according to Parker,[6] and migrated to America in 1796. He
arrived in Norfolk, but remained there only a short time, removing to
Alexandria, where the abundant cultural life already showed a perceptible decline in its sphere of influence, since the new republic tended
to discount the strongly English complexion of its society. The pilgrim in search of a home next visited Baltimore, and then Philadelphia,[7] but his stay in these towns was not of long duration; he seems
to have made a definite settlement in Elizabethtown, New Jersey, however, before arriving in New York where he remained for several years
in active and constant employment as teacher and organist. For part

5 Graupner did not leave Germany until 1788.
6 St. Andrew's is at St. Andrews, Scotland; there is no such college at either
Cambridge or Oxford, but the Scottish University is an ancient and honorable institution.
7 See L. C. Madeira, *Annals of Music in Philadelphia* (1896).

of that time, at least, he resided at 278 Bowery and carried on a business at 17 Dey Street.[8]

Marriage in 1787 to the eldest daughter of Dr. Samuel Rogers, physician, of London, resulted in the birth of eleven children to the couple. It would be contrary to the tendency of the time, in which the mortality rate was distressingly high, to infer that all survived, but since Dr. Jackson was above the exploitation of his progeny for the purpose of recitals on all and sundry instruments there is no juvenile record of their ages or nomenclature. Samuel, Charles, and Edwin W. were arrived at maturity in 1822, and the last two resided in Boston.[9]

Custom may have tempered these things, but in 1810 the comparative equality of Boston and New York in respect to size and importance palpably influenced many persons to regard the other city as more desirable. James Hewitt vacillated between the two, and for a time Mrs. Von Hagen, Miss Sophia Hewitt, and S. P. Taylor seemed undecided as to which was center and which circumference of their activity. According to report, Boston was represented to Dr. Jackson as being a more favorable place for his professional well-being, and he removed from New York early in September, 1812, an act requiring no further argument that New York had proved disappointing in its net contribution to his success. The most sympathetic defender of Boston's august merits cannot but feel that Dr. Jackson would have escaped much of the indignity visited upon him almost immediately had he remained in New York, where sympathies were broader and political feelings did not run so high.

An encouraging scene awaited the arrival of this paragon of musicality. He was assuredly not unheralded, and his reputation, like a strong wind caused by a large moving object, must have aroused great anticipation and instilled a little fear in the bosoms of the earnest band met to greet him. Imagination would like to fancy the populace turning out en masse to view the mighty man, come like a ship under full sail with many children, bound volumes of Händel's celebrated oratorios, grand pianoforte, and other paraphernalia incidental to a private musical establishment. And yes, in the background, somewhere

[8] The materials for study of Dr. Jackson's career in New York are quite as readily available as are those for his Boston experience; that important phase may well provide a chapter of its own. However, in view of consistent adherence to the New England scene in this study, the intervening period is omitted.

[9] There is no evidence to support the statement that "two of his [Jackson's] sons came to Boston before him and established a music store in 1800."

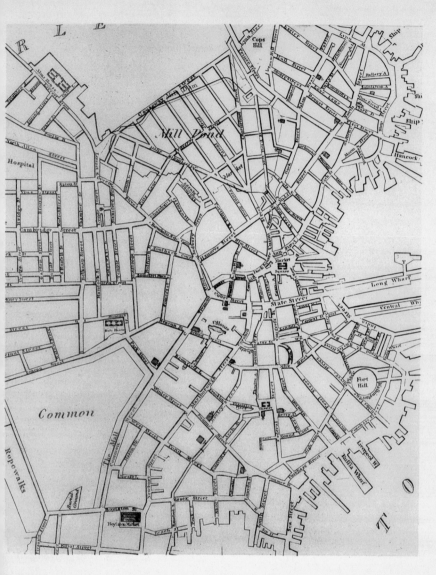

MAP OF BOSTON, 1809

in the entourage, Mrs. Jackson, although that patient lady does not figure once in the accounts of her celebrated spouse. The procession moved along the main thoroughfares, passing up Cornhill, before the State House (where Governor Jones may have looked up from his desk to review the procession), and arriving at 18 Pinkney Street where the great man descended and took up residence near the *foot* of Beacon Hill. Within a few weeks he was engaged by the neighboring congregation of Brattle Street Church, where he continued until the dissembling of his triumph and the dark hours of March, 1813. Yet his joy could not have been truly complete in this post, had he remained, for the organ was a tiny one, installed in 1774; however he soon acquired other parishes, as was the custom, and, of course, he taught privately.

There were some friendships to be formed with the resident musicians, first of all with Gottlieb and Catherine Graupner. This charming couple, recognized leaders of the musical life in Boston, richly deserved the high esteem lavished on them; Mr. Graupner's business was at the commencement of its most active and successful phase, while Mrs. Graupner had within a year given up her long career in the theater and retired to the less hurried activities of benevolence through assisting in charitable concerts, and an interest in truly classical music. Their children were either quite grown or in middle childhood and the Graupner home was an hospitable rallying place for all the musical intelligentsia of the town. Francis Mallet's musicianship was hardly on a par with that of either of these three luminaries, but he was a person of dignity and charm, according to Henry K. Oliver of Salem and Boston, and could recall the memorable associations of the Handel Commemoration a quarter of a century earlier. James Hewitt was surely no stranger to Dr. Jackson; at least his abilities gave him entrée, even though his personality would not maintain it, as events soon proved. Around these hovered the audience of worshipful followers, those humble and faithful members of the Philharmonic and the visiting members of the theatrical company come to Boston for an entire season or for a few performances. Despite its limited size, the society of Boston musicians was assuredly pleasant and one may be confident that proper deference was paid to this new and brightest star of the constellation.

In one respect circumstances favored Dr. Jackson's first major project, the presentation of a concert revealing the splendors of

George Frederick Händel's oratorios, for no existing choral organization was at hand, and the revelation of such a body of works would
not fail to make a deep impression. Several minor choral organizations had failed for lack of leadership or talent, or both, and the field
was clear. Fortunately there was an orchestra at hand which could
realize the main outlines, if not more, of the accompaniments and a
conductor equal to the task. Mrs. Graupner, Mr. Stockwell, and Mr.
Mallet would take care of certain solo parts, each according to his
abilities—a matter of some latitude. The good Doctor was entirely
equal to the organ accompaniments; in fact, he was the first organist
to appear in Boston with the requisite skill for a proper realization of
these exacting works. As certainly as a new broom sweeps cleanly
through the sectionalism of parties and coteries, Dr. Jackson assembled his chorus and trained them until, by October 20, he was at liberty
to announce that "his oratorio is now in a state of great forwardness"
and would be performed on the 29th. The program (given in full in
Chapter III) embraced selections from *The Messiah, Samson, Saul,*
and *Judas Maccabeus.* The townspeople looked with favor on the
project while the press opened its columns to this persuasive notice:

MESSIAH

We have heard with sincere pleasure, that the celebrated Organist and
Composer, Dr. G. K. Jackson, from New-York, intends to have publicly
performed, some select songs, chorusses, and overtures &c. from Handel's
Oratorios of the Messiah, Sampson and Judas Maccabeus.

As there has not been an Oratorio performed in this town, since the
year 1783, it may not be improper to observe, that all the musical virtuosos,
both in Europe and America, look upon Handel as one of the most sublime composers of sacred harmony—The pages of inspiration furnish the
subject matter for these Oratorios. . . .

What-ever passion in the heart of man, he wished to excite, he has done.
Heroes may be forgotten; nations may become extinct; but the fame of
Handel is IMMORTAL!!!
                  "Now strike the golden lyre again;
                  "A louder yet, and yet a louder strain."
These select votaries of Apollo, with Dr. Jackson as grand leader on
the organ, we hope and trust, will do justice to their beatified composer
Handel!

Do the Bostonians delight in novelty? Repair, then, old and young, to
the Chapel Church, this Evening, (29th instant.) and witness the greatest
musical novelty ever exhibited in this place.

"ANGELS EVER BRIGHT AND FAIR:
TAKE—OH! TAKE ME TO YOUR CARE."
Hark!
"That strain again;—It had a dying fall:
"O, it came o'er my ear like the sweet south
"Breathing on a bank of violets,
"Stealing and giving colour."
Hark!

PHILO-HARMONAE [10]

The overwhelming effect which such an occasion seemed to warrant was not forthcoming, nor would it be until the notable concert by the Handel and Haydn Society in December, 1815. But it was an unmistakable success and warranted repetition on December 1 in Salem, where the reception was respectful but not enthusiastic owing in part to the absence of a full performing body. Dr. Jackson was encouraged by the first exhibition, however, and commenced preparations for another oratorio to be performed on Christmas Day, in the afternoon.

We are happy to hear another Oratorio, under the direction of Dr. JACKSON, will be performed by desire, on Christmas Day, in the afternoon.[11]

This was postponed because it was not "sufficiently mature" to bring before the public. Little wonder the untrained Yankee voices, hardly out of the era of fuguing tunes, were unable to master the "Fly, and Hail-Stone Choruses, from Israel in Egypt, as Chief d'oeuvre" of the program.[12] The long hoped for event was consummated on February 2, 1813, with the program (see page 209) bringing another revelation to the appreciative Bostonians.

[10] Boston *Gazette,* Oct. 29, 1812.   [11] *Independent Chronicle,* Dec. 17, 1812.
[12] An extract from *Gilman's Village Choir,* quoted by Perkins, suggests a few of the problems created for the director who sought a precise English diction to accompany the exacting musical demands of Händel: "The taste and knowledge of musical performers was far from being uniform. While some sang with great beauty of expression and a nice adjustment to the sentiment of the happy modulations of a flexible voice, others made no distinction between the different notes than did the printed singing itself, or any lifeless instrument that gives out the tone required with the same strength and the same unvaried uniformity on all occasions. Nothing, too, could be rougher than the stentorian voice of Mr. Broadbreast, and nothing more piercing than the continued shriek of the pale but enthusiastic Miss Sixfoot. It shall not disclose the name of the man who annoyed us not a little with his ultra-nasal twang; nor of another who, whenever he took the tone pitch, did so by a happy accident; nor of another, who had an ungainly trick of catching his breath violently at every third note; nor of several of both sexes, whose pronunciation of many words, particularly of 'how, now,' etc. was dreadfully rustic, and hardly to be expressed on paper."

No special plea is required for the musician to evaluate the zeal of Dr. Jackson and his associates in bringing these concerts to pass. The chorus was on the way to permanent establishment when a third program was announced by the editor of the *Palladium:* "The sacred drama, which gives so lively a sense of deeds done in old times according to Scripture, being both a rational and novel entertainment in New-England, it is hoped will receive a decided preference from the refined taste of the ladies and gentlemen in Boston." [13]

In view of so sensational an introduction into the musical community it is not surprising that Dr. Jackson was prevailed upon to join with other established musicians in the founding of an academy. This idea of a Conservatoire had haunted the teaching fraternity for more than a decade, and it cropped up again with the usual consequence. The public was not ready for it in 1800, nor were they receptive to the idea in 1812. But Dr. Jackson, Messrs. Graupner, and Mallet made the attempt to unite private practice and centralize activity in Pythian Hall. One announcement in the newspapers sufficed. Dr. Jackson's removal from town halted the project before it got fairly under way, and Mr. Mallet withdrew. Graupner remained, secure in his private clientele and in his flourishing business.

Melodramatic aspects of our story, however, require an interruption of the lofty strain dictated by Händel, and the case of Dr. Jackson and the law must give us pause. Doubtless the entire matter seemed tragic for a quiet, respectable member of the community in his 67th year; the whole procedure nowadays smacks of a witch hunt of the like too frequently recorded in the daily press. The cumulative civil feelings expressed in the Revolution, and since then nearly cold, were warmed over once again, while Dr. Jackson's spacious, but harmless, person suffered the pain which over-wrought emotions inflict on sensitive human creatures. No account could be more explicit than that offered at length in the *Palladium* of March 23, 1813:

FOR THE PALLADIUM

DR. JACKSON

THESE four days past, this celebrated Musical Professor, who is justly considered, both theoretically and practically, the greatest Musician we

13 *New England Palladium,* March 2, 1813.

ORATORIO

A Grand Selection from HANDEL's SACRED ORATORIOS, WILL be performed at the Stone Chapel Church, Tomorrow afternoon—under the direction of Dr. G. K. Jackson, assisted by many respectable Vocal and Instrumental Amateurs and Professors.

Leader of the Orchestra   Mr. Graupner

Part I

Overture	Esther
Duet, Hail Judea	Judas Maccabeus
Chorus, Hail Juda, Happy Land	do.
Air, O Thou that Tellest	Messiah
Chorus, O Thou, that Tellest Glad Tidings	do.
Air, Let the Bright Seraphim in Burning Row	
Air and Chorus, Thou art the King of Glory	Grand Te Deum
Air, I know that my Redeemer	Messiah
Chorus, And the Glory of the Lord	Messiah
Air, Pious Orgies	Messiah (?)
Celebrated Fly Chorus, He spake the Word and there came all manner of Flies from Israel into Egypt.	

Part II

Overture	Saul
Air, Rejoice O Juda	Judas Maccabeus
Chorus, Break forth into Joy	Messiah
Air, In thee O Lord	Messiah
Air, The Smiling Dawn	Jeptha
Celebrated Bell Chorus, with Carillons, Welcome Mighty King	Saul
Air, Sound an Alarm	Judas Maccabeus
Chorus, with Kettle Drums and Trumpet— We hear, We hear	Judas Maccabeus
Air, O, Had I Jubal's Lyre	Judas Maccabeus
Celebrated Hailstone Chorus. He gave them Hailstones for Rain, Israel in Egypt.	
Chorus, Happy we the Star I see.	

Finale

GRAND HALLELUJAH CHORUS, with Trumpet and Kettle Drums.

Tickets to be had at Dr. Jackson's, No. 18, Pinkney-street; at Mr. Graupner's Franklin-st., Mr. Mallet, Federal-street; Exchange-Coffee-House; Centinel Compting Room; and at the Door of Performance—To begin at half past 5 o'clock.

Tickets for a Gentleman, one dollar, and for a Lady and Gentleman, one dollar and fifty cents.[14]

14 Boston *Gazette*, Feb. 1, 1813.

have ever had among us, has been the subject of conversation. On *Friday Evening* he received a notice from the Marshal of the District, to depart from the town on *Monday morning,* with permission to reside at *Northampton.* His loss will be sincerely felt. During the few months he has resided here, he has almost banished that spiritless method of performance, which is too common in Sacred Music; and deep-rooted prejudices, have yielded to well-informed reason and refined taste. We do not hazard much, when we defy the intelligent, in any science, to shew so rapid an improvement in it, in the same period, as has been made here, since the arrival of Doctor JACKSON, in the science of Music. In addition to this peculiar accomplishment, he is a man of that pleasantry in conversation, wit, and good humour, which renders him a most agreeable associate and companion.—Though he is (with the exception of a small annuity) dependent on the daily exercise of his talents for his support, yet the charity of his heart is not limited by the strings of his purse. Grateful for the attention bestowed on him, and for the patronage which has been given to his Oratorios of Sacred Music, from Handel, and which were performed in the spirit of the author; he has of late had many rehearsals of some of Handel's best pieces; which after the amateurs, by whom he has been generously assisted, had become sufficiently perfect in, were to have been publicly performed; and one half of the proceeds, given to some Charitable institution. His intention is defeated; and this inoffensive and unexceptionable gentleman, yesterday morning departed from town, leaving his wife and children, the subjects of that charity his professional powers would have enabled him to have bestowed on others.

Doctor JACKSON has been in this country about *seventeen* years, and came here with the intent to make it his home, and has always so considered it. He, however, knew of no advantage which it would be to an organist, and music master, to be naturalized, and did not subject himself to the cost of it. After the Declaration of War, when the Marshal issued his notice to aliens in New-York, about September last, he reported himself there, where he then resided; and upon his departure for Boston, he requested a Certificate to that effect, of the Marshal; but was told, it would not be necessary, and it was not given. Ignorant of legal forms, he supposed by this act, he had complied with the wishes of the government; and not till after the Marshal's late notice in our papers, upon being told by his friends, of the necessity of it, did he go to report himself here. He then went twice to the office; neither of which times was the Marshal there; but, upon being told by the Clerk, that as he was acquainted with him, he need give himself no further trouble, Dr. J. felt satisfied with this performance of his duty. But the title of the order, had not been complied with, and upon only two days notice, he has been sent into exile.

All the solicitations of the parents of his pupils of the choirs of the several parishes he was instructing, and one of the Members of the Brattle Street Society, whose organist he was, in his behalf, seem but to have fortified the determination of the Marshal; and the interest excited in favor, of a harmless and innocent individual seems but to have raised a presumption of his guilt.

On Saturday an Attorney, who had sent to him from New-York some days since, a demand for collection against the Doctor, for rent, on hearing of the notice of the Marshal, issued a writ with orders to arrest him before his departure; which was done. There was immediately a hue and cry set up, that this was a trick to prevent his compliance with the Marshal's notice, and that the authority of the government was to be resisted under the cover of law; wishing that every cause of irritation might be removed, two gentlemen of the Brattle Street Society became bail for the defendant at the gaoler's house, and thus removed this embarrassment, to his compliance with the Marshal's demand. The Parish Committee, we are informed, intend to petition the President for his return, which we have no doubt will be granted.

The gentleness and courtesy of the Federalist press was emphatically not shared by the *Independent Chronicle* which lashed out with this briefer summary of the situation, a lusty bark published after the object had left the town:

ALIEN ENEMIES

Great interest appears to be taken among *some* federalists in Boston, in favor of a certain English musician, known by the appellation of Dr. JACKSON. We know of no reason why any peculiar favor should be shewn to this man, more than to any other. He had free access to the public papers; he must repeatedly have seen the Marshal's notices, calling upon *alien enemies* to report themselves at his office, or be prepared to meet the consequences of refusal. If he, like others, sneered at the requisitions of government and set them at defiance, it is but just that he should feel the effects of his conduct. One thing is certain, that a more violent British partizan than the above mentioned person, is nowhere to be found. Energy, in time of war, is absolutely necessary. If one *alien enemy* be permitted to return on a particular plea, another plea may be set up for a second, third, fourth, and so on, *ad infinitum*.[15]

Satiric notes in the press thereafter referred to the undignified exodus of this storm center, whose fame was immediately increased and whose influence was considerably enhanced in absentia. It was supposed by some that Dr. Jackson had departed to Worcester, and a British Commissary of Prisoners was ordered to follow posthaste to prevent, if possible, the performing of a Te Deum in gratitude for the

15 *Independent Chronicle,* March 25, 1813.

Russian victories. But Dr. Jackson pushed on to Northampton where he remained inactive until the end of the hostilities. In Boston the concert about to be performed was delayed, but only for the gathering of a steady but determined momentum, for the scandal had given new zeal to the amateurs and the largest and "most Scientifick choir" ever associated together in Boston prepared to flaunt the wishes of the government. The concert was most vociferously applauded toward the end of March, all the music was from Händel, it was sung by two hundred amateurs and the proceeds were given to aid the Russian cause. The *Gazette* recorded its pleasure by remarking:

The ill-timed exercise of the despotic power given to the executive over aliens directed possibly in its application in this case by the malice of party feelings, deprived the public of the services of Dr. JACKSON, who was to have superintended the musical performance.[16]

Even James Hewitt overcame his contrariness and joined Graupner in conducting the concert.

There were no further massed choruses during his absence from Boston. Dr. Jackson made a gala return from the wars in April, 1815, reputation unimpaired among his friends and somewhat mended among his enemies. Immediately the idea of a choral society sprang up again, and the result, as has been chronicled elsewhere, was the formation of the Handel and Haydn Society. In the process of organization Dr. Jackson's candidacy as conductor was discussed, and I would venture the opinion that Mr. Graupner's absenteeism from the list of officers of the new organization was due, in part, to his displeasure at the failure of his candidate to obtain the post of conductor. It is quite possible that the political theorem exercised an important part in rejecting him except in an advisory capacity. That the British lion was battered but unbowed is shown in his later refusal to have anything to do with the society unless he could take absolute control of its concerns or, in other words, be president. A previous series of negotiations had come to naught because of his demand for an excessive salary for playing *The Messiah*, and the society, demonstrating that his services were not essential to the performance of this grand work or to that of *The Creation*, engaged S. P. Taylor to come on from New York.[17]

The wisdom of Dr. Jackson's position might have been apparent

16 Boston *Gazette,* March 29, 1813.
17 Not Raynor Taylor from Philadelphia, as given by Perkins.

had anyone seen it in the seasons to come, for the custom of requiring
the president—elected for his personal qualifications rather than for
his musical abilities—to conduct had a most unfortunate effect on the
progress of the repertory. With Jackson to conduct and another to
hold the honorary post of president all would have been well; as it was,
Amasa Winchester, as officiating officer, merely occupied the podium
but made no effort to control the performance. The violin of Mr.
Ostinelli became guiding influence. Undoubtedly, Jackson saw the
ridiculousness of such a situation.

On his return to Boston, Dr. Jackson was restored to some favor
and found immediate employment as organist to the fashionable (and
Federalist) King's Chapel, after which he played at Trinity Church
where his friends, the Graupners and the Parkers were communicants.
Here he succeeded James Hewitt on April 15, probably holding the
position, together with that of King's Chapel, at a salary of two hundred dollars per annum, the same salary, by the way, as that given to
P. A. Von Hagen in 1807. The amusing story of his high-handed buf-
foonery is related by Perkins:

Whenever opposition was offered to his will the doctor sent in his resignation, as at Brattle Street Church, when complaint was made that he made
too great a display of his accomplishments, and at Trinity when Dr.
Gardiner requested him to shorten his voluntaries, and he replied by ad-
vising the reverend gentleman to curtail his sermons. On the following
Sunday, he gave vent to his ill-humour by picking out the psalm tunes with
one finger, and on Easter Sunday, in assertion of his dignity as sufficient to
exempt him from interference, appeared in the choir attired in the dress of
an English Doctor of Music, with plum-colored coat, yellow breeches, and
a square cap. This filled the measure of his offences and brought about the
acceptance of his resignation.[18]

These offenses were not sufficient to prevent him from being sought
after by the parish of St. Paul in Common Street, for on the erection
of its new edifice he was engaged at an extraordinarily high salary,
and maintained the post from 1820 until his passing.

Of Dr. Jackson as an organist, we have the most glowing reports.
Parker writes that "His voluntaries were elaborate and replete with
chromatic harmonies, embracing the most scientific and classic modulations . . . and until his residence in the metropolis of New-
England, chanting the church service was little practised and less

18 *History of the Handel and Haydn Society,* Vol. I, p. 49.

understood." Dr. Bentley of Salem wrote in his Diary: "The celebrated Dr. Jackson, an Englishman, performed on the organ with
great power and pure touch. . . . Mr. Jackson's voluntaries were beyond anything I had heard, and the best music of the evening was before the second Chorus when the organ was the accompaniment only
with the violins." [19]

A new era opened up for him at this time. If not as exciting as the
previous six months of residence in Boston, it was more productively
worth while, for both town and academic gown put away all strife
for an era of good feeling. Dr. Jackson's talents were unrivaled in
Boston, and he stepped forth into positions as adviser and friend;
his Chants were republished and copyrighted on March 9, 1816, and
followed by an elucidation [20] which made them available for the use
of the slow-witted in churches and for private families in private; he
resumed teaching advanced pupils and he benignly attended visiting
songbirds in the humble role of pianoforte accompanist. With an appropriately British attitude, he held aloof from the common herd and
assumed a halo of divinity. Only mankind inclined to celebrity met
him on the same footing; the remainder inclined with a metaphysical
bow and scrape. In early October, 1821, he received a request from the
Handel and Haydn Society to pass on the sheaf of hymn tunes brought
by a young bank clerk from Savannah, Lowell Mason by name, and
the good Doctor's flattering approval convinced the trustees that,
after revision by Dr. Jackson, publication was feasible. The recommendation is expressed with the utmost graciousness:

I have been highly gratified with the examination of the manuscript of the
Handel and Haydn Society Collection of Music. The selection of tunes is
judicious; it contains all the old approved English melodies that have long
been in use in the church, together with many compositions from modern
English authors. The whole are harmonized with great accuracy, truth, and
judgment, according to the acknowledged principles of musical science.
I consider the book as a valuable acquisition to the church, as well as to
every lover of devotional music. It is much the best book I have seen published in this country, and I do not hesitate to give it my most decided
approbation.

Very respectfully yours,
G. H. Jackson. [21]

[19] December 1, 1812.   [20] Copyright Jan. 31, 1817, and March 5, 1817.
[21] *History of the Handel and Haydn Society,* Vol. I, p. 81 f.

By a bold stroke of luck, the Collection eventually made a fortune for the society and for Mason, but Dr. Jackson's profit in so short a time was negligible—assuming that his reimbursement was other than a flat fee for services rendered—and his estate amounted to $99.86, including 129 volumes of old music books, valued at six cents each. The society purchased his edition of the complete works of Händel, by Dr. Samuel Arnold, from his widow.

This final act of recommendation, however, had a salutary effect on the progress of American music, for Lowell Mason richly deserved the cordial approbation given him by the scientific Englishman.[22] The events stemming from that fortunate act are well known; the society laid broad foundations for permanency in its financial structure, and Mason later came to Boston, where his influence rebounded to the remotest musical community in the nation.[23] Dr. Jackson knew talent when he met it; the starvation diet of Boston had whetted his appetite!

The deplorably minute inventory, however, may be partly explained by the fact that two sons, Charles and Edwin, had recently been set up in business. The extent and value of their stock is not known, but the suggestion may be fairly advanced that the close of Graupner's business and the opening of Jackson's may have had some bearing on each other in so far as a possible transfer of certain items of stock is concerned. The brothers opened their store at 44 Market Street in March, 1821, and submitted these prices on instruments which represent a substantial investment:

22 See Dedication, Chap. VIII, p. 236. Ten selections by Dr. Jackson were in the first edition, three were retained for the second, but only one (Tune "Linton") is in the third.

23 These factors do not of necessity imply successive states of progress in the development of American music. There are many who hold that the colonial church music of New England and the early 19th-century fuguing tunes and revival hymns are more interesting than the more harmonically correct European models which were widely adopted through the reforming zeal of Lowell Mason and his associates. Many humble publications continued to appear, finding widespread acceptance in the rural communities, for the most part, having an influence and generating an enthusiasm among their adherents which is a particularly healthy expression of a native, or folk, response. The entire subject is worthy of extended investigation and discussion in relation to the sociological problems involved. The Mason brothers found that their publications were acceptable in parts of the Middle West only as they were issued with "buckwheat" notes. To group the advances in the spread of this new European sacred music under the name of Lowell Mason is to give only the leading figure in the movement. Charles Zeuner (1795–1857), who arrived in Boston in 1824, had considerable ability as a composer, marking the transitional stage to Mason. His "Missionary Chant" survives in many hymnbooks.

C. &. E. W. JACKSON

Elegant Cabinet Piano Fortes by Clementi & Col.		$475.
do	Tomkinson	425.
do rosewood with brass inlay, and drawers		425.
do horizontal mahogany with drawers		320.
do plain		250.
do American with drawers		225.
Elegant Broadwood		275.
Barrel organs 18 key'd w/four stops, drum and triangle in elegant gothic case		325.
15 key'd organs in do. w/stops as above		235.

Violins from 7 to 30 dollars. Clarionets 9 to 20 dollars.
Flutes from 1.50 to 60; Flute Flageolets 12 dolls.
Flageolets, 2.75 to 18 dolls. Violoncellos 25 dolls.
Bassoons 30 dolls. Trumpets 22 dolls.
French horns with additional crooks, pair 140 dolls.
Kent bugles 45 dolls. C dol. w/B crooks, 20 dolls.
Fifes from 50 cents to 2.25 cents
Ladies tamborines, 12 dolls. do. triangles, 2.25 to 2.75 cts.
Pandean Reeds, 2.25 cents [24]

A catalogue of popular songs was published without delay, each bearing the imprint of the firm at this address or at 64 Market Street. (See Appendix III) The enterprise seemed destined for success, but there is strong evidence to the contrary. Neither brother figured in the musical life of the city as performer or as leading member in the official concerns of any existing musical organization; this condition implies something less than intimate knowledge of music's domain, and it mitigated against success in a business which profits by personal contact with practitioners of the art. The passing of Dr. Jackson, as sole contact with the artistic fraternity, destroyed this helpful connection. In August, 1826, all was over.

Notice

The copartnership heretofore existing between C. &. E. W. Jackson is this day dissolved by mutual consent. Accounts of the firm which are unsettled will be adjusted by Charles Jackson by whom the business will be continued.

CHARLES JACKSON
EDWIN W. JACKSON [25]

[24] *Columbian Centinel,* Nov. 24, 1821.   [25] *Ibid.,* Aug. 12, 1826.

Like the second American generation of the Von Hagen and Graupner families, the Jackson boys either turned to other professions, or held so obscure a place in the trade of music that their names ceased to share even the slightest luster of that attached to their distinguished father. Charles announced in October, 1824, that he was about to resume his business as counsellor at law at 12 State Street, adjoining the offices of C. S. Loring.

DIED

> Yesterday, G. K. JACKSON, Mus. D.—Funeral this afternoon at half past 2 o'clock from his late residence, No. 44 Market street. The friends of the deceased are requested to attend.[26]

There were scanty memorials, but few of the sad thoughts which passed through the minds and hearts of closest friends found expression in such a manner as to be of service to us. Many of the tributes continued to reflect that qualified approval which attended every step of the good Doctor's way in life. Chiefest was that of Parker, which rose above the influence of temperament and personality and saw the true stature of the man. A survey of his accomplishments, published in the *Centinel* in the course of a discussion on the merits of sacred song books, is in all likelihood a fair enough estimation of the subject's talents.

Although Dr. Jackson is entitled to great praise and was perhaps the first organist in the Republic, yet I presume there are more than one in Europe who were his rivals at least. As a composer he was, in my opinion (I speak with deference) below mediocrity. Something more than mere mechanical performance or scientific acquirements are necessary to make a great or unrivalled musician. A certain quality called genius is required which I see very little proof that Dr. Jackson possessed. [27]

Times were changing rapidly in Boston, and it is unlikely that Dr. Jackson would have been made happier by any of the events to come. His brief six years in Boston, however, left their impress on all those who knew him, and on sacred music for some time to come; he gave a much needed dignity to the profession of musician, and securely justified his place as the first bona fide Doctor of Music to have a direct influence on American musical life.

26 *New England Palladium,* Nov. 19, 1822.   27 *Columbian Centinel,* Oct. 22, 1823.

COMPOSITIONS BY DR. GEORGE K. JACKSON

1. A Choice Collection of Chants in 4 voices with a Gloria Patri, Sanctus, with the whole figured with a thorough Bass for Organ, as used in Cathedrals, Churches, and Chapels, selected and arranged and composed by G. K. Jackson. . . . Copyright March 9, 1816. 50 pp. Price one dollar.
   (Contains one chant each by Nares, Dr. Blow, Purcel, Boyce; the remainder are by Dr. Jackson)
2. The Choral Companion . . . elucidation of Dr. G. K. Jackson's Chants   Boston, printed by Ezra Lincoln. Copyright March 1817, adv. April 4, 1817. 28 pp. Price fifty cents.
3. Close Cannon for Six Voices for the Use of Masonic Lodges. Printed for the Author. 2 pp.
4. Content, a Favorite Canzone for 3 Voices, Composed for the Apollo Musical Society, New York. 2 pp.
5. David's Psalms, set to Music Expressly for Use of Churches, Chapels, Meetings & Private Families   Adapted, composed, and arranged for a single voice with an accompaniment for the Organ by Dr. G. K. Jackson, Organist of St. George's Chapel, New York. Copyright secured 1804.
6. Dr. Watts's Divine Songs set to Music in an easy and familiar stile for one, two, three & four Voices   London, Printed for the Author. 43 pp.
7. The Dying Christian to His Soul, see Pope's Universal Prayer.
8. Duo . . . Composed by Dr. G. K. Jackson   Philadelphia, Printed for G. Willig & sold at his Musical Magazine, no. 12 South 4 Street. 2 pp.
9. A Favorite Canzone for 1, 2, or 3, Voices. . . . Composed by G. K. Jackson   Written by Mrs. Jackson. 4 pp.
10. A Favorite Collection of Songs and Duets for the Voice, Harpsichord or Pianoforte. Op. 3. London, Printed by Longman and Broderip. 27 pp.
11. A Favorite Sonata for the Harpsichord or Piano Forte   op. 4. London, Printed for the Author. 13 pp.
12. Freedom and Our President. The words adapted to a new composition called Washington's March. Sung by Mr. Hodgkinson, composed by Dr. G. K. Jackson. Printed for the author. New York. (Song with flute or violin and pianoforte accompaniment. First line: Immortal Washington in tuneful lays.)
13. Freedom and Our President. For the Voice & Piano Forte. The Words Adapted to a New Composition called Jefferson's March. . . . N. Y. Printed for the Author. 3 pp.
14. Hear My Pray'r, O Lord, Canon. In Handel and Haydn Society Collection, Vol. I.
15. I Rudimentia da Musica, or Complete Instructor for the Piano Forte. (See Jackson publications, Appendix IV.)

16. The Multiplication Table, voice and pianoforte, composed in familiar style "for juvenile improvement." Printed for the Author. 7 pp. Fifty cents.

17. A Musical Coalition, a humorous compilation of national airs, French, English, and American. Piano Forte and Flute. 2 pp.

18. New Bagatelles for the Voice & Piano Forte. Calculated for Juvenile Improvement . . . various paging.

19. A New Miscellaneous Musical Work, consisting of songs, serenades, cantatas, canzonetts, canons, glees, composed by Dr. G. K. Jackson.
      I   *The Cricket
      II   Song for 2 voices in canon (Waft Me Some Soft)
      III Song "Huzza for Liberty"
      IV   Sweet are the Banks, duet
      V   American Serenade, words by Mrs. Jackson
      VI   Cancherizante [sic.], a song to be sung forward and then back-
              wards beginning at the last note and ending with the first
              [Canorizans].
    Published for the Author. 9 pp. with cover.

20. *Ibid.* with these additions:
      *A Winter's Evening
      *New York Serenade
      *Ah! Delia
      *Dirge for General Washington (Dead March)
      *The Fairies to the Sea Nymphs Sung
      *Glee (Gentle Air)
      (22 pp.)

21. A New Musical Score of Easy Canons for 1, 2, 3, 4, up to 12 Voices. Sacred to Masonry. Invented and Composed by G. K. Jackson. 13 pp.

22. Ode for the Fourth of July. Written by M. Townsend, set to music by G. K. Jackson & sung at the Presbyterian Church in New York, N. Y. Engraved by W. Pirsson. 2 pp.

23. Ode for Gen. Hamilton's Funeral for four voices composed by G. K. Jackson and dedicated to the New York Musical Society. 4 pp.

24. One Kind Kiss, A favorite song composed by Dr. Jackson and sung by Mrs. Hodgkinson [Philadelphia] Printed at Carr's Musical Reposi-tories. 2 pp.

25. O 'Twas a Joyful Sound, canon in three voices   In Handel and Haydn Society Collection, Vol. I.

26. Petit duo, for Miss Clarkson, Miss Cosby. 3 pp. } Three Petit Duos. New York, Copy-

27. Petit duo, for Miss H. Hogan and Miss Burrell. } right Dec. 23, 1807. Engraved E. Riley.

28. Ponder My Words. An Anthem for 3 Voices taken from the 5 Psalm,

* Also published separately.

with three canons For the Use of Country Churches   Op. 2 London. Printed for the Author. 7 pp.

29. *Ibid.* In Handel and Haydn Society Collection, Vol. I.

30. Pope's Universal Prayer and his Celebrated Odes "The Dying Christian to his Soul" set to music by Dr. G. K. Jackson (Two pieces bound, 9 and 12 pp., price $2) First line of Universal Prayer, "Father of all in every age," for solo voice; second work has solo followed by chorus.

31. A Prey to Tender Anguish, composed by the late G. K. Jackson, Mus. Doc. Copyright Nov. 8, 1824, by Charles Jackson.

32. Sacred Music for the use of Churches & Consisting of Two Chants, Sanctus, Gloria Patri & Three Psalm Tunes. 2 pp.

33. The Sylph, Written by T. Moore, Esqr. Composed by G. K. Jackson.

34. The Task, A Whimsical Cannon (sic.) on the Eight Notes. Printed for the Author. 1 p.

35. A Treatise on practical Thorough Bass, with general rules for its composition and modulation, Op. 5, by G. K. Jackson   London: Longman & Broderip [1795]. 40 pp.
    Tunes: Nativity, Malden, Ongar, Jersey, Wood Street, Hull, Linton. (All four part.)

36. A Winter's Evening, A Cantata, composed by the late G. K. Jackson, Mus. Doc. Copyright Dec. 17, 1824. See A New Miscellaneous Musical Work.

Note: The following items, found in the British Museum, may be compositions of Dr. G. K. Jackson, although the initials of the composer are not given:

Dafne, a favorite song; printed for the author

The Inconstant, a favorite song; printed for the author

Sylvia, a favorite song; printed for the author

Part IV

THE ENTERPRISES

VIII. PUBLISHERS

I love a ballad but even too well, if it be doleful matter merrily set down, or a very pleasant thing indeed, and sung lamentably.—WINTER'S TALE, *Act IV, Sc. 3*

THE BUSINESS of music publishing and the nineteenth century arrived in Boston almost simultaneously; or, as one might say with closer application to our purpose, music publishing became a successful enterprise in the very years that Gottlieb Graupner settled there. There were few predecessors, and only a few crude publications of sheet music or music books occurred before the Von Hagens and Graupner issued their works in quantity.

The history of music publishing in Boston—as in any similar community—is a record of cultural ripening which causes the demand, establishes the quality, and regulates the quantity and form of imprint. The business methods of distribution and marketing in that day were far different from the elaborate promotional schemes of today, but the early music publishers of the nineteenth century succeeded in following the demand for their wares throughout New England and, in some instances, over a far wider area.

Whereas music-making and gaiety, so constant in Philadelphia and New York, had only begrudgingly found an occasional outlet in the Puritan stronghold, the publication of music as a business concern of the musician awaited the development of the theater and the popularity of the singing actor. These forms of entertainment, both in the proper stage setting and in the concert hall, denoted the rise of striking personality among public performers and the arrival of public entertainment on a professional level, circumstances brought about by the new secular tunefulness of the English ballad opera or, in a similar style, the American patriotic song. The style of catchy melody which induces the hearer to purchase the printed music comes chiefly through the medium of popular entertainment and is essentially different in its approach to, and effect on, an audience from that brought about by sacred melody. This secular tunefulness catered to a wider range of moods than the limited sacred song, for the latter type consorted but slightly with the cheerful aspects of faith, preferring to deal with the most solemn and lugubrious sentiments of unyielding doctrine.

The theatrical pieces ranged from the gay patter song, the height of comicality in its time, to the sentimental ballad on milady's eyebrow, then unplucked. Solos, duets, glees, and catches in various forms provided the major part of each evening's diversion in the theater, while the concert hall received a transplanting of identical numbers, together with the same singers, and added to them pianoforte and orchestra works of wide variety. The dancing schools were surprisingly popular in Boston and required music for quadrilles, cotillions, *et alia* for private enjoyment and social gatherings. It is no generalization to state that the vast majority of the songs published in the earliest years were known to the public by means of the theater where they had been performed in the course of an opera, in an "afterpiece," or independently between the acts, and it is worthy of note that the first music publishers of importance in Boston arrived as members of a theatrical company.

The publication of books of music naturally found a place in the program of the booksellers, and one looks today to them quite as readily as to the music publishers for hymn books. The single folded sheet of approximately $9\frac{1}{2}$ x 12 inches, customary format of all secular works, is far enough removed from the narrower classification of books to require the attention of one connected with the practical aspects of the music profession rather than the trade of bookmaking. Whereas the market for tune books and sacred music through history has been relatively small but constant, the popularity of the timely song, and frequently of the instrumental work, is brief and flourishing; after its heyday the old stock is virtually worthless. Secular music, particularly when dependent for its popularity on the theater, belongs in the class of "best sellers," here today and gone tomorrow. The booksellers of the day, both in America and in England, had long since recognized the distinction between music and books with respect to problems of marketing and manufacture, and the final releasing of the theatrical restrictions toward the close of the eighteenth century at once set in motion a system in Boston which was similar in all respects to that current elsewhere, notably in Philadelphia, Charleston, Baltimore, and New York.

The evidence gained from exhaustive perusal of surviving collections, and from newspaper announcements of the day, bears out the primacy of Von Hagen's and Graupner's entrance into the field. Few ballads or snatches from theatrical sources are to be found in America before the turn of the century; thereafter there was no need to import them from abroad, since the same works became immediately current in the major cities of America and were reprinted here. To these should be added the confident effusions of native Massachusetts bards who published independently of business firms, contributing an occasional or spasmodic production of ballads for the most part on patriotic subjects designed for special celebrations.

Instrumental music was confined to the keyboard, reflecting the rising interest in the pianoforte and stimulated by extensive importation of instruments from England and an increasing American manufacture. Mention of the harpsichord was rare after 1800, although the simplicity of the published works rendered them suitable for any keyboard instrument. The addition of a part for the German flute, violin, "guittar," or other instrument of the woodwind variety was greatly to the contemporary taste; these were placed at the end of the piece rather than over the staff, as recent custom has served the ukulele by fretted or obbligato parts. An unmistakable standardization adheres to the majority of the sheet music, and it is often possible to detect the publisher from the style of printing, or from the type of paper used, although it must be recognized by the researcher that condition of paper is not sufficient evidence for allocation of date or source. One or two pages were the limit in the works issued by the Von Hagens, without cover design or frontispiece title, and the composer's name was often omitted; the printing was of the crudest, and notes unevenly spaced and the words so crowded together that they have only an oblique relation to the proper note.

A complete survey of the publishers of secular music in Boston is possible within the scope of this study, and a fairly complete listing of their productions may be gained from a combination of sources. Some attempt is made to assign publications to an approximate date, and the following pages unfold the devious methods employed to relate the music to the proper social or political atmosphere which brought it forth and which, in turn, was affected by it.

As prologue to a survey of the major publishers at the turn of the century, Linley [1] and Moore will detain us only a moment. A handful of songs constitute their outturn and few copies of these have survived. The firm was not listed in any directory, but advertised its wares in the newspapers in 1799 giving the address "opp. Faneuil Hall (Market Place)."

Deserving of extended discussion because of their real importance to the musical life of Boston are the Von Hagens, father, son, and mother. The Von Hagen family constitute the first music dealers and sheet-music publishers of importance in Boston; [2] these were branches of several careers which included virtually every aspect of the art and science of music. Mr. Sonneck has listed a number of their publications and these, with others since found, are known in sufficient quantity to give a representative survey of the fashionable taste and the musical trend of Boston in the five years beginning 1797.

The Von Hagen's interest in patriotic songs is worthy of some attention, for although of Dutch descent—the original name was Van Hagen—they had lived in America during a remarkable period. Political feeling during the administration of the beloved Washington was comparatively like-minded, but his passing was a signal for renewed struggle which brought forth conspicuous sectionalism, with Jeffersonian democracy on the one hand and Hamiltonian imperialism on the other. New England conservatism (by now, a recognized political influence!) and its fear of loss of power in an ever expanding nation was eventually appeased and once again felt secure with old John Adams at the helm of government, as it breathed easily once more when young John Quincy assumed the same office. While there are no records to specify the effect of patriotic songs on the pulse of the voting citizenry, or testimonials from winning candidates, such as John Adams, that the songs commemorating their administrative prowesses were responsible for election, or reëlection to public office, the songs

1 Francis Linley and John Moore. Linley was a British organist who made a brief stay in this country.
2 The principal New York publishers were Charles Gilfert, after 1795, and John Paff, after 1798.

themselves are plentiful evidence that music was a useful accessory to the Mumbo Jumbo of campaigning.

The threat—as New Englanders would have termed it—of Jeffersonian democracy challenged the unanimity of the country by the display of patriotic emotion which found frequent and intense expression in popular songs and bore a far greater influence on the immediate issues than we of the present day can readily estimate. With words by Thomas Paine,[3] "Amyntas," or "Amateur of Salem," as set by leading tune smiths—several of them of so recent a residence in this country that their political sentiments were hardly formed—the songs produced an effect calculated to influence the public mind strongly by appeal to the emotions rather than to the reason, an appeal spurned at no time since the days of the Romans.

The Von Hagens sponsored this type of song, among others, and their catalogue is conspicuous for that fact, since later publishers with rare exceptions, quite dropped it. In view of these facts, therefore, it will be worth our while to mention several songs not ordinarily discussed in existing bibliographies.

Among the first was "Adams and Liberty," to the tune of the "Star-Spangled Banner"[4] ("To Anacreon in Heaven"), with words by Thomas Paine, A. M. of Boston, written for the Anniversary of the Massachusetts Charitable Fire Society, sung on June 1, 1798, and first printed by Thomas & Andrews, the booksellers, on the following day; a third edition, revised and corrected by the author was issued by the Von Hagens at 3 Cornhill. "Adams and Liberty" became famous as the "Boston Patriotic Song"; the words, in part, have this burden; there are ten verses in all:

2

While France her huge limbs bathes recumbent in blood,
 And society's base threats with wide dissolution,
May peace like the dove who returned from the flood,
 Find an ark of abode in our mild constitution.
  But though peace is our aim,
  Yet the boon we disclaim,
 If bought by our sovereignty, justice, or fame;

[3] Thomas Paine petitioned Congress to have his name changed, and he was known thereafter as Robert Treat Paine, Jr.
[4] This entire subject is authoritatively treated by Joseph Muller in *The Star-Spangled Banner;* words and music issued between 1814–1864. New York, G. A. Baker & Co., Inc. 1935.

(Refrain)

For ne'er shall the sons of COLUMBIA be slaves
While the earth bears a plant, or the sea rolls its waves.

5

Let our Patriots destroy Anarch's pestilent worm,
    Lest our liberty's growth should be checked by corrosion,
Then let clouds thicken round us—we heed not the storm;
    Our realm fears no shock but the earth's own explosion;
        Foes assail us in vain
        Though their fleets bridge the main,
    For our alters and laws, with our lives we'll maintain;
For ne'er, etc.

6

Let Fame to the world sound America's voice,
    No Intrigue can her sons from their Government sever;
Her pride is her Adams—his Laws are her choice,
    And shall flourish till Liberty slumber forever!
        Then unite heart and hand,
        Like Leonidas' band,
    And swear to the God of the ocean and land.
For ne'er, etc.

7

Should the tempest of war overshadow our land,
    Its bolts could ne'er rend Freedom's temple asunder;
For unmoved at its portals would Washington stand,
    And repulse with his breast the assaults of the thunder.
        Of its scabbard would leap,
        His sword from the sleep
    And conduct, with its point, every flash to the deep!
For ne'er, etc.

"Adams and Washington," a new patriotic song, was published in December, 1798, with words plainly reflecting the sentiments of the people with regard to France, a feeling so intense at a later time that a state of war actually existed, but was never declared. "Adams & Washington" has six ecstatic verses, of which this is the first:

Columbia's brave friends with alertness advance
    Her rights to support in defiance of France;
To volatile fribbles we never will yield
    While John's at the helm and George rules the field.

No subsequent patriotic songs were more popular than these; the tunes sufficed long after the immediate political issue had passed, with other timely words replacing those by Paine. Not all of them were published as sheet music by any means, but they are mentioned in the press of the day, and the words assigned to a well-known tune. In this class belongs "Columbia's Bold Eagle" with words by a gentleman of Salem and music by Mr. Graupner, sung at a concert in Salem on June 25, 1799. Mr. Graupner, in all probability, adapted the words to an existing tune; at any rate, he did not publish the song. "Rule, New England" reached publication by the Von Hagens with words by Mr. Paine and music by F. Schaffer of Boston, as did "To Arms Columbia," with words by Paine and music by Von Hagen. "A Funeral Dirge on the Death of General Washington" is given as illustration in John Tasker Howard's *Our American Music*. The words for "Rule, New England" reveal the strong sentiments of a militant patriotism current at the time:

1

What arm a sinking State can save
   From Faction's Pyre, or Anarch's grave;
Pale Liberty with haggard eyes,
   Looks round the realm and thus replies:

Chorus.

Rule, New England, Rule!
   New England Rules and Saves.
      Columbians never never shall be Slaves.

5

Alone, amid the coil serene
   NEW ENGLAND, stands, and braves the scene;
Majestic as she lifts her eyes,
   The stars appear—the daemons fly.

Chorus.

7

Old Massachusetts' hundred hills,
   Awake and chant the matin song;
A realm's acclaim the welkin fills,
   The Federal SUN returns with STRONG.

Chorus.

8

And thou, pale orb of waning light,
Democracy thou changing moon,
Art doom'd to wheel thy maniac flight
Unseen amid the cloudless Noon.

Chorus.

The words of the remaining patriotic songs are scarcely less ennobling
in purpose.

Gottlieb Graupner published patriotic songs throughout his career,
the majority in celebration of the Birthday of American Independence; these included "A New Ode" for July 4, 1802, "National Ode,
Arouse, Arouse, Columbia's Sons, Arouse!" with words by Robert
Treat Paine Jr. for the Squantum celebration in 1811, and "National
Song for the 4th of July" (1815), with words by Susanna Rowson and
the tune of "To Anacreon in Heaven." "Columbia, Land of Liberty"
was written by John Barker and composed by John Bray for publication in 1819 by Graupner, and while the references are less timely,
they show no diminution of ardent feeling.

And shall we ever dim the fires
That flame on Freedom's kindred shrines?
Shall glory's children shame their sires?
Shall cowards spring from Heroes loins?
NO, etc.

Other songs, reflecting the same trend, bore the title of Washington,
Lafayette, a current governor of the states, or president of the nation.

Late in 1797 (or early in 1798) the Von Hagens—Peter Albrecht
and his son, Peter Albrecht Jr.—opened a Musical Magazine and
Warehouse at 62 Newbury Street; issuance was rapid, with about one
hundred selections ultimately bearing their imprint, of which half are
announced in the press as "published this day"; in all cases, the addresses are on the music and it is therefore possible to determine the
year, if not the day, of issuance. Many Von Hagen imprints contain
notices of the firm which reveals a far-flung enterprise; there is frequent change in the actual wording, but the attached is a typical example:

BOSTON, Printed and sold at Von Hagen's Imported Piano
Forte Warehouse, No. 3 Cornhill—Sold also by G. Gilfert

New York—D. Vinton Providence—W. K. Wilder Newport—B. R. Macanulty Salem—E. M. Blunt Newburyport—I. Stanwood Portsmouth & A. Jenks Portland

The booksellers of the day, advertising their stock in great detail,
were burdened with books on theology, classics, history, and travel,
with the first class quite outnumbering all the other departments combined; music and the fine arts were neglected, with a very occasional
mention of a favorite collection of a locally published hymnody or
book of words. Little wonder, therefore, that the idea of a musical circulating library should occur to Messrs. Mallet, Graupner, and Trajetta in connection with their Conservatory even though in this, as in
other instances, nothing seems to have come of the idea. The several
newspapers carry notifications promising "the terms of subscription,
with other particulars . . . as soon as arrangements can be made." [5]
It is likely that the stock belonged to Graupner rather than to Mallet
or Trajetta, for he advertises a large quantity of musical merchandise
for sale immediately after the dissolution of partnership, and if one
may pry into the financial probabilities regarding the three men, it
might be supposed that Mr. and Mrs. Graupner were better favored
by reason of their several remunerative professional connections than
either Mallet or Trajetta.

In 1812 James Hewitt announced a similar library according to a
European plan, outlined the difficulties and inconveniences of procuring works abroad, and claimed to have the largest collection of
musical compositions by celebrated authors in the country, in all numbering several thousand volumes. The rate was six dollars for annual
subscribers, $3.50 for the half year, and two dollars for the quarter,
but the conditions under which one might borrow are not given. The
same announcement took occasion to remind prospective students of
the existence of his school and added this notice, presumably for the
benefit of their elders: "For Sale as above—An assortment of Spanish
CIGARS, in boxes of 250 each, of a superior quality." [6]

No further mention of his circulating library is made by Hewitt,
but in June, 1813, S. H. Parker informs the public that he has received
a library containing several hundred volumes and proposes to add
them to his rolling stock; these included vocal and instrumental music
and many pieces for the pianoforte. Parker was a shrewd business man

[5] *New England Palladium*, Feb. 3, 1801.   [6] *Repertory*, Sept. 11, 1812.

with a clientele in distant parts; he advertised in many newspapers throughout the States and garnered a considerable business by owning the largest circulating library in Boston, a collection consisting of seven thousand volumes in 1818. Under the title of the Boston Union Circulating Library he dispersed catalogues in the modern manner. (S. H. Parker should not be confused, by the way, with either Matthew S. Parker, secretary of the Handel and Haydn Society, or John Rowe Parker, proprietor of the Franklin Music Warehouse and editor of *The Euterpeiad*.)

There are two possibilities as to the source of Parker's acquisitions; either they mark the abrupt end of Mr. Hewitt's original plan, which characteristically exaggerated the number of volumes, or they were the stock of Dr. Jackson, who disposed of his worldly goods and retired to Northampton during the height of the war period. At any rate, the time was apparently not ripe for a musical circulating library, despite the appeal of the general idea, and it is a curious commentary on the difference in methods employed to further the two arts, music and literature, that such libraries, while thriving in respect to popular novels, have never proved successful when constituted of music.

The booksellers of Boston made a brave show by publication of certain favorite English operas and of several amazing librettos performed occasionally, and usually not more than once, written by Bostonians. The English operas were reprints, of course, carried out without benefit of protecting copyright law for the owners and amounting to plagiarism. Thus *The Blind Girl, or a Recipe for Beauty*, by Thomas Morton, and *Tid Rei I! or the Irish Wedding*, a musical opera in two acts by a young gentleman of Boston, were issued in 1808. A *Musical Dictionary* by Mr. Pilkington, the flutist, was brought out by Watson & Bangs in 1812, but an abridged edition of Busby and Arnold's work of the same title, first printed in 1786, would be a more accurate description of the work. "The disciples of Apollo should not be destitute of so useful and convenient a manual" one enthusiast wrote.[7]

Publication of music took two distinct forms; the booksellers confined themselves to frequent issuance of collections of sacred music and occasional opera scores or miscellaneous works, while the music deal-

[7] *New England Palladium and Commercial Advertiser*, Aug. 21, 1812.

ers neglected the sacred repertory almost entirely and confined themselves to the secular realm. There is every reason to suppose that both branches of the field did a reasonably flourishing business. A typical newspaper advertisement shows the stock of music books for sale by a leading bookseller; most of these were published by Boston concerns.

Music for Singing Choirs

Bridgewater Collection 6th ed. Village Harmony, 14th ed. Lock Hospital Collection, $3; Handel's Messiah, $3; Harmonia Sacra, $3; First Church Collection 50¢; Musical Reader, or Practical Lessons for the Voice, with Rudiments of Music, 50¢; Instrumental Preceptor, by Whitely, $1.25; Old Colony Collection, 11 numbers; Read's N. E. Selection, 75 cents; Suffolk Selection, $1, and a variety of Thanksgiving Anthems. Just published, the favorite Anthem by the celebrated Mr. Leach, entitled Canaan—price 12 cts. For Sale at James Loring's Bookstore, No. 2, Cornhill.[8]

Manning & Loring, leading booksellers, published the *Old Colony Collection of Anthems* (copyright February 5, 1814) in several parts, containing music by "authors of the first celebrity" as Purcell, Wanley, Kent,[9] Williams, Mason, Händel, Nares, Stephens, Boyce. The price was 37½ cents per volume. Numbers 10 and 11 of the same work, issued in October, 1818, contained two choruses from Beethoven's *Mount of Olives* [10] and *The Mariners at Anchor* by Mozart; according to the editors these were considered "a very fine specimen of the Author's superior talents in the composition of Music." [11] In the same year Oliver Shaw compiled his *Sacred Melodies*, containing two selections by Händel, three by Haydn, one by Mozart, and two by Beethoven; [12] there were numbers by lesser composers, and a new selection by the esteemed Mr. Shaw. Miller & Hutchins, Providence, were printers for the compiler.

These volumes were "best sellers" in quantity lots and helped to spread the musical influence of New England far and wide. Other collections of the same type published from 1760 onward show the chang-

8 *Columbian Centinel,* Nov. 28, 1818.
9 James Kent (1700–1776), English ecclesiastical composer of indifferent quality. James Nares (1715–1783), composer of miscellaneous glees, catches, anthems, etc.; onetime organist of the Chapel Royal. John Stephens (d. 1780), organist of Salisbury Cathedral and composer of a volume of cathedral music published 1805.
10 The Society first sang the final chorus on Nov. 24, 1818.
11 *Columbian Centinel,* Oct. 10, 1818.
12 One of the melodies by Beethoven is an arrangement from a Romanza in G Major, Opus 40, composed in 1803 for violin and orchestra.

ing style of church music from the psalm-tune era to a latter and not in all respects better day. The period under consideration here, however, is of particular interest since the works of the Vienna classicists became known in the choir loft as well as in the concert hall. The history of sacred music is a subject of parallel interest, but too vast for proper consideration in these pages.[13] *The Bridgewater Collection* (1802), *Norfolk Collection of Sacred Harmony* (Oct. 22, 1805), *The Norfolk Harmony* (Sept. 22, 1805), *The Sacred Minstrel* (Nov. 1, 1806), *Middlesex Collection of Church Music* (Jan. 5, 1807), *The Columbian Harmony* (Oct. 29, 1810), and *Harmonia Sacra* (May 2, 1812) are a few of the several hundred Boston collections sponsored after 1800 by denominational interests. Neighboring cities likewise sponsored their own compilations, but this flood of chorus material, much of it fundamentally the same in scope and purpose, was stopped when the *Handel and Haydn Collection* (1820) proved its superiority over all its predecessors. The Handel and Haydn Society likewise undertook a partial sponsorship of the *Old Colony Collection of Anthems* by entering into a joint copyright with James Loring on December 12, 1817.[14]

A collection of catches and glees was brought out by S. H. Parker with the crafty suggestion that "a book of this kind introduced into those Societies where psalm singing alone is practised (merely as music for practise) would have a tendency to promote the taste and cultivate the expression so necessary to give effect to any musical performance." This book of the Gods-at-play was thus virtually laid on the altar, and the way made easier for the inevitable step from psalm-tune singing to the newer type of anthem, less severe in musical texture, if not outrightly secular. However, to what extent the profane advice was heeded remains a matter of conjecture.

A new and uniform plan of printing was gradually adopted during these prolific years, for the remarkable impetus given to music printing here and in Europe, the vastly improved facilities for transportation and importation of books, and the emergence of the several business aspects of the entire field of music resulted directly in improved standards of teaching and publishing, as it resulted indirectly in fa-

[13] See Henry Wilder Foote, *Three Centuries of American Hymnody* (1940) and Hamilton C. MacDougall, *Early New England Psalmody* (1940).
[14] The dates are those on which copyright was granted by the Clerk of the District Court in Boston, Massachusetts.

voring improved professional and amateur performances. For the most part, the change, or "New Plan," most calculated to facilitate the progress of the musician was the adoption of the treble clef for the alto part and the printing of words with the music, since interchange of tunes was less common with the new and more exact science of hymnody. Hence, the advertisement, though fantastic and rather commercial at first glance, is not so far-fetched as it might seem:

These Collections are printed on a new plan, and a number of Teachers, who have given it a fair trial, say that it saves one half of the time which is required in learning the old way; it then will save one half of the expense of tuition. Should this plan become universal, it would be a yearly saving to the United States of fifty or sixty thousand dollars, and soon hundreds of thousands.[15]

The far-flung advantages of the plan refer, oddly enough, to a new edition of Andrew Law's *Church Music*, truly an instance of old wine in new bottles.

Meanwhile the fame of Dr. Watts was spreading with many editions of his psalms and hymns printed in various types and on several qualities of paper. The Methodists, Congregationalists, Universalists, and Presbyterians advanced new hymn books, featuring, for the most part, Dr. Watts's settings while side by side copies of the new idea and the old were demanded. The old style, however, had lost its popularity in the urban centers for the primitive custom of "lining out" became unnecessary with the installation of organs. In the smaller communities, or in those presided over by narrow and unmusical doctrinaires, ancient practices gave way slowly, particularly at a period when so many of the current changes were based on an alteration of fundamental belief. It is significant that the newer faiths, the contemporary "dissenters," were most advanced in their choice of sacred music and these grew most rapidly in the cities. (It will be remembered that at this time the enlivening spirit of a new thought had not disturbed the serenity of Concord.)

Much emphasis has been placed on the importance of *The Handel and Haydn Society Collection*, selected by Lowell Mason and approved by Dr. Jackson, an undertaking destined to stimulate the formation of choral societies throughout the country. There is some confusion of dates regarding the publication of this famous volume, but

[15] *Columbian Centinel*, Oct. 10, 1818.

order may be brought out of chaos by setting the several editions down. The copyright was granted by the Clerk of the District Court, Boston, as follows: "Joseph Lewis, as Secty. of the Handel and Haydn Society, The Boston Handel and Haydn Society Collection of Sacred Music, June 15, 1820." This was one of six musical copyrights in the state during the year. The preface to the first edition is dated 1821, as is the long and affectionate dedication.

THE HANDEL & HAYDN SOCIETY
OF BOSTON
Dedicate
Their Collection of Church Music
to
GEORGE K. JACKSON
Mus. Doct.
not only
as a tribute of gratitude
for his great care and attention in revising and correcting their work
but also
as a testimony
of the esteem in which he is held
for his
exquisite taste, profound knowledge,
and
unrivalled skill
in
the art and science of music

Boston, October 12, 1821

In March, 1821, *The Euterpeiad* carried an extended review of the volume "just published" discussing the rising taste in music of the church, and the salutary influence of the Handel and Haydn Society throughout New England. Considering the work in its most favorable light, obeisance was made to the president of the society, Amasa Winchester, and to the editors. The following issue of *The Euterpeiad* in April contained a notice by the publishers, Richardson & Lord, that copies awaited the subscribers. Thereafter the newspapers announced this volume and the following issues. A bulky work of 320 pages, there are 253 psalm and hymn tunes, many of them derived from Beethoven, Haydn, Mozart, and Pergolesi; there is one by Gluck, and several are by Dr. Jackson. The seventeen anthems are selected variously from Kent, Mason, Dr. Jackson, and Händel.

Following the complete issue of the first volume, the second and third came out in parts, a custom enabling singing societies to purchase anthems and hymns in smaller units and bind them later. The first number of the second volume was out in August, 1821, and contained half a dozen selections toward the complete work.

The story of Dr. Jackson's participation in this project is well known. Lowell Mason, an obscure Georgia bank clerk, submitted his collection to the officers of the Handel and Haydn Society; the manuscript was turned over to Dr. Jackson for advice, and his warm approval spurred the society to a quick decision with the result that a tidy fortune was made by author and sponsor, thus paving the way for Mason to come to Boston in 1827 and exert a leading influence on America's musical development.

Internal evidence gained from perusal of the volume shows that Dr. Jackson revised the selections most carefully, with such a stamp of personal authority and so much completeness that Mason and his collaborator, F. L. Abel, were virtually forgotten. In the first volume Mason's name occurs hardly at all, and then only in the fine print of the preface, while Dr. Jackson's praises are spread over an entire page. This was owing to Mason's desire that his respectable profession of bank clerk be not endangered by association with music. A correspondent wrote *The Euterpeiad* in 1822 granting the responsibility of Dr. Jackson for the harmonic revisions but pointing out the fact that Mason was properly responsible for the idea and for the selection of the majority of the 253 members. There must have been some extraordinary lifting of eyebrows, therefore, when the second edition (copyright July 7, 1823, and so dated) which had twenty more pages, "additions and improvements," omitted the preface and one of the good Doctor's anthems. There was, indeed, no mention of that good man! He had passed on during that very year, but that fact does not entirely explain the failure of the society to carry on a dedication so elaborately made. It is certain that Dr. Jackson always had enemies in Boston who could be relied upon to check any excess of egotism.

Let us return to the lesser publications of the time and to the secular as championed by other prominent figures in the Boston of these fruitful days.

Joseph Tinker Buckingham, publisher, editor, commentator—in all respects Boston's *enfant terrible*—confined his musical works to a few discreet volumes which found wide circulation. Among them was *The Boston Musical Miscellany*, a selection of modern songs, sentimental, amatory, humorous, anacreontick, adapted for the voice, violin, and German flute." This work of 190 pages was first printed by Mr. Buckingham in 1811 in one volume with the melodies given only above the words. The songs were universal favorites from the theater and concert repertory, and for this reason constitute an important source book to the popular music of the day. "Faithless Emma," "I Knew by the Smoke That So Gracefully Curl'd," "Why Does Azure Deck the Sky," "I Sold a Guiltless Negro Boy," "Old Towler," "Black-eyed Susan," "Life Let Us Cherish" are among them. No author's names are given, but the volume shows the shrewd judgment of the publisher, for it is the sort of omnibus which meets with ready approval and soon finds its way (as did the saccharine "Heart Songs" of a more recent day) into every home.

The success of this collection prompted a revision in two small volumes issued under the same title but adding to the sub-title the word "National" to the types of songs found in its pages. As before, it was printed and sold by Buckingham himself and issued from 5 Marlborough Street in February, 1815. The format is more attractive and there are charming decorations throughout. Many of the same songs reappear but Volume II contains in addition "Jubilee," "Freedom" (Arise, Arise, Columbia's Sons, Arise), "America, Commerce, and Freedom," "Adams & Liberty," "Columbia, Land of Liberty," and "Yankee Thunders," the latter written for a dinner given by the citizens of Boston to Captain Isaac Hull and officers of the "Constitution" in honor of their victory over the "Guerriere." The words hardly bear out the promise of the patriotic titles in any of the above instances, but the sentiments are beyond question.

Mr. Buckingham also girded his loins for sponsorship of "The Vocal Companion" in two parts consisting of "Songs, duetts, Glees, Catches &c. and Choruses" from Händel's *Dettingen Te Deum* and Haydn's *The Creation*. Verily, it would seem that Mr. Buckingham's collecting instincts were well developed and that the success of his ventures inspired others to do likewise. The same gentleman's publication of *Sacred Music*, composed by George C. Sweeney and William

Cooper, copyright in 1810, and *Hymns Suitable for Devotions of Families and Churches*, set to music by F. Schaffer, M. P. (Professor of Music?), in the same year are evidence of his catholic tastes.

In the same category belongs *The Songster's New Pocket Companion*, with engravings and musical appendix "containing a number of new and much admired melodies, and the most popular new Songs, singing at the different Theatres in the U. S., many of which have never before been published here." This little volume is a source mine for more than one hundred sets of words and tunes, many of them English, many of them known to be of American origin, and others which, thus far at least, defy identification; the volume was announced on March 15, 1817,[16] and was sold by every stationer and bookseller in the town. Booksellers often emulated the music publishers by bringing out occasional anthems for such special days as Thanksgiving and Christmas; in this manner Cooper's anthem, "The Lord Hath Done Great Things for Us," was advertised in 1815 by Manning & Loring, and Chapple's "Anthem from the 95th Psalm," in 1817.

Many publishing ventures, in a similar manner to the concerts, were approached by means of a subscription list, a custom well known to Beethoven in these same years. Subscription gave the advantage both of reduced prices and of mention as a patron on the introductory leaf. One of the largest proposals of this nature concerned the republication of the Vocal Works of Händel in the edition of Dr. John Clarke of Cambridge, England; the Franklin Music Warehouse secured right to the plates and stated that the sixteen oratorios and smaller vocal works has gone through three editions in England. The proposal was made in the spring of 1818, and the publication in separate volumes commenced in June of the same year. Surviving volumes are not uncommon in Boston libraries today.

Subscription papers were out at the same time for Haydn's *The Creation* sponsored by Farnum & Badger, a handsome edition of 160 pages with "accompaniment affixed to all the Airs, Recitatives, Duets, Trios, and Chorusses, and the Author's Introduction of the Representation of Chaos"; the work was issued May 1, 1818, at the price of $2.75 to subscribers and seventy-five cents additional to non-subscribers. The Great Society performed *The Creation* on the thirtieth

16 *Columbian Centinel.*

of the month, and the composer received further honor by a similar subscription plan for an edition of L. A. C. Bombet's [17] *The Life of Haydn*, in a series of letters written at Vienna; this was a reprint of the London edition with notes by William Gardiner, published in 1817.

The firm of Mallet & Graupner came into being as an adjunct to the Conservatory in 1802, and immediately following the termination of Trajetta's brief association with them. This announcement, appended to an advertisement, occurred in the Boston *Gazette* on March 29, and thereafter in other newspapers:

They have the satisfaction likewise to announce, to the Amateurs of this country, that they have established a Printing Office for the correct and elegant execution of all kinds of Music—and from the long experience they have had of the taste and judgement of their patrons and employers, they flatter themselves, that the production of their press will be pleasing and satisfactory.

They have now ready for sale, the Battle of Prague, and a few selected Songs—and in a few days will be published the Death of Anna, and Go Gentle Zephyr.

Approximately twenty selections bear the imprint of "Mallet & Graupner at their Conservatorio or Musical Academy" with few variants in the title. The Academy was located in Rowe's Lane, and the proprietors made constant use of an "apparatus that enables them to dispatch business with great neatness and celerity," in other words, a printing press with musical type. Among the earliest publications was the "Attic Bower" with words by Mr. Paine and music by Mr. Graupner. The newspapers regularly announced songs and pianoforte pieces "just published," but a word of caution should be observed in regard to the interpretation of the phrase "Just published" as it appears in advertisements. Of the music dealers only G. Graupner was absolutely faithful to the correct usage, for he noted "Just published" exclusively before those works bearing his own imprint, heading those issued by others, but for sale by him, as "Just received." Other dealers employ the words to signify consignments which they have received for sale. This notice of the Franklin Music Warehouse requires some explanation, however:

[17] Pseud. of Henry Beyle (1783–1842). *The Life of Haydn* was translated by R. Brewin, mainly as a plagiarism of Carpani's *Le Haydine* (Milan, 1812).

Just published, the much admired Song from Moore's sacred Melodies, "There's nothing true but Heaven," composed, and sung by Mr. O. Shaw, at the Oratorios, at the
King's Chapel.[18]

The song bears the stamp of Oliver Shaw, for this was the year in which
Graupner moved his business to the Franklin Music Warehouse, publishing a few songs there without address. In this case, Graupner's
press produced the song for Mr. Shaw, and not as one of his own publications. The later song "Mary's Tears" belongs in the same category.

With the dissolution of partnership in November, 1802 (treated
on pages 181–182, above), the publishing of music remained the chief
concern of Mr. Graupner. Therefore, except for works currently in
the press at the time of dissolution, the imprint of Mallet and Graupner may be interpreted as referring to music issued within the nine-
month period of their partnership.[19] Graupner advertises on November 11 that he has removed to his "Musical Academy, No. 6,
Franklin-street," and that form of title is used consistently until
1809, with the slight variant of "Repository" in place of "Academy."
After this date the word "Music Store" is used, and the lack of any
further identification than "G. Graupner, 6 Franklin street" (with
few variants) leads me to attribute all works not otherwise accounted
for to the long period which brought forth the majority of his publications. The few having no address I apportion to the early twenties, following the bankruptcy of his business. A half dozen imprints
bear the address of the Franklin Music Warehouse, where Graupner
set up briefly from early April to August, 1817. In the Appendices to
this volume, all possible aids to identification are entered, but no at-
tributive date is given on surmise. Furthermore, each piece of music
has been actually handled by the compiler and examined carefully for
all identifying marks. A brief list of works advertised by the Von Hagens and by Graupner, but not located, is added in the hope that
information may be forthcoming which will aid in completing a bibliography of these publishers.

A number of the plates on Graupner publications bear the added
information "Engraved by S. Wetherbee"; most of these are other-

18 *Columbian Centinel,* April 5, 1817.
19 Messrs. Mallet and Graupner united once more, in 1812, but for purposes of
teaching only.

wise identifiable as belonging to the year 1820, and I therefore incline to the belief that all Wetherbee-engraved works were made in this year. Wetherbee is listed in the directory as engraver for only one year, 1820; otherwise he is classed as a "Musician." Eight selections engraved by him were advertised as published on June 3, 1820.

A very large number bear the legend "and Sold for him by John Ashton, 197 Washington street," added to Graupner's name or placed at the bottom of the sheet. John Ashton Jr. took over the instrument and umbrella business of Elna Hayts, 18, Marlboro' Street in December, 1818; after a slow start he expanded his business and began publishing. Throughout the twenties Ashton advertised on a more elaborate scale than any other Boston musical warehouse and published more than fifty pieces of sheet music under his own name, in addition to the very many issued in connection with Graupner. The composers of his own imprints often show the progress of a generation over those characteristic of Graupner, but the style and type of selection are approximately the same and there is evident deduction that the example of the older man, independently and during their association, guided Ashton in his later career. Several editions of Graupner's successful imprints exist, of course, and frequently the later editions carry Ashton's name and address, added, in some instances, to the original plate; at other times, new plates were made to meet the higher standards of music printing or, presumably, to replace worn plates. The exact nature of this association is not yet clear from the evidence at hand, and no advertisements of either party refer to the two jointly. In my judgment, the Ashton legend establishes the imprints at a date subsequent to 1820 when Graupner anticipated giving up his place of business but planned to continue publishing, adding his stock of music for sale in conjunction with the very complete stock of instruments maintained by Ashton. This is an interpretation open to further enlightenment, but the first advertisement of John Ashton Jr., wherein music is conspicuously featured is dated February 6, 1820.

The question of plate numbers has given some concern to the examiner of Graupner's publications in the endeavor to discover the precise order of each work. The writer has preferred to make use of the newspaper advertisements and the addresses given on the music in so far as they are obtainable; in some cases the phrase "sung by Mr.——" has been of assistance, since it was customary to take ad-

vantage of a favorite singer's local engagement by publishing some
of the songs in his repertory. The larger problem concerns those published at 6 Franklin Street, for they cover a period of many years.
Here the question of plate numbers, studied in connection with those
definitely advertised according to date reveals no absolute method of
usage. Mr. J. Francis Driscoll, of Brookline, whose collection of
Graupneriana is unusually extensive urges the importance of plate
numberings, maintaining that Graupner used two sets.

The sheet music from the "Conservatorio or Musical Academy" by
Mallet & Graupner has no plate numbers whatever, nor have those
bearing the address "1 Province House Court," about eighteen pieces
in all. The imprint "15 Marlboro' (or Marlborough) street," appearing on fewer than fifteen pieces, need not concern us, since it represents
a brief period. Certain convincing deductions may be made from the
plate numbers to bear out the reasonableness of Mr. Driscoll's theory,
but it must be borne in mind that plate numbers, like opus numbers,
may not represent the exact order of issuance. A nearly complete set
of numbers from 70 to 103 may be attributed by reasons of other evidence—some of them mentioned above—to 1817–1820; the few dupli-
cate numbers belong to the parallel set, but the few plate numbers
from 1 to 70 cover a wide period from the days of the Musical Academy to 1816. Of the other series, some of the numbers from 80 onward
were published in 1811, or those in the one hundreds, in 1813, and
those in the first half of the two hundreds, in 1815; there are exceptions and complications in abundance, and this method soon becomes
a backward one of justifying the plate number by the music, rather
than identifying the music by the number.

From the beginning of his career as publisher, Graupner was interested in larger works than those requiring a single folded sheet, and
his outturn contains several collections and preceptors. The first was

The Musical Magazine

being a collection of the most Modern & Favorite Songs,
Airs, Marches, Etc.   taken from the Works of the most
celebrated authors and adapted to the Voice, with Bass &
key'd instruments.

These are songs of one page each, for the most part, from the favorite
ballad operas of the day. Volume I, published early in April, 1803,

contained songs by Arnold, Mazzinghi, Shield, Storace, and Moulds; the second and third volumes went further afield in the selection of composers but still remained true to the spirit of the series. Volume II added Dibdin, Hook, and Reeve to the list, while Volume III included Mr. Graupner's own "Attic Bower," without the composer's name, and Haydn's "A Prey to Tender Anguish." Many of these selections had been issued separately by him; always the collections represented numbers known elsewhere, if not in Boston, and not the newer works coming to the stage. Each volume sold for $2.10.

Graupner's second large undertaking was the *Monitor or Celestial Melody*, announced in January, 1806:

SACRED MUSIC

Proposals for publishing by Subscription, a valuable collection of Sacred Music.

G. Graupner, respectfully informs the Public in general, and the admirers of Divine Harmony in particular, that he intends publishing a collection of Psalm and Hymn Tunes, taken principally from a celebrated work lately published in London, and used at the Chapel of the Lock Hospital, and other places of Public Worship there.—To which will be added, some of the most favorite, at present in the United States. The work will be adapted for four voices and Organ for Public Worship, and as the full harmony, or thorough bass is annexed to the treble, in small notes it will be equally calculated for the Piano Forte with one or two voices. The whole work will contain the names of the subscribers. The first number (which may be considered as a fair specimen of the whole) will be published on the first day of March, and continued monthly. It will consist of 8 pages folio, printed on good music paper, and neatly engraved.

The price to subscribers will be 50 cents, to nonsubscribers 75 cents. Any person procuring subscription for 12 copies, shall be entitled to one gratis. As this valuable work is offered to the public at half the usual price of Music and as no collection of Sacred Harmony of equal utility, has yet been printed in America, it is presumed that the above will meet with their patronage and support.

Subscriptions received at G. Graupner's Musical Academy, Franklin Place, and at this Office.[20]

The first part was available on April 10, and the others came along regularly as promised until the concluding number, issued on November 3, 1806; there were sixty-nine hymns of the new style in the ninety-six pages of the Collection.

[20] Boston *Gazette,* Jan. 16, 1806.

The story of Boston's musical development must take into account the numerous preceptors which filled an immediate and long-continuing need in New England and elsewhere. The first preceptor, compiled and published by Graupner, attained the greatest influence of any of the three bearing his name and was given to the musical public about the time the several parts of the *Monitor or Celestial Melody* were completed.

Rudiments
of the Art of Playing
on the
Pianoforte
Arranged by Gottlieb Graupner
etc. . . .

Printed and sold by Gottlieb Graupner at his
Musical Repository, 6 Franklin street
Entered according to Law

Following the customary instructional material, there are thirty examples for practice, ranging from the most elemental and unidentified composers to the world's most venerable masters ; the names of Händel, Corelli, Pleyel, Hook, Scarlatti, Haydn, and—happy culmination!—Sebastian Bach, represented by a Polonaise from the Sixth French Suite, are included. The arranger's own name is given among the simpler examples, but these would hardly conspire to make out a strong case for Graupner as composer. A second edition, dated May, 1819, was "Improved and enlarged" according to the Foreword, or "Note," explaining the omission of 20 pages of "exercises which were generally considered difficult of execution," but the total runs to 51 pages, whereas the first edition had but 40 pages. Yes, the example by Bach was omitted.

Some confusion exists in the accounts already given of this work, but careful perusal of all the editions reveals that the first edition, with plate numbers 219-258, was published in April, 1806, in accordance with this announcement:

NEW INSTRUCTION BOOK FOR THE PIANO FORTE

Published this day and for sale by G. Graupner, at his Musical Academy, No. 6, Franklin-street. Rudiments of the art of playing on the Piano Forte—containing Elements of Music, Preliminary Remarks on Fingering, with

examples in thirty fingered Lessons, and a plain Direction
for Tuning. The whole arranged by

GOTTLIEB GRAUPNER [21]

In the second edition each page had the plate number 520, the word
"Repository" was changed to "Warehouse," and "Copyright Secured" is given in place of "Entered according to Law." The date is
May, 1819. Thereafter the date of the Introduction is often changed,
representing further printings of the second edition. "Jan. 1, 1825,"
and "Jan. 1, 1827" have been found, and it is possible that other
printings were made. The volume sold for $2.50 in all editions. For
further discussion, see Appendix II.

In these active years, Graupner also brought out *The Anacreontic
Vocalist* consisting of glees, catches, canons, duets, rounds, etc. by
Jenkins, Battishall (hill), Linley, Smith, Ives, Hilton, Hayes, Playford, Webb, Purcell, Harrington, Byrd, Calcott, Arne, Warren,
Green, Aldrich, Boyce, Atterbury, Webbe, Dibdin, Haydn, etc.—in
all, fifty-three pieces of which thirty are catches. This work, "elegantly engraved upon copperplate, and containing from 70 to 80
pages" is a rather crude volume, 11 by 8½ inches, containing 80
pages. The proposal was made on February 21, 1809, and the books
were available on June 30 at the price of $1.50 to subscribers and two
dollars to non-subscribers. Many selections contained in the volume
are familiar today, but this interesting verse is given in "Drink to Me
Only with Thine Eyes":

> Speak to me only with thine eyes,
>   And language read from mine,
> For sad adieu give heaving sighs,
>   Mute eloquence divine;

These lines are given in place of the four commonly used: "I sent thee
late a rosy wreath"; otherwise the poem remains unchanged.

With the remarkable interest in the several varieties of flute, it was
not surprising that *G. Graupner's Complete Preceptor for the German Flute* "containing accurate scales and examples of the best
Fingering to which is added a Collection of the most popular airs,
Marches, &c. &c. and a Dictionary of Musical Terms" should follow
a similar work for the pianoforte. Directions for beating time with the
foot were likewise included! The flute preceptor bears the Ashton

[21] *Repertory*, Sept. 2, 1806.

mark and contains 49 pages. *A New Preceptor for the German Flute*
"printed and sold by G. Graupner at his Music Store, No. 6 Franklin
street" is quite a different affair of 34 pages, with some new examples,
and smaller pages; it is my surmise that this volume was predecessor
of the other, owing to the Ashton mark and the inclusion of an example from Rossini's *The Barber of Seville* in the other volume.
Neither preceptor has plate marks.

Graupner likewise arranged his flute preceptor to assist the student
of the clarinet, and advertised it on July 14, 1826; this work is difficult to locate, but the Library of Congress has a copy.

Only one other large work appears to have the Graupner imprint.
A Collection of Country Dances and Cotillions, in four volumes, contains thirty-three short dances suitable for the purpose mentioned in
the title; all four volumes must have enjoyed popularity in view of
the large number of dancing instructors and schools operating in
Boston. On September 26, 1821, this work was copyright by Graupner as *Collection of Cottillions,* "selected from the best composers by
F. D. Mallet, arranged for pianoforte by F. C. Shaffer."

Other than his own compilations, few large works were issued by
Graupner, but the *Gentlemen's Pocket Companion,* "being a collection
of the most favorite Marches, Songs, Rondos, &c. adapted as Duettinos for two German Flutes, or Flute and Violin, by Frederick
Granger, price 1 dol. 50 cts." is an exception; Granger was one of
Boston's veteran composers and arrangers. The *Companion* was first
advertised on October 22, 1803.

Graupner's all-inclusive interests as a musician may be seen in the
larger publications emanating from his press. The sacred song, the
secular (the latter both from the theatrical aspect and that of private
entertainment), the instructional, and the dance are represented;
moreover, all are designed for a large public in the beginning stages of
musical development. To these must be added the various collections of
group songs. If the standard does not often maintain a notable elevation, one must consider the times, in relation to both youthful America
and the older Europe.

It should be apparent from the leisurely survey of the major publishing houses in Boston and from the extensive Appendices at the end
of this volume that the influence of the Von Hagens and Graupner was
of utmost importance during these formative years. Contemporane-

ously, however, a large number of smaller enterprises flourished under circumstances of manufacture and sale which are not in all respects clear; few were dealers, but the booksellers, musical instrument warehouses, and repositories provided outlet for publications of any individual whose enthusiasm for a given work encouraged him to have his name imprinted on a handful of ballads or marches. These included Simeon Wood, S. H. Parker, Thomas Badger Jr., John Ashton Jr., Dr. Jackson, Thomas Spear, Francesco Masi, and others duly listed in the Appendix.

Inasmuch as there were nearly thirty periodicals having regular issue in Boston in 1820, there is reason to expect that at least one of these would give intelligent concern to the subject of music. Actually, the literary periodicals of the day gave slight attention to music, but some discussed the theater. While the old *Massachusetts Magazine* [22] religiously included a selection of music in many of its issues, no discussion as to their value to the subscribers was permitted in the columns and one may sense the same faint disapproval with respect to the musical illustration that was expressed with regard to the handsome engravings used as frontispieces. In the first number of the second year (January, 1790) the editors discussed the reception of the first volume and stated the complaint of one reader who considered engravings a waste and expense since eight pages of reading matter could be inserted to improve the mind for the same expense of an illustration which is of no improvement whatever; henceforth the quality of the illustrations became inferior and, after a few months, the selections of music disappear. Despite so much faithfulness, the small print and poor condition of the plate had nullified much of the service which otherwise might have been accomplished by introducing music to a literary audience. The selections, however, show a rare discernment in adhering to the avowed title of the publication, for they admitted, with few exceptions, only works by Massachusetts composers; hence the pages of the *Massachusetts Magazine* are a valuable source of information for the works of Hans Gram, John Selby, E. Mann, and

[22] Established by Isaiah Thomas and Ebenezer Andrews in January, 1789, and published until 1796; a few publications of music by this firm belong to the turn of the century. Isaiah Thomas is likewise famous for his connection with the *Spy,* and he was the first to print extensively from musical type. In 1812 he founded the American Antiquarian Society, leaving his large collection of newspapers as an invaluable nucleus.

others who never achieved separate issue or wide sale, since no other form was existent at the time. A complete list of the forty-four selections is given at the end of this chapter.

By 1812 Boston had the *Polyanthus*,[23] "a Monthly Magazine, consisting of History, Biography, Romance, Criticism, Poetry, &c. &c." and published by Joseph T. Buckingham. Mr. Buckingham's forte was criticism, and Boston was the livelier for his ungallant and irreverent commentary; furthermore, there is every reason to suppose that he knew what he was talking about, and none whatever to persuade the reader that Heinrich's disparaging lines were true: [24]

> To Mr. Buckingham
> Hurl'st thou thine arrows at a rock?
> They will themselves receive the shock,
> And fall divested of their point.

When the editor of the *Polyanthus* announced summarily that "The hoyden is Mrs. Poe's forte," [25] that "From Mr. Poe's BARNWELL we expected little satisfaction, and of course we were not disappointed," [26] and "Little Pickle, by Mrs. Poe, if we may be allowed the use of a pun, was a very green Little Pickle. We never knew before that the Spoiled Child belonged to that class of beings termed hermaphroditical, as the uncouthness of his costume seemed to indicate," [27] it is not surprising that Mr. Poe called at the home of the writer "to chastise my impertinence" as the editor gleefully reported, adding that the would-be assailant went away without effecting his purpose.[28]

Beginning with the issue for August, 1812, a selection of music was included each time, with only two exceptions, for which profuse apologies were made. The composer's name was not always given, but the majority of the selections were popular ballads sung at the theater and chosen, one may be sure, by the careful hand of the editor whose interest, if not his education, was extraordinary when unleashed in defense of the muse. A complete list of these selections may be found at the end of this Chapter.

The most formidable periodical to come into being was the *North American Review*, established in 1815. To such a work one looks ex-

---

23 The *Polyanthus* was begun in 1805, but in 1812 a new and enlarged periodical was commenced by the same editor.
24 *Columbian Centinel*, March 19, 1825.
25 *Polyanthus*, 1806, Vol. V, p. 66.   26 *Ibid.*, 1805, Vol. IV, p. 281.
27 *Ibid.*, 1805, Vol. IV, p. 212.   28 Buckingham, *Memoirs*, p. 57.

pectantly for mention of the Handel and Haydn Society, established in the same year, and for recognition of the active forces permeating the life of Boston in these wonderful times. Only disappointment is there, however, for not until 1822 is there a discussion of any phase of musical life, and the result in this case is not a forward-looking article on the extensive secular activities—the Philharmonic Society, the Handel and Haydn Society, the manifold publishing interests, or the growing concert life—of Boston, or of the country at large, but a long and extremely tiresome "Dissertation on Musical Taste," a review of a volume by Thomas Hastings, he of the reactionaries, one of the Psalm-tune survivalists.

An earlier literary group had propounded the *Monthly Anthologie* from 1803 to 1811, a rather pathetic attempt to encourage American talent, but its direction was in the hands of clergymen suffering from the prevailing melancholy of Presbyterian belief, then making some headway in New England. Music played no part in it, for there were none to write on that subject and few readers to understand reviews of anything more secular than hymn-tune publications.

No, none of the literary periodicals showed an inspired concern for the art of music, but there were poets and poetesses who evidenced an unnecessary familiarity with its terminology. In the *Monthly Anthologie*, Robert Treat Paine Jr. labels each verse in an effusion entitled "Spirit of the Vital Flame" with such titles as "Air-adagio," "Recitativo," "Air-largo maestoso," "Allegro," "Allegro assai," but there was no assault on the muse in the body of the poem. Mrs. Morton brought forth a poem containing a stanza "to be sung by those who have been restored to life from apparent death." The few composers of the time were not of this number, for no music was volunteered as fitting counterpart to so overwhelming a conception. While the *Monthly Anthologie* reviewed Andrew Law's *Musical Magazine,* and Buckingham's *First Church Collection of Sacred Music,* occasional reference to the jew's harp and hand organ are more typical references. Such talents as there were seem to have been embodied in the clergy, but theological disquisitions, however acceptable in pamphlets and pulpits, are seldom desirable as specimens of literature per se.

A certain evidence of any "movement" is the appearance of a periodical. Accordingly *The Euterpeiad, or Musical Intelligencer, De-*

voted to the Diffusion of Musical Information and Belles Lettres, was founded in 1820 under the editorship of John R. Parker, proprietor of the Franklin Music Warehouse, No. 6 Milk Street, later widely known authority on semaphoric signals, and was published by Thomas Badger Jun., printer, formerly proprietor of an evening school. The first issue was dated Saturday, April 1, 1820. Parker's name did not appear until the end of the first quarter, but it is apparent that he was responsible for the policies of the magazine from the beginning, and evidences of his ownership and flavorsome personality may be found on every page, that is, every page not bodily reprinted from other books or periodicals. The magazine had four quarto pages, invariably adding a fashionable song or other musical example.[29] The price was three dollars per annum payable half-yearly in advance. The *Euterpeiad*, which must be recognized, therefore, as the first musical periodical published in this country, aimed to present:

a brief history of music from the earliest ages, Cherish a classical taste, watch progress of the art, Excite the emulation of genius, record the transactions of society, Examine and impartially review new musical works, Stimulate professional gentlemen to explore new traces in the regions of science, etc.

The mainstay of the publication was "A Brief History of Music," which continued for nearly two years, and which was unblushingly appropriated without acknowledgment from the voluminous pages of Dr. Burney. Anecdotes, biographical articles on Corelli, Samuel Webbe, Padre Martini, Henry Purcell, etc. with constant, unfailing, and enthusiastic references to George Frederick Händel comprised the main body of the paper. Local news and criticism of concerts had an important place, and these comprise the first attempts at professional criticism in this country.

This Lady's last Concert (Mrs. French's) on Thursday Evening at Boylston Hall was numerously and fashionably attended with a genteel assemblage of Ladies and Gentlemen.

A benefit, lovingly tendered Mr. Granger Sr. was recommended as worthy recompense for one

who, having outlived his abilities, is now descending the vale, and may be denominated a *decayed musician.*

[29] A list, nearly complete, of these supplements may be found at the end of this chapter.

Or Mr. Christiani, who gave a concert of music in the Italian style:

his exertions to please, were received with an universal degree of complacency.

Even the Great Society was not free from criticism:

We regret not having it in our power to express an approval of their performance, but it would be a dereliction of principle, as well as the forfeiture of a duty we owe the public, not to declare our unequivocal dissatisfaction of what we heard from all quarters instrumental and vocal. It is not our duty to trace the causes which had a tendency to deteriorate from the merit usually displayed at these exhibitions, neither can we refrain from an avowal of the conviction, that, an apparent want of individual exertion, was too glaringly manifested on this occasion, and while we regret the existence of so palpable a neglect of duty towards public expectation, we are brought to the recollection, from the effect produced upon our minds, of the following effusion of an ancient native Bard of our metropolis on jargon.

> Now horrid jargon splits the air
> And rends my nerves asunder,
> Now hateful discord, greets the ear,
> As terrible as thunder.

Or a report of Mme. Catalani:

Mme. Catalani sings about a dozen airs with which she travels over Europe. It is a tissue of embroidery for the most part, in very bad taste. Mme. Catalani is still very handsome by candlelight.

Mr. Cartwright's exhibition on the musical glasses was treated as a musical performance eliciting rapturous letters to the paper, to which a special note of praise was appended by the editor. One enthusiast wrote a poem. Mr. Cartwright also gave "Philosophical Fire-Works," a form of amusement unknown to the present day under that title.

Beethoven was not unknown in Boston, for several distorted tunes were to be found in the Handel and Haydn Collection.[30] Otherwise few of his other works were mentioned in the lists of the day. "When Bee-

30 One of the most tantalizing questions in connection with the early life of the Handel and Haydn Society concerns a commission offered to Beethoven for a musical work. No authorization of such an important step is contained in the records of the society, but Perkins believes that Samuel Richardson and two or three members made the offer unofficially in 1823 when a Boston bank had occasion to correspond with Geymüller, bankers, of Vienna. Richardson was a charter member of the society, elected librarian and purveyor at the first meeting, and by pro-

thoven nods like Homer" was a phrase used frequently by those who did not hesitate to censure the harmonic "errors" contained in his works. News items regarding the famous gift of the Broadwood piano, a gift, by the way, which reaped its full value in publicity, were copied from the English periodicals. A later number contained a rhapsodical sketch of a "Translation of Beethoven's Trio, Op. 70, No. 1," but there could have been no immediate application to any Boston performance of the work. Its inclusion was undoubtedly directed by the prevailing love for flowery description, a trend more than topped by the writings of the Rev. William Gardiner, soon to sweep over the musical world under the title of *The Music of Nature*.

High hopes indulged at the start were only partially realized by the end of the first year. The *Euterpeiad* was still "devoted to the diffusion of Musical and Belle Lettre information" but—to come to the point—art did not pay, and the editor was receiving no profit from his venture. Either the subscription list was largely constituted of ladies whose further interest promised a revival of prosperity, or it was not constituted of ladies whose potential support promised a mine of unclaimed riches, for the only perceptible change in its conduct was the introduction of a "Ladies' Gazette" into the body of the magazine. The many anecdotes, bits of homely philosophy, and news items from abroad, all dealing with sweet womankind, are amusing by reason of their naïveté, but it must be admitted that articles on "Scheme for Getting a Husband," "Pleasures of a Married State," and "Second Bliss of Matrimony" hardly live up to the promise of the suggestive titles. They are not to be compared, for instance, with the full revelations obtainable, with illustrations, in the twentieth century from the corner newsstand.

---

fession a banker; his act would probably been considered well within the bounds of propriety by the members. It was conveyed by Schindler.

Alexander Wheelock Thayer was at this time a boy of five years living in Natick, but in 1853 he made a further search into this matter while Consul at Trieste, and he concurs in the explanation as given by Perkins. Beethoven's conversation books contain this passage in answer to a question by Bühler, "The Oratorio for Boston?" "I cannot write what I should best like to write, but that which the pressing need for money obliges me to write. This is not saying that I write only for money. When this period is past, I hope to write what for me and for art is above all, Faust." A periodical notice in 1823 listed three works in progress by Beethoven, one of them the oratorio with English words for Boston. Nothing came of it, of course, for Beethoven's remaining years were few, and his immediate work in hand, coupled with domestic troubles prevented any further steps being taken.

Our interest in the first musical magazine printed in this country, however, concerns those portions which gave information regarding the leading musicians of the community. While the *Euterpeiad* was a house organ in the sense that it was sponsored by the Franklin Music Warehouse, of which John Rowe Parker was proprietor, there was no effort made at any time to secure particular advantage for the merchandise or publications of that firm. All interests were united in the encouragement of amateur and professional societies, and in the diffusion of general knowledge, all objectives impartially outlined in the first issue. Mr. Graupner, formidable competitor of the Franklin Music Warehouse, was given such attention and praise as he deserved, evidence both of the universal affection which that worthy gentleman inspired, and of the fair-minded recognition of local merit on the part of Mr. Parker. Mr. Graupner did not advertise in its columns, but during the years 1820–1822 his business was practically closed and there are no indications that he was in public life other than as teacher and conductor. Other merchants and private teachers had cards in the *Euterpeiad,* and their names and occupations are duly recorded in Leporello's best manner at the end of Chapter X.

John Rowe Parker was more than an amateur musician and more than a merchant. His wide interests, and apparent influence, were based on a modest, thoughtful, and credibly accurate application of general knowledge. From the pages of the *Euterpeiad* plentiful confirmation of these faculties is available. When an inquiry asks for advice on musical instruction, Mr. Parker recommends Dr. Miller's book on thorough bass,[31] Kollmann's essay on musical harmony,[32] and Holden's *Treatise,*[33] all works of scholarly merit. He comments on the publication of the lives of Mozart and Haydn in Boston with the statement that such noble talents are worthy of finer bindings and bet-

[31] Edward Miller (1731–1807), Mus. D., Cambridge. Studied under Dr. Burney, became organist of Doncaster, and composed in small forms. *The Elements of Thorough-Bass and Composition* was published in 1787.

[32] August Friedrich Christoph Kollmann (1745–1829) was born in Hanover but lived in England, where he composed much and was author of at least theoretical works on music. The volume referred to by Parker is probably *Essay on Practical Harmony,* published in 1796.

[33] While the name Holden suggests that of Oliver, the Charleston carpenter who made a name in the field of psalmody, the reference by Parker is probably to Rev. William Holder, D. D. (1616–1697) who wrote in 1694 *A Treatise on the Natural Grounds and Principles of Harmony,* which had a second edition in 1731. This is considered a very able work. Interest attaches to Holder because of his marriage to the sister of Sir Christopher Wren.

ter print than the new cheap editions. In befitting acknowledgment of
Mr. Ostinelli's concert, he describes it as "certainly the most genteel
thing of the kind ever witnessed in Boston," but remarks that Mr.
Granger's claims were complacently received on an occasion more
notable for its charitable intent than its musical importance.

The musical criticism throughout the career of the *Euterpeiad* aims
to be helpful to the organizations involved. The Handel and Haydn
Society is given high praise and some good advice, and the Philharmonic Society also benefits by Parker's almost fatherly interest in the
fortnightly concerts. With a grateful regard for the disparity between intention and fulfillment he usually omits mention of the solo
performers, particularly if they be of local vintage, a consideration
doubtless appreciated at that time, but regrettable to us at a safer
remove. Biographies of the great and near great are useful for reference purposes; these included Mr. Gillingham of Philadelphia, Dr.
Jackson, Miss Hewitt, and Miss Eustephieve of Boston. Parker's
tribute on the passing of Mrs. Graupner is just and moving in its sincerity.[34] He also envisioned the place of an orchestra in the cultural
life of a major city and showed a real understanding of the rising
estate of the professional musician. In the issue of February 2, 1821,
Mr. Parker wrote: "It appears that a COLLEGIATE ESTABLISHMENT
for the education of youth, designed for the profession of Music, is
the grand desideratum. As we are not yet prepared to go into the detail for such a foundation, we shall resume this subject on a future
occasion." Thrice misfortunate that Mr. Parker did not find opportunity for a full discussion of his ideas on this subject! There already
existed institutions called "conservatorios" in the sense that several
teachers were banded together to provide musical instruction, but
none which by the remotest stretch of the imagination could be called
collegiate in purpose or accomplishment. With Harvard near at hand,
and Mr. Parker sufficiently literate to wield a florid pen, the imagination is provoked into wonderment as to the precise mold into which his
conception of a musically educated person would be dipped before
carrying the gospel of Haydn, Mozart, and Beethoven to the remotest borders of a new world.

Throughout these pages much small gossip attendant on the New
England musician's daily fortunes has been set down with the object of

34 See pp. 192–93.

making our study as complete as possible. The social position of the musician had been changing rapidly during these very decades in Europe. Mozart and others in his situation had stampeded from the overweening authority of the patronage system, and the whole situation of the musician's social world had crumbled at that daring interview between Hieronymus of Salzburg and a hot-tempered and exasperated genius. Mozart had fled to Vienna, the one place where a free soul might hope to find self-respecting employment without sacrificing the social position to which his art entitled him. The subsequent story, one of the saddest in all music, is embarrassingly familiar, while similar tales may be recounted of others for many years afterward. In the very years when the New England worthies were striving to achieve a respectable place in human society, Franz Schubert was knowing the same poverty and the same inability to make tangible profit from scores which his genius poured forth; he, too, finally succumbed to the same fate from an accumulation of troubles caused by want of the small things in life.

The conditions under which music had flourished in Europe were manifestly impossible in America where freedom of mind and body, and equality before the law were cornerstones of national policy. No self-respecting American could bind himself as servant to a merchant, political figure, or shipowner, whose vaster wealth and equal social position were without hereditary tradition or title, and whose mode of living was modest and plain compared with the courtly magnificence of the European nobility. A different scale of values throughout the American social system forbade duplication of the older system, even if the distraught musician had been willing to consider such a form of degrading patronage. But the problem of the social eligibility of the musician was one which concerned both the musician and the upper classes who comprised a circle no less aristocratic in feeling and, in many respects, in culture than that of the courts of Europe. New England, Virginia, Philadelphia, and New York were "Society conscious"; in many respects they were socially conscious, in the modern sense, as well. Was not America a democracy? It was, notwithstanding Alexander Hamilton and the widely accepted theories which survived him.

The *Euterpeiad* entered no lengthy discussion of this pertinent subject, but the fact of a single article in defense of the musician's worthiness provides a commentary on the alertness of the editor. A correspondent found the article worthy of a reply, in which he wrote: "Let me assure you, Sir, that you will find probity and character, eloquence and economy, united in many professors . . . who are distinguished ornaments of the country."

With the third year there came a parting of the ways, with the *Euterpeiad* continuing under its own rapidly diminishing power, and the ladies' department springing, truly like Minerva, into a full-fledged magazine. The two were issued in reduced size, of eight pages each, and at the price of two dollars each yearly, the combination for three dollars. Volume I of the *Minerviad* and Volume III of the *Euterpeiad* bear the date of March 30, 1822, but the former came out the following week, and both continued fortnightly thereafter. There was no perceptible change in the contents of either, but the new arrangement was manifestly less satisfactory than the old, and after six months both publications were discontinued. Mr. Parker stated in the *Euterpeiad* that "publication will be conducted by others" a reference to the subsequent ambitions of Charles Dingly, whose career at this point is somewhat obscure. Two issues of the "New Series," Volume I, Nos. 1 and 2 of May and June, 1823, are in the American Antiquarian Society but no proof of the title or author are to be found in Boston annals, nor did they deserve greater favor, for they are more poverty-stricken of material than the later issues under Parker. Dingly revived the *Euterpeiad* in New York in 1830.

The first conclusion with regard to the failure of a musical magazine at this period may be that the public was not yet ready to support one, a just conclusion in so far as Boston and New England are concerned. However, Parker listed forty-four distributing points from Montreal, Canada, to Augusta, Georgia, where the magazine might be obtained, and his failure to treat local events in the several communities more fully—except for the nationally famous Handel and Haydn Society—may have been in recognition of the wide geographical distribution over which the musical public was scattered. In view of modern periodicals, however, one may analyze the chief fault as a want of concern for local news in the several capitals where musical life was quite as active as in Boston. Occasional reprints from Philadelphia or New York papers, served over again a month later, hardly supplanted the value of direct correspondence with musical enthusiasts, an asset immediately recognized by John Sullivan Dwight while editor of the *Harbinger* and, later, of his *Journal of Music*.

Elsewhere in New England publishers were active with collections of sacred and secular words and music. Word books were familiar, of course, and a far less expensive undertaking than engraved tune books. It is difficult, if not impossible, to give a complete list of these trivia at so early a period in the research among American communities, but a few have been reported in various books lately published, and mention of others is scattered through these pages. Nathaniel Heaton Jr. issued *The Columbian Songster* in Wrentham in 1799; William & Daniel Treadwell were booksellers of Portsmouth, and their *Nightingale, a Collection of the Most Popular Ancient and Modern Songs* set to music, selected by Samuel Larkin, contained the rather surprising number of 288 pages and bore the date 1804. There were 109 songs with the melody given, but no harmony, nor were the authors mentioned.

The Songster's Companion, published at Brattleboro, Vermont, in 1815 contained words only, with tunes indicated; *The Songster's Museum, or a Trip to Elysium* was printed at Northampton by Alpheus Wright for S. & E. Butler, and sold at their bookstore in 1803; the hundred pages comprised folk-songs from Scotland, Ireland, and England, with a few which may be true Americana; several tunes were by Uri K. Hill. Only the melody was given except in one instance, "The Nymph's Complaint" by Mr. Swan, which was "accompanied by the base." The popularity of the Handel and Haydn and Bridgewater Collections led Colton, Warren & Sproat of Fairhaven, Vermont, to republish them without leave, and Richardson & Lord, Boston printers of these copyrighted works, made open protest. Herman Mann, of Dedham, is remembered for his printing of Oliver Shaw's earliest works, but he was a compiler, with others, and editor of collections on his own behalf in a few instances. He must not be mistaken for E. Mann of Worcester whose compositions were printed in the *Massachusetts Magazine*.

In concluding a study of Boston music publishers in the first quarter of the nineteenth century it may be useful to append brief identifications of the lesser names occasionally imprinted on works listed in Appendix IV.

Samuel Stockwell has been mentioned frequently in these pages as actor and singer, member of the Boston Theatre troupe, and fellow organizer of the Handel and Haydn Society until his death in 1818.

Thomas Badger Jr. (formerly of Farnum & Badger) was a printer with few claims to musical competence beyond the fact that he set many collections of music from 1815 onward and the *Euterpeiad* during the three years of its existence. He had ambitions to engage in printing, however, and advertised in 1821: "Music, vocal and instrumental, typographically executed, on the most reasonable terms." The reasonableness of his prices for printing doubtless gave strong encouragement to the several congregations throughout New England to make their own selection of Psalm tunes and have a collection bearing their own name. Badger quotes these rates in 1821:

Common Psalmody at 75 cents per page, common Singing book form.

Quarto common, Psalmody at One Dollar fifty cents per page.

Music of the above sized page for the Organ, Piano Forte, Flute, Clarionet, &c. will be enhanced a mere trifle, and can be procured 150 per cent cheaper than plate music . . .

The Franklin Music Warehouse at 6 Milk Street undertook a very small amount of printing, except in the six month period of Graupner's hegira, but sold the publications of all Boston, New York, Philadelphia, and Baltimore houses; no purchase stamp is more familiar than that of this firm, which must have done a thriving business under the guidance of John Rowe Parker; the single item listed in the Appendix was actually printed by Bacon & Co. of Philadelphia for the Franklin Music Warehouse.

The single sheet bearing the name of the "Gazette Office, 32 Congress street," suggests a musical supplement at a time unknown, and by no means denotes a regular music-publishing business by the Boston *Gazette*.

Simeon Wood was a bassoon and double-bass player in the Philharmonic and Handel and Haydn Society orchestras, but there is no record of his owning a music store or other direct outlet for the dozen selections printed for him; these belong to the period 1815 to 1822, the year in which he died at the age of thirty-eight years.

The several Masi brothers were on hand, if not prominent, during the period treated in this survey. Vincent was a dancing master, and one-time confectioner; Francesco was a musician.

Samuel Wetherbee is remembered as a player in the orchestras of Boston and as engraver of Graupner's publications in 1820 ; the directories list him as "copper plate printer and musician" for that year only, thereafter returning to the description "musician." His career as publisher must have commenced at a later date, however, for "Home, Sweet Home" must of necessity belong after 1823. America first heard *Clari, Maid of Milan* in 1828.

Considering the overwhelming size and importance of Dr. Jackson as an omniscient paragon, it is remarkable that he would demean himself by selling music. Dr. Jackson in trade? With parental concern, however, he was responsible for setting up his sons, Charles and Edwin W., in business when they came to Boston in 1821. "Dr. George K. Jackson, Doctor of Music, business 64 Market street house Hancock" is given in the directory for 1821, and the opening of their store was announced in the papers of March 31 ; after their father's death the sons carried on by themselves, moving to 44 Market Street.[35] After the first year or two it appears that Edwin carried on alone, but the firm is listed in the directories until 1826, when the partnership was dissolved. The extent of their publishing is indicated in the forty-six selections listed here.

Thomas Spear had a brief career as teacher of piano and publisher from approximately 1820 to 1822 and, as a representative pupil of Dr. Jackson, endeavored to profit from that association by offering testimonials of Charles and Edwin Jackson. His address was given as 21 School Street, but no further importance can be attached to his career in Boston.

The history of the house of Hewitt is of more than local interest, and the interrelationships between the Broadway headquarters and the Boston and Philadelphia branches require fuller treatment than is accorded them here.[36] A list of publications bearing the Boston address would number more than 150 items and provide a sizeable study. James Hewitt's first Boston imprints of the year 1813 have the address 58½ Newbury street and extend through several changes of address over a period of nearly twenty years. During his peregrinations, James A. Dickson acted as agent.

35 It is possible that the street was renumbered.
36 John Tasker Howard has given the fullest account of the Hewitt family in his *Our American Music.*

The Massachusetts Magazine

by Isaiah Thomas and Ebenezer T. Andrews

1789

The Pursuit, duetto; set by a Student at the University at Cambridge	Jan.
How cold it is! a Winter song ——	Feb.
Bright Dawns the Day, a Hunting song; set by a Student at the University at Cambridge	Mar.
On Musick; set by William Selby	April
The Invitation; set by the author of Pursuit	May
also Ode on Spring; set by Abraham Wood	
Hunting Song; Hans Gram	June
Ode for American Independence; Horatio Garnet	July

> " 'Tis done! the edict past, by Heav'n decreed,
> And Hancock's name confirms the glor'ous deed.
> On this auspicious morn
> Was Independence born:
> Propitious day!
> Hail, the United States of America!"

Sally, a Pastoral; S. Holyoke	Aug.
Marlborough's Ghost; E. Mann of Worcester	Sept.
also Pensive Shepherd; S. Holyoke	
The Rural Retreat; William Selby	Oct.
also Ode to Columbia's Favorite Son	
also Ode to the President of the United States by a Lady; Hans Gram	
Song; set by a Gentleman in the County of Worcester	Nov.
Andre's Ghost; Mr. Mann of Worcester	Dec.

1790

Ode for the New Year; William Selby	Jan.
A Song; Philo Musico [James Hulbert Jr.]	Feb.
The Charms of Nature; Philo Musico	Mar.
The Charming Creature; H. J.	April
Tereminta, a Song; S. Holyoke	May
Rosy Nell; Philo Musico	June
The Lovely Lass; William Selby	July
Song—When all the attick fire was fled; William Cooper	Aug.
Washington—A Song; S. Holyoke	Sept.
A Shape alone let others Prize; Hans Gram	Oct.
Fidele, song ——	Nov.
The Grasshopper; E. Mann	Dec.

MUSIC PUBLISHED IN
Polyanthus
by Joseph T. Buckingham

1812

The Billow Song; C. A. of Boston	August
Awake my fair, the morning Springs; Dr. Calcott	September
Yankee Thunders, a song; L. M. Sargeant, Esq. with appropriate music for the Piano Forte by Calcott	October
The Steeds of Apollo	November
The Poor Exile of France	December

1813

The Fearless Tar; Tune the same as The Origin of Gunpowder; from the Siege of Tripoli	January
Death of Crazy Jane; Hook	February
Love and Friendship; W. Reeve	March
Wilt thou my farewell, Love (Will thou say farewell); Thomas Moore	April
Ellen of Windermere	May
Go, lovely Rose! W. Reponah	June
Ye Ling'ring Winds	July
The Yellow Leaf	August
Go to my Love, enchanting Rose, (Rondeau) ——	September
——	October
Perry's Victory	November
——	December

1814

Naval Song	January
They played in air, (Glee)	May
Columbia, Land of Liberty	June
The Road Side Cottage	August

Euterpeiad

The Nightingale's Warble, a favourite Irish air

A favourite Song as sung by Mrs. French ("Believe me if all those endearing young charms")

* Can I again that look recall, composed by Thomas Moore, Esq.

* Embosom'd in a Shadowing Bow'r, an air composed by T. Cooke, arranged for three voices by T. Philipps, and dedicated by him to the Boston Glee Club

Why Ella dear, adapted to the favourite Venetian air, Mamma mia

* Henry

* Anacreontic Glee, composed by George Gillingham

* Catch, by Webbe; also Canon by Byrd
* Ode to the memory of Commodore Perry, words by H. C. Lewis, music by
    A. P. Heinrich
* Auld Robin Gray, a favourite Song as sung by Mrs. Holman
* All Alone, lines by Henry Kirk White, set by Roderick Roundelay
* Fair pupil of the tuneful Muse, an original song from ms. of A. P.
    Heinrich, composed and addressed by him to Miss Eustaphieve
  Charlie is my Darling, a scotch song as sung by Mrs. Holman at the
    opera of Montrose
* Original sacred music, composed by Lowell Mason, Esq. Savannah, for
    the *Euterpeiad:* Andover, L. M.; Bridgeport, C. M.
* Examples of sacred music from Whitaker's Seraph
* Examples, referred to in musical Student, No. 3 (eight selections by
    Lotti, F. Durante, Haydn)
* Clementi's Grand One Fingered Waltz, published by desire
* Oh! no, not e'en when first we Lov'd, a Cashmerian air, with symphonies
    and accompaniment by Henry R. Bishop, words by T. Moore
  also Porcellian Clubs March, composed and arranged for 2 German
    flutes by John Hart.

  * Those marked with an asterisk bear the words "Printed for the Euterpeiad";
all are the same in format.

IX. MUSIC DEALERS AND MANUFACTURERS

O NE MAY hardly expect to find an extensive list of dealers in music
and musical instruments in a country where very little sheet
music is published and few instruments are made, and while
trade is based on the importation of every item from a distance of
more than three thousand miles. Under such difficult and unsatisfactory conditions success may be won only by the fortunate combination of able business man and experienced musician, a combination
rarely encountered. In Boston there were few such persons at the
turn of the century, but these few were sufficient to satisfy the needs
of a public whose musical interests required the wares of the bookseller rather than the music dealer, for even today the largest stock
of hymn and word books is to be found elsewhere than in a music store.

Figures may not represent an accurate comparison between these
times and our own, particularly in a large city of the East which acts
as central agency for a country-wide market; but with a population
of 25,786 in 1800, Suffolk County (Boston, Revere, Winthrop) listed
five individuals or firms engaged in the several branches of the music
publishing, dealing, and manufacturing business. In 1810 eight firms
accommodated 34,381 persons, and in 1940 approximately fifty-four
instrument makers and repairers and forty-four dealers and publishers were in Boston proper and the population numbered close to
900,000. This represents a merchant for each 5,000 persons in 1800
and one for each 4,300 in 1810; few firms employed more than two
or three persons, while most of them were partnerships. At present
the figure is nearly doubled, with firms employing scores of assistants
to serve a network of national representatives.

It may be supposed that the growing popularity of the pianoforte in America—the earliest musical development directly traceable to the Western Hemisphere which had recurring effect on the musical life of Europe—was due to the absence of the older type of keyboard instrument in American homes. It has enjoyed a far greater popularity in this country than in any other, including those nations whose musical culture is older, owing principally to the greater prosperity enjoyed by the average worker. We have come to regard piano lessons as indispensable to childhood education, along with the prescribed reading, writing, and 'rithmetic sponsored directly by the state. Music in general, and the piano in particular, is the one art spontaneously adopted by society as essential to good-breeding, cultural development, and amateur entertainment. To be sure, it was known as a lady's instrument, and the earliest evidences of its cultivation are in the advertisements of female seminaries where the piano was always taught along with needlework and drawing, an "extra" for which Mr. Graupner, one of the tribe Von Hagen, or Miss Hewitt was employed for a day each week. The male animal fancied the German flute.

Incidental, but not-to-be-overlooked factors, are the stable tuning of the pianoforte over those instruments of the string family and the greater pleasure derived by the amateur with elementary skill, whereas the violin requires accompaniment for fullest effect and a fidelity to pitch which the inexpert ear of the New England child probably did not possess. No arguments are needed to make plain the practicability of the pianoforte for use in America or the rapid expansion of instrument building as an industry at a historic moment when the change from one medium of keyboard expression to another was in process.

Mozart was always curious about the pianoforte and his music shows a development of pianoforte style as his acquaintance with the instrument becomes more complete. In 1777 he was first introduced to the pianos of Stein, which charmed him, and he wrote his father a lengthy description which praises their virtues but reveals the deficiencies of this and other instruments of the same type: The touch, he writes,

never blocks, and never fails to sound—as is sometimes the case with other pianos. On the other hand, it never sounds too lòng, and the machine pressed by the knee (to act as a forte pedal) is prompt to raise the dampers, or, on discontinuing the pressure ever so little, is as prompt to let them down upon the strings again.[1]

Beethoven was more the adventurer than Mozart and found at hand an instrument of far better quality than his predecessor, but one wonders now that the deep sonorities of his late sonatas could have been discerned with the aid of the contemporary Broadwood, presented him in 1817, or his earlier Clementi.

As early as 1789 Philadelphia had Charles Albrecht,[2] a pianomaker who copied English pianos with improvements of his own. In Europe fundamental changes were continually being advanced. Christofori's design had provided for a lever, now known as the "underhammer," or "escapement," between the hammer and its string after the blow is struck, necessary for its vibration, but a marked advance came with the so-called "double escapement" made by Sebastian Erard of Paris in 1808, enabling the blow of the hammer to be repeated without its falling back into the original position.

Before this date, however, John Geib whose "hopper and underhammer actions" were used in the square piano, had come to Boston and settled in 1804; later he went to New York. His public notice as organ and piano builder read "merchandise to be seen at 15 State street, but orders received in New York," but he probably concerned himself with the development of the upright pianoforte which became popular after the turn of the century.

While the mechanical action of the instrument improved, the cases were taking on new forms considered attractive to the public, and one advertisement reveals the importation of an instrument, probably by William Stodart, in the shape of a bookcase. The upright piano having a special action of its own was further developed about 1800 in Philadelphia when John Isaac Hawkins [3] (British-born American resident) carried the strings down to the bottom of the tall case and called his instruments "cottage grands" or "portable grands," presumably on the model of Stodart's "upright grand." Although the

[1] Letter, Oct. 17, 1777.

[2] Spillane cities 1775 as the date of the first pianoforte in Philadelphia and that city as the seat of pianoforte development up to 1835. It must be remembered that, on the continent at least, the principal features of harpsichord and pianoforte were combined in one instrument.

[3] Hawkins' inventions also include the ever-pointed pencil. He was civil engineer, poet, preacher, phrenologist as well, Spillane states. A friend of Thomas Jefferson and Charles Wilson Peele, he was an important figure.

cabinet piano was introduced by Southwell of London in 1807, and the cottage piano by Wornum of London in 1811, both with success, they appear to have achieved slight popularity in America, where the resident makers forged ahead with improvements soon destined to influence the entire industry and eventually to provide the world's finest instruments. The evolution of the pianoforte frame is marked by constant invention during the first quarter of the century, but the most far-reaching advance was made with the complete iron frame, or metal plate, in 1825 by Babcock of Boston. Lewis and Alpheus Babcock had been in business at 18 Winter Street in 1809,[4] but Lewis died in 1817 and Alpheus carried on as employee of Jonas Chickering.[5] Thus it is apparent that Boston shared with Philadelphia the distinction of being the most important center in the new world for the advancement of construction ideas. The most influential builder, however, was John Osborn, a Crehore-trained man, who in turn had Chickering, the Gilberts, and John Dwight as apprentices, and Stewart for a partner; the latter removed to London and became closely associated with Collard & Collard. By this time, the manufacture of American instruments commanded a large market, and a large export business resulted from the expanding industry as furthered by Chickering and MacKay. By 1829 an amazing productivity was achieved; 717 pianofortes were made in Boston, 900 in Philadelphia, and 800 in New York, with a total value of $750,000, according to Spillane.

The harpsichord and the clavichord received scant usage in the homes of America for, while there are notable exceptions—and the mind leaps immediately to Williamsburg—the fact remains that not until the advent of the pianoforte were keyboard instruments found in great quantity in homes of the middle classes in any country.[6] In public places, as the theater, summer garden, or concert hall, an orchestra or band performed without harpsichord, and in 1800 there was no market whatever for the harpsichord, except as an occasional

4 Not 1810 as Spillane states.
5 A fine example of pianoforte "Made by A. Babcock for R. MacKay Boston" is in the Belle Skinner Collection of Old Musical Instruments at Holyoke, Mass. MacKay was the financial backer of Babcock, becoming partner of Chickering in 1829; this instrument (numbered 252) apparently belongs to the period between 1817 and 1829. It is probably a late model.
6 In the Essex Institute, Salem, there is but one harpsichord method preserved, a London publication; very many pianoforte preceptors are on hand, however.

second-hand instrument might become available; a gradually enlarging public was showing marked interest in the pianoforte. Instruments of the hand-and-mouth variety were especially popular and—important consideration for the importer—they were easily portable. The extent and diversity of these promised a greater popularity than was apparent in group performance for, other than the Boston Brigade Band, the ensembles were few and feeble indeed. At least, this complaint would seem to bear out the assumption:

Field Music in Boston

Mr. Russell,—It is a singular fact, that the Boston Brigade Band is probably the worse off for field music than any other in the State. Martial music in the town of Boston is astonishingly scarce, excessive high in price, and with few exceptions, the most miserable. In proof of these assertions, I will state that four or five musicians engross all the playing for company trainings—and regulate their own fees—which they could not do were drummers and fifers plenty. As it regards the expense, they obtain from one to two dollars for two or three hours drill—four dollars for an half, and five dollars for one day's duty in uniform. I trust the mention and knowledge of these facts will operate to correct the procedure. M.[7]

Two dealers advertised extensive lists of instruments from 1815 onward, and it is likely that the Franklin Warehouse had as large a stock as Graupner and the store over Callender & Son's, operated by Dickson; the attached is selected from the latter firm's announcements:

A few elegant PIANO FORTES, of a superior fine tone, made by Clementi & Co. London.   —ALSO—
    Violins—Violincellos—English and French Flageolets—Clarionets, B, C, and E,—French Horns—Harp Lutes—Trumpets—Bugles—Hunting Horns—Castinets—Patent Flutes, with 4 or 6 Keys—Florio Flutes—Plain English and German Flutes—English and Spanish Guittars—Patent Harmonicas—Patent Kent Bugles, with Keys—Concert Trumpets, with Slides—Plain Trumpets—Concert Horns—Violin Strings, Roman and English—Violincello Strings—Harp Strings, in sets—Piano Forte Strings, in sets—English and Spanish Guittar Strings, in sets—Tuning Forks—Tuning Hammers—Violin and Violincello Bows—Bridges—Pegs—Finger Boards—Tail Pieces—Bassoon, Clarionet, and Oboe Reeds—Cases, for do.—boxes of Steel and Brass Wire—Pocket Music Desks—Piano Forte Covers—Violin, Violincello and Guittar Cases, mahogany or common—Pleyels, Haydens, Mozarts, &c. Quartets—all the lates and most fashionable Glees, Duetts, Songs, &c. &c.[8]

[7] Columbian Centinel, June 18, 1817.   [8] New England Palladium, Oct. 27, 1815.

In 1790 it was estimated that there were approximately twenty-seven pianofortes in Boston, all of them London made, and Spillane noted two teachers of harpsichord and piano in the previous year; the number increased by 1800, but the public that required the services of a music dealer was still a very limited one and it is not surprising that musicians combined many callings in the day's work in an effort to gain a mere livelihood.

The Von Hagen family were among the first to establish a sizeable business as dealers and publishers, opening a Musical Magazine and Warehouse at 62 Newbury Street in 1797. Public announcements cited only the ballads of the day, whose titles are indicative of the musical culture of their time, and the list of Von Hagen publications may be found in Appendix I. These publications from the Von Hagen catalogue show the preference for music of English origin current in the Bostonian taste of the winter of 1802:

Anna
Poor Blind Girl
He Has Left Me
When You Tell Me Your Heart
  Is Another's
My Love to War Is Going
Poor Adeline
Can Joy That Wretched Bosom
  Cheer?
The Grave of Love
Poverty's No Sin

To Banish Life's Troubles
Blue Bell of Scotland
Mark When beneath the Western
  Sky
Willy Is a Bonny Lad
Oh, Red Look'd the Sun
The Triumph of Love
Durham Hunt
Love and War
I've Lovers Kind, and Suitors
  Many [9]

One may assume that these were among the first works heard on the new instrument, the pianoforte, as it found its way into the stately homes of New England.

The frequency of the Von Hagen's removals, however, suggests that their stock was small, for in March, 1799, both "Sr. & Jr." removed to the head of the Mall, and in May to No. 3 Cornhill; there they remained, but for a time conducted both establishments and began a far-flung empire throughout most of New England (see page 162); Benjamin Crehore joined them in partnership under the firm name of P. A. Von Hagen jun. & Co. "for the purpose of importing from London instruments of the first quality and the best makers. Also from Amsterdam by the justly celebrated Meyer [10] formerly of the City of

[9] *Columbian Centinel,* Jan. 30, 1802.   [10] Not Conrad Meyer.

London," but the association lasted only thirteen months, culminating in this very definite manner:

Take Notice

The Copartnership between P. A. Von Hagen, senior, junior, and Benjamin Crehore trading under the firm of P. A. Von Hagen jun. & Co. being this day the 28th of June 1799 dissolved by mutual consent, all persons having demands will please to apply at P. A. Von Hagen's musical magazine, No. 3 Cornhill; and those indebted are solicited to pay their respective balance to P. A. Von Hagen, he being duly authorized to settle the concerns of said company.

This day is published by P. A. Von Hagen and son, the song of "How tedious Alas! are the hours," also the new Answer in the Comedy of the Stranger.[11]

Thereafter Crehore was affiliated with several Boston and outlying dealers and builders, including Mallet and Graupner, and Babcock, to whom he taught the trade of instrument building and for whom he afterwards worked.

Benjamin Crehore, accounts to the contrary, was well known in Boston, New York, and Philadelphia as a maker of violins, violoncellos, guitars, drums, and flutes as early as 1791. He spent one year, at least—that of 1797—as stage carpenter for the Federal Street Theatre in Boston and became acquainted with the Von Hagens at that time. His activities brought him in touch with every important pianoforte maker of his day.

The Von Hagens did not deal extensively in the larger items of the musician's stock, probably through lack of capital and through the concentration of interests on the practical aspects of their art. This is a typical family notice:

Notice

To those ladies who have called at the Warranted Imported Pianoforte Warehouse, No. 3 Cornhill for instruction on the pianoforte, singing, and theoretical knowledge of music,

Mrs. Von Hagen, respectfully informs That she was returned from New York and will be happy to attend those ladies who have honored her with their application during her absence. Mrs. Von Hagen also informs that the musical academy in the different branches of the science of music will also be attended by Mr. Von Hagen who by his residence in Holland has passed through five public examinations and obtained the principal place as organist.

11 *Columbian Centinel*, July 3, 1799.

N. B. The School will be opened for the reception of scholars on the first Tuesday in October next to instruct the grammatical practical and theoretical knowledge of music—also the art of singing.[12]

The junior member of this active partnership was organist for many years, serving Trinity Church [13] as successor to William Belsted from April 6, 1801, until 1809 with such satisfaction that his salary was raised from $125 to $150, and eventually to $200; this annual stipend included tuning and repair of the organ, but the bellows blower and the singing leader were paid separately. All were under the careful supervision of Major Higginson, John Rowe Parker (later editor of the *Euterpeiad* and proprietor of the Franklin Music Warehouse), and the Reverend Gardiner.

After the elder Von Hagen's passing in 1803 Mrs. Von Hagen and Peter Albrecht jr. continued the business; in 1806 the son purchased the stock of J. & M. Paff in Boston, a branch of the New York firm, and went under the name of the "Boston Piano Forte Ware-House," corner of Short and Essex Streets, "opp. Glass House." Paff had come to Boston in 1805, locating in Winter Street "at the 'Sign of the Golden Eagle,' " with a small stock of Clementi, Ditmor, Dall, Astor & Co. pianofortes, displaying them temporarily before taking them to New York, but had lingered for nearly two years, continuing, it would seem, for a year after sale to the Von Hagens. Another Von Hagen, come to maturity in 1809, announced [14] that "John E. Von Hagen's Blank Book Manufactory, Stationery, and Music Shop" was in business at 16 Court Street, Cornhill Square, with a stock which included some of the late P. A. Von Hagen's compositions.

A number of minor dealers appear at the beginning of the century, but their progress over a period of years eliminates them from serious consideration as contributors to the musical life of the day; many of these, such as John West, Greenleaf and Larkin, became booksellers; many of them sold music paper and supplies. The gradual emergence of the music dealer, however, is clearly shown in the advertisements of the day, and by the time G. Graupner and the Franklin Music Warehouse were fully established, the booksellers had ceased to feature "wind instruments, instrumental supplies" and other items which

12 *Ibid.,* Aug. 7, 1799.
13 Trinity Church has kindly permitted examination of its treasurer's and clerk's reports during the first quarter of the century.
14 *Columbian Centinel,* Aug. 6, 1809.

gave a department-store aspect to their businesses, combining stationery, cigars, billiard balls, glassware, cloth, mariner's supplies,
shoeblacking, elephant's teeth, and combs—"every Article usually
kept in a Music Store," according to John Ashton.

The firm of Mallet and Graupner as dealers in music did not reach
its stride until the Conservatory was well under way. At the first
emphasis was placed on their publications, since the selection and importation of stock from Europe required several months, but by the
close of the year 1801 a remarkably full supply was on hand:

MESSRS. MALLET AND GRAUPNER

Respectfully acquaint the Public that [they] have lately received from
London several Musical Instruments, of the latest and most improved
workmanship, which are now ready for sale at the Conservatory Hall,
Rowe's Lane, and consist of Grand Piano Fortes, Harpsichords, small do.
double action, best English Guitars, &c. Also, for sale at the above place,
a large assortment of American Piano Fortes, manufactured by Mr. Benjamin Crehore, whose genius and experience, cannot fail of producing as
correct and elegant work, in this line, as any imported from abroad; and
it is hoped will insure him the patronage and encouragement of his fellow
citizens. His instruments will be warranted by Messrs. M. & G. for six
months. The Hall will be opened for the sale of Instruments from 12 till
2 o'clock.[15]

There is no record of the number of American pianofortes sold by
Graupner, nor of his interest in Boston builders other than Crehore.
The merits of the latter's instruments required special recommendation, however, for it was alleged that the fashionable world preferred
the imported variety so much that purchasers of American manufac-
tures had been known to erase the real name and substitute that of a
celebrated English musical instrument maker, disposing of them as
the "best English Piano Fortes" for which they creditably passed.

Graupner properly regarded advertising of his new publications as
of greater interest for the public than repeated inventories of his
stock, but it is certain that no dealer in Boston was so well provided
with selected merchandise, while his first-hand knowledge of London
and continental dealers and publishers, together with his own informed
musicianship, made his Repository at once the major establishment
of its kind in Boston and probably in the United States.[16] Guitars,

15 Boston *Gazette,* Nov. 23, 1801.
16 The writer cannot refrain from suggesting a parallel with the bookshop kept

violins, flutes, and clarinets were among the instruments most in demand; in fact, the number and variety of flutes are astounding to this later age. Graupner's patronage of Crehore proved his genuine interest in the mechanical improvement of several instruments, but the piano and organ builder's business associations never lasted very long, it would seem, and Graupner's active interest in Crehore was of short duration. There is evidence to support the argument that the noted craftsman was a difficult person in so far as business relations were concerned. His record suggests that he was first and finally a craftsman with neither ambition nor ability to create an industrial empire. However, a subsequent notice by Graupner "offers the Public, a specimen of a Piano Forte, made under his direction, after a plan of the Germans by Messrs. Crehore and Babcock of Milton. It is particularly convenient to accompany the voice on such an instrument as it may be put in one moment (by its movable key board) several notes above or below Concert pitch, as best suits the compass of the voice." [17] No further information regarding this transposing piano keyboard or its success with the public is mentioned.

In 1812 Graupner drew the attention of his public to "The Glassichord," a European instrument consisting of plates of glass struck by hammers and operated by a keyboard. This was a German instrument, often called the "Glaschord" invented in 1785 by a German named Beyer, living in Paris; Benjamin Franklin had made improvements on the musical glasses as early as 1788, and called his instrument the harmonica. There is an example in the Skinner Collection and one in the Crosby-Brown Collection at the Metropolitan Museum of Art. The compass is three octaves from the first C below to the second C above middle C.

The newly-invented celestina, "which embraces the full deep tone of the Grand Piano with all the convenience of the Square Piano" was advertised in 1813. Among his importations, Graupner advertises three portable compositor's organs, with patent ornamental swells, "the pipes and action enclosed within a writing desk so that the fingers can neither touch nor injure the action." This detailed description was given with an invitation for the curious to visit the store.

---

by Elizabeth Peabody in Boston at a later date, which furnished a similar center of intellectual concourse for the literary figures of that day.

[17] *Independent Chronicle,* March 23, 1807.

No. 1   Has a flute stop as extensive and powerful as any Church Organs on the same stop—price 300 dolls.

No. 2   Has five octaves of keys, to F F. The flute extended down into the Diapason Stop—Price 400 dolls.

No. 3   Has two stops equal to four; additional keys, five and an half octaves; the Stop and Open Diapason—price 500 dolls.[18]

The "Panharmonicon" has acquired a certain fame in connection with Beethoven and Maelzel, and the latter gentleman actually visited these shores to further distribution of the instrument. Its success in Boston was without the aid of his presence, nor does this one-time friend of Beethoven appear to have visited the city. Installed at the Columbian Museum in Boylston Hall along with a varied assortment of curiosities, the "Panharmonicon" amused the town for months on end playing regular programs which formed a small repertory skillfully rearranged in order to provide semblance of a new program each night. Works by Haydn, Mozart, Steibelt, Ries, and lesser lights of the musical firmament gave Bostonians their first hearings of certain works of the classical school and may be credited with some influence in establishing better taste for orchestral music among the townspeople. The instrument consisted of flutes, trumpets, drums, cymbals, triangle, and strings struck by hammers, clarinets, violins, and violoncellos; the mechanism was worked by weights acting on cylinders, the whole being perfected about 1812, although an earlier variety had been in circulation.[19] A farewell announcement was made on May 3, 1817:

> Last Week of Grand Concerts by the Panharmonicon At Boylston Hall, South-end of Boston. Music to commence at 8 o'clock precisely, on Monday, Wednesday, Thursday and Friday evenings.
>
> The Panharmonicon will be packed up and there is no probability it will ever be exhibited again in Boston. Price of Tickets 50 cents.[20]

[18] *Repertory*, Sept. 7, 1810.
[19] For the program, see Chap. III, "Concert Life." The instrument had been shown at the Exchange Coffee House in 1811 without achieving much success. Mr. Goodrich tried to make it work, but the weather got into the pipes and caused a few gratuitous wheezes on the opening night. Profound apologies in the newspapers, coupled with promises of improved behavior in the future—at $1 admission—were unavailing, and the Panharmonicon was packed away.
[20] *Columbian Centinel.*

In an age of experimentation along many lines of instrument construction, many of which eventually proved themselves blind alleys, it is not surprising that the "Apollonicon" should follow the "Panharmonicon" in 1818; built by Flight and Robson, it was considered a masterpiece, with five manuals available for separate players, and controllable by automatic machinery through three shifting cylinders, revolving at the same time under steam power. Various instruments of percussion were sounded in the same way, adding to the orchestral effect.[21] Of only temporary interest, none of these strange species of barrel organ were heard of again.

The "Apollino" was invented by an American, Plimpton, in 1820, probably after the order of the "Apollonicon"; the *Euterpeiad* gave notice of its exhibition at the Columbian Museum, with a picture of the imposing contraption on September 2, 1820, but no further details are available. No lack of invention is apparent in the titles or in the supplementary features of the instruments put forward in this eventful period. The "Androides" was mentioned as a musical instrument and exhibited by Mr. Haddock in 1821 to the delight of 16,000 persons who viewed it in Boylston Hall. No details are at hand as to the nature of its musical anatomy, but attached were "images, so formed and regulated, as to bring any article of fruit desired by the spectator." [22]

The New York Museum had featured the "Musical Clock," made by Mollinger, of Mannheim, "which plays a solo on the first and second Flute and Piano Forte, and a variety of delicate airs," [23] and at another time presented a concert by Mr. E. Reynolds, late from Ireland, and his "Irish Union Pipes." We have elsewhere mentioned the "spiccato," a strictly private matter of Mr. Schaffer which played by means of common nails arranged in some strange manner; probably there were others whose sudden fame is not worth renewing here.

In view of the extensive discussion of the manufacture of instruments given by Miss Ayars [24] and, previously, by Mr. Spillane, there is no need to enter into a more lengthy examination here; the subject of

---

21 Galpin, *A Textbook of European Musical Instruments and Their Origin, History, and Character* (1937), on "Barrel Organs."
22 Felt, *Annals of Salem,* III, 90.   23 Boston *Gazette,* Nov. 4, 1811.
24 Christine Merrick Ayars, *Contributions by the Music Industries of Boston (1640–1936).*

dealers, however, is one which may benefit by elaboration. Graupner's shipments from abroad in 1811 numbered two grand pianos and eight square, made by Broadwood & Sons, London, and an organ valued at $1,400; his major importations appear to have been made once a year, for the most part, directly through the agency of Clementi & Co.[25]

Some impetus was given to the manufacture and sale of American-made instruments by reason of the embargo incident to the War of 1812, and Mr. Graupner, as the shrewdest and best-informed merchant in New England, was equal to the situation. He traveled to Philadelphia and New York—one of his very few departures from home—to purchase pianofortes and, according to announcement, opened a correspondence useful for future dealings with the leading musical houses of those cities.

After the sudden parting of the ways by Francis Mallet and Gottlieb Graupner, the former set up "F. Mallet's Musical Academy" in Congress Street; Mr. Mallet [26] survived for a number of years, coming before the public as teacher, singer, or manager until the spring of 1813, shortly thereafter leaving Boston, but his business had languished long before that time and one may suppose that as a music shop his was not very important.

In so far as the association of Hayts and Schaffer was concerned, it was the umbrella maker who survived the longest, for he had been in business before 1808 and continued for nearly two decades to join himself with brotherly fidelity to musical instrument dealers; he represents, more than any other of the strange affinities of these years, a consistency which must have been sanctioned by custom and accepted without remark. However, in their way umbrellas and musical instruments are no farther removed than some of the peculiar combinations displayed by twentieth-century "drug" stores in those very communities where specialization represents the ultimate in business acumen. The Schaffer of this temporary engagement was William, the instrument maker, presumably brother to Francis, whose son George was dancing master.

[25] All existing shipping records of the Boston port were destroyed in the Custom House fire of 1879.
[26] The F. D. Mallet, teacher of dancing, in Boston from 1824 onward was unrelated to Francis M., teacher of music and organist at First Church.

The Hayts brothers, Charles and Elna, were at 19 Marlboro' Street in 1811, joined in this mysterious union, but they became affiliated with Babcock and Appleton in 1815, moving to 6 Milk Street and assuming the name "Boston Musical Instrument Manufactory." The firm returned to the earlier address in the fall of 1816, but in December, 1818, John Ashton Jr. took over the business and began a career of some moment in an ever expanding field, perpetuating indefinitely the ridiculous combination hallowed by his predecessors. Ashton's stock in 1815 comprised:

> A general assortment of Flutes—Clarinets—Bassoons—Violins—Bass viols—Guitera—Hand organs—Horns—Trumpets—Bugles—Drums—Fifes—Cymbals—Flageolets &c.
>
> A large collection of the most approved music for the Piano-Forte–Instruction books for all instruments.
>
> Silk and cotton umbrellas and Parasols, of their make and imported.
>
> A number of first rate chamber organs finishing.
>
> Pianofortes and organs repaired.
>
> N. B. Church organs made and warranted to be equal in every respect to the English and much cheaper.
>
> A few tons of Ebony of superior quality.
>
> Journeyman Cabinet makers wanted.[27]

Following the removal of Hayts, Babcock, and Appleton, the Milk Street address was continued by J. R. Parker as "The Franklin Music Warehouse," with an increased emphasis on the smaller items of music trade and of imported pianofortes rather than ones made on the premises. The firm vied with that of Graupner in cultivating the purchaser of sheet music, while music of distant publishers, John Cole and George Willig Jr. of Baltimore, E. Ripley, Dubois & Stoddart, or James Hewitt of New York, John G. Klemm, G. E. Blake, or Bacon & Co. of Philadelphia, was sold there; many of the same titles were also published by Graupner. These two firms were always among those selling tickets to Boston concerts, and the newspaper notices added these instructions for those desiring to purchase them: "for sale at the Bookstore of O. C. Greenleaf, Court-street; West & Richardson, and Munroe & Francis, Cornhill; S. H. Parker's Circulating Library, No. 1, Water-street; Franklin Musical Warehouse, Milk-

[27] *New England Palladium*, Feb. 28.

street; G. Graupner's Franklin-street, David Francis's Bookstore and Library, Newbury-street, and at the Door of the hall."

The brief transference of Graupner's stock to the Franklin Music Warehouse in 1817 has been discussed elsewhere; he returned to his "old established Stand" [28] early in September with a renewed stock of fashionable music from London, Philadelphia, and New York, which was available to dealers in music, that is, wholesale as well as retail. This last aspect of Graupner's business is deserving of some comment, since it is likely that his clientele was not confined to the narrow limits of Boston; there are occasional evidences of a wider scope of activity and several law suits attempt to recover payment from persons resident in the South.

All dealers made the most of a noted singer's presence to import or publish selections from his repertory and announce them in the press, an illustration of the "best seller" method carried on in music today no less effectively than in the case of books.

All the Songs sung by Messrs. Phillips and Incledon, Miss Johnson and Mr. Tailor, at New-York, for sale at the Franklin Music Warehouse, No. 6, Milk-street among which are the celebrated Serenade of "Lilla come down to me," " 'Tis but Fancy's Sketch," "The Last Words of Marmion," "The death of Abercrombie," "Tho' Love is warm awhile," "My heart with love is beating," "Sweeter to be loved again," "When thy bosom heaves a sigh," "Ah such a pair was never seen," ALSO—Several new airs with variations, "Blue eyed Mary," and "Pray Goody" &c.[29]

One of the most interesting advertisements made by Graupner & Co. occurred in 1818:

NEW MUSIC

MOZART'S SONGS, a further supply; Mozart's celebrated opera of DON JUAN; Handel's Songs; select SCOTCH AND IRISH SONGS, with accompaniments by Haydn, Beethoven, &c. elegantly printed in numbers. Nicholson's FLUTE PRECEPTOR; do. select FLUTE BEAUTIES.

ORATORIOS viz:—The Creation, by Haydn; MOUNT OF OLIVES, by Beethoven; Jeptha, Israel in Egypt, Samson, Messiah, and Redemption by Handel;—Together with a great variety of Sonatas, Variations, &c. for the Piano Forte.[30]

---

28 Mr. Driscoll informs me that 6 Franklin Street and 6 Milk Street backed into each other; a map of Boston in 1810 shows them in the same block but with other property between.

29 *Columbian Centinal*, March 14, 1818.   30 *Ibid.*, Oct. 28, 1818.

In all likelihood, other dealers in Boston maintained much the same stock, but none other than Graupner had the judgment to feature those works of greatest importance.

George Cushing joined Gottlieb Graupner in 1818 as the "& Co." and moved the business to 15 Marlborough (or Marlboro') Street for a brief moment, but the partnership was terminated on February 17, 1820, and a sale of the large stock was followed by an auction early in March; the remainder, consisting of music and musical instruments, was offered for sale at reduced prices, and the store was "To be Let," possession given immediately. The same notice, however, announces eight new publications ready for sale and establishes Mr. Graupner's eventual continuance as publisher and dealer in sheet music at the same address; he no longer was dealer in instruments, and in that fact is the secret of change worked by his bankruptcy.

Mr. Graupner had been in public life for so many years that a sudden withdrawal comes as a surprise, and the effect must have been one felt throughout the entire musical community. For two years his name does not appear, although the Philharmonic Society meetings continue; but certain personal considerations explain his temporary relinquishment of public duties from so active a business life. Either his business had acquired a reputation which made special promotional methods unnecessary, or his resumption of business was on a smaller scale than hitherto, for the advertisements are fewer and new issues are rarely announced. These notify the public that he has on hand a supply of vocal and instrumental music and is active as a teacher, but their laconic manner suggests somewhat less of the urge and shrewdness which typified the years from 1815 to 1820 when the first flush of the Great Society and the remarkable success of the orchestra gave promise of an extensive market for musical merchandise.

A further clearance sale is mentioned in September, 1829, when a large stock of the best European authors is offered wholesale or retail at reduced prices; "persons wishing to examine same may have the privilege of trying it with the assistance of a Piano Forte at the Academy."

Many dealers were fortunate in disposing of their stock and good-will to other firms, and the table at the end of this chapter shows a surprising number of individuals and firms which had envisioned success in the field of publishing and dealing in music. Graupner's business, however, gradually lost its identity; the stock was finally disposed of, but the deduction is inevitable that much of that remaining at the last had lost its claim to fashion long since; the copyrights of his own publications were of little value in view of the changing taste which had passed beyond the pretty ballads of past decades and in view also of the insufficient protection offered the publisher through copyright. Devotion to Haydn and Mozart, and a discerning recognition of Beethoven had characterized his personal enthusiasms, but as a publisher his exalted taste seldom influenced sound business considerations, and the large majority of his imprints had a temporary interest for the buying public. There is no evidence to prove that he ever went abroad again, and other and younger minds and bodies, more sensitive to the rapid advance of the times, forged ahead in the business of dealing, manufacturing, and publishing; capital was increasingly necessary, and Mr. Graupner had never made large sums to warrant extraordinary investment in new enterprises; in fact, there is strong reason to attest his conservatism. His family was musical, but none aspired to follow him in business, although one son, John Henry Howard, finally settled down as an engraver for Ditson.

The principal dealers and manufacturers are listed here in as complete a manner as the newspapers and the directories permit.

1797. P. A. Von Hagen's Musical Magazine and Warehouse, 62 Newbury street (Peter Albrecht and son)
    May 1798, P. A. Von Hagen jun. & Co. with Benjamin Crehore as partner
    March 1799, removed to 55 Marlborough street, head of the Mall
    May 1799, removed to No. 3 Cornhill, and 4 Old Massachusetts Bank
    June 28, 1799, Partnership with Crehore dissolved; title now P. A. Von Hagen's Musical Magazine, sometimes referred to as Warranted Imported Pianoforte Warehouse
    1803, located on Common street
    1806, Boston Piano Forte Ware-House, cor. Short and Essex streets
1798. Green & Bent, musical instrument makers, 90 Newbury street
    May 1799, partnership dissolved; thereafter William & Adam Bent, 26 (or 24) Orange street
    July 1807, William Bent at 49 Newbury street "makes, tunes instruments, and sells London-made instruments"
    1809 Adams and Bent went out of business (Spillane)

1799. Linley & Moore, "opp. Faneuil Hall (Market place)," one grand piano and smaller instruments

William Callender, 59 State street, bass viols and other instruments, musical instrument maker; also sold guns, canons, musket cartridges, and large elephant's teeth

    1806, Middle street (hitherto given as home address)

    1815, J. Callender & Son, 40 Marlboro' street

    1825, Salem street, near Prince, ivory turner and musical instrument maker

1800. Josiah Leavitt, bottom of Rowe's Landing, organ builder (barrel)

    December 1803, moved to 18 Winter street

1801. Mallet & Graupner, Rowe's Lane

    November 11, 1802, G. Graupner's Musical Academy, sometimes referred to as "Repository," 6 Franklin street

    From @ 1809, G. Graupner's Music Store

    April 1, to August 1, 1817, moved to Franklin Music Warehouse, 6 Milk street; returned to 6 Franklin street

    January 1, 1818 to February 17, 1820, G. Graupner & Co. (Geo. Cushing), 6 Franklin street; thereafter G. Graupner.

    1826 to 1836, Academy, 1 Province House Court

1803. Museum, Milk street, pianofortes, and instrumental supplies

Kentner and Von Harten and Co. 6 Marlborough street, instrumental supplies

    October 1803, 26 Newbury street

    October 1804, 54 Marlboro street

John Cushing & Co. (no address) pianofortes imported from London

1804. John Geib, organ and piano builder, merchandise to be seen at 15 State street, but orders received in New York

1808. Ebenezer (Eben) Goodrich, Cambridge-street, Organ builder

    1811, manufacturer of church and chamber organs, Water street

N. H. Henchman's Music Shop, 79 State street, instruments

    April 1813, sold out to Frederick Lane, 79 State street

    1820, No. 93 Court street (opp. Old-Court House) bass drums and wind instruments; also violins

1809. Mr. Dyke, "lately from London" (no address) "setts up," tunes, organs.

J. E. Von Hagen (John), Cornhill-square, blank book manufactory and music

Lewis & Alpheus Babcock, 18 Winter street, piano warehouse, organs, songs

    1813, Appleton & Babcock partnership formed, same address

    1815, Hayts, Babcock & Appleton partnership formed; moved to Milk street, umbrellas, instruments

1810. Thomas Appleton, Somerset place, musical instrument maker

1811. James & Charles Everett, 11 Broad street, London-made pianos

1812. J. Hewitt's Musical Repository, 58½ Newbury street, published and
   sold music and instruments (see J. A. Dickson 1816)
   36, 70, and 150 Market street given on publications

1813. Paul Lamson, 23 Court-street, woodwind instruments and violins
   F. Hofmaster (from Europe), 1 Water street, repairs musical instruments

1815. John Osborn, "back of 3 Newbury-street," instrument builder
   (pianoforte)
   1819, moved to Orange street
   1822, advertised as Osborn and Stewart
   1823, at Market street, under the Pantheon
   1824, April, sold stock of 25 pianofortes
   1826, April, final sale of 36 pianofortes; Henry Niebuhr purchased stock and continued business

1816. James A. Dickson (formerly Manager Boston Theatre) 1 Marlboro'
   place, music salloon
   1820, 34 Market street, music seller
   1823, "Salloon and variety store"
   1824, James L. Hewitt & Co. (James A. Dickson), 34 Market
   street (upstairs)
   1826, 36 Market street (probably the same)
   Franklin Music Warehouse, 6 Milk street (November)
   May 1822, moved to 2 Milk street

1818. John Ashton, jr. 18 Marlborough street, musical instrument and
   umbrella maker (December 19)
   1822, in directory only as umbrella maker
   1825, umbrella maker and music store, 197 Washington street
   (same address; change of street name in 1823)

1820. A. Mathieu, 60 Newbury street, lyres, harps, pianofortes, music,
   repairs instruments, teaches Spanish Guitar

1821. Charles and Edwin W. Jackson, 64 Market street (March 31)
   1822, 44 Market street, Music Warehouse and Variety store,
   "Ladies indispensibles of every description, perfumes, soaps,
   etc."
   August 12, 1826, partnership dissolved by mutual consent.

1824. Hooten & Powell (James Hooten, Snelling Powell), 154 Washington street, music and fancy goods
   Henry Prentiss, 23 Court street, musical instruments and umbrellas

X. TEACHERS

FEW ASPECTS of research in the musical development of New England during the commencement of the nineteenth century are so elusive as that which concerns the profession of teaching; oftentimes those who did the most advertising were those most in need of pupils, while then, as now, certain reputable professors carried on a lively practice without recourse to advertising in the public press. In other instances, those musicians most in the public eye, especially if they were connected with the theater, were not available as instructors, and might have made very poor ones, had they sought a public following.

In a primitive, or—to say the least—extremely localized community of musicians, many persons constantly engaged in the societies of the town were amateurs, occupied during the day with other pursuits, which ranged from clerking in banks to the cutting of hair—the day of dressing wigs having but recently passed. In the course of a quarter century, the numbers increased and, doubtless, the quality of teaching improved, but Boston was well enough furnished with teachers to satisfy the limited demand. We may gain some enlightenment from the fact that there is an inevitable relation between the sale of instruments and instruction in playing them, although that exact relation cannot be established. As flutes were being imported by the hundreds, the schools for teaching of flute increased, and the same ratio applies to the pianoforte.

Music was indispensable to the curriculum of the ladies' seminary which never failed to include it, at an extra charge, in the same category with needlework and the French language, but in the majority of instances this implied pianoforte only, for the names of the instructors make that fact plain, particularly in the case of Mr. Graupner, who never taught singing. The standard charge for instruction during the first decade of the century was seventy-five cents per lesson with the better teachers, of whom Mr. Graupner is fairest example. Changing money values probably altered this at a later time, but one can hardly fancy Dr. Jackson bestowing his august presence on any household for ever-so-brief an hour for that minute sum.

No information is available for the period of William Selby's influence to suggest the number or extent of the instructional opportunities in his day, but the deduction is inevitable that until 1800, or the opening of the Graupner-Mallet-Trajetta Conservatorio, the teaching of secular music was not very scientific, with the possible exception of that given after 1797 by the Von Hagen family.[1] Granting the widespread enthusiasm and varied talent of the day, it is unlikely that one person could teach reading, English, grammar, sewing, tambouring, also pianoforte and guitar, harpsichord, and to "accompany the above insts. with the voice," with entire success in all branches, although several tried to do so. One is most likely to judge the merit of a teacher on the ground of participation in community activity; hence, organists of leading congregations and members of the theatrical band possess an a priori right to consideration as representative musicians of a community, whether or not they functioned as teachers to the youth of the land.

The Boston Directory of 1798 ennumerated sixteen musicians, some of them of no mean reputation in the history of their time. They are as follows:

Belstead William, organist, Common street
Berkenhead John L. organist, Prince street
D'hattentot Lewis, musician, No. 9 Jarvis's buildings
Gram Hans, musician, Belknap's lane
Granger Frederick, musician, No. 10 Jarvis's buildings
Graupner, Gotleb, musician, No. 10 Jarvis's buildings
Green & Bent, musical instrument makers, No. 90 Newbury street
Greenleaf Jonathan, organist, Cold lane
Mallet Francis, musician, Orange street
Pick Jacobus, musician Sweetser's Alley, Newbury street
Rozier Etienne, musician Orange street
Selby William, organist Tremont street
Schaffer Francis, musician, No. 21 Newbury street

[1] Dr. Carleton Sprague Smith mentions C. T. Pachelbel in the 1730's, Peter Pelham in the next two decades, and W. S. Morgan, pupil of Giardini, in the 1770's as able teachers in other parts of the country, and there was John Selby whose work in Boston and thereabout has never been properly stressed.

Smink Peter, musician and Dyer, Wing's lane
Vechner Joseph, musician Hanover street
Von Hagen P. A. jun. and co. Musical magazine, No. 62 Newbury street

D'hattentot does not figure in the lists of the day, but his residence in
Jarvis' Buildings suggests that he, together with Graupner and Leaumont, were caught in the melancholy fire of 1799, the last information
available with regard to one of the three victims. Hans Gram is no
stranger, of course, for his publications appear frequently in the
Massachusetts Magazine, and his *Massachusetts Compiler* (1795)
earned him some fame. Peter Smink carried on music instruction as a
sideline to a dyeing and scouring business in Wing's Lane, and em-
phasized military music as his choice:

> Any gentlemen who may incline to form a Military Band,
> will please apply to Mr. Smink, who will give them the
> proper instructions for carrying their object into effect,
> upon reasonable terms. Music taught as usual.[2]

By 1800 Mr. Smink had ceased to proclaim himself a musician; he
does not, therefore, qualify for a place in this company of scholars.
In view of the fact that the theatrical orchestra at this time was a
good one, it is likely that most of the names mentioned here with the
noncommittal designation "musician" were engaged therein. The un-
certainty of the season's duration prevented these nomadic tribes
from becoming integrated into the community, or building up a large
clientele. The list is interesting, however, for the conjunction of names
representing the old and the new musical leadership of Boston; by
1805 Gram, Berkenhead,[3] and Selby [4] had disappeared from the Boston directory, but they had long since failed to attract a single dis-
coverable notice in the musical life of the new century.

The Von Hagen family came to Boston in 1797, immediately commencing a career of teaching. Mrs. Elizabeth Von Hagen taught at
Mrs. Rowson's Academy, Medford, on Tuesdays and Fridays in 1800,
charging the usual seventy-five cents per lesson. This advertisement
gives full particulars:

[2] *New England Palladium,* May 26, 1801. "Peter Smink, the silk-dyer, furnished
the comedy of those earliest days. He had come over as a 'Hessian,' his figure was
'orbicular,' and he played profoundly on the bassoon. They compared him to Fal-
staff." (Esther Forbes in *Paul Revere*)
[3] Moved to Newport, R. I., in 1796 although his name is still in the 1798 directory.
[4] Died Dec. 12, 1798; a son, aged 18, had died on July 28 of the same year.

Mr. and Mrs. Von Hagen etc. . . .
  terms by the quarter 5 dollars entrance
  3 times a week 17 dollars per quarter
  2 times a week without singing 14 dollars
  singing alone once a week 8 dollars
Out of town each lesson one dollar with proper conveyance.[5]

The custom of requiring entrance by the quarter with an advance de-
posit of five dollars was general and denotes the seriousness of purpose envisaged by the instructors; however, there are few instances to
show the fruits of intensive training implied in three lessons a week
over a long period of time.

Mr. Mallet enjoyed a considerable respect during his early years
in Boston, but he seems to have declined in popularity after better
musicians took up residence there. He advertises in this manner in
1798:

FRANCIS MALLET

offers his respects to the families from those he is indebted for their past
favors and kindnesses to him and assures them of his zeal and punctuality
to the pupils intrusted to his care in the several branches of his profession,
viz: Forte piano, vocal music, Guitar, &c.—He is removed to South end
4th house beyond Liberty Pole same side.[6]

During the uncertainties of the theatrical season, Mr. Graupner,
then a member of the Federal orchestra, offered his services as teacher
of oboe, German flute, violin, etc., and as repairer of instruments,[7]
but a sudden reverse of fortune took him to Salem, and his eventual
career as teacher in Boston was deferred. In the course of that sojourn Mr. Von Hagen advertised in the Salem papers. In the fall,
Mr. Graupner resumed teaching in Boston, and continued to do so independently until the founding of the Conservatorio or Musical
Academy early in 1801. He was joined by Mallet and by Filippo Trajetta, son of the celebrated composer of operas. The triumvirate issued a long statement on the value of music as a polite amusement,
arriving at the point with this specific declaration:

Conservatory or Music Academy
at the Hall, (formerly Duport's) in Rowe's Lane

Messrs. Mallet, Graupner, & Trieta, have jointly agreed, wishing to be
useful to this metropolis, and sensible that many will be able (by this

[5] Aug. 24, 1799.   [6] Boston *Gazette*, Feb. 21, 1798.   [7] March 3, 13, 17, 1798.

way) to satisfy their wishes in accomplishing the education of their children, intend to open a new institution (for this country) but on the same foundation of the first Conservatories of Europe, where order and the progress of their pupils shall be their principal rule.

The date of the opening will be announced in future papers. The books for subscription, are open at Mr. Mallet's, Court-street nearly opposite Concert Hall, Mr. Trieta's, State street, corner Wilson's Lane, and Mr. Graupner's Sweetser's Alley, Newbury street.

Boston, November 24, 1800.

Since Mr. Graupner's address is given at the end, it is likely that he composed the announcement; at any rate, the subsequent career of the institution makes it plain that he was the leading spirit of the partnership. A modest plea for credit in establishing the first conservatory of music in this country is implied.

An interesting announcement concerns the presence of U. K. Hill in Boston:

MUSIC

Vocal and Instrumental, will be taught in Devonshire-Street, two doors northwest of the corner of Water and Devonshire-Streets, in a stile perfectly novel, and better adapted to instill into the minds of the susceptible, the meliorating influence of this divine art, than any heretofore practiced.

At the same place, Profile likenesses will be elegantly taken in gold * * * Piano fortes tuned in a new method.

U. K. HILL [8]

Hill, father of the celebrated Ureli Corelli, later identified with the New York Philharmonic Orchestra as first conductor, gained some fame at this moment by the publication in Boston of his *Sacred Minstrel*, a collection of Psalm tunes; recently come from Northampton, he did not linger in Boston, but removed to New York about 1819.

Dr. Jackson loomed on the Boston horizon in 1812; his talents, like his person, were prodigious, and it is unthinkable that he should remain long in Boston without commanding a clientele of earnest, if occasionally awestruck, neophytes. It should be noted, however, that Dr. Jackson did not follow the custom of ordinary mortals in soliciting patronage. No indeed! With evident reluctance he signified his willingness to accommodate the many prospective pupils who cast themselves before him:

[8] Boston *Gazette,* March 13, 1806.

DOCT. JACKSON

Professor of Musick

HAVING been solicited by many of the most respectable families in town to open a School for the purpose of instructing young Ladies in that beautiful science, and what is esteemed one of the most fashionable parts of education. He proposes to commence as soon as a sufficient number of Pupils offer to make it an object, at the Hall now occupied by Mr. Turner as his Dancing Academy.—Terms 5 dls. at entrance and 15 dls. pr. quarter, two lessons a week, and *no pupil taken for less time than a quarter.*

Subscription papers are with Mr. TURNER, at his Academy; at Mr. O. C. GREENLEAF's Book Store, and at Doctor JACKSON's, No. 18 Pinkney-street.

Boston, March 4th, 1813.[9]

This followed a venture of Jackson, Graupner, and Mallet with headquarters at Pythian Hall which apparently came to naught. It will be noted that in this instance, as in all, Dr. Jackson's name was placed head over all with Mr. Graupner gracefully stepping down in order of priority; I would not attempt in words to span the great divide between Jackson and Mallet.

James Hewitt embraced every field of activity—if not every fellow musician—in the course of his rounds, and it is not surprising to find his card in the newspaper even before he acquired a permanent address. In the course of a brief visit in 1808–1809 when he conducted at the theater, he was available for instruction on the pianoforte, violin, and violoncello, and in 1811, when he had really settled in Boston for good, he joined forces with Mr. Stockwell in a Musical Academy. Both gentlemen were employed at the theater.

No figure of sublime importance followed those already mentioned until the arrival of Samuel Priestly Taylor from New York, and he did not leave any marked impression by reason of the number of pupils to come under his tutelage. He made periodic visits in connection with his official post as organist to the Handel and Haydn Society and it may be supposed he taught at those times, but he did not linger in Boston beyond them. He had come for a fortnight in the spring of 1817 and had given a recital, but returned for the season beginning in November, 1818, and remained until January, 1820, advertising himself as teacher of pianoforte, organ, and singing. Boston had dealt kindly with him, apparently, for he returned in 1822 to resume

[9] *Independent Chronicle,* March 4, 1813.

as organist in several churches, but the majority of his many years were spent in association with New York and Brooklyn churches, where he was active until after the Civil War.

Among the younger generation, Miss Sophia Hewitt and Mr. Paul Louis Ostinelli were the leaders. By reason of their prominence as pianist and violinist respectively, their popularity increased and brought to their doors a very large number of pupils. Miss Hewitt was employed at a number of schools and academies, while Mr. Ostinelli coupled leadship of the theater orchestra with playing for the Philharmonic Society and teaching; both were in demand as recitalists throughout New England. After their marriage [10] the couple was at home at 32 Federal Street, where Mrs. Ostinelli, organist at the Catholic Church, gave instruction on organ, pianoforte, and harp, and Mr. Ostinelli on the violin, Spanish guitar, lyre, and in singing. "Will also devote one day to accompany Mrs. Ostinelli's scholars on the violin." On one occasion, at least, Mrs. Ostinelli offered her services as teacher of the French language.

No mention has been made of the singing schools devoted to sacred music which prospered throughout this section of the country, a strong fortress bravely withstanding the newer style of music represented by the urban societies, of which the Handel and Haydn was the most important. Nathaniel D. Gould (Elnathan Duren), Samuel Holyoke, Andrew Law, all descendents of the genus Billings, associated themselves with the god-fearing plainness of the psalm tune, made the church choir loft ring with its forthright sound, and thundered ancient theology with no less emphasis than did the fundamentalist preachers of the time. Each group engraved its name on a collection of tunes, tunes which were simple enough musically but were subject matter for endless study by the completely untutored voice of the New England church member. The fact that many of the leaders were without musical background was secondary to the fact that they had the faculty of inspiring these hardy groups to burst forth in lusty praise to God; in New England the tunes were of the plainest kind, some of them fuguing, but quite unlike the moderately difficult and extremely interesting fuguing tunes which were meet for the skill of Pennsylvania Dutch societies. Often these singing

[10] MARRIED: Mr. Paul Lewis Ostinelli to Miss Sophia Henriette Hewitt, daughter of Mr. James Hewitt.—*New England Palladium*, Aug. 27, 1822.

schools were also schools for "plain and ornamental writing." [11]

Frequently the choirs of the several churches were united into societies for the purpose of utilizing the newer psalm-tune collections and attracting a noted director for weekly rehearsal. Thus the above-named musicians were constantly occupied in the outlying towns. There is no way of telling the size, importance, or length of time over which these groups held sway, but a list of singing societies is appended, derived from all available sources; they are given with the date of first mention, which does not signify the date of formation by any means. There are doubtless many more to be added.

Stoughton (Mass.) Musical Society, 1786
Handel Society at Dartmouth College soon after 1800
Franklin Musical Society, Boston, ca. 1803
St. Cecelia Society, Boston, 1805
Massachusetts Musical Society, Boston, 1807–10
Musical Societies of Middlesex, Hanover, N.H., 1811
Sacred Harmonick Society, Boston, 1813
Park Street Singing Society, Boston, 1814
Old Colony Musical Society, East Bridgewater (Mass.), 1814
Handel and Haydn Society, Boston, 1815
Hancock (Maine) Musical Association, 1816
St. David Musical Society, Framingham (Mass.), 1817
Beethoven Musical Society, Portland, 1819
New Hampshire Musical Society, Concord, 1820
The Handel Society of Bath, Maine, 1820 circa
Harmonic Society, Boston (A. Law), 1820
Augusta (Maine), Union Society, 1819 circa
The Psallonian Society, Providence (Oliver Shaw), 1821
Neponset (Mass.) Sacred Music Society (G. Graupner), 1821
Pleyel Society, Nantucket (first concert June 9), 1822
Union Musical Society, Guilford (N.H.), 1822
Central Musical Society, Concord (N.H.), 1822
Martin Luther Society, Boscawen (N.H.), 1822
Phil Harmonic Society, New Haven (Conn.), 1822
Canaan (Conn.?) Musical Society, 1822
Jubal Society, Hartford, 1822
Musical Society in Amherst (N.H.?), 1822
Waltham (no name), 1822
Springfield (no name), 1822

[11] A fuller account of these sacred collections, together with an accurate listing, may be found in the American Supplement to Grove's Dictionary, edited by Waldo Selden Pratt and C. N. Boyd.

Worcester (no name), 1823
Charleston Harmonic Society, 1824
Charleston Pleyel Society, 1824
Union Sacred Singing Society, Brighton, 1824
Harmonic Society, Westborough, 1824
Apollo Society, Boston (Hewitt), 1824
Harmonic Society, Worcester, 1826
Boston Mozart Society, 1827
Norfolk Musical Society, no date
Exeter Musical Society, no date
Haverhill Singing Society, no date

The list of instructors which follows is gathered from all available sources, of which the newspapers and, for a brief period, the *Euter-peiad* are chief. Many of these names do not appear in the town directories, but that is a matter of no great consequence since those irregular volumes were far from comprehensive. Over a period of a quarter of a century the more important members of the musical community emerge, however, by virtue of their persistence or by reason of other relationships affecting the musical life of Boston. As evidence of Graupner's place in the scheme, it may be remarked that he is the only teacher to practice his profession constantly throughout the period; he may, in fact, claim a liberal margin at both extremes.

Directory of Teachers of Music

1800

The Musical Academy, or Conservatorio, F. Mallet, G. Graupner, F. Trajetta, Professors, Rowe's Lane (disbanded Nov., 1802). All branches of music. (Home addresses: Mallet, Court Street; Graupner, Pond Street. For further addresses, see individual teachers)

Peter Albrecht Von Hagen Sr., Elizabeth Von Hagen, Peter Albrecht Von Hagen, Jr. No. 3 Cornhill for Senior, Essex Street for Junior. All branches taught

1803   Mrs. Von Hagen, pianoforte and singing
1805   P. A. Von Hagen (Jr. now become Sr.), "Instructor of Vocal and Instrumental Music, removed to corner of Short and Essex-streets, opp. Glass House"
1807   Elizabeth Von Hagen, 7 Winter Street
1809   P. A. Von Hagen, Myrtle Street; leave orders at John E. Von Hagen's Book Manufactory
1810   P. A. Von Hagen; leave orders at G. Graupner's, 6 Franklin Street

1813   "After four years from Boston," leave names at G. Graupner's, 6 Franklin Street

1801

"A Lady," a Native of England, 32 Federal Street. Reading, English grammar, sewing, and tambouring; also pianoforte and guitar. In later advertisements, harpsichord, and to "accompany the above instruments with the voice"

Mr. Smink, Wing's Lane. "Music taught as usual"

Thomas Harris, "at the Tavern kept by the said Harris, 2 Cross Street." Singing school

Hans Gram, Common Street

1802

Jonas P. Barret, "Call at Mrs. Makean's, Elm street." Clarinet, Hautboy, Flute, Bassoon, Violin, and Bass Viol

Mr. Law (Andrew), "in Mr. Payne's School-Room, opposite the Rev. Mr. Popkin's Meeting-House." Singing school. $4 per quarter, $2 at time of entrance

Mr. Mallet (Francis), house "lately occupied by Dr. Jackson in Congress street." English and Spanish Guitar, Pianoforte, and singing with accompaniments

     1798   Feb. South end, 4th house beyond Liberty Pole same side

     1803   Aug. removed to 61 Cornhill

     1805   Resided Devonshire Street, as "The Boston Musical Academy"

     1808   Removed "centre of Myrtle-street, facing South Russel-street, back of Mount-Vernon"

     1809   Resided Spring Lane

     1810   Resided Summer Street

     1810   Removed to Central Court, Newbury-Street; "intends resuming" teaching

     1810   Takes a house in Winter Street, opp. Trinity Church

     1811   March 18, at Summer Street, opp. Trinity Church

     1811   July 8, Mr. Yarnold and Mr. Mallet's School at Concert Hall; Mr. Mallet lived in Congress Street

     1824   469 Washington Street. Pianoforte, harp, singing &c. "References to Mr. Mallet having led many to suppose him to be the same person who recently taught dancing in this city, he begs leave to caution the public against this mistake." (*Columbian Centinel,* Nov. 8, 1824)

1803

Miss Burgess, Ladies' Academy, Woburn. Music—pianoforte, 75 cents per lesson

Music and dancing taught at Gentlemen's Academy, Medford, by John Hosmer

1805

John N. Rudberg. No address. Continues to teach English Guitar
    1812   In Charlestown, Main Street
    1818   Pitts Lane, Boston
Wm. H. Manning, Music Shop in Charlestown, near Dr. Morse's Meeting-house. Organist . . . continues to teach Organ, Piano Forte &c.
    (1807—Listed in Boston Directory as "baker")
no name   Instructor in German Flute, "apply at Printer's"
U. K. Hill, Devonshire Street, two doors northwest of the corner of Water and Devonshire. Vocal and Instrumental Music
    1806   April, removed to Joy's Buildings, corn. Congress and Water Streets; teaches violin, violoncello, viola, German Flute and other instruments. School for Vocal Music opening
    1810   Removed to New York

1807

R. Shaw, No. 6 Newbury Street. "Late Singing Master in Theatre Royal, Drury Lane, London, last from Philadelphia, teaches Piano Forte, Singing, German Flute &c."
    1808   Removed to Milk Street, opp. Old South
M. Masi (Francisco), No. 3 Hanover Street, Music Master of the Italian Band, teaches Piano Forte, Clarionet, Violoncello, Violin, French Horn, Trumpet, Flute, French Guitar &c. Produces certificates from Church of St. Peter in Rome
  —— Removed two weeks later to No. 2 State Street
    1811   9 Newbury Street. "His three Sons will be happy to perform as Musicians at Balls, Assemblies, &c."
    1812   Nov. 83 Newbury Street. "Singing in Italian mode"

1808

Mr. Delarue, "Row No. 3, opposite to the sign of the Lamb, in Newbury street." Violin, 6 to 9 o'clock, Tues. Sat. evenings. $9 per quarter, $3 entrance
L. Boucherie, Apply at Mr. Graupner's. Lately from Europe, Piano Forte, Harp, and singing accompanied in the Italian manner. F. Fontaine, a friend, repairs instruments
James Hewitt (from New York). Leave commands at Mr. Labottiere's, No. 6 Cambridge Street, or at Mr. Graupner's Music Store, Franklin Street. Piano Forte, Violin and Violoncello
    1810   At Mr. Dall's House on the Neck, near So. Boston
    1811   Hewitt & Stockwell Musical Academy, Round-Lane, 3 doors

from Atkinson-street, South side. Piano Forte. Terms 12 dolls. per Quarter, and 5 dolls. Entrance

1812 Apply Pond Street, next door to Duport's Dancing Hall
Sept.   58½ Newbury Street

1813   19 Water Street

1814   May   South Bennett Street, last house, left hand

1816   Washington Street

1809

N. Foster, School Street, near the Old South. German Flute

1810

Wm. Cooper, No. 3 West Street. Sacred Music School

1811

Mons. P. C. Louvrier, 18 Distil-House Square. Instructor in the French Language, and on the Piano Forte
—— March 6, 17 Pinkney Street

Nathaniel Ruggles, Esq., Roxbury, German Flute and Piano Forte "while being kept out of his property in the West-Indies"; also "French and Spanish Languages and Writing"

1812

Mr. Yarnold, with Mallet at Concert Hall (see Mallet). Taught at Mrs. Davis' School

1813   Removed to No. 15 Charles Street

Dr. George K. Jackson, with Graupner and Mallet, Pythian Hall; resided, 18 Pinkney Street. All branches of music, including theory, Psalmody, English and Spanish Guitar

(1813   March 20, to April, 1815, at Northampton)

1815   Bowdoin Square

1816   37 Hanover Street

1817   Removed to Middlecot Street

1822   Living at 44 Market Street

J. Bailey, singing school at North School House. Sacred Music

1819   Located opposite Old South Church

1820   At Boylston School House, Fort Hill

H. Pilkington, 19 Marlboro' Street. German flute

1813   Nov. at 12, Court Street, opp. Franklin's Head. Also taught flageolet

1813

Mr. Goss, No address. Singing School

Jonathan Huntington, Boylston Market House, No. 2. Sacred Music School

1818   Water Street. School for Flutes, Sacred music taught

1820	Cornhill Square. School for Singing, Music of Handel, Haydn, Mozart, and Beethoven

1814

P. Ribes, 13 Congress Street. Pupil of Reuitzer (Kreutzer). Violin, Vocal Music, Piano Forte, French. Only pupils received "who have already acquired a certain degree of perfection on that fine instrument"

S. Holyoke, 88 Newbury Street. Vocal Music

1817

Luke Eastman, No. 11 Tudor's Buildings and at School Room at Province House. School for Sacred Music. Some classes for gentlemen only

Philip Lewis (from England), 14 Charles Street. Pianoforte, singing, violin, Piano fortes tuned

    1819	Removed to 1 Hamilton Place, opp. Park Street meeting house. Added Pedal-harp, organ, English & Spanish Guitars to list of instruments taught

"A Gentleman from England," Apply Franklin Music Warehouse. German Flute, single and double barreled Flageolet.

Mr. Mocenig, lately from Trieste, 64 Court Street. Teacher of violin

1818

M. Antoine Mathieu, lately from Italy. Residing in Salem, but starting class in Boston. Address at Mr. Fleury's. Lyre, Spanish Guitar, and vocal music

    1819	At 60 Newbury Street; sells Spanish cigars in addition to the above

Samuel Priestly Taylor, from New York. Charles Street. Pianoforte, organ, and singing. Music tuition and board later, Leverett Place, West Boston

Miss Hewitt. Addresses may be supposed to parallel those of her father, James Hewitt, until

    1818	Mrs. Rowson's, Hollis Street. Piano forte or harp

    1823	Mrs. Ostinelli (late Miss Hewitt), 32 Federal Street

    1823	April, 2 High Street

1820

Geo. Pollock, 3 Scollay's Buildings, Tremont Street. Teacher of flute

Nathaniel D. (Duren) Gould, 40 Marlboro' Street. School for sacred music

M. Christiani, Marlborough Hotel. Singing in the true Italian style, as taught by him in Europe, Washington, and Philadelphia

1821

John Hart, 7 Cornhill Square. Organ, pianoforte, flute, clarinet, horn, trumpet, and Patent Kent Bugle

Eben Goodrich, Market Street. Principles of harmony and modulation (or thorough bass) and organ playing on the system of the Italians

R. W. Wyatt, 23 Newbury Street. Pianoforte or singing

Charles Nolcini, from Europe, 3 Province House Row, entrance through the arch; tuning. Use of the piano forte, singing &c. (Moved to Portland, but returned to Boston in 1829)

A. Lyon, No. 9 Newbury Street ("Music")

1822

"Mr. Nichols of the theatre"; 74 Court Street. Instruction in vocal music

Thomas Spear, Pianoforte. Recommended by Dr. Jackson and by his sons in advertisements placed in the *Euterpeiad* and signed by Samuel, Charles, and E. W. Jackson

J. J. Wilson and Son, 31 Brattle Street. Piano Forte and singing

1823

George Prince, No address. German flute

1824

William M. Pease, "late from London and organist of the 1st Church, Malden" teaches pianoforte and organ. Terms $13 per quarter

Kent B. Stratford, Roxbury. Pianoforte. A pupil of Dr. Jackson

1825

Miss Ann Ross, No address. Pianoforte. A pupil of Dr. Jackson

NOTE: The street names as given above are misleading when applied to present-day locations. The following will serve to correct some of the names as they were changed during the period covered by this survey.

Newbury Street is now a part of Washington Street

Common Street is now known as Tremont Street

Cornhill is now a part of Washington Street

Market Street is now Cornhill

Marlboro' Street is now a part of Washington Street

Pond Street is now Bedford Street

APPENDICES

APPENDIX I

VON HAGEN PUBLICATIONS [1]

X ——— A New Federal Overture, for the opening of the season (Oct. 12, 1799). 3 Cornhill. (Adv. July 3, 1799).

1 ——— Adams & Liberty; words by Thomas Paine, A.M. Set to the tune of "To Anacreon in Heaven" 3d edition, revised and corrected. 2 pp. 3 Cornhill. (First printed by Thomas & Andrews, June 1, 1798.)

2 Von Hagen Jr. Adams & Washington; a new patriotic song. 2 pp. 62 Newbury Street. ("This day publ." Dec. 29, 1798.)

3 ——— Adams March. German flute or violin part. 1 p. 3 Cornhill.

4 ——— Alknomook, the death song of the Cherokee Indians; printed by Gilfert, also to be had at P. A. Von Hagen's Music Store, 3 Cornhill.

5 ——— Alone beside a Stream. 2 pp. 3 Cornhill.

6 Hook, James. Alone by the Light of the Moon. German flute or guitar part. 2 pp. 62 Newbury Street.

7 Von Hagen Jr. Anna; Words by "Amyntas." Clarinet or guittar part. 2 pp. 3 Cornhill & 4 Old Massachusetts Bank.

8 ——— Answer to the Favorite Song in *The Stranger* ("Poor suffering soul"). 1 p. 3 Cornhill & Gilfert.

9 ——— Arabella. 2 pp. 62 Newbury Street.

10 ——— Arise My Fair. 3 Cornhill. ("This day publ." June 23, 1803.)

11 Hook, James. As Forth I Ranged the Banks of Tweed. 2 pp. 3 Cornhill. ("This day publ." May 29, 1799.)

12 [Viguerie, B.] Battle of Maringo. ("This day publ." Ind. Chron. August 5, 1802.)

13 ——— The Blue Bells of Scotland (words by Mrs. Jordan). 1 p. 3 Cornhill. ("For sale" Jan. 30, 1802.)

X ——— Can Joy That Wretched Bosom Cheer?

14 ——— The Captive of Spilberg; favorite romance. 3 Cornhill. (Adv. June, 29, 1799.)

15 ——— Come Buy My Daffodillies. 2 pp. 3 Cornhill.

[1] For listings preceded by "X," see p. 303. A dash indicates that composer is not known.

16 ——— Come Buy My Wooden Ware; new song. 55 Marlborough Street. (Adv. June 29, 1799.)

17 ——— The Cottage in the Grove. 1 p. 3 Cornhill.

18 ——— The Cottager's Daughter. 1 p. 3 Cornhill.

19 ——— Crazy Henry to Crazy Jane. 3 Cornhill and 4 Old Massachusetts Bank. ("This day publ." May 8, 1802.)

20 ——— Crazy Jane. 2 pp. 3 Cornhill. ("A few copies of" May 8, 1802.)

21 ——— Death of Crazy Jane. 2 pp. 3 Cornhill. ("A few copies of" *Centinel,* May 8, 1802.)

X ——— Durham Hunt

22 ——— Ellen the Richmond Primrose Girl. 2 pp. 62 Newbury Street. (1798.)

23 ——— Ere Sorrow Taught My Tears to Flow. 2 pp. 3 Cornhill.

24 ——— The Fashions; sung by Mrs. Graupner. 2 pp. 3 Cornhill.

25 ——— A Favorite Song in *The Stranger* "I Have a Silent Sorrow Here." 1 p. 3 Cornhill.

26 Von Hagen, Jr. A Funeral Dirge on the Death of General Washington, Author, Von Hagen Sr. 3 Cornhill.

27 [Reeve] The Galley Slave. 2 pp. 3 Cornhill.

28 Von Hagen, Jr. Gentle Zephyr. "By the author of Anna" (Amyntas). 1 p. 3 Cornhill & 4 Old Massachusetts Bank. ("This day publ." *Pall.,* Mar. 3, 1802.)

X ——— The Grave of Love

X ——— He Has Left Me

X Pleyel. Henry's Cottage Maid

29 ——— Henry's Return, or the sequel to Crazy Jane. 2 pp. 3 Cornhill & 4 Old Massachusetts Bank.

30 ——— Honest Colin; ballad.

31 ——— How D'ye Do. 2 pp. 62 Newbury Street.

32 ——— How Tedious, Alas! Are the Hours. 2 pp. 3 Cornhill. (Adv. July 3, 1799.)

33 ——— I Never Would Be Married. 2 pp. 62 Newbury Street.

34 Von Hagen, Jr. I'm in Haste; song. 1 p. No address. Printed for G. Gilfert, N.Y.

X ——— I've Lovers Kind, and Suitors Many.

35 ——— Jeremy. 3 Cornhill.

36 ——— Jockey of the Green (Scotch Song). 2 pp. 3 Cornhill & 4 Old Massachusetts Bank. ("This day publ." *Gazette,* May 31, 1802.)

37 Von Hagen. Kiss the Brim and Let It Pass. 2 pp. 4 Massachusetts Bank. Guittar or clarinet accompaniment. Words by Mrs. Rowson. (Copyright Aug. 21, 1802.) (Announced, *Centinel,* Sept. 1, 1802.)

38 Naegli, J. H. G. (Naegeli, Hans Georg). Life Let Us Cherish, 2 pp. (3 Cornhill in advertisement, no address on music.)

39 ——— Lillies and Roses; song. 55 Marlborough Street. (Adv. April 17, 1799.)

40 ——— The Linnets. Clarinet or guittar accompaniment. 2 pp. 3 Cornhill.

41 ——— The Little Singing Girl. 55 Marlborough Street. (Adv. Apr. 17, 1799.)

42 ——— The Little Sailor Boy; sung by Mrs. Graupner. Clarinet accompaniment. 2 pp. 3 Cornhill. Words by Mrs. Rowson. (For opening of the Federal Theatre, Oct. 14, 1799.)

X ——— Love and War.

43 ——— Lucy or Selim's Complaint. Guitter part. 2 pp. 3 Cornhill.

44 ——— Lullaby. 1 p. 62 Newbury Street.

45 ——— Mary's Bower. 2 pp. 3 Cornhill.

46 ——— Mary's Dream or Sandy's Ghost. 1 p. 62 Newbury Street.

X ——— Mark When beneath the Western Sky.

47 Von Hagen. May Morning. 2 pp. Clarinet or Guitter part. 4 Old Massachusetts Bank. ("This day was publ." *Centinel,* Mar. 22, 1802.)

48 [Kelly, M.] Song in the Castle Spectre (Megen Oh!, Oh Megen Ee!). 1 p. 55 Marlborough Street (Adv. Mar. 13, 1799.)

49 ——— The Midshipman, in the opera of *The Rival Soldiers.* 3 Cornhill.

50 Von Hagen. Monody; words by "Amyntas" (Copyright Sept. 25, 1802.) (Adv. *Centinel,* Nov. 6, 1802.)

51 ——— Mounseer Nong tong paw (sung by Mr. Hodgkinson). 2 pp. 55 Marlborough Street. ("This day publ." March 30, 1799.) Words by "Amyntas."

X ——— My Love to War Is Going.

52 [Cramer, Taylor or Hook?] The Nightingale. 3 Cornhill. (Adv. Nov., 1800.)

53 ——— No, Not Yet.

54 ——— Now Is the Time to Sing and Play. 2 pp. 3 Cornhill.

X ——— Oh, Red Look'd the Sun.

X Von Hagen, Jr. Overture to be played at the Haymarket Theatre, Oct. 25, 1797.

X ——— Poor Adeline.

55 ——— The Poor Blind Girl. Flute or violin part. 1 p. 62 Newbury Street. ("For sale" Jan. 30, 1802.)

X ——— Poverty's No Sin.

56 Von Hagen. The Pride of Our Plains. Guitter or clarinet part. 2 pp. 3 Cornhill & 4 Old Massachusetts Bank.

57 L'Abbé Vogler. The Request. 1 p. 3 Cornhill.

58 ——— Roslin Castle. 1 p. 3 Cornhill.

59 F. Schaffer. Rule New England; words by Thomas Paine, A.M.

guittar and clarinet part. 2 pp. 4 Old Massachusetts Bank. (Adv. Feb. 2, 1808.)

60 ——— The Sailor's Orphan Boy. 2 pp. Published for Gilfert by Von Hagen, 3 Cornhill.

61 Von Hagen. 2 de Marsch. 2 pp. Published for Zutphen.

X ——— Poor Adeline.

X ——— Poverty's No Sin.

62 ——— She's Quite the Thing. Guittar part. 2 pp. 3 Cornhill.

63 Hook, James. The Silver Moon. German flute and violin part. 2 pp. 62 Newbury Street.

64 Dibdin. The Soldier's Adieu. Guittar, flute, or clarinet part. 2 pp. 3 Cornhill.

65 ——— Somebody. 1 p. 3 Cornhill.

66 ——— The Sweet Little Bird. 2 pp. 3 Cornhill. (". . . has this day published A New Echo Song," *Centinel,* July 17, 1802.)

67 ——— Sweet Passion of Love. 1 p. 3 Cornhill.

68 ——— The Tear.

69 ——— Tell Me It Is Love. 1 p. 55 Marlborough Street.

X Steinbelt (Steibelt) Three Progressive Lessons.

70 Von Hagen. To Arms Columbia; words by Thomas Paine. 2 pp. 3 Cornhill. 25¢ (Adv. *Col. Centinel,* June 29, 1799.)

X ——— To Banish Life's Troubles.

71 ——— To Morrow. German flute part. 2 pp. 4 Old Massachusetts Bank & 3 Cornhill.

X ——— The Triumph of Love.

72 ——— Truxton's Victory, written by Mrs. Rowson. 55 Marlborough Street. (Adv. March 13, 1799.)

73 Haigh. When the Hollow Drum, in *The Mountaineers.* 3 Cornhill. ("Has this day published . . . as a Rondo for the Piano Forte" *Centinel,* July 10, 1802.)

74 ——— When the Stars Can Be Told. 2 pp. 3 Cornhill. ("This Day publ. . . ." *Independent Chronicle,* May 13, 1802.)

X ——— When You Tell Me Your Heart Is Another's.

75 (Paisiello, G.) Whither My Love, in the Haunted Tower. Flute or violin part. 2 pp. 3 Cornhill.

76 Von Hagen. Will Not Dare to Tell (or, Will Not, Dare Not, Tell). 2 pp. 4 Old Massachusetts Bank. ("Just printed" Sept. 18, 1802.) Words by Mrs. Rowson. (Copyright Sept. 10, 1802.)

X ——— Willy Is a Bonny Lad.

77 ——— Within a Mile of Edinburgh Town. Flute, violin, or clarinet part. 2 pp. 62 Newbury Street.

78 ——— The Wood Robin. 1 p. 3 Cornhill.

79 ——— The Wretched Slave (from *Paul and Virginia*). 2 pp. Published for Gilfert by Von Hagen, 3 Cornhill.

80 (Storace) Ye Streams That Round My Prison Creep. 2 pp. 3 Cornhill.

81 ——— Young Jemmy Is a Pleasing Youth. 1 p. 3 Cornhill. (Adv. May 1799.)

Von Hagen Imprints Not Found

A New Federal Overture, for the opening of the season, Oct. 12, 1799.

* Can Joy That Wretched Bosom Cheer?

Daranzel; or, the Persian Patriot"; written by a gentleman of Boston; music by Mr. Von Hagen. (*Columbian Centinel,* Jan. 29, 1800.)

* Durham Hunt.

* The Grave of Love.

* He Has Left Me.

* I've Lovers Kind, and Suitors Many.

Love and War. 3 Cornhill. (Adv. Nov., 1800.)

* Mark When beneath the Western Sky.

* My Love to War Is Going.

* Oh, Red Look'd the Sun.

Overture to be played at the Haymarket Theatre, Oct. 25, 1797. By Peter Von Hagen Jr.

* Poor Adeline.

* Poverty's No Sin.

* To Banish Life's Troubles.

* The Triumph of Love.

* When You Tell Me Your Heart Is Another's.

* Willy Is a Bonny Lad.

Three Progressive Lessons, for the Forte Piano. By D. Steibelt (spelled Steinbelt in *Centinel,* Aug. 4, 1802, "this day publ.") 3 Cornhill, 4 Old Massachusetts Bank.

Wild Flowers Shall Deck Thy Hallow'd Tomb; words by Amyntas. 4 Old Massachusetts Bank. ("this day publ." Oct. 12, 1802.)

* These were advertised together in the *Columbian Centinel,* Jan. 30, 1802, as "for sale." Probably they were published much earlier, or were published by others than the Von Hagens. We may accept those publications announced as "just published," although they do not survive, but we may well be hesitant in considering them as authentic Von Hagen imprints until they can be identified as such.

APPENDIX II

LEADING VOCALISTS APPEARING IN BOSTON

(Where no specific month is given, the entire season is implied)

Mrs. Burke	1816	Mrs. Mills	1808–09
Mr. Darley	1802–04	Mrs. Oldmixon	June 1807
Miss Dellinger	January 1810	Mr. Phillips	April 1818
Mr. Fox	1805–07		January 1822
Mrs. French	May 1819	Mrs. Poe	1809
	August 1820	Mr. Phipps	1824
Mrs. Graupner	1796–1818	Mr. Spiller	1813
Mrs. Holman	August 1822	Mr. R. A. Taylor	August 1817
Mr. Incledon	June 1818		September 1823
Mrs. Jones	1801–04	Mr. Story	1801–02
Mr. Keene	1819	Mr. Vining	1807
Miss Kelly	November 1824	Mr. Webster	1807
Mr. Labasse	1822	Mr. Williamson	1797–98
Mr. McFarland	1811	Mr. Williamson	1823

APPENDIX III

CATALOGUE OF GRAUPNER PUBLICATIONS

Every piece of music listed has been in the hands of the compiler except sixteen marked JFD. Those were accepted from the card catalogue of Mr. J. Francis Driscoll who owns copies of them, and is, apparently, the only possesssor of those particularly rare imprints. Seven imprints to which reference has been found, but which have eluded the compiler in his search, are entered in their proper order, but not numbered. They will be found together at the end.

n.pl. signifies "no plate number"

1 A Highland Lad My Love Was Born, sung by Mrs. Holman (in Boston, 1822). 2 pp. n.pl. 6 Franklin Street.

2 A New Ode, sung by Mr. Eaton at the celebration of the Anniversary of American Independence, July 4th, 1802. Words by "Amyntas" (music by F. Mallet?). 2 pp. n.pl. Mallet & Graupner at their Conservatorio ("This day published. . . ." Boston *Gazette,* July 19, 1802.)

3 A Prey to Tender Anguish. Music by F. J. Haydn. 1 p. n.pl. Mallet & Graupner at their Conservatorio or Musical Academy.

Another, with arrangement for two guitars. 2 pp. n.pl. Mallet & Graupner.

Another, with Spofforth's "Death of Anna," ballad, sung by Mr. Incledon. 3 pp. n.pl. 30¢ 6 Franklin Street. *See* No. 92.

Also in the *Musical Magazine,* Vol. III.

4 A Soldier to His Own Fireside, sung by Mrs. Jones at the Federal Theatre in *The Wife of Two Husbands.* Music by F. Granger. 2 pp. n.pl. Musical Academy, 6 Franklin Street. 25¢ (". . . lately published" Boston *Gazette,* April 10, 1806. Copyright Nov. 16, 1805.)

5 Absence, words adapted to the favorite air of Rousseau's "Dream." [Music by J. Cramer.] 1 p. n.pl. 6 Franklin Street.

Another, "and sold for him by John Ashton, 197 Washington Street."

6 Address to Spring, and Providence March. Music by Oliver Shaw. 2 pp. pl. 31–2. 6 Franklin Street.

7   Adventures of Paul Pry, sung by Mr. Hilson. 2 pp. n.pl. 6 Province
      House Court.

8   Aeolian Harp, sung by Mrs. Graupner at his Concert Hall. Music
      by F. C. Schaffer. Violin part. 2 pp. pl. 36–7. Musical Academy,
      6 Franklin Street. 35¢. ("Lately published" Boston *Gazette*,
      April 10, 1806. Copyright Feb. 3, 1806.)

9   The African Dance, and Aria in *The Brazen Mask,* and Rondo. 2 pp.
      pl. 516. 6 Franklin Street. [Music by Davy.]
      Another, without rondo.

10   Ah! Little Blind Boy! Music by M. Kelly. 6 Franklin Street, 3 pp.
      pl. 303–5. (JFD)

11   Ah, Sure a Pair Was Never Seen, favorite song as sung by Mr.
      Phillips. 2 pp. pl. 121. 15 Marlboro Street.

12   Ah! What Is the Bosoms Commotion, in the grand dramatic romance
      of the *Forty Thieves,* sung by Mr. Darley. Music by Michael
      Kelly. 3 pp. pl. 306–08. 6 Franklin Street.

13   Ah Where Can I Turn for Relief, sung by Mrs. Mills in the grand
      melodrama of the *Forty Thieves.* Music by Michael Kelly. 2 pp.
      pl. 316–17. 6 Franklin Street.

14   A Favorite Air in *Oscar And Malvina. See* the *Musical Magazine,*
      Vol. I.

15   A Favorite Air with Six Variations for Pianoforte. *See* No. 117.

16   Aria in *The Brazen Mask. See* No. 9.

17   L'Amour est en enfant trompeut [!]. Music by Johann Dussek. 3 pp.
      with cover. n.pl. 6 Franklin Street.

18   Anchors Weighed, sung by Mr. Braham. Music by John Braham.
      3 pp. pl. 60–62. 6 Franklin Street. Sold by John Ashton.

19   Araby's Daughter, sung by Mr. Williamson. Words by Thomas
      Moore. Music by George Kiallmark. 3 pp. n.pl. 1 Province House
      Court. Sold by John Ashton.

20   Arioso. Music by G. F. Handel. *See* No. 149.

21   Arouse, Arouse, Columbia's Sons, Arouse! *See* No. 240.

22   As Wrapt in Sleep I Lay. *See* the *Musical Magazine,* Vol. I.

23   Attic Bower, sung by Mrs. Graupner. Words by Thomas Paine.
      Music composed by Gottlieb Graupner. 1 p. n.pl. Printed and for
      sale at the Conservatorio, or Musical Academy. 1802. 25¢. Copy-
      right Oct. 4, 1802.
      Also, in the *Musical Magazine,* Vol. III.

24   The Augusta Waltz. Composed and arranged for the piano forte
      by James Hewitt. Respectfully dedicated to Miss E. Andrews.
      1 p. n.pl. 6 Franklin Street.

25   Auld Lang Syne, for pianoforte or harp, with variations. Music by
      John Ross. 4 pp. n.pl. 6 Franklin Street. Sold by John Ashton.
      Another, simplified. 1 p. n.pl. 6 Franklin Street.
      Another, as above. Sold by John Ashton.

26 Awake, Ye Dull Sluggards, sung by Mrs. Mills at the Boston Theatre. 2 pp. n.pl. 6 Franklin Street.

27 Away with Melancholy (O dolce concento). Music by Mozart. 1 p. n.pl. 6 Franklin Street. Sold by John Ashton.

28 Bangor March. Music by Oliver Shaw. 2 p. n.pl. 6 Franklin Street.

29 Bath Waltz, rondo. Arranged as a rondo for piano forte by Thomas Tomlins. 4 pp. pl. 90. 6 Franklin Street. Engraved and printed by S. Wetherbee. ("Just published . . ." June 3, 1820, Boston *Gazette.*)

30 Battle of Maringo, Op. 8. Music by B. Viguerie. Accompaniment for violin. 13 pp. n.pl. 6 Franklin Street, near Tontine Buildings. ("Publ. and ready for delivery" Nov. 22, 1802, Boston *Gazette.*)

31 Battle of New Orleans, dedicated to the American nation. Music by D. Etienne. 20 pp. n.pl. 6 Franklin Street. Published for the author. (Copyright Oct. 26, 1816.)

32 The Battle of the Nile, favorite British song. 2 pp. n.pl. 6 Franklin Street.
Another. pl. 156–57.
Another, for piano or harpsichord, with cover. 8 pp. n.pl. Mallet & Graupner at their Conservatorio, or Musical Academy ("now ready for sale . . ." March 29, 1802.) (First announcement of printing office.)

33 Battle of Prague, sonata for piano forte. Music by Kotzwara. 8 pp. pl. 485–92. Printed and sold by G. Graupner, 6 Franklin Street. (Lithograph cover with portrait of Washington.) $1.
Another. pl. 124–32. Printed and sold by G. Graupner at his Conservatorio, or Musical Academy, near Tontine Buildings. $1.
Another. n.pl.
Another. Violin part. 2 pp. Issued separately, or with one of the above editions.

X The Beggar Boy.

X The Beggar Girl.

34 Behold in His Soft Expressive Face, sung by Signorina Garcia in *Devil's Bridge.* Music by John Braham [and C. E. Horn]. 2 pp. n.pl. G. Graupner; sold for him by John Ashton.

35 The Beautiful Maid, from *The Cabinet.* [Music by Thomas Dibdin, son of Charles.] 2 pp. n.pl. 6 Franklin Street.
Another. pl. 79–80.

36 Believe Me, If All Those Endearing Young Charms. Words and music by Thomas Moore. 2 pp. pl. 79–80. 6 Franklin Street.
Another. Sold for him by John Ashton.
Another, with variations.

37 The Bird Waltz, for piano or harp. Music by Francis C. Vanormo, Jr. 3 pp. pl. 74. 6 Franklin Street. (Copyright Jan. 16, 1819.)
Another. n.pl.

38 A Blessing on Brandy And Beer, in *Magician No Conjurer*. *See* the *Musical Magazine*, Vol. I.

39 A Favorite Mad Song, or Blest Were the Hours, from *Men and Manners*. [Music by James Hook.] 4 pp. pl. 169–70. 6 Franklin Street.
Another. n.pl.

40 The Blue Bells of Scotland, sung by Mrs. Graupner at the Federal Theatre. Words by Mrs. Jordan. Mallet & Graupner. ("Just published" June 14, 1802.)

41 Blue-eyed Mary, song. 2 pp. pl. 77. 15 Marlborough Street.
Another. n.pl.

42 The Blue-ey'd Stranger, written by Wm. Currell. Music by Wm. Slapp. 2 pp. pl. 33–34. 6 Franklin Street.

43 Bonaparte's Coronation March. 1 p. pl. 155. 6 Franklin Street.
Another, with Bonaparte's March Crossing the Rhine. 1 p. pl. 155. 6 Franklin Street. Sold by John Ashton.

44 Bonaparte's Favorite Waltz. 2 pp. pl. 84–5. Musical Academy, 6 Franklin Street.

45 The Bonny Boat (O Swiftly Glides . . .), Scotch melody. 1 p. n.pl. Gottlieb Graupner; sold for him by John Ashton.

46 Bonny Charlie, a favorite song. Music attributed to Neil Gow. 3 pp. pl. 438–39. 6 Franklin Street.
Bonny Charly, a favorite Scotch song. 2 pp. n.pl. 6 Franklin Street. Sold by John Ashton.

47 Bonny Doon. Music by James Millar. 2 pp. n.pl. Musical Academy, 6 Franklin Street. "Pianofortes for sale, to let, and tuned in town and country at shortest notice." 25¢.
Another. 2 pp. pl. 71. 6 Franklin Street.

48 Boston Brigade March, as performed by the Brigade Band at the reception of General Lafayette, written for the pianoforte. Music by James Hewitt. 2 pp. n.pl. 1 Province House Court. Sold by John Ashton. (Lafayette in Boston, 1824. *See also* General Lafayette's Grand March.)

49 Boston Cadet's March; also, Favorite Spanish Air, arranged for piano. 2 pp. n.pl. 6 Franklin Street. Sold by John Ashton.
Another (March only). 1 p. pl. 450. 6 Franklin Street.

50 Bounding Billows, written by Mrs. Robinson in crossing from Dover to Calais. [Music by James M. Elliott.] 1 p. pl. 49. Musical Academy, 6 Franklin Street. 12¢.
Another. n.pl.

51 Brazen Mask, The. For aria in, *see* the African Dance (No. 9).

52 Brazilian Waltz, with accompaniment for flute, flageolet, violin, or clarinet. 6 pp. pl. 504. 6 Franklin Street.

53 The Bride's Farewell. Words by Miss M. L. Beevor. Music by

Thomas Williams (probably Thomas E.). 2 pp. n.pl. 1 Province House Court.

54 Bristol March, and Country Dance. By Oliver Shaw. Flute or violin part. 2 pp. pl. 419–20. 6 Franklin Street.

Another, without Country Dance. 1 p. pl. 419–20. 6 Franklin Street.

Another, with Caravan March. Flute or violin part. 2 pp. n.pl. 6 Franklin Street.

55 Bruce's Address to His Army, favorite Scotch song, sung by Mr. Incledon. 2 pp. pl. 92. 6 Franklin Street. [Engraved S. Wetherbee.] ("Just published" June 3, 1820.)

Another, without "Engraved S. Wetherbee."

56 The Bugle Quickstep. 1 p. pl. 72. 6 Franklin Street. [Engraved S. Wetherbee.] ("Just published" June 3, 1820.)

57 The Bugle Call, with variations. Music by T. Latour. 3 pp. n.pl. Gottlieb Graupner; sold for him by John Ashton.

58 Buonaparte's Grand March, and Washington's Assembly. 1 p. pl. 30 (or 32). Musical Academy, 6 Franklin Street, near Franklin Place. 12¢.

59 The Calendonian Hunt, with four variations. Music by T. Latour. 4 pp. pl. 102. 6 Franklin Street.

60 A Canadian Boat Song, song. [Music by Thomas Moore.] 1 p. pl. 48. Musical Repository, 6 Franklin Street. (Original published in England, 1805.)

Another. pl. 81. 6 Franklin Street.

61 The Capture, song in *The Pirates*. *See* the *Musical Magazine,* Vol. II.

62 Canna Muna Marry Yet, written by Mr. R. Burns. Music by James Hook. Flute part. 2 pp. n.pl. Musical Repository, 6 Franklin Street.

63 Caravan March. *See* No. 54.

64 The Carrier Pigeon, sung by Mrs. Holman. Music by P. K. Moran. 4 pp. n.pl. Gottlieb Graupner; sold for him by John Ashton.

65 O Cease Sweet Girl, a canzonet. Music by D. D. Roche. 4 pp. pl. 203–06. 6 Franklin Street. ("Lately published" *Columbian Centinel,* Feb. 10, 1813.)

66 Celebrated Andante with Eleven Variations for Pianoforte with Accompaniment for German Flute ad libitum by T. Latour. [Theme by Pleyel.] 9 pp. pl. 521. 6 Franklin Street. ("Just published" June 3, 1820.)

67 Celebrated Concertante, in four movements, with accompaniment for violin. By Pleyel. 9 pp., with cover. pl. 226. 6 Franklin Street.

68 Charlie Is My Darling, Scotch song, sung by Mrs. Holman in the opera *Montrose*. [Music by Sir Henry R. Bishop.] 2 pp. n.pl. 6 Franklin Street.

69 The Chase, for pianoforte. By Moler. 2 pp. pl. 453–54. 6 Franklin Street.

70 Cherry Ripe, ballad, sung by Mrs. Burke in Boston. [Originally sung by Mme. Vestris.] Music by Charles E. Horn. 3 pp. n.pl. Gottlieb Graupner; sold for him by John Ashton.

71 The City Guard's Grand March and Quickstep, performed by the Brigade Band. 2 pp. n.pl. 1 Province House Court. Sold by John Ashton. (JFD)

72 Claudine Liv'd Contented, sung by Mrs. Bolton in *Two Faces Under One Hood*. Music by William Shield. 2 pp. pl. 514. 6 Franklin Street.

73 Clementi's Favorite Waltz. By Clementi. 2 pp. n.pl. 6 Franklin Street.
Clementi's Grand Waltz. 2 pp. n.pl. 6 Franklin Street.
Another. 3 pp. n.pl. 6 Franklin Street.
Another. 2 pp. n.pl. 6 Franklin Street. Sold by John Ashton.

74 La' Clementina Waltz, arranged for the pianoforte with accompaniment for flute. 2 pp. n.pl. 6 Franklin Street.
Another. 6 Franklin Street. Sold by John Ashton.
Another, without flute. 2 pp. n.pl. 6 Franklin Street.

75 Collection of Cottillions, selected by F. D. Mallet, arranged for pianoforte by F. C. Shaffer. 12 pp. with cover. n.pl. 6 Franklin Street. (Copyright September 26, 1821.)

76 A Collection of Country Dances and Cotillions, never before published and to be continued monthly. 6 Franklin Street.
Vol. I: 9 Short Dances. pl. 213–16. (Sept. 31, 1821).
Vol. II: 7 Short Dances. pl. 259–62.
Vol. III: 9 Short Dances. pl. 465–68.
Vol. IV: 8 Short Dances. pl. 469–72.

77 College Hornpipe (or Coledge Hornpipe). *See* No. 123 and No. 218.

78 Col. Orn's March. 1 p. pl. 128. 6 Franklin Street. ("Lately publ." *Columbian Centinel,* Feb. 10, 1813.)
Another. Sold by John Ashton.

79 Columbia, Land of Liberty, favorite patriotic song, written by J. N. Barker. Music by John Bray. 3 pp. pl. 109. 6 Franklin Street. (Copyright Jan. 23, 1819.)

80 Come Haste to the Wedding, and Russian Dance. 1 p. n.pl. Gottlieb Graupner; sold for him by John Ashton.

81 Come Rest in This Bosom. Words by Thomas Moore, Esq. Set to the air "Fleuve du Tage," by Kiallmark. 2 pp. n.pl. 6 Franklin Street. *See* No. 83.

82 Comin' through the Rye, Scotch ballad, sung by Mrs. Knight, and adapted to the air "Fleuve du Tage." 2 pp. n.pl. 1 Province House Court. Sold by John Ashton. *See* No. 82.

83 Copenhagen Waltz, with variations for the pianoforte. By Saml. Webbe. 4 pp. pl. 117. 6 Franklin Street.
Another, with Pleyel "Favorite Divertimento." *See* No. 95.

84 The Cottage in the Grove. By James Hook. 2 pp. pl. 58–59. Musical Academy, 6 Franklin Street. 25¢.

85 The Cottage Rondo. By Holtz (Holst, M.). 4 pp. pl. 99. 6 Franklin Street and the Franklin Music Warehouse (1818–19).
Another. 4 pp. pl. 506. 6 Franklin Street.

86 Country Dance. *See* No. 54.

87 Dance, in *Cinderella*. *See* No. 225.

88 Danish Waltz, with variations for the pianoforte. By George Kiallmark. 5 pp. n.pl. 6 Franklin Street.

89 The Dashing White Sergeant, sung by Mrs. Knight. Music by H. R. Bishop. 3 pp. n.pl. 1 Providence House Court. Sold by John Ashton.

90 The Day of Marriage, sung by Mrs. Jones. 2 pp. pl. 23–24. Musical Academy, 6 Franklin Street. 25¢. (". . . for sale" Oct. 22, 1803, *Columbian Centinel,* but "just published" Sept. 24, 1804, Boston *Gazette.*)

91 Death of Anna, ballad, sung by Mr. Incledon. Music by Reginald Spofforth. 3 pp. n.pl. Conservatory, or Musical Academy, 6 Franklin Street. 30¢. ("Just publ. . . ." June 14, 1802.)
Another, with Haydn's, A Prey to Tender Anguish. *See* No. 3.

92 Dear Wanderer. *See* the *Musical Magazine,* Vol. I.

93 Diana, a Favorite Hunting Cantata; and a Favorite Waltz. By James Hook. 5 pp. n.pl. 6 Franklin Street.

94 A Favourite Divertimento, and Copenhagen Waltz. By Pleyel. 1 p. n.pl. Gottlieb Graupner; sold for him by John Ashton.

95 Does the Harp of Rosa Slumber, sung by Miss Dellinger. By Thomas Moore. 2 pp. pl. 82–83. 6 Franklin Street.

96 Donshier Quick Step. By Oliver Holden. 1 p. pl. 274. 6 Franklin Street.

97 The Downfall of Paris. 1 p. pl. 39. Musical Academy, 6 Franklin Street. 13¢. ("Lately published . . ." April 10, 1806, Boston, *Gazette.*)
Another. n.pl. 6 Franklin Street. Sold by John Ashton. 12½¢.

98 Draw the Sword, Scotland! Sung by Mr. Williamson. 3 pp. n.pl. G. Graupner. Sold by John Ashton. (JFD)

99 The Duke of York's March. 1 p. pl. 31. Muscial Academy, 6 Franklin Street, near Franklin Place.
Another, with Swiss Guard's March. 1 p. 12¢.
Another, at Hewitt's Musical Repository, 59 Maiden Lane, New York.

100 Each Moment Blew Softly Away, translated from the French by an amateur of Salem.

101 The Echo, duet, sung by Mr. Braham and Miss Kelly in *The Americans.* Music by John Braham. 4 pp. pl. 413–16. 6 Franklin Street.

102   Edward and Maria, canzonet. Music by James Hook. 2 pp. pl. 363–64. 6 Franklin Street.

103   Egyptian Air, rondo. By H. Butler (Thomas Hamly). 2 pp. n.pl. 6 Franklin Street.

104   Ellen Aureen, sung by Mr. Williamson. By J. Monro. 3 pp. n.pl. 6 Franklin Street. Sold by John Ashton.

105   Ellen of the Dee, for pianoforte. By John Ross. 3 pp. n.pl. 6 Franklin Street. 25¢. ("Lately publ." Boston *Gazette*, Apr. 2, 1806.) (JFD)

106   Emperor Alexander's Waltz. *See* No. 312.

107   'Ere Around the Huge Oak. *See* Vol. II, The *Musical Magazine*, Vol. II.

108   Erin Go Brah. 1 p. pl. 25. Musical Academy, 6 Franklin Street. 12¢. Another. n.pl. 6 Franklin Street.

109   Eveleen's Bower, or Maid of Derby, arranged by J. B. Logier with variations for the pianoforte. 6 pp. n.pl. 6 Franklin Street.
      Another, as sung by Mr. Phillips. 3 pp. pl. 134. 15 Marlborough Street.
      Another. n.pl.

110   The Evening Star, quickstep. 1 p. n.pl. 1 Province House Court.

111   Faithless Emma, sung by Mr. Spray (Liverpool). Music by Sir John A. Stevenson. 2 pp. pl. 222. 6 Franklin Street.
      Another edition, different plate. [Sung by Mr. Webster at Concert Hall, Sept. 18, 1809.]

112   Fancy's Vision, composed and sung by H. F. Keene. 2 pp. pl. 81. 6 Franklin Street.
      Another. Sold by John Ashton.

113   Far, Far at Sea. By C. H. Florio. 1 p. n.pl. 1 Province House Court. Sold by John Ashton.

114   Farewell! Words by Thomas Moore. Music by Sir John A. Stevenson. 3 pp. pl. 101. 6 Franklin Street. [Engraved S. Wetherbee.]

115   Farewell My Love, ballad dedicated to Lady More. Introduced by Mrs. Sterling, Covent Garden. Music by Wm. M. (Mineard) Bennett. 4 pp. pl. 462–64. 6 Franklin Street.

116   The Farmer's Wife, from the opera of the same name. Music by Sir Henry R. Bishop [with Reeves and Davy].

117   A Favorite Air with Six Variations for Pianoforte. By T. Latour. 4 pp. pl. 105. 6 Franklin Street.

118   A Favorite Mad Song. *See* No. 39.

119   The Favorite Song in the Opera *Traveller in Switzerland*. *See* the *Musical Magazine*, Vol. II.

120   A Favorite Waltz. By W. A. Mozart. 1 p. n.pl. 15 Marlboro Street.
      Another. 2 pp. pl. 78. 15 Marlboro Street.
      Another. 2 pp. pl. 78. 15 Marlboro Street. Sold by John Ashton.

Another, Favorite Waltz, accompaniment for German flute. 2 pp. pl. 231. 6 Franklin Street.

121 A Favorite Waltz. By Daniel Steibelt. 2 pp. pl. 508. 6 Franklin Street.

122 Finale in the Pantomime of *Oscar and Malvina*. *See* the *Musical Magazine*. Vol. II.

123 Fischer's Hornpipe and Coledge Hornpipe. 1 p. pl. 33. No publisher's name, but advertised by Graupner, April 10, 1806, as published.

124 Five Waltzes, by the author of "There's a Bower of Roses." By R. W. Wyatt. 5 pp. n.pl. Published for the author by Gottlieb Graupner, 6 Franklin Street. [Engraved S. Wetherbee.] (Copyright R. W. Wyatt, April 5, 1820.)

125 Fly Not Yet. Words by Thomas Moore. Music by Stevenson. 2 pp. n.pl. 6 Franklin Street. (JFD)

126 Follow, Follow thro' the Sea, sung by Miss Kelley. Music by Vincente Martini. Arranged by Bishop. 5 pp. n.pl. 6 Franklin Street. Sold by John Ashton.

127 Follow, Follow over Mountain, sung by Mrs. Hackett. Music by S. T. Smith. 4 pp. n.pl. 1 Province House Court.

128 The Foray. Words by Walter Scott. Music by Dr. John Clarke of Cambridge, England. 5 pp. with cover. n.pl. Gottlieb Graupner; sold for him by John Ashton.

129 Friend of My Soul. Words by Thomas Moore. Adapted to the air "Sul Margino d'un Rio (!)" 2 pp. n.pl. 6 Franklin Street.

130 From Childhood's Dawn to Noon of Youth, sung by Mr. Philipps. From *Lionel and Clarissa,* as additional air. [Music by Charles Dibdin.] 2 pp. pl. 82. 15 Marlboro Street.

Another. n.pl.

131 The Gallant Troubadour, a favorite song. 2 pp. n.pl. 6 Franklin Street.

Another. 6 Franklin Street. Sold by John Ashton.

132 The Galley Slave, in *The Purse*. Music by W. Reeve. 1 p. n.pl. 6 Franklin Street.

Another, in the *Musical Magazine,* Vol. II.

133 Garland of Love, sung by Mrs. Claude in the grand melodrama of *Tekeli*. Music by James Hook. 2 pp. pl. 301–02. 6 Franklin Street.

Another. n.pl.

134 Gem of Aberdeen. *See* Vol. II, the *Musical Magazine,* Vol. II.

135 General Coburg, Trumpet March. 2 pp. pl. 97. 6 Franklin Street, and Franklin Music Warehouse, 6 Milk Street.

(". . . just published" Jan. 1, 1817.)

136 General Lafayette's Grand March, as performed by the Boston

Band. Music by James Hewitt. 3 pp. with cover. n.pl. 6 Franklin Street.

137 General Lafayette's Light Infantry March. Arranged by Granger. 1 p. n.pl. 6 Franklin Street.

138 General Washington's March at the Battle of Trenton, and Yankee Doodle. 1 p. pl. 1. 6 Franklin Street.
Another. n.pl. 6 Franklin Street. Sold by John Ashton.

139 Gentleman's Pocket Companion; Collection of Marches, Airs, Songs, Rondos, adapted for two German flutes, or flute and violin. No. 1. Arranged by Fr. Granger. n.pl. Musical Academy, 6 Franklin Street. $1.50. (Advertised in the *Columbian Centinel*, Oct. 22, 1803.)

140 A German Waltz, with variations. 1 p. pl. 64. 6 Franklin Street.
Another. n.pl. 6 Franklin Street. Sold by John Ashton.

141 The Girl of My Heart, sung by Mr. Webster. Music by William Shield. 2 pp. pl. 220. 6 Franklin Street.

X Go, Gentle Zephyr.

142 Governor Brooks Favourite Scotch March. Composed and dedicated to Miss Swan and young ladies at her Academy, Medford, by Gottlieb Graupner. (Copyright Oct. 9, 1820.) With part for flute. 2 pp. pl. 106. 6 Franklin Street. (Engraved S. Wetherbee.)
Governor Brooks Favourite Scotch March, and Favorite Polish Waltz. With Two Variations. Engraved and composed by G. Graupner. 2 pp. pl. 119. G. Graupner & Co. ("Just publ. . . ." June 18, 1820.)

143 Governor Jones's March. By Oliver Shaw. 1 p. pl. 9. 6 Franklin Street. (Govr. Wm. Jones, 1811–17.)

144 Governor Knight's March. By Oliver Shaw. 2 pp. pl. 93. Published for the author by Gottlieb Graupner, 6 Franklin Street. [Governor Nehemiah Knight, 1817–21.]

145 Governor Strong's March. 1 p. pl. 129. 6 Franklin Street. (". . . Lately published" *Columbian Centinel,* Feb. 10, 1813.)

146 The Guard's Song, as composed and sung by a member of the Guard at Savin Hill, 1823. 2 pp., with lithograph cover. n.pl. (Copyright 1835, at District Court of Massachusetts, Clerk's Office.)

147 Had I a Heart, song. Music by Thos. T. Linley Jr. 2 pp. n.pl. 15 Marlboro Street.

148 Hallelujah Chorus, by Handel. Sung by Trinity Choir. n.pl. 5 pp. 6 Franklin Street. (JFD)

149 Handel's Water Music, Hornpipe, and Arioso. By G. F. Handel. 2 pp. n.pl. 6 Franklin Street.
Another, pl. 29–30. Musical Academy, 6 Franklin Street.
Another, at Francis Mallet, Devonshire Street, opp. Spring Lane. 25¢.
Another. pl. 108–09.

150 The Harper's Song. Words from *Rokeby*. Cottage Melodies No. 1. Composed and arranged by T. V. Weisenthal, with accompaniment for harp or pianoforte. 2 pp. n.pl. 6 Franklin Street. (Copyright Feb. 6, 1821.)

151 Have You Not Seen the Timid Tear, sung by Mrs. Holman. Dedicated to Mrs. Holman. Music by James Hewitt. [Words by Thomas Moore.] 2 pp. n.pl. 6 Franklin Street.

152 Haydn's Celebrated Military Andante. By F. J. Haydn. 2 pp. n.pl. 1 Province House Court. Sold by John Ashton.

153 Henry's Cottage Maid. *See* the *Musical Magazine,* Vol. III.

154 Here We Meet Too Soon to Part, sung by Mr. Williamson, adapted to Rossini's air "di tanti palpiti" with new symphonies and accompaniments by T. Phipps. 2 pp. n.pl. 6 Franklin Street.
Another. 6 Franklin Street. Sold by John Ashton.

155 Hey Dance to the Fiddle And Tabor. *See* the *Musical Magazine,* Vol. III.

156 The Hindoo Girl. 1 p. pl. 360. 6 Franklin Street.

157 Home! Sweet Home! Sung by Miss M. Tree in *Clari, or the Maid of Milan, London.* [Words by John Howard Payne.] Music by Sir Henry R. Bishop. Key of E. 3 pp. n.pl. 6 Franklin Street. Sold by John Ashton. (*Clari* first produced in London, 1823; in New York, 1828.)
Another. Key of F. 1 p. n.pl. 6 Franklin Street. Sold by John Ashton.
Another, Sicilian air with variations. 4 pp. n.pl. 6 Franklin Street. Sold by John Ashton.

158 Hope, or Hope No More Thou Soft Beguiler. Poetry by J. Townsend. Music by J. T. Burrowes (probably John Freckleton). 3 pp. pl. 408–10. 6 Franklin Street.

159 Hours There Were, song. Music by Joseph Wade. 2 pp. n.pl. 1 Province House Court.

160 Hull's Victory. *See* No. 316.

161 Hungarian Rondo. By S. Von Rosenberg. 2 pp. n.pl. 6 Franklin Street.

162 The Hungarian Waltz, as danced in the admired ballet *Love among the Roses* (1818). 1 p. n.pl. 6 Franklin Street.
Another. 6 Franklin Street. Sold by John Ashton.

163 The Hussar's Adieu, and Providence March. By Oliver Shaw. 2 pp. pl. 446–47. 6 Franklin Street. *See also* Nos. 6 and 292.

164 Hymn to the Evening Star. Written by Lord Byron. Arranged for organ or pianoforte by T. V. Weisenthal. 2 pp. n.pl. 6 Franklin Street. (Copyright May 12, 1821.)

165 I Have Lov'd Thee, Dearly Lov'd Thee, written by Mrs. Robinson. With flute part. Music by James Hook. 2 pp. pl. 139–40. 6 Franklin Street. ("Lately publ." *Columbian Centinel,* Feb. 10, 1818.)

166 I Knew by the Smoke That So Gracefully Curl'd. Words by Thomas

Moore. Music by J. Willson. 2 pp. pl. 367–68. 6 Franklin Street.

167   I Love Thee, a duetto sung by Miss Bishop and Mr. Braham in *Circassian Bride.* Music by Sir Henry R. Bishop. 4 pp. pl. 510. 6 Franklin Street.

168   I Owe You One. From *63rd Letter.* Music by Arnold. 1 p. n.pl. Musical Academy, 6 Franklin Street, near Franklin Place. 12¢.

169   I Sold a Guiltless Negro Boy, ballad. *See* the *Musical Magazine,* Vol. I.

170   I That Once Was a Ploughman. *See* the *Musical Magazine,* Vol. II.

171   I Won't Be a Nun! 1 p. n.pl. 6 Franklin Street.

172   Isabel, Spanish serenade, sung by Miss Stephens. Music by Sir Henry R. Bishop. 2 pp. n.pl. Gottlieb Graupner; sold for him by John Ashton.

173   Is There a Heart, sung by Mr. Philipps. [By J. Braham.] 2 pp. pl. 122. 15 Marboro Street.

174   'Tis But Fancy's Sketch, in *The Devil's Bridge.* Music by Braham [with Horn]. 2 pp. n.pl. G. Graupner; sold for him by John Ashton.

175   'Tis Love in the Heart, rondo, sung by Mr. Williamson, from *The Bride of Abydos* (probably *The Magic Bride*). Music by Charles E. Horn. 4 pp. n.pl. 6 Franklin Street.

X   'Tis Lovely Woman Governs All.

176   'Tis the Last Rose of Summer. Words by T. Moore. 1 p. pl. 221. 6 Franklin Street.

177   The Jealous Don. *See* the *Musical Magazine,* Vol. II.

178   The Jersey Blue. *See* the *Musical Magazine,* Vol. III.

179   Jessie, the Flower o'Dumblane, favorite Scottish song, sung by Miss Johnson at the Boston Theatre, and dedicated to James McFarland. [Composed 1808.] Music by R. A. Smith. 3 pp. with cover. pl. 101. 6 Franklin Street, and at Franklin Music Warehouse, 6 Milk Street.
Another, without cover.

180   Jonathan's Account of the Pilgrim People. By F. Granger. Words by the Boston Bard. 2 pp. n.pl. G. Graupner. Sold by John Ashton. (JFD)

181   The Jubilee, dedicated to Miss P. Baker. By John Gildon. 6 pp., with cover. pl. 207–12. 6 Franklin Street.

182   Julia to the Wood Robin, canzonet. By Reginald Spofforth. 4 pp. n.pl. Printed and sold by G. Graupner at his Conservatorio, or Musical Academy. (" 'Julia . . . a Favorite New Song' is this day published . . ." *Columbian Centinel,* Aug. 21, 1802.) ("*Sighs;—Or, the Daughter* with a song for the first time in Boston, called, 'Julia to the Wood-Robin.' " *Columbian Centinel,* Nov. 3, 1802.)

183 Kate Kearney, famous Irish air. [By Wm. H. Webster.] 2 pp. pl. 441. 6 Franklin Street.

184 The Knight Errant, translated from the French by Walter Scott. Music by Hortensia, Queen of Holland. 2 pp. pl. 104. Published for P. Muck, Charleston, S.C. by G. Graupner & Co., Boston. Sold by John Ashton, 197 Washington Street. ("Just published" June 18, 1820.)

185 Knox's March. 1 p. pl. 175. (No publisher's name, but probably Graupner, by reason of the plate number. Driscoll accepts it as so.)

186 Lafayette, a parody. 2 pp. n.pl. 6 Franklin Street.

187 Lafayette's March, in honor of Lafayette, August 30, 1824. For Boston Independent Cadets. By Miss Caroline Clark. 2 pp. n.pl. 6 Franklin Street, for the author. (Copyright by Miss Clark, Sept. 9, 1824.)

188 Laurette, a much admired Italian dance arranged as a progressive rondo. Arranged by T. V. Weisenthal. Dedicated to Miss Maria Blake. 3 pp. pl. 75. 6 Franklin Street. (Copyright Jan. 11, 1819.) Another, n.pl.

189 The Lavender Girl. 1 p. n.pl. 6 Franklin Street. Another. 6 Franklin Street. Sold by John Ashton.

190 The Lee Rigg, with variations. [Arranged by D. Corri.] 3 pp. pl. 3–5. 6 Franklin Street. Sold by John Ashton. Another. n.pl. 6 Franklin Street.

191 The Legacy—When in Death I Shall Calm Recline. [Words by T. Moore.] 2 pp. pl. 444–45. 6 Franklin Street.

192 Let This Brow, on Thy Bosom Reclining. By C. E. Phillips. 2 pp. n.pl. 6 Franklin Street.

193 Life Let Us Cherish, an air with variations. By Johannes Hans Georg Naegli. Arranged by Mozart. 4 pp. pl. 511. 6 Franklin Street. Another. pl. 513.

194 The Light House, ballad. Words by Thomas Moore. Music by J. Willson (organist, the Rev. Dr. Porter's Church, Roxbury). 2 pp. pl. 513. 6 Franklin Street. Sold by John Ashton. Another. 6 Franklin Street.

195 Like the Gloom of Night Retiring, sung by Mrs. Holman. Music by Henry R. Bishop. 4 pp. n.pl. 6 Franklin Street.

196 Little Sue, sung by Mrs. Bland at Vauxhall. Music by James Hook. 2 pp. pl. 217–18. 6 Franklin Street. Sold by John Ashton. Another. n.pl. 6 Franklin Street.

197 Lorade in the Tower. *See* the *Musical Magazine,* Vol. I.

198 Lord Wellington's Grand March and Waltz. By M. Holst. 5 pp. pl. 84. 6 Franklin Street, and at Franklin Music Warehouse, 6 Milk Street. ("Just publ." Jan. 1, 1817.)

199 Love and Glory, from the comic opera, *The English Fleet.* Music by John Braham. 4 pp. pl. 1–4. 6 Franklin Street.

200 Love and Time, sung by Mrs. Holman. Music by Michael Kelly. 3 pp. n.pl. 6 Franklin Street.
Another, with cover.

201 Love Has Eyes, ballad, from *The Farmer's Wife.* Music by Henry R. Bishop [with Reeve and Davy]. 4 pp. pl. 509. 6 Franklin Street.
Another. n.pl. 6 Franklin Street. Sold by John Ashton.

202 The Love Letter, in *Family Quarrels.* Music by John Braham. 5 pp. pl. 477–81. 6 Franklin Street.

203 Love, My Mary Dwells with Thee. Words by Thomas Moore. Music selected from the ancient ballads, and arranged by Stevenson. 2 pp. pl. 365–66. 6 Franklin Street.

204 Love Sounds the Trumpet of Joy, sung by Mrs. Holman. 2 pp. n.pl. 6 Franklin Street.

205 Love, Soft Illusion. *See* the *Musical Magazine,* Vol. II.

206 Love's Young Dream. Words by Thomas Moore. Music by Sir John A. Stevenson. 2 pp. pl. 411–12. 6 Franklin Street.
Another. n.pl.

207 Lullaby. By Storace. 2 pp. pl. 72–73. 6 Franklin Street.
Also, as lullaby in *The Pirates,* in the *Musical Magazine,* Vol. III. (Marked "printed for W. Norman, 75 Newbury Street.)

208 The Madrigal, in *The Fortress,* sung by Mrs. Darley, Mrs. Graupner, and Mr. J. Darley. Music by James Hook. 1 p. pl. 6. Music Store, 6 Franklin Street.

209 The Maid of Erin, ballad. Music by Thomas Thompson (Gen. Thos. Perronet). 2 pp. pl. 7–8. 6 Franklin Street.

210 The Maid of Lodi, accompaniment for harp or pianoforte, from music collected by Mr. Shield in Italy, 1791. [Sung by Mr. Webster at Concert Hall, Sept. 25, 1809.] Music by William Shield 2 pp. n.pl. 6 Franklin Street. 25¢.
Another. pl. 61–62.

211 The Manly Heart, selected from the German *Erato.* Composed by Sigr. Mozart. 2 pp. pl. 225. 6 Franklin Street.

212 A Favorite March by Mozart, "Pandeon Band." By W. A. Mozart. 1 p. pl. 29. 6 Franklin Street [Engraved by Wetherbee.]
Another. n.pl. Also known as Mozart's March.

213 March from *Masaniello.* By Auber. Arranged by Chaulieu. 2 pp. n.pl. 1 Province House Court.

214 March in *Blue Beard,* and Waltz. By Michael Kelly. 1 p. n.pl. 6 Franklin Street.
Another, followed by Little Wood. 1 p. pl. 44. 6 Franklin Street.

215 March in the *Forty Thieves.* By Michael Kelly. 2 pp. pl. 318–19.

(No publisher shown, but plate number suggests the likelihood of issuance from Graupner's press.)

216 March in *God of Love. See* No. 351.

217 March in the Melodrama *Der Freyschütz.*

218 March in *Pizzarro,* and College Hornpipe. By Alexander Reinagle. 1 p. n.pl. 6 Franklin Street. ("Lately published—"Fisher's and College Hornpipe, 12½¢." April 10, 1806.) *See also* No. 123.

219 March in *Richard the Third* with the Bugle Quickstep. 1 p. pl. 74. 6 Franklin Street [Engraved by Wetherbee.] ("Just publ." June 3, 1820.)

220 March of the Tartars, at a Distance, in *Timour the Tartar.* By Matthew Peter King. 1 p. pl. 459. 6 Franklin Street.

Another. 6 Franklin Street. Sold by John Ashton.

221 March of Victory, in *Timour the Tartar.* By Matthew Peter King. 2 pp. pl. 460–61. 6 Franklin Street.

222 Marches and Dances in *Tekely* (8 numbers). By James Hook. 6 pp. pl. 324–29. 6 Franklin Street.

223 Marianna, favorite air with variations for pianoforte and German flute. By A. Howship. 7 pp. pl. 507. 6 Franklin Street.

224 Marian's My Lily, and Flora's My Rose, ballad, sung by Mrs. Jones at Vauxhall. 2 pp. pl. 518. 6 Franklin Street.

225 Massachusetts March, and Dance in *Cinderella.* By F. Granger. 1 p. pl. 30. 6 Franklin Street.

X May Morning.

226 The Meeting of the Waters. 2 pp. pl. 451–52. 6 Franklin Street.

227 Megen Oh!, Oh Megen Ee!, from *Castle Spectre.* By Michael Kelly. 1 p. pl. 60. 6 Franklin Street. 12¢. (Sung in Boston before 1800; advertised "with original music" Jan. 8, 1801.)

Another. n.pl. 6 Franklin Street. Sold by John Ashton.

228 A Military Waltz. By Charles Nolcini. 1 p. n.pl. 6 Franklin Street. (Copyright May 3, 1821.)

229 The Minstrel's Harp, a cantata from the *Lay of the Last Minstrel.* Words by Sir Walter Scott. Music by Dr. John Clarke. 5 pp. pl. 269–73. 6 Franklin Street.

230 Mme. de Neuville's Waltz. 1 p. n.pl. 1 Province House Court.

231 The Celebrated Mocking Bird Song, sung by Miss O. Stephens in the opera *The Slave* by J. R. Planché. Music by Sir Henry R. Bishop, with flute accompaniment. 6 pp. pl. 118. 15 Marlboro Street.

232 Moorish March. *See* the *Musical Magazine,* Vol. I.

233 Moran's Favorite Variations on the Suabian Air, arranged for harp or piano-accompaniment. By P. K. Moran. 6 pp. n.pl. G. Graupner; sold for him by John Ashton. 50¢.

Another, without Ashton.

234   The Musical Magazine, in three volumes. *See* "Larger Works," p. 334.

235   My Bonny Lowland Laddie. *See* the *Musical Magazine,* Vol. III.

236   My Heart and Lute, ballad. Words by Thomas Moore. Music by Sir Henry R. Bishop. 2 pp. n.pl. 1 Province House Court.

Another, written and arranged by Thomas Moore. 2 pp. n.pl. 1 Province House Court. Sold by John Ashton.

237   My Heart's in the Highlands. 1 p. n.pl. 6 Franklin Street. Sold by John Ashton.

238   My Lovely Maid Forget Me Not, from *Narensky, or the Road to Yaroslaf* produced at the Theatre Royal, Drury Lane. Music by John Braham. 3 pp. pl. 219. 6 Franklin Street.

239   Nancy, or the Sailor's Journal. By Charles Dibdin. 2 pp. n.pl.

Another, in the *Musical Magazine,* Vol. II.

240   National Ode: Arouse, Arouse, Columbia's Sons, Arouse! Sung by Mr. McFarland at the Concerts in Boston. Written by Robt. Treat Paine Jr. 2 pp. pl. 453–54. 6 Franklin Street. ("This day published by Mr. Graupner" Boston *Gazette,* Aug. 5, 1811.)

241   The Negro's Humanity. By F. Mallet. With Guittar part. 2 pp. n.pl. Mallet & Graupner at their Conservatorio, or Musical Academy. ("Just publ." June 14, 1802.)

242   The Nightingale, favorite rondo. By J. B. Cramer. 1 p. n.pl. 6 Franklin Street. Sold by John Ashton.

243   Nobody Coming to Marry Me, sung by Mrs. Poe. Music by Mr. Cooke (Thomas Simpson Cooke). Flute part. 2 pp. pl. 122–23. 6 Franklin Street. (". . . in the course of the evening, (by desire,) the new song . . ." Boston *Gazette,* Mar. 24, 1808.) (". . . just published" Boston, *Repertory,* October 7, 1808.)

244   No, 'Twas Neither Shape nor Feature. By J. Bach Sr. 1 p. n.pl. 6 Franklin Street. (JFD)

245   No, That Will Never Do. *See* the *Musical Magazine,* Vol. III.

246   Now at Moonlight's Fairy Hour, duet. By Thomas Thompson (Gen. Thomas Perronet). 6 pp., with cover. n.pl. 6 Franklin Street. 62½¢.

247   O Can I Cease to Love Her. *See* the *Musical Magazine,* Vol. I.

248   [A Duet for Two Performers on One Pianoforte in Which Is Introduced the Air with Variations] "O Dolce Concento." By Mozart. Arranged by T. Latour. 10 pp., with cover. n.pl. 6 Franklin Street. Sold by John Ashton.

Another. 6 Franklin Street.

249   O Give Me a Cottage, composed and arranged for the pianoforte by T. V. Weisenthal. 2 pp. pl. 98. 6 Franklin Street.

Another. 2 pp., with cover. n.pl. 6 Franklin Street. (Copyright Mar. 1, 1819.)

250   O Say Bonny Lass. *See* the *Musical Magazine,* Vol. II.

251 O! Sing Sweet Bird, sung by M. Incledon. 2 pp. pl. 361–62. 6 Franklin Street. (JFD)

252 O Swiftly Glides the Bonny Boat. *See* No. 45.

253 Ode (Gluck). *See* the *Musical Magazine,* Vol. I.

254 Oft in the Stilly Night, sung by Mr. Williamson in *The Lady of the Lake.* Music arranged by Sir John Stevenson. 2 pp. pl. 222.
Another. 2 pp. n.pl. G. Graupner; sold for him by John Ashton.

255 Oh Ever in My Bosom Live. *See* the *Musical Magazine,* Vol. II.

256 Oh! My Baby, sung by Mrs. Mills, in the *Forty Thieves.* Words by Michael Kelly. 2 pp. pl. 313–14. 6 Franklin Street.

257 Oh, My Love's Like the Red Rose. Arranged by John Davy. 2 pp. n.pl. 6 Franklin Street.

258 Oh! Nanny, Wilt Thou Gang with Me, ballad. By Thomas Carter. Guittar or clarinet part. 2 pp. n.pl. Printed and sold by G. Graupner at his Musical Academy, 6 Franklin Street. 25¢.

259 Oh, Ne'er Can I the Joys Forget. By J. Smith. 2 pp. n.pl. G. Graupner; sold for him by John Ashton.

260 Oh No, My Love, No, in the musical entertainment *Of Age To-Morrow.* Music by Michael Kelly. [Words by M. G. Lewis.] 2 pp. pl. 73–74. Musical Academy, 6 Franklin Street. 25¢.
Another. 2 pp. pl. 417–18. Music Store, 6 Franklin Street.
Another. n.pl.

261 Oh! Say Not Woman's Heart Is Bought, sung by Mrs. Holman. Music by John Whitaker. 2 pp. n.pl. 6 Franklin Street.

262 Oh! the Sweet Little Village. 1 p. pl. 67. 6 Franklin Street. Sold by John Ashton.

263 Oh Strike Again! [From *Oh this love, or the Masquerader.*] Sung by Miss Griglietti. Music by Matthew Peter King. 2 pp. pl. 482–83. 6 Franklin Street.

264 Oh Tis Love (C'est l'Amour), sung by Mr. Keene. Music by J. R. Planché. Adapted by G. W. Reeve. 2 pp. n.pl. 6 Franklin Street.
Another. 6 Franklin Street. Sold by John Ashton. (Composer and adaptor obviously should be reversed.)

265 Oh! Why Should the Girl of My Soul Be in Tears? By Thomas Moore. 2 pp. pl. 371–72. 6 Franklin Street. Sold by John Ashton.

266 On the Lightly Sportive Wing, song in *My Grandmother.* Music by Storace. 3 pp. pl. 130–32. 6 Franklin Street. ("Lately publ." Feb. 10, 1813, *Columbian Centinel.*)

267 On the Rock Where Hangs the Willow, sung by Mrs. Nunn at Vauxhall. Music by D. Corri. 4 pp. pl. 124–27. 6 Franklin Street.

268 Orphan Nosegay Girl. Words by Mrs. Rowson. 1 p. pl. 45. Musical Academy, 6 Franklin Street.

269 O'er Dales and Mountains Stray, duett, sung by Mr. Bernard and Mrs. Mills, in the *Forty Thieves.* [Music by M. Kelly.] 2 pp. pl. 320–21. 6 Franklin Street.

270   The Favorite Overture from *The Blind Boy.* By John Davy. Harp
        solo. 5 pp. pl. 503. 6 Franklin Street.
271   Overture to *The Blaise of Babbet.* [By Dezede.] 6 pp. pl. 263–68.
        6 Franklin Street.
        Another, *Blaise et Babet.* 5 pp. pl. 90–94. 6 Franklin Street.
        Another, *Blaise et Babet.* 3 pp. n.pl. Musical Academy, 6 Franklin
        Street.
272   Overture to *The Caravan* (La Caravane du Caire). By Gretry. 4 pp.
        pl. 427. 6 Franklin Street.
273   Overture to *The Deserter.* By Pierre Alexandre Monsigny. [Adapted
        by Dibdin.] 2 pp. pl. 442–43. 6 Franklin Street.
        Another. n.pl.
274   Overture to *Lodoiska.* By Krietzer (Kreutzer). 6 pp. pl. 505. 6
        Franklin Street.
275   The Favorite Overture to *Timour the Tartar.* By Matthew Peter
        King. 8 pp. pl. 493–500. 6 Franklin Street.
276   Overture to *The Turnpike Gate.* By W. Reeve. 4 pp., with cover.
        pl. 86–89. Musical Academy, 6 Franklin Street. 50¢.
277   Pandean Band. *See* No. 212.
278   Panharmonicon March, and La Pantalon Waltz. 1 p. pl. 2. G. Graup-
        ner; sold for him by John Ashton.
279   Pas Re Double, as played by the Boston Brigade Band. 1 p. n.pl.
        G. Graupner; sold for him by John Ashton.
280   A Pastorale. *See* the *Musical Magazine,* Vol. I.
  X   The Peerless Maid of Buttermore.
281   Picknickery, favorite comic song. 3 pp. pl. 133. 15 Marlboro Street.
282   The Pilgrim of Love, sung in the comic opera called *The Noble
        Outlaw!* Music by Henry R. Bishop. 2 pp. n.pl. 6 Franklin Street.
283   Polish Waltz. *See* No. 138.
284   Pollacca, song. Music by John Braham. 4 pp. pl. 40–43. Musical
        Academy, 6 Franklin Street.
285   Poor Little Child of a Tar. 2 pp. n.pl. 6 Franklin Street, nr. Frank-
        lin Place. (Advertised in the Boston *Gazette,* Sept. 9, 1803.)
        (JFD)
286   Poor Little Gypsy, in the comic opera, *Wags of Windsor.* [Music by
        Arnold.] 2 pp. pl. 77–78. 6 Franklin Street. Sold by John Ashton.
        25¢.
        Another. Musical Academy, 6 Franklin Street.
287   The Poor Orphan Maid, ballad, sung by Mrs. Graupner. Music by
        M. P. King. 1 p. pl. 315. 6 Franklin Street.
  X   Post Captain.
288   President Monroe's Trumpet March, as performed in his review of
        the garrison on the day of Independence, July 4, 1817. By I.
        Briljan. Arranged for pianoforte by P. A. Von Hagen. 2 pp.
        pl. 103. 6 Franklin Street.

289 Pretty Black-ey'd Sally. By James Sanderson. 2 pp. pl. 200–201.
6 Franklin Street. ("Lately publ." *Columbian Centinel,* Feb. 10,
1813.)

290 The Pride of Our Plain. Words by "Amyntas." Music by Francis
Mallet. Accompaniment for harp or pianoforte. 1 p. n.pl. Mallet &
Graupner at their Conservatory, or Musical Academy. ("Just
publ." June 14, 1802.) (Mrs. Graupner sang this selection on
April 23, 1802, at her benefit in the Federal Theatre.)

291 The Primrose Girl. *See* the *Musical Magazine,* Vol. III.

292 Providence March. *See* No. 6 and No. 163.

293 Prussian March in *Abelino.* 1 p. pl. 68. Musical Academy, 6 Franklin
Street.
Another. n.pl. "Boston, printed and sold by J. Hewitt and at G.
Graupner's, 6 Franklin Street."

294 The Queen of Prussias and the Russian Waltz. By F. C. Vanormo,
Jr. 2 pp. pl. 100. 6 Franklin Street and the Franklin Music Warehouse, 6 Milk Street.

295 Quick March in *Oscar and Malvina. See* the *Musical Magazine,*
Vol. I.

296 The Rangers Grand March of Parade, as performed by the Brigade
Band. 2 pp. n.pl. 1 Province House Court. Sold by John Ashton.

X Reel, in *Rob Roy.*

297 The Reply, a divertimento. By T. Latour. With flute part. 6 pp.,
with cover. pl. 110. 6 Franklin Street. ("Just publ." June 3, 1820.)
Another. n.pl.

298 The Request. By Abbé Vogler. 1 p. pl. 227. 6 Franklin Street.

299 Resignation March. *See* the *Musical Magazine,* Vol. II.

300 Ripe Cherries. *See* the *Musical Magazine,* Vol. III.

301 Rise Columbia. *See* the *Musical Magazine,* Vol. I.

302 Robin Adair, sung by Mr. Braham at the Lyceum Theatre. Music by
W. Reeve. 2 pp. n.pl. 6 Franklin Street. ("Lately publ." Feb. 10,
1813.)
Another. 2 pp. pl. 153–54. 6 Franklin Street. Sold by John Ashton.

303 The Rosary. *See* the *Musical Magazine,* Vol. I.

304 The Rose, sung by Mr. Vining at the theatre in Boston. ("To a
Shady Retreat") (Music by John Bray.) 2 pp. pl. 63–64. 6
Franklin Street. 25¢.

305 The Rose, from *The Blind Girl, or the Queen.* By Mazzinghi and
Reeve. Accompaniment for German flute. 2 pp. n.pl. Mallet and
Graupner at their Conservatory, or Musical Academy. ("Just
publ." June 14, 1802.)

306 The Rose Had Been Washed, ballad. By Mr. Knowles (Boston).
Guitar part. 2 pp. pl. 133–34. Musical Repository, 6 Franklin
Street.

307 Roslin Castle. 1 p. pl. 26. 6 Franklin Street, near Franklin Place. 12¢.

308 Rousseau's "Dream," with variations. By J. B. Cramer. 7 pp., with cover. n.pl. 6 Franklin Street.
Another. Sold by John Ashton.

309 Roy's Wife, favorite Scotch song. By John Watlen. 2 pp. pl. 73. 6 Franklin Street. ("Just publ." June 3, 1820.)
Another. 6 Franklin Street. Sold by John Ashton.

310 Rule New England. Words by Paine for the anniversary of the Massachusetts Charitable Fire Society, May 28, 1802. Music by Francis Mallet. 2 pp. n.pl. Mallet & Graupner at their Conservatorio, or Musical Academy. ("Just publ." June 2, 1802.)

311 Russian Dance. *See* No. 81.

312 Russian March, and Emperor Alexander's Waltz. 2 pp. n.pl. G. Graupner; sold for him by John Ashton.

313 Said a Smile To a Tear, sung by Mr. Braham, Boston. [From *False Alarms.*] Music by John Braham. 6 pp. pl. 106–11. 6 Franklin Street.

314 The Sailor Boy, favorite glee. 4 pp. n.pl. 6 Franklin Street. (JFD)

315 The Sailor-Boy's Dream, ballad. Composed and arranged for the pianoforte by T. V. Weisenthal. 3 pp. n.pl. 6 Franklin Street.
Another. 3 pp. pl. 133. 6 Franklin Street. Sold by John Ashton. (Copyright Jan. 29, 1819.)

316 Salem Cadet's March, and Hull's Victory. 2 pp. n.pl. 6 Franklin Street.

317 Salutation, a duett. 2 pp. pl. 1–2. 6 Franklin Street.

318 Sandy and Jenny. Music by James Sanderson. Accompaniment for German flute. [First sung by Mr. Gardner, Oct. 1813, Federal Theatre.] 2 pp. pl. 224. 6 Franklin Street.

319 Sappho on the Rock of Lucate. By Fonbrune de la Rose. 2 pp. pl. 367–68. 6 Franklin Street.

320 The Scotch Air. *See* the *Musical Magazine,* Vol. III.

321 See from Ocean Rising, duett. [From *Paul and Virginia.*] Music by Joseph Mazzinghi. 2 pp. pl. 456 (?). 6 Franklin Street.
Another. 6 Franklin Street. Sold by John Ashton.

322 See How Beneath the Moon Beams Smile. [Written at sea.] By Oliver Shaw. 1 p. pl. 48. 6 Franklin Street.

323 See, Sister, See on Yonder Bough. *See* the *Musical Magazine,* Vol. I.

324 A Selection of Favourite Waltzes Composed for the Charleston Circus, and adapted for pianoforte. 12 pp. pl. 176–83. 6 Franklin Street.

325 The Serenade. By F. Mallet. 2 pp. n.pl. 6 Franklin Street.

326 Set of Mons. Labasses Quadrilles. Danced at his Academy and quadrille parties. Proper figures by Mr. Mann. Arranged by Mal-

let (not Francis). 3 pp. n.pl. G. Graupner; sold for him by John Ashton.

327 Sett of Mon. Labasses Quadrilles, with their proper figures, arranged for pianoforte by Wm. Slapp Jr. By Wm. Staunton Jr. 5 pp. G. Graupner; sold for him by John Ashton.

328 Shipwrecked Seaman's Ghost. *See* the *Musical Magazine,* Vol. I.

329 Sicilian Air with Variations. *See* No. 157.

330 Siciliano. *See* No. 73.

331 Sigh Not For Love, sung by Miss Dellinger. Music by M. P. King. 4 pp. pl. 90–93. 6 Franklin Street.

332 The Silver Moon. *See* the *Musical Magazine,* Vol. III.

333 Since Then I'm Doomed, song in *The Spoiled Child.* 1 p. pl. 18. 6 Franklin Street.

334 Six Bacchanalian Waltzes. 8 pp. pl. 116–23. 6 Franklin Street.

335 Six Progressive Sonatinas for Pianoforte or Harpsichord with Accompaniment for Violin. By Pleyel. 29 pp., with cover. pl. 276 on cover. 6 Franklin Street.

336 Smalilou. *See* the *Musical Magazine,* Vol. II.

337 Snatch Fleeting Pleasures, trans. from the German. [Music by Hans Georg Naegeli.] 1 p. pl. 228. Musical Academy, 6 Franklin Street.

Another. n.pl. Mallet & Graupner.

Another. pl. 228. 6 Franklin Street.

338 Soft As Yon Silver Ray That Sleeps. Words by Anne Radcliffe. Music by John Bray. 3 pp. n.pl. 6 Franklin Street.

339 Softly Waft Ye Southern Breezes. By James Hook. Sung by Mrs. Graupner. 2 pp. n.pl. (No imprint, but probably Graupner.) (JFD)

340 The Soldier's Adieu, from *The Wags.* Flute or violin accompaniment. By Charles Dibdin. 2 pp. n.pl. Mallet & Graupner.

Another, 1 p. pl. 24. 6 Franklin Street.

Also in the *Musical Magazine,* Vol. III.

341 The Soldier's Bride, sung by Mr. Phillips. Arranged by T. Phillips. 2 pp. pl. 91. 6 Franklin Street.

Another, 3 pp. n.pl. 6 Franklin Street. Sold by John Ashton. [Engraved S. Wetherbee] ("Just publ. . . ." June 3, 1820.)

342 A Soldier's Gratitude, sung by Mr. Keene. Music by Henry R. Bishop. 2 pp. pl. 108. 6 Franklin Street.

Another, n.pl.

343 Soldier's Rest, from *The Lady of the Lake.* Music by James Hook. 2 pp. pl. 457–58. 6 Franklin Street.

344 A Favorite Sonata. By Johann Dussek. 4 pp. n.pl. 6 Franklin Street.

345 Sonatas for the Piano Forte, Op. 21. Accompaniment for Violin. By Valentino Nicolai. (6 Sonatas, 2 movements each, with cover.) 31 pp. pl. 321–51. 6 Franklin Street. $3.

Another, published separately. 38¢ each (2 editions with different covers.) ("Lately publ. . . . 'Two Sonatas from Nicolay'" Boston *Gazette,* Apr. 10, 1806.)

346 A Sonata for the Pianoforte or Harpsichord (No. II). By Valentino Nicolai. 3 pp. with cover. pl. 5–7. 6 Franklin Street.
Another, n.pl.

347 Song in *The Spanish Barber.* Music by Dr. Arnold. 1 p.
Another, as favorite song in the opera, *The Spanish Barber,* in the *Musical Magazine,* Vol. II.

348 Song in *The Travellers In Switzerland.* Music by William Shield. 2 pp. n.pl. 6 Franklin Street.
Also published in the *Musical Magazine,* Vol. II.

349 The Song of Fitz Eustace, sung by Mrs. Ashe at Bath Concerts. Poetry from "Marmion." Music by Dr. John Clarke. 8 pp. n.pl. 6 Franklin Street. 75¢.
Another. 6 Franklin Street. Sold by John Ashton.
Another, as sung by Mr. Webster. 5 pp. pl. 515. 6 Franklin Street.

350 Favorite Spanish Air. *See* No. 49.

351 Stamitz' Air, arranged for pianoforte. By Johann Stamitz. 1 p. pl. 6. 15 Marlboro Street.
Another, with march in *The God Of Love.* 1 p. pl. 35. Musical Academy, 6 Franklin Street.
Another. n.pl.

352 The Sports of the Village, ballad. Music by Alfred Moxley. 3 pp. pl. 85. 15 Marlboro Street.
Another. n.pl.

353 Star of Bethlehem, sacred song. Words by Henry Kirke White. Music by F. Granger. Sung by a female amateur at the oratorios of the Handel and Haydn Society. 4 pp. n.pl. G. Graupner, published for the author. (Copyright April 9, 1821.)

354 The Stop Waltz. 1 p. n.pl. 6 Franklin Street.

355 The Storm Rondo. By Daniel Steibelt. 10 pp., with cover. n.pl. 1 Province House Court. Sold by John Ashton.

356 Stranger Think Me Not too Bold, from *Il Bondocani.* By John Moorehead. 1 p. pl. Mallet & Graupner. ("Just publ." June 14, 1802.)

357 The Streamlet. *See* the *Musical Magazine,* Vol. III.

358 Strike the Cymbal, as performed at the oratorios in Boston. Song and part chorus. Music by Vinc. Pucitta. 4 pp. pl. 116. 6 Franklin Street. (Performed July 5, 1817, before President Monroe, at Concert Hall.)

359 Strike! Strike! the Chord; Raise! Raise! the Strain! (National song for the 4th of July, 1815, the birthday of American independence.) Words by Mrs. Rowson. Music adapted by Dr. Arnold. 2 pp. pl. 223. 6 Franklin Street. (Copyright Sept. 25, 1815.)

360 Sweet Gratitude. By James Sanderson. 3 pp. n.pl. 6 Franklin Street.

361 The Sweet Little Girl That I Love. *See* the *Musical Magazine,* Vol. II.

362 Sweet Is the Vale, duet sung by Mrs. Wignell and Mrs. Woodham. Music by the Duchess of Devonshire. 2 pp. pl. 143–44. 6 Franklin Street.
Another. n.pl.

363 Swiss Guard's March. *See* No. 100.

364 Swiss Waltz, with variations for harp or pianoforte. 3 pp. n.pl. 6 Franklin Street.
Another. 6 Franklin Street. Sold by John Ashton.

365 A Favourite Swiss Waltz, arranged for two performers on one pianoforte. 1 p. pl. 107. 6 Franklin Street.
Another. 6 Franklin Street. Sold by John Ashton.

366 The Tank, favorite air with variations. By T. H. Butler. 3 pp. n.pl. 6 Franklin Street. (JFD)

367 The Tears of Mary. By James Hooton. 2 pp. n.pl. 6 Franklin Street. (JFD)

368 Thanksgiving Anthem. By Nolcini. Published for the Philharmonic Orchestra (no address). 10 pp. n.pl. (JFD)

369 There's a Bower of Roses, from *Lalla Rookh.* By R. W. Wyatt. 2 pp. n.pl. 6 Franklin Street. (Copyright April 5, 1820.)

370 They Tell Me Thou Art Cold of Heart, from *Airy Dreams.* 2 pp. 6 Franklin Street.

371 Thine Am I, My Faithful Fair, sung by Messrs. Phillips, Keene, and Taylor. Music by John Whitaker. 2 pp. n.pl. 6 Franklin Street.

372 Think Your Tawny Moore Is True. *See* the *Musical Magazine,* Vol. I

373 The Thorn. Words by Robt. Burns. Music by Wm. Shield. Sung by Mr. Smalley. 2 pp. pl. 194–95. 6 Franklin Street.

374 Tho' You Leave Me Now in Sorrow, duet, sung by Mrs. Holman and Mr. Howard. 2 pp. n.pl. 6 Franklin Street.

375 Though Love Is Warm Awhile, sung by Mr. Phillips, in *The Devil's Bridge.* [Music by Braham and Horn.] 2 pp. pl. 123. 15 Marlboro Street.
Another. n.pl.

376 Three Walses (for Pianoforte). By J. Friedheim. 2 pp. n.pl. 1 Province House Court. Dated 1835.

377 Thy Blue Waves O'Carron, ballad. Music by John Ross, organist at Aberdeen. Accompaniment for pianoforte and guitar. 3 pp. pl. 153–55. Music & Instrument Warehouse, 6 Franklin Street.
Another. n.pl.

378 'Tis the Last Rose of Summer. *See* No. 176.

379 To Me a Smiling Infant Came. *See* the *Musical Magazine,* Vol. I.

380 Tom Tackle. *See* the *Musical Magazine,* Vol. II.

381   Tomorrow. By Michael Kelly. Clarinet part. 2 pp. n.pl. Mallet & Graupner. (Advertised in the Boston *Gazette,* June 14, 1802.)

382   Too Late for Redress. By S. Stockwell. 3 pp. pl. 664–66. 6 Franklin Street. ("Lately publ." *Columbian Centinel,* Feb. 10, 1813.)

383   The Trumpet Echo of the Duke of Wellington. 1 p. pl. 96. 6 Franklin Street. Sold by John Ashton.

     Another. Franklin Music Warehouse, 6 Milk Street.

384   A Favorite Turkish March. By J. B. Cramer. 2 pp. pl. 73–4. 6 Franklin Street.

     Another, Turkish March. 2 pp. n.pl. 6 Franklin Street. Sold by John Ashton.

385   Twenty-five Duettinos for 2 Clarinetts, being a collection of favorite songs, marches, waltzes. Arranged by Frederick Granger. 12 pp., with cover. pl. 421–35. 6 Franklin Street. (Contains a waltz by Mozart.)

386   Tyrolese Song of Liberty. English words arranged by Thomas Moore. 3 pp. pl. 517. 6 Franklin Street.

387   Tyrolese Waltz. *See* No. 420.

388   Variations on Hummel's Favorite Waltz. By Gelinek. 10 pp., with cover. n.pl. G. Graupner (no address).

389   Vienna Grand Waltz.

390   The Village Holyday, song. [Music by Pleyel.] 1 p. pl. 334. 6 Franklin Street. ("Just publ." June 14, 1802, Boston *Gazette.*)

     Another. pl. 7. Mallet & Gr.

     Another in the *Musical Magazine,* Vol. III.

391   Walter's Sweethearts. *See* the *Musical Magazine,* Vol. I.

392   The Waterloo March and Introduction, dedicated to the Duke of Wellington. By Joseph Dale. Accompaniment for violin and flute by F. Granger. Also trumpet and bugle parts. 6 pp. n.pl. 6 Franklin Street. ("Just publ." Jan. 1, 1817.) (Copyright Dec. 20, 1816.)

393   Waving Willow. By William Shield. 2 pp. pl. 436–37. 6 Franklin Street.

394   Welcome Lafayette. By Joseph Wilson, organist at the Rev. Dr. Porter's Church in Roxbury. (Lafayette came in 1824.) 2 pp. n.pl. 6 Franklin Street.

  X   Wha'll Be King, but Charlie.

395   When Bidden to the Wake. *See* the *Musical Magazine,* Vol. II.

396   When First I Slipped My Leading Strings. *See* the *Musical Magazine,* Vol. I.

397   When First to Helen's Lute. *See* the *Musical Magazine,* Vol. I.

398   When He Tells of a Lover, ballad. Music by James Sanderson. 6 Franklin Street.

399   When in Death I Shall Calm Recline. *See* No. 191.

400   When Nights Were Cold. *See* the *Musical Magazine,* Vol. II.
401   When O'er Life's Sunshine Clouds Are Cast, duet, sung by Mrs.
      Darley and Mrs. Mills, in the *Forty Thieves.* Music by Michael
      Kelly. 4 pp. pl. 330–333. 6 Franklin Street.
402   When Pensive I Thought of My Love, admired song. Mallet &
      Graupner "at their Conservatorio, Rowe's Lane, and at Messrs.
      Blake's, No. 1, Cornhill." (Boston *Gazette,* July 26, 1802.) 2 pp.
      n.pl.
      Another, from *Blue Beard.* Music by Michael Kelly. 2 pp. n.pl. Con-
      servatory, or Musical Academy, 6 Franklin Street.
403   When Shall We Three Meet Again, ballad. By Wm. Horlsey, Mus.
      Bac. Oxon. Accompaniment for pianoforte or harp. 2 pp. n.pl.
      6 Franklin Street.
      Another. 6 Franklin Street. Sold by John Ashton.
404   Where Can Peace of Mind Be Found, a duett. Music by John Bray.
      5 pp. n.pl. 6 Franklin Street. (Copyright June 19, 1821.)
405   Why Does Azure Deck the Sky, ballad, sung by Mr. Webster at New
      York. Written by Thomas Moore. Music by R. Humfrey. 2 pp.
      pl. 322–23. 6 Franklin Street. [Sung by Mr. Webster, Boston,
      Sept. 25, 1809.]
406   Will You Rise My Belov'd to Inhale the Fresh Air? Words by Mrs.
      Rowson. Music adapted to "Will You Come to the Bower"
      (T. Moore). Accompaniment for German flute. 2 pp. pl. 448–49.
      6 Franklin Street.
407   William Tell, the Swiss Patriot, sung by Mr. Keene. Music by John
      Braham. 4 pp. n.pl. G. Graupner; sold for him by John Ashton.
408   Willis' Grand March and Quick Step, as performed by the Brigade
      and West Point Bands. By John Willis. 2 pp. n.pl. 1 Province
      House Court. Sold by John Ashton.
409   Wilt Thou Say Farewell, Love? Music and words by Thomas Moore.
      2 pp. pl. 156–57. 6 Franklin Street. ("Lately publ." *Columbian
      Centinel,* Feb. 10, 1813.)
      Another. 6 Franklin Street. Sold by John Ashton.
410   Windsor Park. 4 pp. pl. 141. 15 Marlboro Street. Two editions; one
      spelled Grauner, and one, Graupner.
411   The Winterville Waltz, dedicated to Miss S. Burrell. By James
      Hewitt. Arranged for pianoforte. 1 p. n.pl. G. Graupner (no ad-
      dress).
412   The Withered Rose, ballad. Poetry by John Stewart. Music by Dr.
      John Whitfield Clarke. 2 pp. pl. 94. 6 Franklin Street.
413   Within a Mile of Edinburgh, with four variations for harp or piano-
      forte. By Augustus Meves (James Hook). 7 pp. pl. 111. 15 Marl-
      boro Street. Sold by John Ashton.
      Another. n.pl. 15 Marlboro Street. ("Just publ." Dec. 18, 1818.)

414   The Wood Pecker, ballad, sung by Mr. Braham, Drury Lane. Words by Thomas Moore. Music by Michael Kelly. 4 pp. pl. 229. 6 Franklin Street.

       Another. 6 Franklin Street. Sold by John Ashton.

415   The Wood Robin, for pianoforte. By Reginald Spofforth. 1 p. n.pl. 6 Franklin Street.

416   The Wreath, pastoral glee. By Mazzinghi. 6 pp., with cover. n.pl. 6 Franklin Street, and Franklin Music Warehouse, 6 Milk Street. 50¢.

417   Wreaths for the Chieftan, sung by Mr. Huntington, Feb. 22, 1815, in Stone Chapel. Music by F. Granger. [Adapted] to an air by Sanderson. 3 pp. pl. 230. 6 Franklin Street.

418   Yankee Doodle. *See* No. 138.

419   Ye Streams That Round My Prison Creep, from *Lodoiska*. Music adapted by Storace. (Opera by Kreutzer.)

       Also in the *Musical Magazine*.

420   The Yellow-hair'd Laddie, Song, and the Tyrolese Waltz. [Gelinek.] 2 pp. pl. 98. 6 Franklin Street, and at the Franklin Music Warehouse, 6 Milk Street.

COMPOSER INDEX

(*Graupner Publications*)

LARGER WORKS PUBLISHED BY GRAUPNER

Rudiments of the Art of Playing on the Piano Forte. Arranged by Gottlieb
Graupner. Printed and sold by Gottlieb Graupner at his Musical Repository, 6 Franklin Street. 40 pp. Entered according to Law. Plate
nos. 219–258. (Copyright Aug. 29, 1806. Advertised "Published this
day . . ." Boston *Gazette,* Sept. 4, 1806.)

Contains thirty lessons and examples from Graupner, Handel, Corelli,
Pleyel, Hook, Scarlatti, Haydn, and a Polonaise from the Sixth French
Suite by Sebastian Bach.

Copy in Boston Public Library has no plate numbers on last three
pages. Two copies in the Essex Institute have no plate numbers; a third
copy has them all. Some copies have the words "Graupners Art of Playing on the Piano Forte" at bottom of many pages, and on these pages
the plate number is at the side. Two copies of this work are bound with
a dozen or more copies of sheet music published in the earliest days of
Graupner's business.

Another, Second Edition Improved and Enlarged. "Copy Right Secured"
at bottom of frontispiece, which is otherwise the same as the above.
51 pp. Preface dated "Boston, May 1819." Plate No. 520 on all pages.
The Thirtieth Lesson, by Sebastian Bach, is omitted.

Some copies bear this note: "This edition differs from those heretofore
published by him in the omission of 20 pages. This was done and this
edition of my instruction book published at the request of several instructors of music. The pages thus omitted contained exercises which
were generally considered difficult of execution."

Another, Second Edition Improved and Enlarged. Preface dated Jan. 1,
1825, but otherwise the same as the above, except that the word "Warehouse" instead of "Repository" is used.

Another, Second Edition Improved and Enlarged. Preface dated Jan. 1, 1827. Otherwise the same as the above.

New Instructor for the Clarinet, containing elements of music, fourteen progressive lessons with a collection of airs, songs, marches, duets, &c. Selected by Gottlieb Graupner, Boston. (Copyright Jan. 15, 1811.) (Copy in Library of Congress.)

G. Graupner's Complete Preceptor for the Clarinet, containing an Accurate scale and examples of the best fingering to which is added a collection of the most popular Airs, Marches, &c. &c. and a concise Dictionary of Musical Terms. 28 pp. Dated, July 14, 1826.

G. Graupner's Complete Preceptor for the German Flute, containing accurate scales and examples of the best Fingering, to which is added a Collection of the most popular arias, Marches, etc. &c. and a concise Dictionary of Musical Terms. Boston. Published by G. Graupner and sold for him by John Ashton, No. 197 Washington Street. 50 pp. n.pl. (Contains directions for beating time with the foot.)

A New Preceptor for the German Flute. Boston. Printed and sold by G. Graupner at his Music Store, No. 6 Franklin Street. (This is entirely rewritten, and contains new examples with more on each page.) 36 pp. n.pl.

The Anacreontic Vocalist. Published by G. Graupner, Boston. (Glees, catches, canons, duets, rounds, etc. by Jenkins, Battishall (-hill), Linley, Smith, Ives, Hilton, Hayes, Playford, Webb, Purcell, Harrington, Byrd, Calcott, Arne, Warren, etc. 30 catches, 14 glees, 6 duets). 80 pp. n.pl. 11 x 8½ c.m. (Proposals in the Boston *Repertory,* Feb. 21, 1809; books ready for subscribers, June 30, 1809.) Price $1.50 to subscribers; $2 to non-subscribers.

Monitor, or Celestial Melody. Collection of psalm and hymn tunes based on Lock Hospital. 95 pp. pl. 47–142. 50¢ to subscribers; 75¢ to non-subscribers. (Proposal: Boston *Gazette,* Jan. 16, 1806. Second part available "this day," April 10, 1806; sixth part available "this day," Nov. 3, 1806.)

The Musical Magazine, being a Collection of the Most Modern & Favorite Songs, Airs, Marches . . . Taken from the Works of the Most Celebrated Authors and Adapted to the Voice, with Bass & Key'd Instruments. To be continued. Printed and sold by Gottlieb Graupner at his Musical Academy, Boston, No. 6 Franklin Street near Franklin Place. Price 2 dollars ten cents each volume. N.B.: all may be had singly.

Volume I:

Arnold. When First to Helen's Lute, in *Children in the Woods* (1791).

Arnold. See, Sister, See on Yonder Bough, in *Children in the Woods* (1791)

[Reeve and Shield]. A Favorite Air in *Oscar and Malvina* (1791)

Mazzinghi. A Blessing on Brandy and Beer, in *Magician no Conjurer* (1792)

Shield. The Rosary, ballad, in *Midnight Wanderer* (1793)

Arnold. Walters Sweethearts, in *Children in the Woods* (1791)

Storace. Shipwrecked Seaman's Ghost, in *The Pirates* (1792)

Arnold. Think Your Tawny Moor Is True, in *Mountaineers* (1795)

Moulds. I Sold a Guiltless Negro Boy, ballad.

Arnold. Moorish March, in *Mountaineers* (1795)

Shield. Dear Wanderer, in *Midnight Wanderer* (1793)

Shield. When First I Slipped My Leading Strings, in *The Woodman* (1791)

Arne. Rise Columbia (Paine).

Storace. O, Can I Cease To Love Her.

Gluck. Ode.

—— To Me A Smiling Infant Came, ballad.

[Reeve and Shield]. Quick March, in *Oscar and Malvina* (1791)

Storace. Ye Streams That Round My Prison Creept, etc.

—— A Pastorale.

Arnold. Lorade in the Tower, in *The Mountaineers* (1795)

Moulds. Sterne's "Maria."

Volume II:

—— Resignation March.

Dibdin. I That Once Was Ploughman.

Shield. When Bidden To The Wake, from *Rosina* (1783)

Reeve. The Galley Slave, from *The Purse* (1794)

Shield. Smalilou, from *The Picture of Paris* (1790)

Shield. 'Ere Around the Huge Oak, from *The Farmer* (1789–92)

Hook. Gem of Aberdeen.

Storace. The Jealous Don, from *The Pirates* (1792)

Reeve and Shield. Finale in the pantomime of *Oscar and Malvina.*

Storace. The Capture, song in *The Pirates.*

Hook. The Sweet Little Girl That I Love.

Reeve and Shield. Oh Ever In My Bosom Live, from *Oscar and Malvina.*

Dibdin. Tom Tackle.

Arnold. O Say, Bonny Lass, from *Inkle & Yarico* (1787)

Arnold. Love, Soft Illusion, from *Castle of Andalusia* (1781)

Dibdin. Nancy, or the Sailor's Journal.

Shield. The favorite song in the opera *Travellers in Switzerland* (1794)

B. Carr. When Nights Were Cold, in *Children of the Wood* (1793)

Arnold. Favorite song in opera *The Spanish Barber* (1783)

Volume III:

—— The Village Holyday.

Hook. The Silver Moon.

Hook. My Bonny Lowland Laddie.

Hook. Ripe Cherries.

Storace. Lullaby in *The Pirates* (printed for W. Norman, 75 Newbury Street).

Hook. No, That Will Never Do.

Pleyel. Henry's Cottage Maid.

—— The Primrose Girl.

Storace. The Scotch Air, in *The Pirates*.

General Howell. The Jersey Blue.

Spofforth. The Death of Anna, ballad, sung by Mr. Incledon.

Haydn. A Prey to Tender Anguish.

[Graupner]. Attic Bower (Paine), sung by Mrs. Graupner.

[Dibdin]. The Soldier's Adieu.

—— * As Wrapt In Sleep I Lay.

—— * A New Ode.

—— * Hey Dance to the Fiddle and Tabor.

—— * The Streamlet.

[M. Kelly]. * When Pensive I Thought of My Love.

Note: Boston *Gazette,* April 4, 1803 "Gottlieb Graupner . . . informs . . . that he has published, ready for delivery as above, the first three volumes of a work entitled, the *Musical Magazine.*"

Undiscovered Graupneriana

The Begger Boy. Musical Academy, 6 Franklin Street (Advertised in the *Columbian Centinel,* Oct. 22, 1803).

The Beggar Girl. Musical Academy, 6 Franklin Street (Advertised in the *Columbian Centinel,* Oct. 22, 1803).

Go, Gentle Zephyr. Music by Von Hagen ("Now published," Boston *Gazette,* April 12, 1802). Mallet & Graupner. [Another, published by Von Hagen.]

'Tis Lovely Woman Governs All. Musical Academy, 6 Franklin Street (Advertised in the *Columbian Centinel,* Oct. 22, 1802.)

May Morning. Music by F. Mallet. Mallet & Graupner (Advertised in the Boston *Gazette,* Apr. 12, 1802.)

The Peerless Maid of Buttermere. Printed and sold by G. Graupner. (Advertised in the *Columbian Centinel,* Oct. 22, 1803.)

Post Captain. [Music by Shield.] Printed and sold by G. Graupner. (Advertised in the *Columbian Centinel,* Oct. 22, 1803.)

* Listed in the indexes of all three volumes as part of Volume III, but missing from the only copy available, that in the New York Public Library.

Graupner's Addresses

First performance in Boston, Jan. 23, 1797

1798	March	Lodgings at Mrs. Granger's, Orange-Tree Lane
	Later,	According to Directory, "Gotleb Graupner musician No. 10 Jarvis' buildings" between 76–77 Newbury Street
1799	May 8–10	Burned out in fire which swept Jarvis' buildings
1800		Sweetser's Alley (Directory)
1801	Feb. 5	Musical Academy, Rowe's Lane
1802		"Removed frome Rowe's Lane to 6 Franklin street," newspaper advertisement, Nov. 24
1803		Pond Street, according to Directory (Rowe's Lane changed to Pond Street; the Directory, therefore, refers to the old address)
1802–17		House and music store at 6 Franklin Street, verified by advertisements and directories
1817	April?	Moved business to the Franklin Music Warehouse, 6 Milk Street
1817	Aug. 1	Moved from 6 Milk Street to his "old stand," 6 Franklin Street
1818		"Teacher of music," 6 Franklin Street (Directory)
	Jan. 1–15	Moved business to 15 Marlboro Street
1819		(Gottlieb Graupner & Co. (Geo. Cushing), store 15 Marlborough street (Directory)
	May 1	G. Graupner & Co. No. 6 Franklin St. (Removed from 15, Marlboro' St.) (*Columbian Centinel*)
1820–23 *		Music store 6 Franklin; (Directory)
1825		Music store 6 Franklin; house 469 Washington (Directory)
1826–27		House Province house Court (Directory)
1828–34		No. 1 Province house Court (Directory)
1835		Professor of music (Directory)
1836	Apr. 20	Died, No. 1 Province House Court
		Buried

* "To be let, Store No. 6, Franklin-street—possession given immediately" (*Centinel*, June 3, 1820). Graupner stayed on, however.

APPENDIX IV

LESSER PUBLISHERS IN BOSTON

This list makes no claim to completeness, since it represents the by-products of research on the main subject of Graupner. In several instances these were also the by-products of other businesses, or even other professions, and not a substantially remunerative undertaking. Badger was printer of the *Euterpeiad;* Wetherbee, an engraver; Simeon Wood, the bassoon or bass player; Stockwell, an actor and singer; Masi, a dancing teacher; and Spear, a teacher of pianoforte; Hayts, Babcock, and Appleton were musical instrument and umbrella makers; and Thomas & Andrews, booksellers. None, excepting the firm of E. W. Jackson, boasted a place of business where musical merchandise in large quantity could be procured. S. H. Parker was for long time proprietor of the Franklin Music Warehouse, and Francis Mallet is remembered as earliest partner of the short-lived firm of Mallet and Graupner.

THOS. BADGER JR.

Haydn, Josef.   The Creation. Arr. Clementi. 169 pp. Published 1818.
—— Miriam's Song—Sound the Loud Timbrel. Sung at the Oratorio by the Handel and Haydn Society.
Webbe, Samuel.   Ode for New Years. ("Just Publ." Jan. 3, 1821, *New England Palladium.*)
Also see Chap. VII for list of Supplements issued with the *Euterpeiad,* printed by Badger.

FRANKLIN MUSIC WAREHOUSE

Bray, John.   God Is There; sacred melody written by a Lady and originally sung at the oratorios performed by the Handel and Haydn Society at Boylston Hall, Boston. 3 pp. 83 pl.

HAYTS BABCOCK & APPLETON'S MUSIC STORE

New England Guard's March. 1 p.

JACKSON

Charles and Edwin W. Jackson, business established 1821 at 64 Market Street; in 1822 at 44 Market Street; partnership dissolved 1826.

Music issued from second address marked "E. W. Jackson" * 64 Market Street † 325 Broadway, New York, by C. & E. W. Jackson.

Attwood, Thomas. The Acacia Bower (Words from Lalla Rookh).

Valentine, Thomas. And We're a Noddin'; Scotch air with variations.

Kiallmark, G. Araby's Daughter; from *Lalla Rookh*.

—— Auld Robin Gray; sung by Mrs. French.

[Viguerie, B.] Battle of Maringo (with cover).

Beethoven. The Bird Let Loose; written by Thomas Moore.

Moran, P. K. The Carrier Pigeon; sung by Mrs. Holman (words by J. G. Percival).

Spear, Thomas. The Charming Portrait.

[Reeve, William.] Cosmetic Doctor; a Comic Song, sung by Mr. Twaits.

—— The Duke of York's March.

Janowski, Edward
(arr. G. K. Jackson). Ermine Waltz. (No publisher given but probably issued from 64 Market Street.)

King, M. P. Eve's Lamentation; from *The Intercession*.

† Williams, R. L. The Fairy Waltz.

* Mozart, W. A. Fare Thee Well! Adapted to "Ah, Perdona." Words by Lord Byron.

Stevenson, John A. Fare Thee Well Thou Lovely One; favorite air.

* Moore, Thomas. Fly to the Desert.

Moran, P. K. The Fortune Teller; sung by Mr. Ritchings at the New York Theatre.

Stevenson, John A. Go, Let Me Weep!

—— Gramachree Molly.

Stevenson, John A. Hark the Vesper Hymn.

Attwood, Thomas. Her Hands Were Clasp'd (Words from *Lalla Rookh*).

Bishop, H. R. A Highland Laddie Heard of War; sung by Mr. Williamson.

Kiallmark, G. Hinda's Appeal to Her Lover.

—— The Hymn Of Eve; sung by Miss Stevens.

* Monro, J. The Joys of Harvest Home.

—— Love and Friendship; words by Thomas Moore.

* Monro, J. May Day

Moran, P. K. The Murderer's Bride.

Clark, Dr. John. Namounas Song; from *Lalla Rookh*.

Moran, P. K. The Nightingale, with Introductory Minuet.

† Martin, Wm. O Nanny Wilt Thou Gang with Me, with variations.

—— Oft in the Stilly Night (Words by Thomas Moore).

Moran, P. K. Pray Papa; sung at the fashionable Le Boulanger private parties, adap. to Prussian March.

* Monro, J.   The Rose in June.

I Rudimenti de Musica

or

Complete Instructor

for the

Piano Forte

including most of the favorite

Airs, Songs, and dances

arranged and fingered in progressive order

also for the

Flute and Violin

the whole composed, selected, and adapted

by

Dr. G. K. Jackson

(22 pp. 3 pages of instruction, 17 of music by Pleyel

and other composers of note)

Stevenson, John A.   Should Those Fond Hopes.

* Taylor, J. B.   They're a'Noddin! Sung by Miss Stephens.

* ——   Tho the Day of My Destiny Over (Words by Lord Byron). ("Just publ." *Euterpeiad,* Sept. 15, 1821.)

Stevenson, John A.   Those Evening Bells.

——   To Ladies' Eyes.

Hewitt, James.   Trip to Nahant, rondo.

Norami, Pietro.   The Washing Day; as sung at the theatre and gardens.

Stevenson, John A.   When the Rosebud of Summer.

——   Yankee Doodle. (Advertised, but no copy found).

* ——   Flow on Thou Shining River; from Moore's Melodies. ("Just publ." Sept. 15, 1821.)

F. MALLET

Mallet, F.   The Flowing Tear, written by John H. Nichols. Music by Mr. M——. 1 p.

Mallet, F.   The High Hills of Detsmas; favorite song, written by "Amyntas." 1 p.

FRANCESCO MASI

Masi, F.   Genl. Boyd's March, and Col. Whiting's March. 1 p.

Masi, F.   The Cotillion Party's Assistant, and Ladies Musical Companion. 6 New Sets of Cotillions and Six New Country Dances. (Copyright April 6, 1818.)

Masi, F.   A Favorite Waltz; arranged for the pianoforte by F. M. 71 Newbury Street.

S. H. PARKER

——   Exult Not Dear Maid; ballad, by D. A. O'Meara Esq., adapted to a favorite Spanish Air.

King, Andrew. Glee-Time Dame Durden, as sung at the Salem Whig Festival, August, 1834.

King, M. P. Hush! Christians, Hush!

Whitaker, John. Oh! Say Not Woman's Heart Is Bought; sung by Mrs. French.

Brown, Bartholomew. (Arr. A. P. Heinrich.) The Pilgrim Fathers; song dedicated for anniversary of the Pilgrim Society celebrated at Plymouth, Dec. 22, 1824.

Bishop, Henry R. Tho 'Tis All but a Dream; words by Thomas Moore (12 Cornhill).

—— Orphean Lyre; No. 2, containing collection of Glees, catches, duetts, with pianoforte accompaniment. ("Published" *Centinel,* Feb. 4, 1824.)

THOMAS SPEAR

Willis, John. Day Is Departing. 21 School Street.

Wade, Joseph. Hours There Were.

—— The London March.

Planche, J. R. (Arr. T. Cooke). Love's Ritornella.

Nolcini, Charles. Op. 1, A March.

—— Mme. De Neuville's Waltz.

SAMUEL STOCKWELL

Webbe, S. Copenhagen Waltz with variations for the piano forte. 4 pp.

THOMAS AND ANDREWS

Wood, Abraham. A Funeral Elegy on the Death of General Washington, adapted to the 2nd of February. (Part song with accompaniment.)

Dibdin. Nancy, or the Sailor's Journal; sung by Mr. Williamson. 25¢. (Publ. 1797.)

Holden, Oliver. Sacred Dirges, Hymns, and Anthems, commemorative of the death of General Washington. An original composition by a citizen of Massachusetts.

WILLIAM & DANIEL TREADWELL

Larkin, Saml. Nightingale, a Collection of the most popular ancient and modern songs. 288 pp. (Jan. 1804.) (Not copyrighted.)

S. WETHERBEE

—— Home, Sweet Home. 1 p.

—— The Hunter's Horn, cavatina; sung by T. Phillips. 4 pp.

—— The New York Serenading Waltz. 2 pp.

—— Picknickery; favorite comic song.

Simeon Wood

Bennett, William.   Anthem for Fast. ("Just publ." *Euterpeiad,* April 13, 1822.)

King, M. P.   Eve's Lamentation; from the oratorio of *Intercession.*

Stevenson (adapted to).   Hark the Vesper Hymn; favorite Russian air.

—— Here Shall Soft Charity Repair; sung by Mr. Phillips published at the request of the Handel and Haydn Society. 7 pp.

Ross, J.   I Am Wearing Awa' to the Land O' the Leal; canzonet.

Whitaker, John.   O Say Not Woman's Heart Is Bought; as sung by Mrs. French. 2 pp.

Jameson, R. F.   Oh! Sweet Was the Scene; sung by Mr. Wheately of the Boston Theatre.

Bray, John.   Peace and Holy Love; sung by Master Ayling at the Handel and Haydn Society; words by Mrs. Rowson. Copyright Secured. 2 pp.

Horn, Chas. E.   Rose of Love! As sung by Mrs. French. 2 pp.

Granger, F.   The Star of Bethlehem; as sung by a female amateur at the Handel and Haydn Society; words by Henry Kirk White. ("Just publ." *Euterpeiad,* March 31, 1822.)

Phillips, T.   This Blooming Rose; ballad. Dedicated to Sir John Stevenson, and sung with unbounded applause; sung by Mr. Brenan. 3 pp.

Hay, James D.   Thy Cheek Has Borrowed from the Rose; sung by Mr. Sharp at the Philharmonic Society Concerts, Boston. 2 pp.

Haydn.   To Sigh Yet Feel No Pain, as sung at the Philharmonic Society's Concerts by Mr. Sharp; words by T. Moore.

Eckherd, Jacob, Jr., of Charleston, S.C. Waltz, also a favorite air played by a musical seal.

Advertised, but no copy found

Beaumont.   The Barren Fig Tree; duet ("Just publ." *Euterpeiad,* Oct. 27, 1821.) S. Wood & S. P. Taylor, Franklin Street.

Arnold, Dr.   Erect Your Heads; chorus, with figured bass. ("Just publ." *Euterpeiad,* Oct. 27, 1821.) S. Wood & S. P. Taylor.

Peene, I.   When First This Destined Orb; anthem for Thanksgiving or Christmas. ("Just publ." Oct. 27, 1821.) S. Wood & S. P. Taylor.

APPENDIX V

COMPLETE LIST OF MUSICAL WORKS FOR WHICH COPYRIGHT WAS GRANTED BY THE CLERK OF THE DISTRICT COURT, BOSTON, BETWEEN JANUARY 1, 1791, AND SEPTEMBER 1, 1827 *

Samuel Holyoke. Harmonia Americana. Jan. 24, 1791.

Isaiah Thomas. Worcester Collection of Sacred Harmony. July 29, 1791.

Thomas & Andrews. Anthem designed for Thanksgiving Day, by William Cooper. Feb. 22, 1792.

Oliver Holden. American Harmony. Sept. 25, 1792.

Geo. Richards and Oliver W. Lane. Psalms, Hymns, and Spiritual Songs. Oct. 15, 1792.

Oliver Holden. Union Harmony, or Universal Collection of Sacred Music (2 vols.). Aug. 1, 1793.

Joseph Stone and Abraham Wood. Columbian Harmony. Sept. 13, 1792.

Jacob Kimball. Rural Harmony. Dec. 3, 1793.

Hans Gram, Samuel Holyoke, and Oliver Holden. The Massachusetts Compiler of Theoretical and Practical Elements of Sacred Vocal Music. Feb. 25, 1795.

Jeremy Belknap. Sacred Poetry, Consisting of Psalms and Hymns. May 26, 1795.

Samuel Babcock. Middlesex Harmony. Dec. 22, 1795.

Benjamin Dearborn. The Vocal Instructor (published in numbers); No. 1, containing rules of vocal music by principal questions and answers. Feb. 28, 1796.

Thomas & Andrews. Laus Deo, the Worcester Collection of Sacred Harmony. Sept. 12, 1797.

Daniel Belknap. The Harmonist's Companion. Oct. 14, 1797.

Elias Mann. The Northampton Collection of Sacred Harmony. Nov. 3, 1797.

James Davenport, Francis Linley, and John Moore. "Columbia and Lib-

---

* The dates are sometimes given as of the year of the Independence of the United States and reckoned to July 4th. This was discontinued after 1806 when the calendar year was observed. Music was often entered as book or engraving.

erty," a new patriotic song written by Mr. Davenport; the music composed by Dr. Arne. Oct. 7, 1798.

Thomas Paine, Francis Linley and John Moore. The Green Mountain Farmer, a new patriotic song written by Thomas Paine, A.M.; the music and accompaniments by the celebrated Shield. Oct. 7, 1798.

Josiah Goddard. A New and Beautiful Collection of Select Hymns and Spiritual Songs. March 25, 1799.

Samuel Holyoke. Hark from the Tombs, &c., and Beneath the Honors, &c.; adapted from Dr. Watts and set to music by Samuel Holyoke (for the Washington Celebration, Newburyport). Jan. 21, 1800.

Solomon Howe. The Worshipper's Assistant. Jan. 25, 1800.

Samuel Holyoke. Instrumental Assistant, containing instructions for violin, German flute, clarionet, bass viol, and hautboy; compiled from European publications. Aug. 30, 1800.

Daniel Belknap. Evangelical Harmony. Aug. 30, 1800.

Jacob Kimball. The Essex Harmony; an original composition. (*See also* Dec. 25, 1802.) Jan. 6, 1801.

Samuel Holyoke. A Dedication Service, Ode, Three Hymns, Doxology, and Anthem. July 20, 1801.

Samuel Holyoke. The Columbian Repository of Sacred Harmony. April 7, 1802.

P. A. Von Hagen. Kiss the Brim and Let it Pass, a new song by Mrs. Rowson; the music composed by P. A. Von Hagen. Aug. 21, 1802.

Samuel Holyoke. Occasional Music. Sept. 1, 1802.

P. A. Von Hagen. Will not, Dare not Tell; words by Mrs. Rowson; music by Von Hagen. Sept. 25, 1802.

P. A. Von Hagen. Monody; words by "Amyntas," music by Von Hagen. Sept. 25, 1802.

Gottlieb Graupner. The Attic Bower; original ode written by Thos. Paine, Esq., and sung by Mrs. Graupner; music composed by Gottlieb Graupner. Oct. 4, 1802.

Daniel Belknap. The Middlesex Collection of Sacred Harmony. Nov. 13, 1802.

John M. Dunham. The Vocal Companion and Masonic Register. Dec. 3, 1802.

Warwick Palfrey. The Evangelical Psalmodist; original work consisting of plain tunes, fugues, and set pieces. Dec. 10, 1802.

Thomas and Andrews and John West. Columbian and European Harmony, or Bridgewater Collection, by Bartholomew Brown and others. Dec. 13, 1802.

Joshua Cushing. The Essex Harmony. Dec. 25, 1802.

Benjamin Holt, Jr. The New England Sacred Harmony. March 1, 1803.

Samuel Holyoke. Masonic Music. May 13, 1803.

Manning and Loring. Original Sacred Music, by William Cooper. July 12, 1803.

Abijah Forbush. The Psalmodist's Assistant. (*See also* Sept. 10, 1806.) Nov. 14, 1803.

Andrew Law. The Art of Singing. In 3 parts: I, Musical Primer; II, Christian Harmony; III, *Musical Magazine,* 4th ed. (*See also* Nov. 5, 1804.) Dec. 10, 1803.

Samuel Holyoke. Christian Harmonist [designed for Baptist Churches of the United States]. Dec. 24, 1803.

Manning and Loring. The Beauties of Church Music, by William Cooper. Jan. 24, 1804.

Andrew Law. *Musical Magazine,* 4th ed. (*See also* Dec. 10, 1803.) Nov. 5, 1804.

Samuel Holyoke. A Dedication Service for the New South Meeting House, Salem. Dec. 7, 1804.

Cushing and Appleton. The Fifer's Companion. No. 1, containing instructions for playing the fife, and a collection of music consisting of marches, airs, etc. May 24, 1805.

Joshua Spalding (minister of Branch Church in Salem). The Lord's Songs. June 8, 1805.

J. T. Buckingham. The First Church Collection of Sacred Music. Sept. 26, 1805.

Amos Albee. Norfolk Collection of Sacred Harmony. Oct. 22, 1805.

Samuel Capen. The Norfolk Harmony, No. 1. Nov. 12, 1805.

Cushing and Appleton. Salem Collection of Classical Sacred Musick. (*See also* Dec. 26, 1806.) Nov. 23, 1805.

Stephen Jenks. Laus Deo! the Delights of Harmony, or Union Compiler, No. 11. Dec. 31, 1805.

Stephen Jenks. The Jovial Songster, No. II. March 4, 1806.

Ensign Lincoln. The Young Concerts Companion, collection of hymns.

Manning and Loring. Psalmodist's Assistant, by Abijah Forbush. (*See also* Nov. 14, 1803.) Sept. 10, 1806.

Samuel Holyoke. The Occasional Companion, No. I. (*See also* Nov. 1, 1808.) Sept. 13, 1806.

Daniel Belknap. The Village Compilation of Sacred Music. Oct. 29, 1806.

Uri K. Hill. The Sacred Minstrel, No. 1. Nov. 1, 1806.

Cushing and Appleton. Salem Collection of Classical Sacred Music; 2d edition, improved and revised. Dec. 26, 1806.

John Kettell, and others. Psalms, Hymns, and Spiritual Songs for the Society of Universalists in Boston. Jan. 5, 1807.

David Palmer. Middlesex Collection of Church Music. Jan. 5, 1807.

Jonathan Huntington. The Apollo Harmony. June 25, 1807.

Walter Janes. The Harmonic Minstrelsy. August 9, 1807.

Thomas and Andrews. Suffolk Selection of Church Music. Oct. 26, 1807.

S. and E. Butler. Complete Fifer's Museum, by James Hulbert Junr., Philo musico. Nov. 10, 1807.

Samuel Holyoke. The Vocal Companion. (*See also* Sept. 13, 1806.) Nov. 14, 1807.

Elias Mann. The Massachusetts Collection of Sacred Harmony. Nov. 21, 1807.

Manning and Loring. The Boston Collection of Sacred and Devotional Hymns. Jan. 22, 1808.

Elijah Pomeroy. "Old Meeks Anthem." April 20, 1808.

Herman Mann. The Drummer's Assistant; instructions for beating English and Scotch duties, calls, marches, and tatoos. May 13, 1808.

William Emerson. A Selection of Psalms and Hymns: "Sing Ye Praises with Understanding." Ps. XIVII, 7. Sept. 6, 1808.

Joel Read. The New England Selection and Plain Psalmodist. Sept. 17, 1808.

Zedikeal Langer, and others. The Meridian Harmony. Sept. 29, 1808.

Samuel Holyoke. The Occasional Companion, No. III. Nov. 1, 1808.

Daniel Hardy, Jun. (author) Thanksgiving Anthem; 8-part chorus, mixed. Nov. 16, 1808.

George Schaffer. Two Sets of New Cottilions, arranged for the pianoforte or violin and bass by G. Schaffer; to be continued. (Published by Manning and Loring, for G. Schaffer, 1809, 16 pp.) Feb. 16, 1809.

Daniel Belknap. Middlesex Songster. Sept. 30, 1809.

Samuel Holyoke. The Occasional Companion, in 12 numbers. Sept. 31, 1809.

Josiah Goddard. A New and Evangelical Collection of Sacred Harmony. Dec. 14, 1809.

Stephen Jenks. The Royal Harmony of Zion, complete. Feb. 5, 1810.

Abner Kneeland. Hymns Composed at the Request of the General Convention of Universalists; 2d ed. April 19, 1810.

Samuel Thomson. The Columbian Harmony. October 29, 1810.

William Wood. Harmonia Evangelica. Nov. 20, 1810.

J. T. Buckingham. Sacred Music, composed by George C. Sweeney and William Cooper. Dec. 3, 1810.

J. T. Buckingham. Hymns Suitable for Devotions of Families and Churches; set to music by F. Schaffer, M.P. Feb. 14, 1810.

Benjamin Leslie. Concert Harmony, or Youths Assistant to Sacred Music. April 8, 1811.

Herman Mann. Psalms of David, by Watts; first corrected edition by H. Mann. May 11, 1811.

James Hewitt (Organist at Trinity Church). Harmonia Sacra. *See* July 2, 1816. May 2, 1812.

H. W. Pilkington, musician, and James Greenwood. A Musical Dictionary. June 6, 1812.

William Collier (minister in Charlestown). A New Selection of Hymns, designed as a supplement to Dr. Watts. August 5, 1812.

William D. Narramore and A. Jewett. The Fifer's Assistant. Aug. 19, 1812.

Manning and Loring. Lord's Day, a hymn tune by N. Mitchell. Feb. 26, 1813.

Another. 4th ed. (Copyright June 17, 1817.)

David Pool and Josiah Holbrook. American and European Harmony. June 11, 1813.

William Bull. Music Adapted to Language, hymn tunes, etc. July 22, 1813.

Samuel T. Armstrong. Sacred Harmony. Sept. 18, 1813.

Solomon Warriner and Bontecue. The Springfield Collection of Sacred Music. Nov. 13, 1813.

Manning and Loring. No. I. Old Colony Collection of Anthems, under the direction of the Old Colony Musical Society. (*See also* Dec. 12, 1817.) Feb. 5, 1814.

Josiah Talcott, Jr. Millenniel Praise; 4-part hymns. June 28, 1814.

Samuel Willard. Deerfield Collection of Sacred Music. August 4, 1814.

Samuel Worcester. Christian Psalmody. Jan. 7, 1815.

Francesco Masi. Ballad of Lake Champlain and Plattsburg, a grand sonata for pianoforte. July 29, 1815.

Thomas Brown. Theatrical Songster and Musical Companion. Aug. 1, 1815.

G. K. Jackson. A Choice Collection of Chants in 4 Voices, selected, arranged and composed by G. K. Jackson. March 9, 1816.

Samuel Holyoke. Instrumental Assistant, containing instructions for violin, German flute, accompanied bass viol, hautboy, and French horn, compiled from late European publications, Vol. I; 2d ed., corrected and enlarged. June 7, 1816.

Flagg and Gould. Harmonia Sacra. July 2, 1816.

West and Richardson. Templi Carmina, Songs of the Temple, or Bridgeport Collection; 4th ed., improved and enlarged. Oct. 26, 1816.

Jonathan Wilson. A Selection of Hymns. Nov. 21, 1816.

G. K. Jackson. The Choral Companion, Elucidation of Dr. G. K. Jackson's Chants; published by him. Jan. 31, 1817.

Another. March 5, 1817.

James Loring. Old Colony Collection of Anthems, under the patronage of the Old Colony Musical Society, Plymouth County, and the Handel and Haydn Society in Boston, Vol. I. (*See also* Dec. 29, 1819.) Dec. 12, 1817.

James Loring. Resurrection Hymn. Dec. 23, 1817.

Luke Eastman. Masonik Melodies. Jan. 21, 1818.

James M. Winchell. Arrangements of the Psalms, Hymns, and Spiritual Songs of Watts. Jan. 23, 1818.

Another, enlarged and improved. Nov. 16, 1818.

West and Richardson. The Chorister's Guide. Feb. 10, 1818.

Joseph Burakin and Amos G. T. Rudock. The American Camp Meeting Hymn Book. March 9, 1818.

Vincent Masi. The Cotillion Party's Assistant, and Ladies' Musical Companion, containing 6 new sets of cotillions and 6 new country dances. April 6, 1818.

West and Richardson. The Choristers Guide. April 18, 1818.

James Loring. Sacred Harmony, supplement to Watts and Winchell. March 10, 1819.

Winchell, Loring, Ensign Lincoln, and Thos. Edmands. Selection of More than 300 Hymns. May 22, 1819.
Another; 2d ed. Feb. 7, 1820.
Another. Sept. 8, 1820.
Another, indexed. August 8, 1820.

Samuel T. Armstrong. Psalms of David, by I. Watts. August 14, 1819.

Jonathan M. Wainwright. A Set of Chants. August 26, 1819.

James Loring. Old Colony Collection of Anthems, Vol. II. (*See also* March 6, 1823.) Dec. 29, 1819.

Joseph Eckley. Ask Why a Blush, altered and arranged for pianoforte by an amateur.

R. W. Wyatt. 5 Waltzes for the Pianoforte (later published by Graupner as "A Selection of Waltzes"). April 5, 1820.

Joseph Lewis, as secretary of the Handel and Haydn Society. The Boston Handel and Haydn Society Collection of Sacred Music. June 15, 1820.

Gottlieb Graupner. Governor Brooks Grand March, composed and dedicated to Miss Swan by Gottlieb Graupner. Oct. 9, 1820.

Richardson and Lord (formerly West and Richardson). Carmina: 8th ed. (Templi Carmina). Oct. 9, 1820. 10th ed., 10/4/22; 13th ed., 1/17/24; 15th ed., 10/3/25; 17th ed., 9/20/27; 18th ed., 7/28/28; 19th ed., 6/29/29.

Simeon Wood and Louis Ostinelli. My Beautiful Maid, a new song; music by P. D. Moran. Oct. 20, 1820.
The Murderous Bride; music by P. D. Moran. Dec. 11, 1820.

Monroe and Francis. The Universalists Hymn Book. April 14, 1821.

Samuel Penniman. A German Waltz, with 9 variations, by Maria Penniman at the age of 13 years. (Pupil of Mr. F. C. Schaffer). May 23, 1821.

Loring, Lincoln, and Edmands. Arrangements of Psalms, Hymns, and Spiritual Songs by Watts, with indexes and supplement. (*See also* May 22, 1819.) Sept. 10, 1821.

Gottlieb Graupner. Collection of Cotillions, selected from the best composers by F. D. Mallet; arranged for pianoforte by F. C. Shaffer. Sept. 26, 1821.

Gottlieb Graupner. Love and Opportunity, ballad, by T. V. Weisenthal. Dec. 20, 1821.

Thomas Phillips. Elementary Practices for Singing, arranged by T. Phillips according to his new and highly approved system.

C. C. Abbott. Young Converts Pocket Companion, with tunes. Jan. 25, 1822.

J. Lewis, secretary, Handel and Haydn Society. Boston Handel and Haydn Society Collection of Church Music. March 5, 1822.
Another; 3d ed. Feb. 10, 1825.

William Bennet. Anthem for Fast. March 30, 1822.

J. Lewis, for the Handel and Haydn Society. Old Colony Collection of Anthems; 3d ed. March 6, 1823.

J. Lewis, etc. The Boston Handel and Haydn Society Collection of Sacred Music, Vol. II. March 12, 1823.
Another, Vol. III. April 28, 1827.

Samuel Gray, chairman, Central Universalist Society in Boston. Christian Hymns, adapted to worship of God. April 15, 1823.

J. Lewis, etc. The Boston Handel and Haydn Society Collection of Church music; 2d ed., with additions and improvements. (*See also* May 4, 1827.) July 7, 1823.

Samuel Armstrong (minister at Salem). Psalms, Hymns, and Spiritual Songs of Watts, to which are added select hymns by Worcester. July 17, 1823.

Nathaniel D. Gould. Social Harmony. July 23, 1823.

Nathan Ardley, Edmund Frost, and George Cowles. Hymns and Sacred Songs for Monthly Concert. Sept. 30, 1823.

Samuel Willard. Regular Hymns. Jan. 16, 1823.

Charles Jackson. A Prey to Tender Anguish, composed by the late G. K. Jackson, Mus. Doc. Nov. 8, 1824.

Charles Jackson. A Winter's Evening, a cantata, composed by the late G. K. Jackson, Mus. Doc. Dec. 17, 1824.

Moore and Prowse. A Musical Biography, by John R. Parker. Dec. 18, 1824.

Samuel H. Parker. The Pilgrim Fathers, song written by Rev. J. Pierpont, music by B. Brown, Esq., with accompaniment by P. Heinrich. Jan. 10, 1825.

Monroe and Francis. Hymns for Children. March 15, 1825.

Gustavus L. Davis. The Young Christians Companion, selection of hymns. June 23, 1826.

Jonathan Dabney. A Selection of Hymns and Psalms; 4th ed. June 20, 1826.

John Wills, organist at West Church, Boston. A Selection of Sacred Melodies. August 26, 1826.

Richardson and Lord. The Boston Handel and Haydn Society Collection of Church Music; 5th ed.; 6th ed. 4/23/28; 7th ed. 5/25/29. May 4, 1827.

Theophilus Manning. Address on Music, delivered October 7, 1826, by Lowell Mason. May 8, 1827.

Hilliard and Brown. Select Hymns. May 16, 1827.

Charles Bradlee. A Set of Quick Marches for a Military Band. Sept. 1, 1827.

INDEX